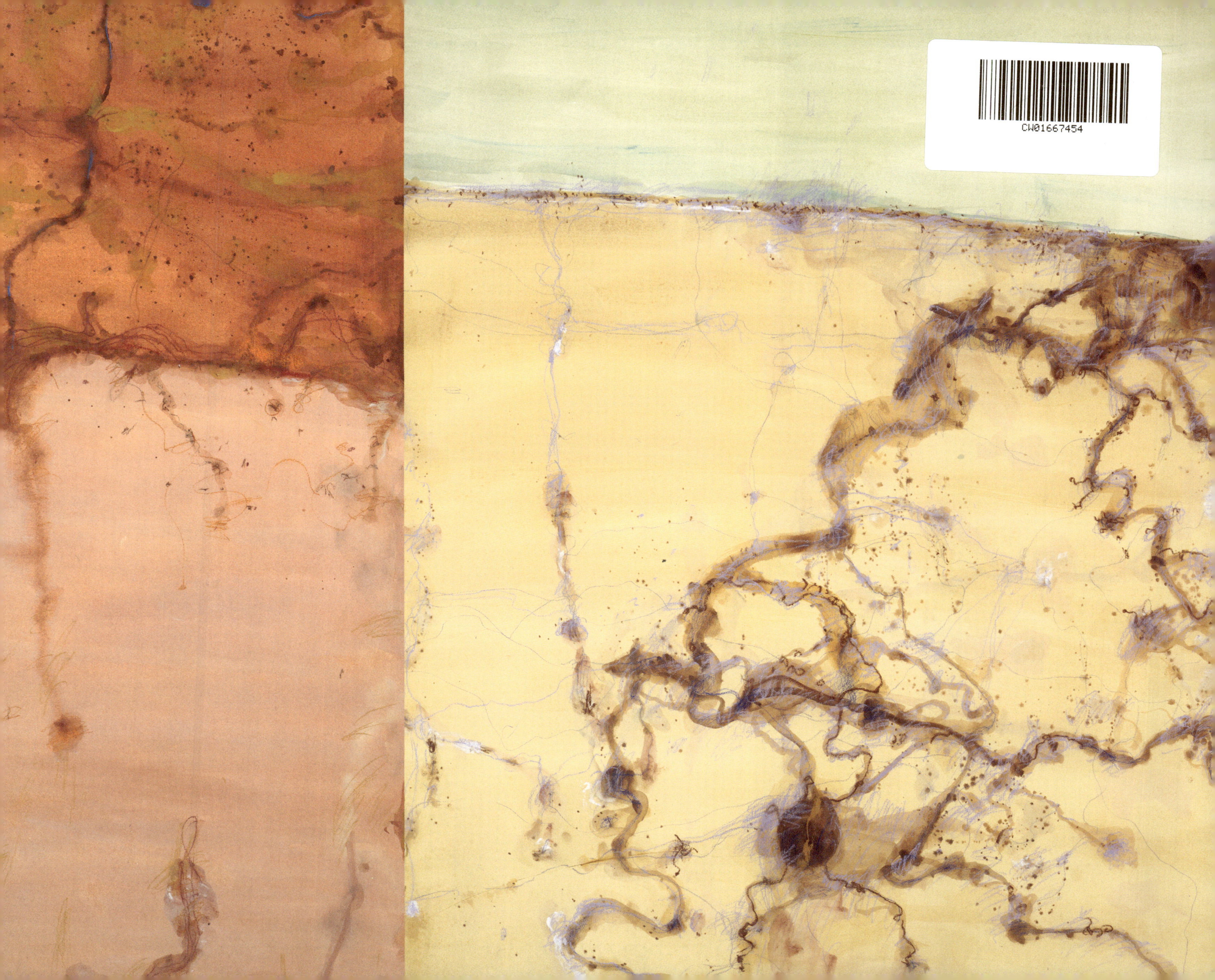

Lake Eyre

A journey through the heart of the continent

ABC
Books

Lake Eyre

A journey through the heart of the continent

Paul Lockyer

Featuring photographs by John Bean and Gary Ticehurst
Additional text by Professor Richard Kingsford

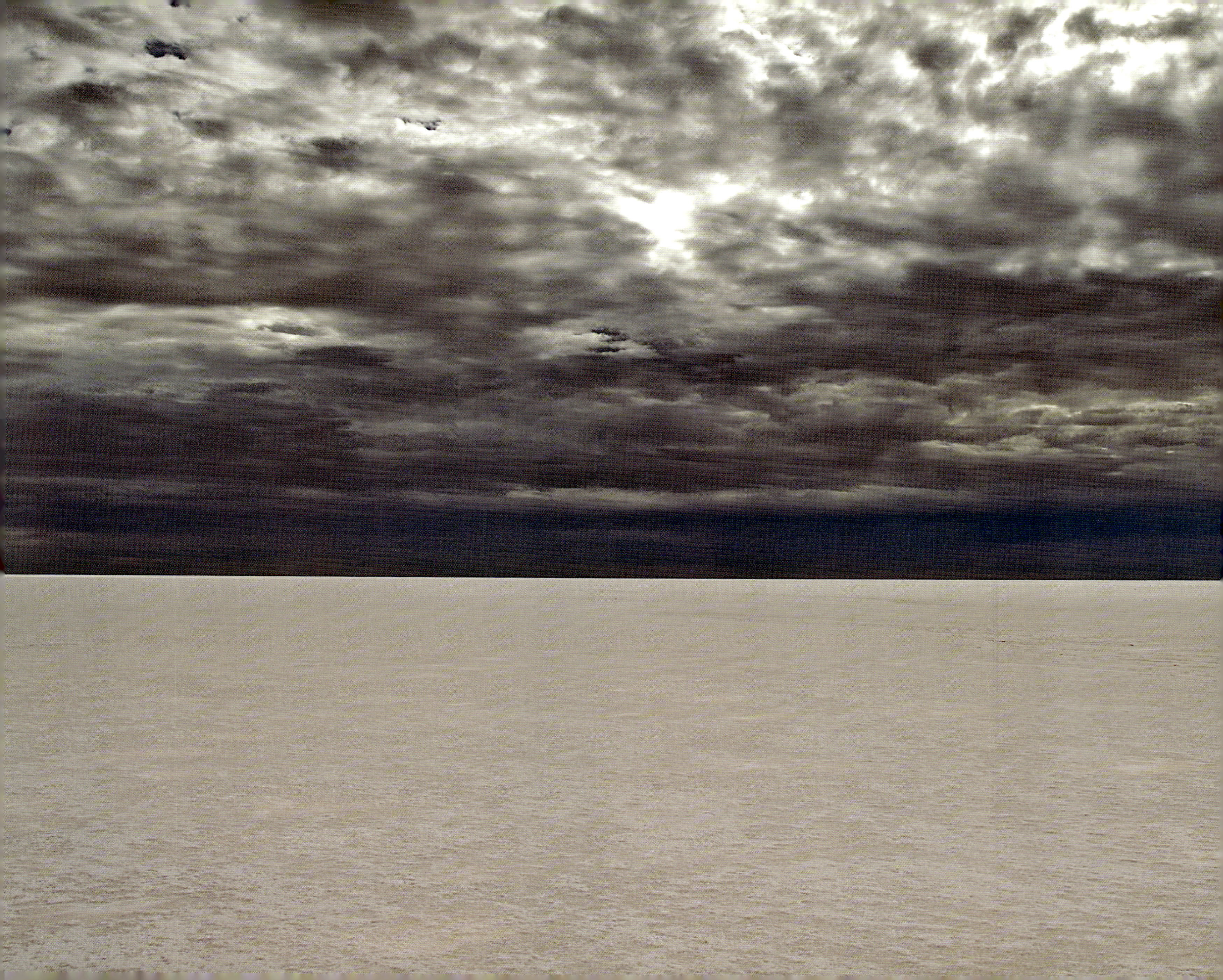

CONTENTS

Previous page: 'This barren, dazzling wilderness...' part of the vast salty expanse of Lake Eyre.
Overleaf: Warburton Creek as it enters Lake Eyre

PUBLISHER'S NOTE

ABC Books is grateful to the following people for their generous contributions to this book:

ABC producer **Ben Hawke**, for making the book possible in the first place.
The **Lockyer** family, **Teresa Ticehurst** and **Pip Courtney**, for their grace, help and enthusiasm.
Richard Kingsford, for original photography and for going above the call of duty on captions, proofreading and editorial advice
Angus Emmott, for original wildlife photography
Kim Wirth, for original photography
The Brook family, for original photography
Peter Elfes, for the cover photograph
John Olsen, for the endpapers from Lake Eyre: *Ruminations on an Empty Landscape.*
(Lake Eyre - The Desert Sea II, Lake Eyre - The Desert Sea IV, Lake Eyre - The Desert Sea III, Lake Eyre - The Desert Sea V, Lake Eyre - The Desert Sea VII, Lake Eyre - The Desert Sea IX)
Rex Ellis, for original photography
Linda Brainwood, for picture research
The publishers warn that this book contains images of the dead which may be offensive to Aboriginal people

Foreword by John Olsen

How lucky we were to have had Paul Lockyer.

Paul was a very special and courageous person who brought the finest presentations of crisis and triumphs of inland Australia to television. With cameraman John Bean and helicopter pilot Gary Ticehurst, he conveyed to the rest of the country the disaster of the Queensland floods, taking enormous risks to do so.

The three of them made two definitive films on the miracle of Lake Eyre in flood. They are the finest films of the region ever done and probably never will be excelled. Paul Lockyer profoundly understood that to interpret nature was to understand its cyclical process. It takes three months for the flood waters from Queensland to reach the huge boundaries of the inland sea and its enormous receptive principle, 'Gaia' the big mother, to receive the requisite rivers which, on arrival, bring with them millions of fish, ducks, pelicans, ibis, cormorants and seagulls, all feasting and nesting.

The loss of Paul Lockyer and his team while filming the third installment of their Lake Eyre series shall remain with all of us forever. They were modern explorers.

John Olsen, Sydney, 2011

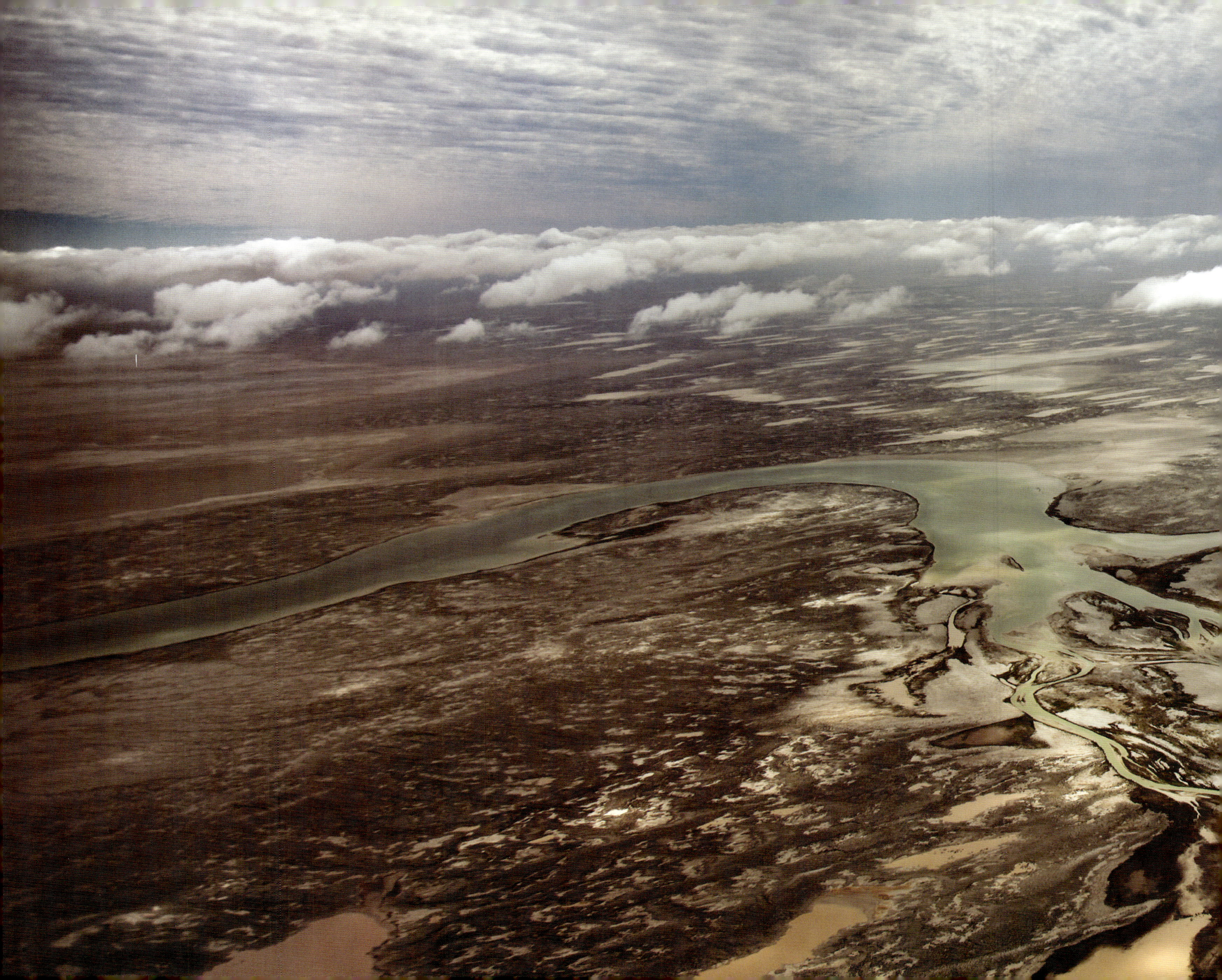

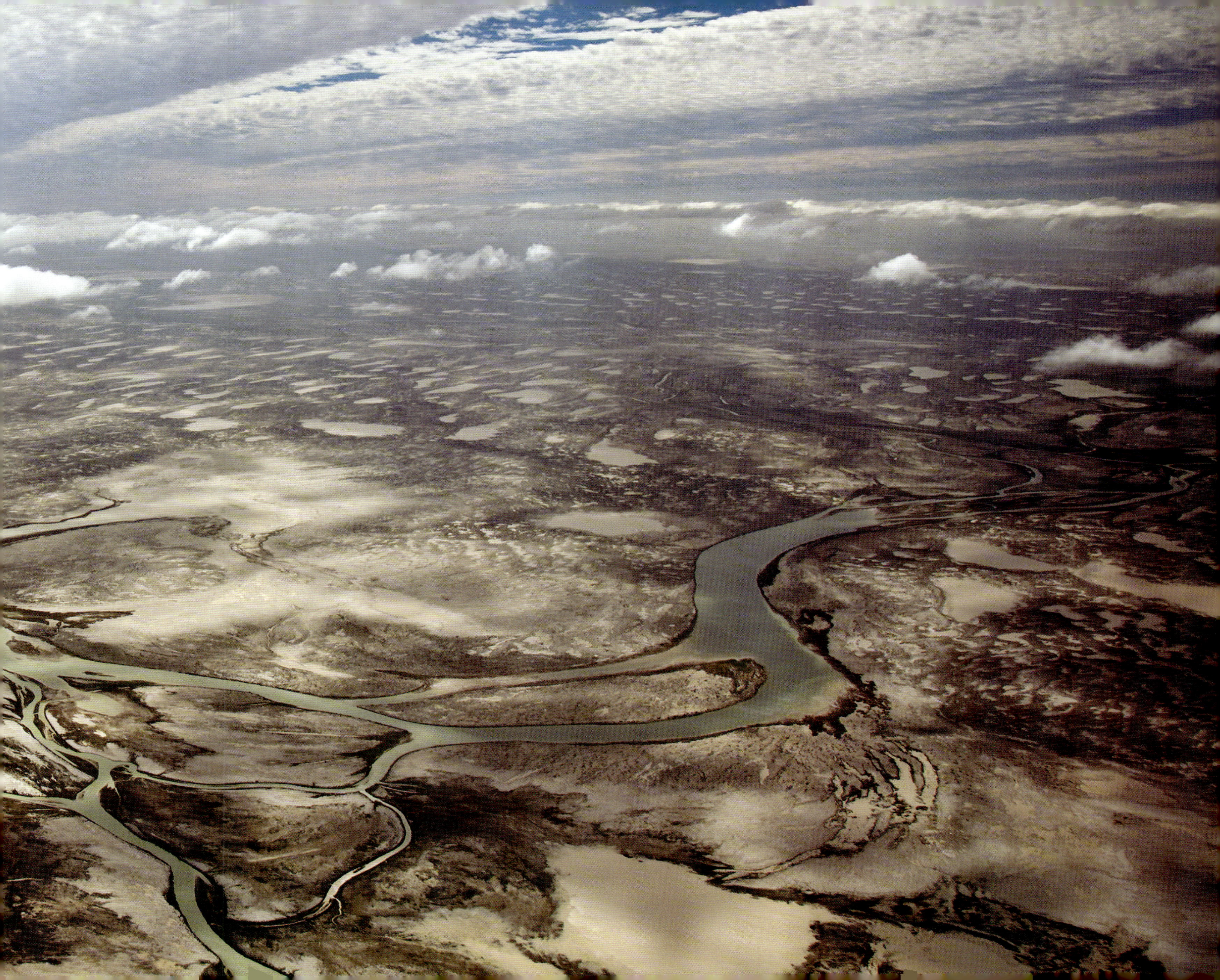

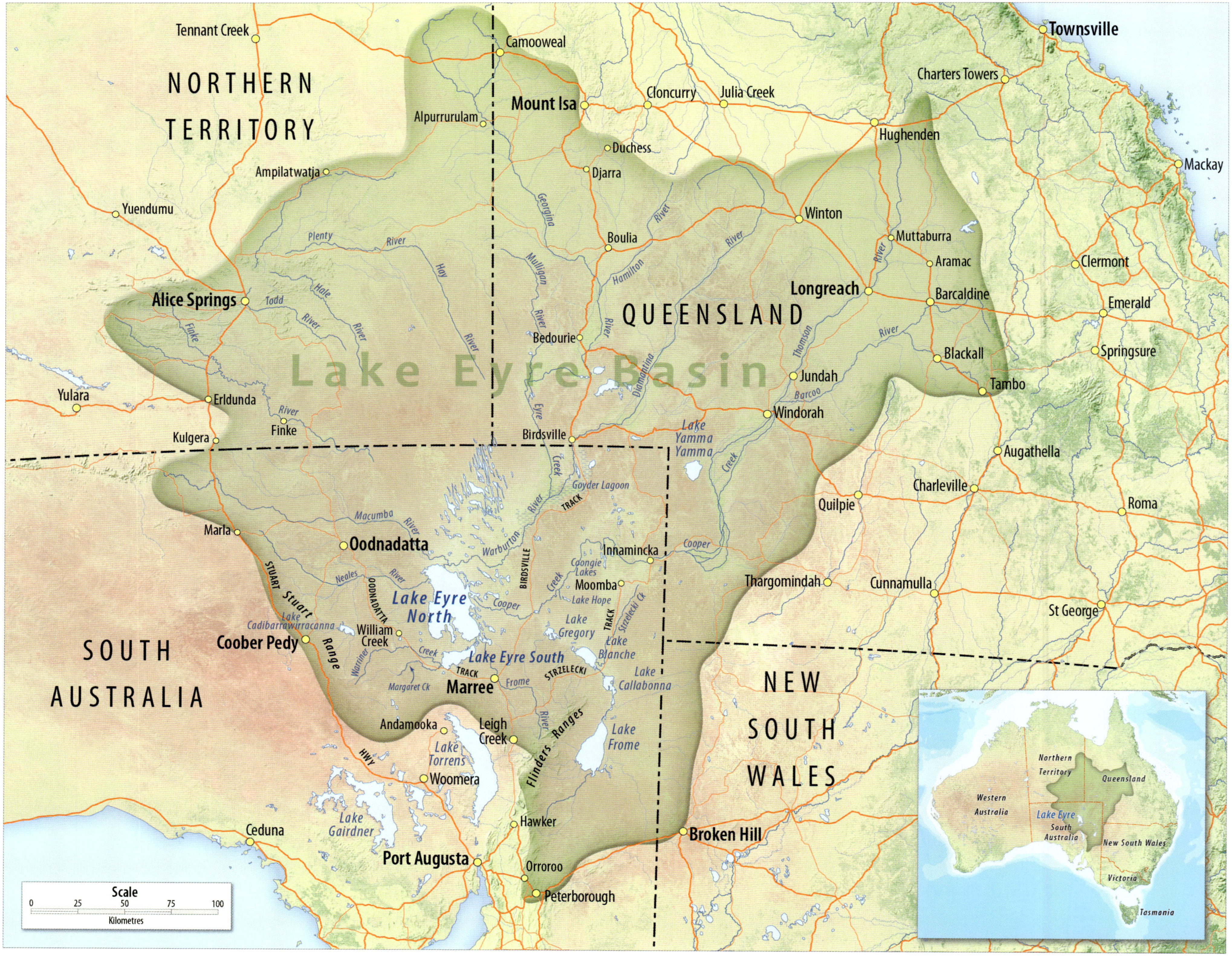
NORTHERN TERRITORY
QUEENSLAND
SOUTH AUSTRALIA
NEW SOUTH WALES
Lake Eyre Basin
Tennant Creek
Camooweal
Mount Isa
Cloncurry
Julia Creek
Townsville
Charters Towers
Hughenden
Mackay
Alpurrurulam
Ampilatwatja
Duchess
Djarra
Yuendumu
Winton
Muttaburra
Aramac
Clermont
Boulia
Longreach
Barcaldine
Emerald
Alice Springs
Springsure
Blackall
Tambo
Bedourie
Jundah
Windorah
Yulara
Erldunda
Finke
Kulgera
Birdsville
Augathella
Charleville
Roma
Quilpie
Marla
Oodnadatta
Innamincka
Moomba
Thargomindah
Cunnamulla
St George
Lake Eyre North
Lake Eyre South
William Creek
Coober Pedy
Marree
Andamooka
Leigh Creek
Woomera
Hawker
Ceduna
Port Augusta
Orroroo
Peterborough
Broken Hill
Lake Yamma Yamma
Goyder Lagoon
Coongie Lakes
Lake Hope
Lake Gregory
Lake Blanche
Lake Callabonna
Lake Frome
Lake Torrens
Lake Gairdner
Lake Cadibarrawirracanna
Plenty River
Hay River
Hale River
Todd River
Finke River
Georgina River
Mulligan River
Hamilton River
Diamantina River
Eyre Creek
Thomson River
Barcoo River
Cooper Creek
Macumba River
Neales River
Warburton River
Warriner Creek
Margaret Ck
Frome River
Strzelecki Ck
STUART HWY
Stuart Range
OODNADATTA TRACK
BIRDSVILLE TRACK
STRZELECKI TRACK
Flinders Ranges
Scale
0 25 50 75 100
Kilometres
Northern Territory
Western Australia
Queensland
Lake Eyre
South Australia
New South Wales
Victoria
Tasmania

PROLOGUE

In many ways, Lake Eyre defines Australia's ancient, arid continent. Nowhere are the extremes of drought and flood more dramatically displayed, framed against the weathered deserts of Central Australia. At the heart of it all is the country's biggest lake — but seldom does it see any water. For years on end it's a starkly desolate place — a shimmering white salt pan under the searing heat of a cloudless sky, deep in South Australia's north. Out on the rock-hard salt, there's an eerie sense of emptiness and unreality, heightened by a shifting, dancing horizon caught in a distorting mirage. Not a creature to be seen, not even a bush fly; there's just the crunch of salt under foot and the whistling of the wind. You imagine you could be on another planet. In this vast void, constructed over millions of years, there's a profound feeling of man's insignificance.

No wonder the Aboriginal people have long had a sense of foreboding about this barren, dazzling wilderness area, ringed as it is by dangerous patches of deep, grasping mud. They have myths and legends about terrifying creatures believed to occupy and guard the region — all adding to the sense of mystery about Lake Eyre.

But then, when the great inland rivers occasionally flow towards the centre of the continent, an amazing transformation takes place. Nature springs into action. The floodwaters trigger a frenetic breeding cycle amongst the native fish that have been sheltering deep in the sparse outback waterholes. Soon the rivers are alive — from the fish right down to the minutest forms of animal life. Before long, the seemingly lifeless desert becomes a carpet of green, abounding in wildlife. Packs of dingoes go on the hunt, and the sky is filled with birds of prey.

Then, seemingly from nowhere, a vast array of other birdlife begins to arrive, including tiny waders, such as banded stilts, scurrying and picking in the shallows of the rivers and lakes, and larger birds — cormorants, egrets, ibis, and squadrons of pelicans and even seagulls. Huge flocks wing their way to the centre of Australia from hundreds of kilometres away to feed and breed. How they know the water has finally arrived remains one of the great puzzles of the Australian outback.

As the water creeps across the wide floodplains on its way to Lake Eyre, long-dormant seed beds burst into life. Soon the dead heart is blooming.

All the newly flowing rivers and creeks stream towards the lowest point in the continent — Lake Eyre — a huge sink in the desert, 15 metres below sea level. As the water stretches across the dry lake bed, nature presents a magnificent display. Swirling patterns of vibrant colour are formed, reflected against the sparkling white of the salt pan. Floods that fill the lake have rarely been witnessed in the history of white settlement.

When it became clear that the water would get all the way to Lake Eyre in 2009, after the outback rivers were set flowing by summer downpours in Queensland's north-west, we went out to the region by helicopter to record the incredible changes to the landscape and the massive influx of birdlife. But the next year even bigger rains fell, over an even bigger area, bringing flooding to much of eastern Australia and finally ending a ten-year drought, one of the driest periods ever recorded. Again the rivers flowed to Lake Eyre. This, we thought, would be nature's grandest performance as huge areas of desert turned to green and were then extravagantly coloured in by blossoming wildflowers. But there was still more to come.

The flooding rains returned for a third year in a row, something that hadn't been witnessed since the 1970s. For the people who make their lives in the harsh interior, in the isolated communities and on the cattle stations dotted around Lake Eyre, the change in the seasons was a godsend. Tourist operators struggled to meet the demand from travellers anxious to observe natural history unfolding in all its glory. And for those of us involved in the ABC filming missions, it was a rare privilege to tell a truly remarkable story.

Lake Eyre South — A huge sink in the middle of desert, the rains that filled the lake in 2009 ended a ten-year drought.

Overleaf: Warburton Creek — One of the many waterways that feed the lake during heavy rains

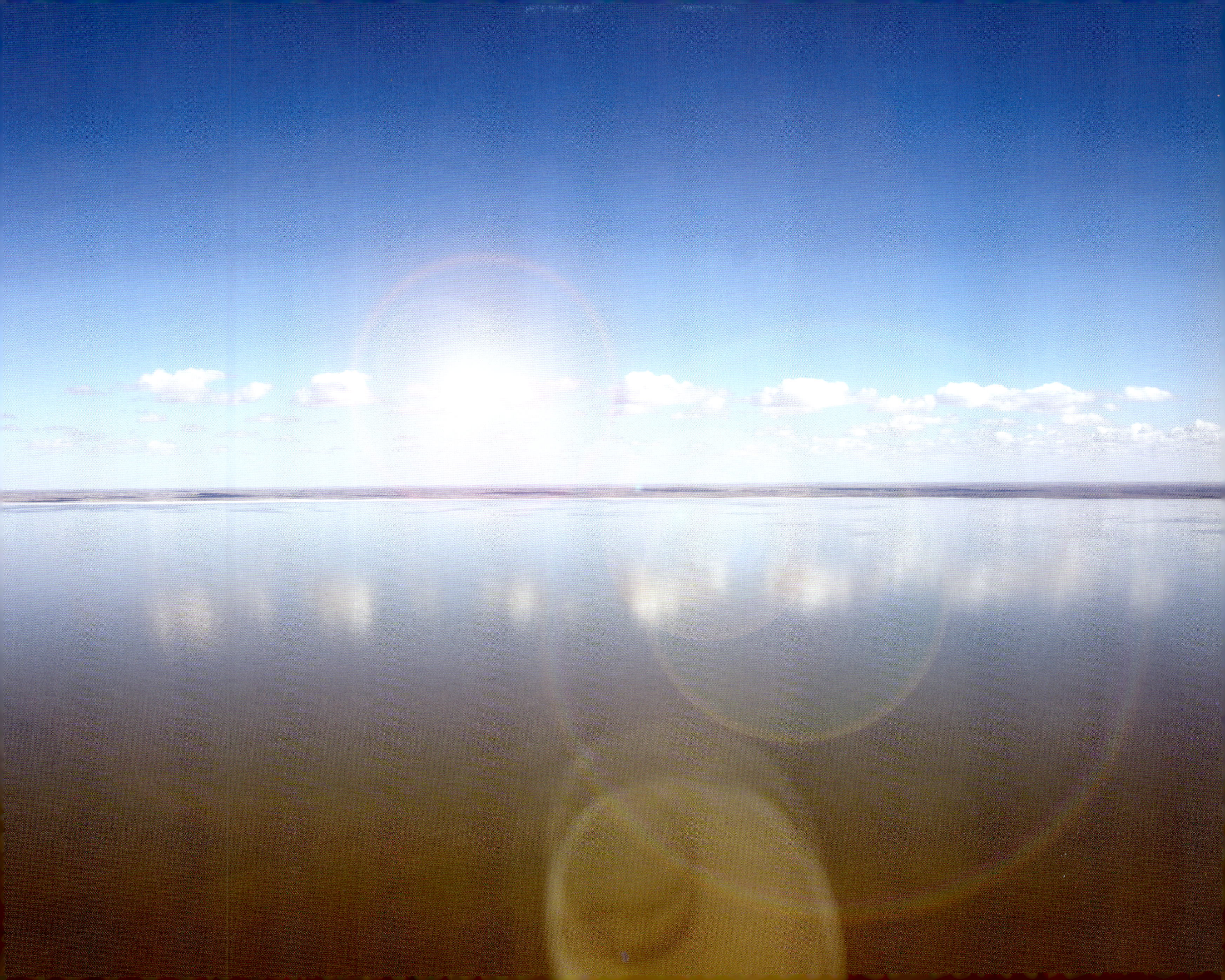

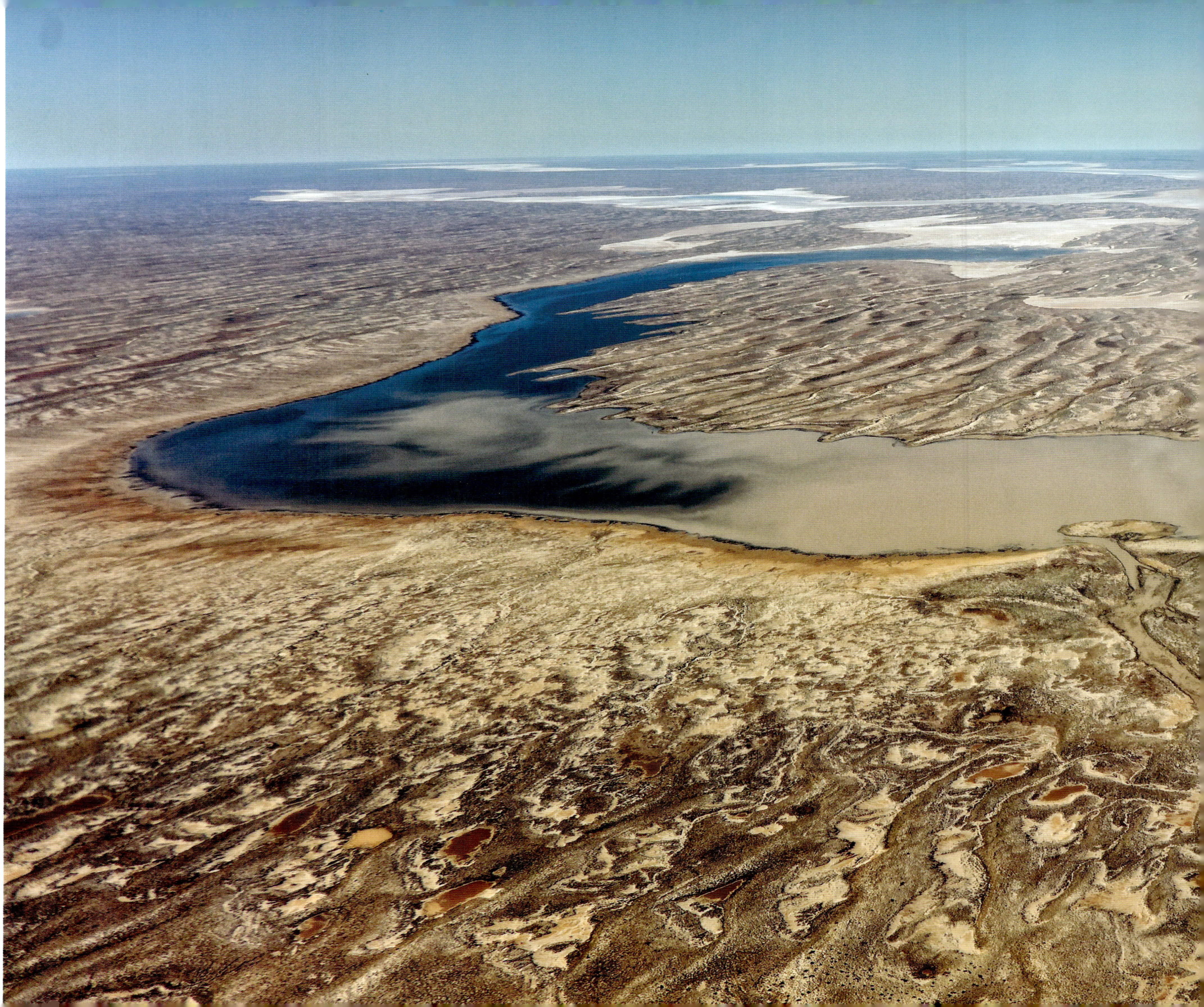

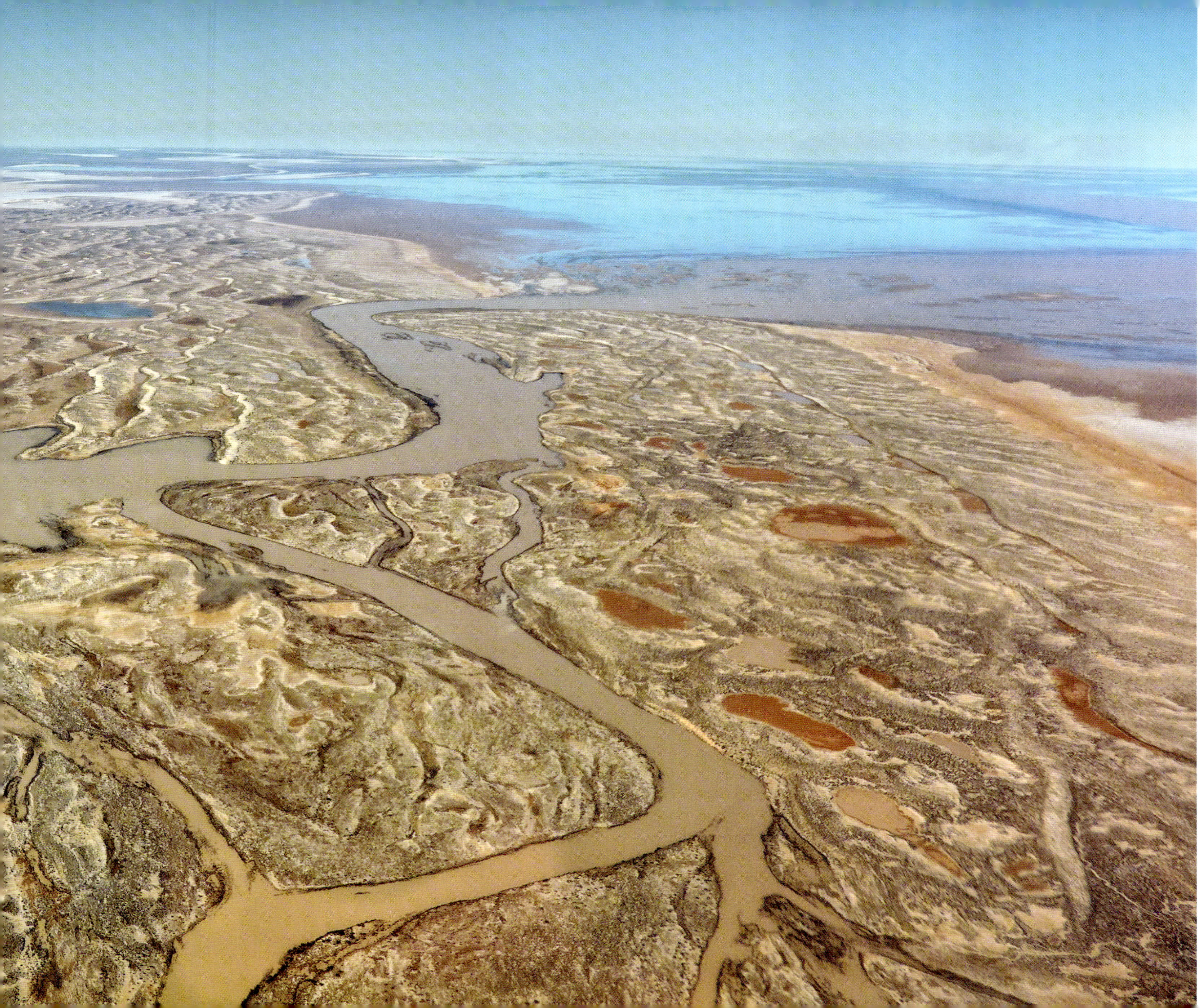

CORE OF THE CONTINENT

What is it about this place in the middle of nowhere that has become such a magnet for Australians? Veteran adventurer and tour guide Rex Ellis, who has travelled to the lake for over forty years, explains it this way: 'Moslems like to go to Mecca — Aussies like to go to Lake Eyre!' And there *is* something of a pilgrimage element to the flow of travellers who feel they must leave the security of the coast, where most Australians live, to journey to the dead heart of the continent. It's motivated not just by a sense of adventure, to follow in the footsteps of the explorers and pioneers, but by a sense of ownership.

Even if the coastal dwellers seldom journey to the interior, they consider the wide brown land to be part of their make-up, to be celebrated and honoured. The Australian landscape artist John Olsen, who has been fascinated and inspired by Lake Eyre ever since he first visited there during the flooding of 1974, describes Australians as 'saucer dwellers' clustered around the edge of the continent, and believes that Lake Eyre has an enormous pull on them. 'It's as though it invades their unconscious, as though there's something else that's so radically different from the sophisticated urban life that most of them live.'

The early settlers who ventured to the Lake Eyre region in the late 1880s struggled to carve out an existence in an extreme environment very foreign to their European backgrounds. But it was the harshness they encountered in the outback that largely moulded the Australian character, creating the tough, laconic, fiercely independent types that fill the pages of bush folklore. Those strong, self-reliant characters are still found today dotted around Lake Eyre in remote communities and

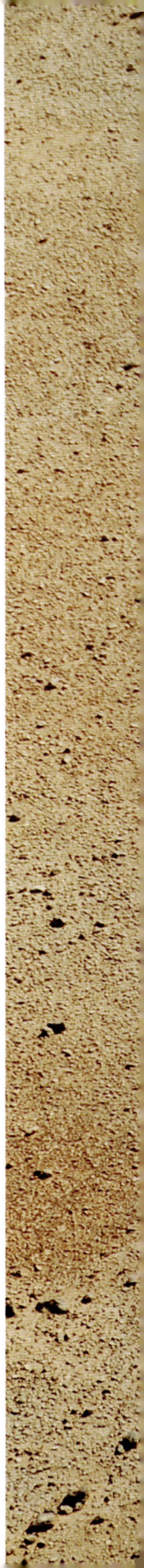

In the Stony Desert south of Birdsville, rocks form a heart-shaped pattern.

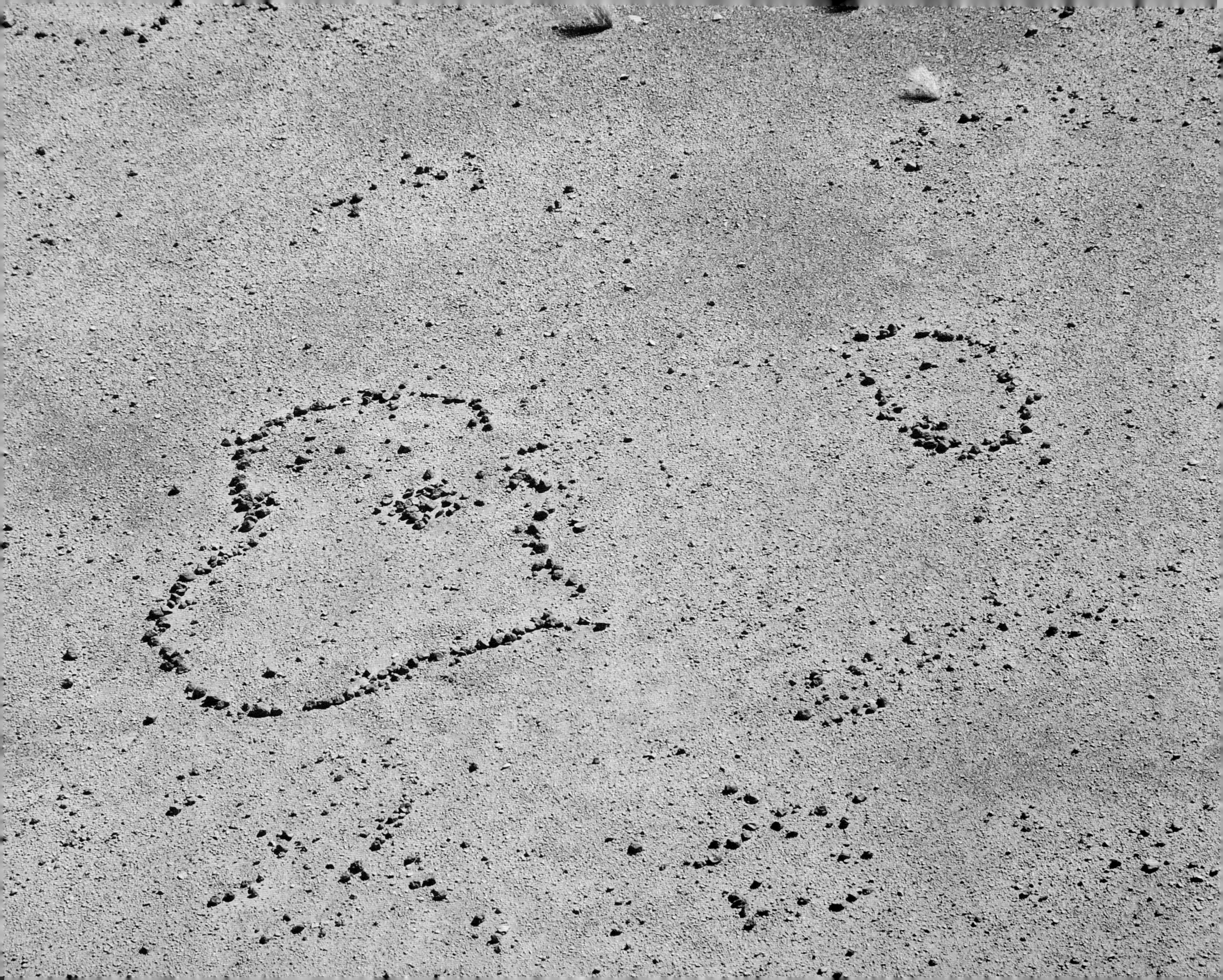

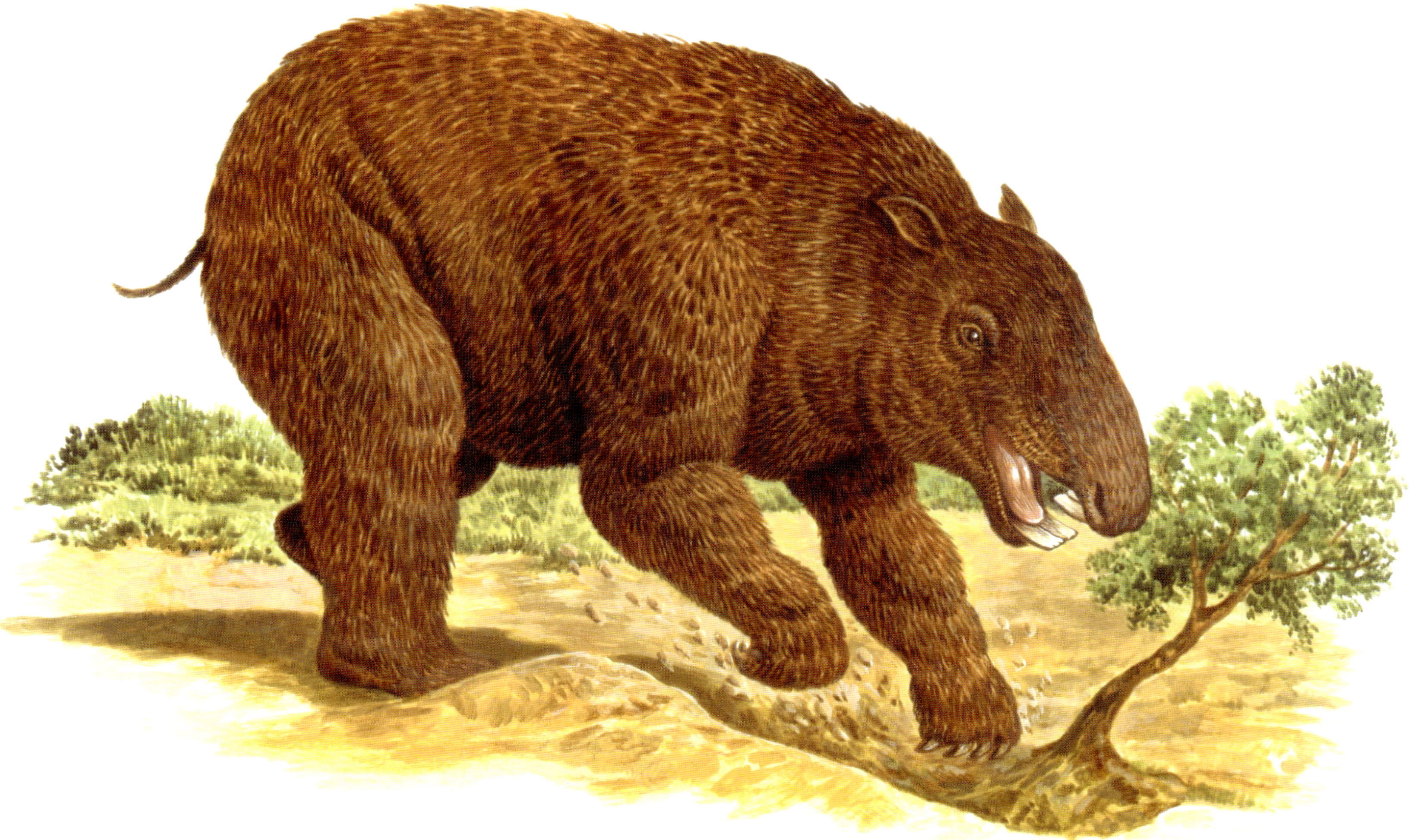

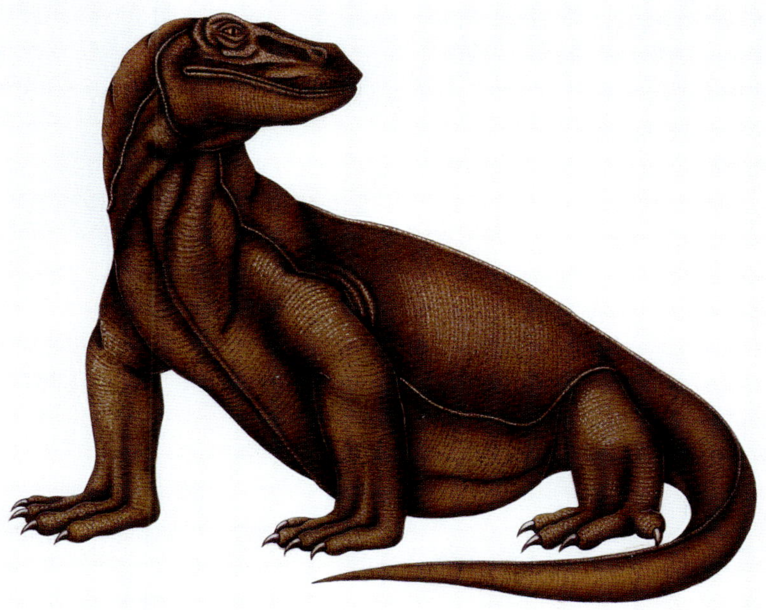

At 3 metres long and 2 metres tall, Diprotodon optatum *(left) was the largest land mammal ever to exist in Australia. The giant carnivorous goanna* Megalania prisca *(above) weighed up to 600 kilograms and grew to almost 7 metres.*

on vast cattle stations. Even as world horizons shrink, with faster communications and easier travel — or perhaps because of it — there's a new thirst to discover the real Australia, and Lake Eyre is high on that list. In many ways, it's one of the last great adventures. Just getting there still requires detailed planning, providing a sense of what the early explorers confronted. Then, as now, travellers are struck by the daunting vastness of the outback. It is still a journey into a frontier land, largely untouched by development, and that's a big part of its attraction to the growing legions of Australians now keen to discover the heart of their own country. And when nature occasionally extends a softer hand to the arid centre, offering a once in a lifetime chance to see the rivers flow and the sand dunes bloom, it sends a ripple of wonder across the continent and the stream of travellers to the centre also turns into a flood.

For a brief interlude the desert presents a deceptively benign appearance. Summers in the centre bring home the stark reality. Travellers wilt as temperatures soar above 50° Celsius and blinding dust storms lash the desert. Faced with the searing extremes that usually prevail in Central Australia it's hard to imagine that this was once a lush wetlands area, with the lake at the heart of the whole system. About 200 million years ago the continent began to sink and was flooded by the ocean. As the climate warmed out of the ice age and the continent drifted north, the centre flourished.

Turn the clock back 100,000 years, just before the desert climate started to take hold, and Lake Eyre would have been an enormous body of deep water, teeming with life, including a wide variety of fish and turtles.

Giant versions of kangaroos, emus, echidnas, koalas, crocodiles and other animals — categorised as megafauna — roamed the floodplains, forests and grasslands that surrounded the lake. There, grazing on the vegetation, would have been the biggest marsupial ever to live in Australia, the Diprotodon. It was like a huge wombat, weighing well over 2 tonnes and standing more than 2 metres tall. But such a size would have offered no defence against the carnivorous goanna, the Megalania. This terrifying animal, like an enormous Komodo dragon, grew up to 7 metres long. The other great threat to the Diprotodon was posed by the

Rocky escarpments such as this, on boulder-strewn Mount Knuckey in the Northern Territory, break up the endless lines of sand dunes in the North Simpson Desert.

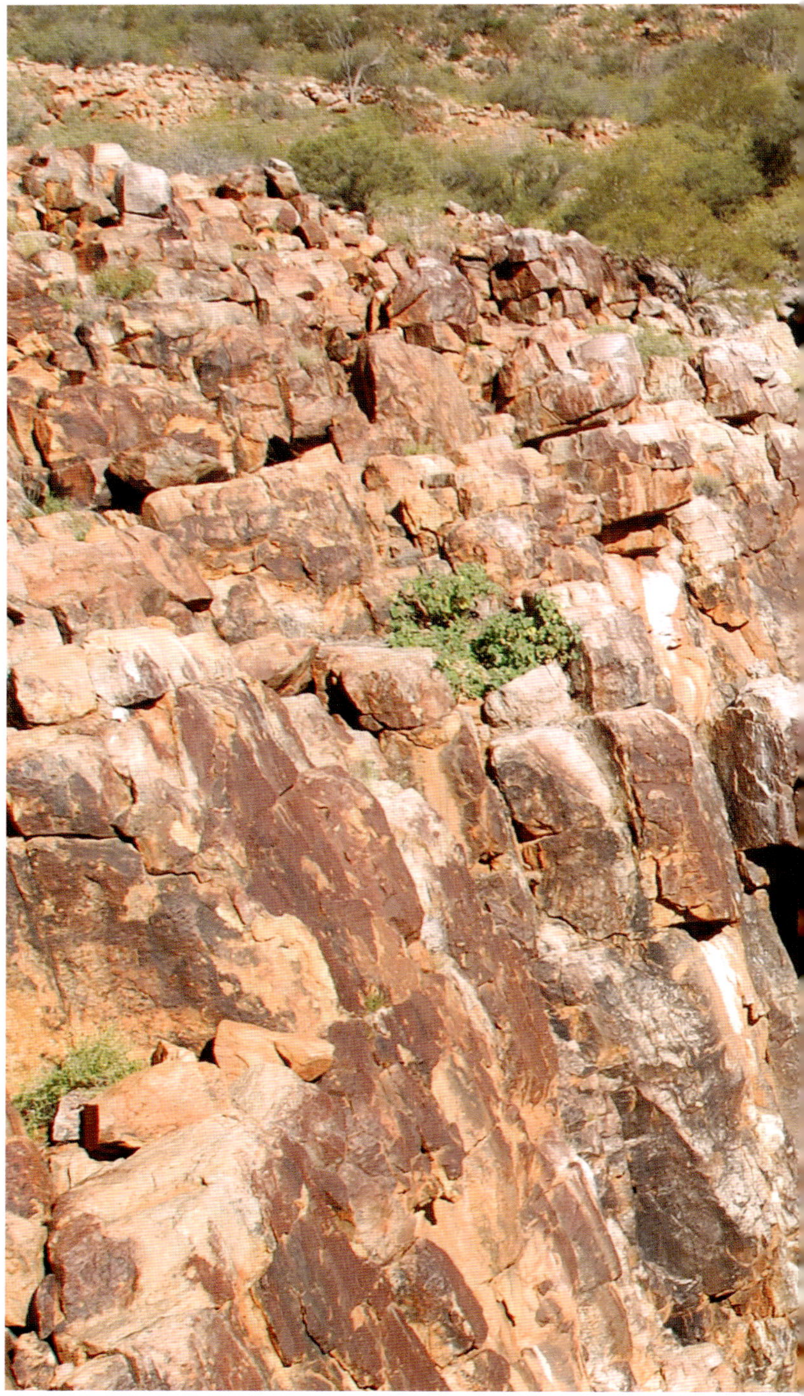

ferocious marsupial lion, Thylacoleo. About the size of a leopard, it could climb trees where it would wait to pounce on its prey.

The megafauna also included a wide array of birdlife including early species of flamingo. In 1893, hundreds of megafauna fossils were found embedded in the mud of Lake Callabonna, south-east of Lake Eyre, exciting great interest in the scientific world. Each succeeding dig has helped to tell the evolving story of Central Australia: gradually the centre had dried out and the more luxurious flora disappeared, and in its place grew hardy shrubs and less nutritious vegetation. Only those animals able to adapt to this stringent new diet survived. Most of the megafauna — the reptiles, birds and marsupials — did not.

Scientists are still unlocking the history held in the lake beds, the sand and the sedimentary rocks of Central Australia. One is Dr Mike Smith, an archaeologist and senior research fellow with Canberra's National Museum. We stood at the foot of a rocky outcrop north of Lake Eyre, deep in the Simpson Desert. Rising steeply above us was a craggy, boulder-strewn escarpment, covered in spindly shrubs and pitted with caves. The ridge runs for several kilometres across the desert, the only feature on the landscape to disturb the long procession of sand dunes, running north-south, as far as the eye can see: 'It's probably one of the world's largest dune fields. There is tremendous regularity in these long sand ridges — they run for hundreds of kilometres across several degrees of latitude.'

Dr Smith knows this country intimately. He has spent more than thirty years tramping across the deserts around Lake Eyre, tracing the human connection with the region. Early research suggested Aboriginal

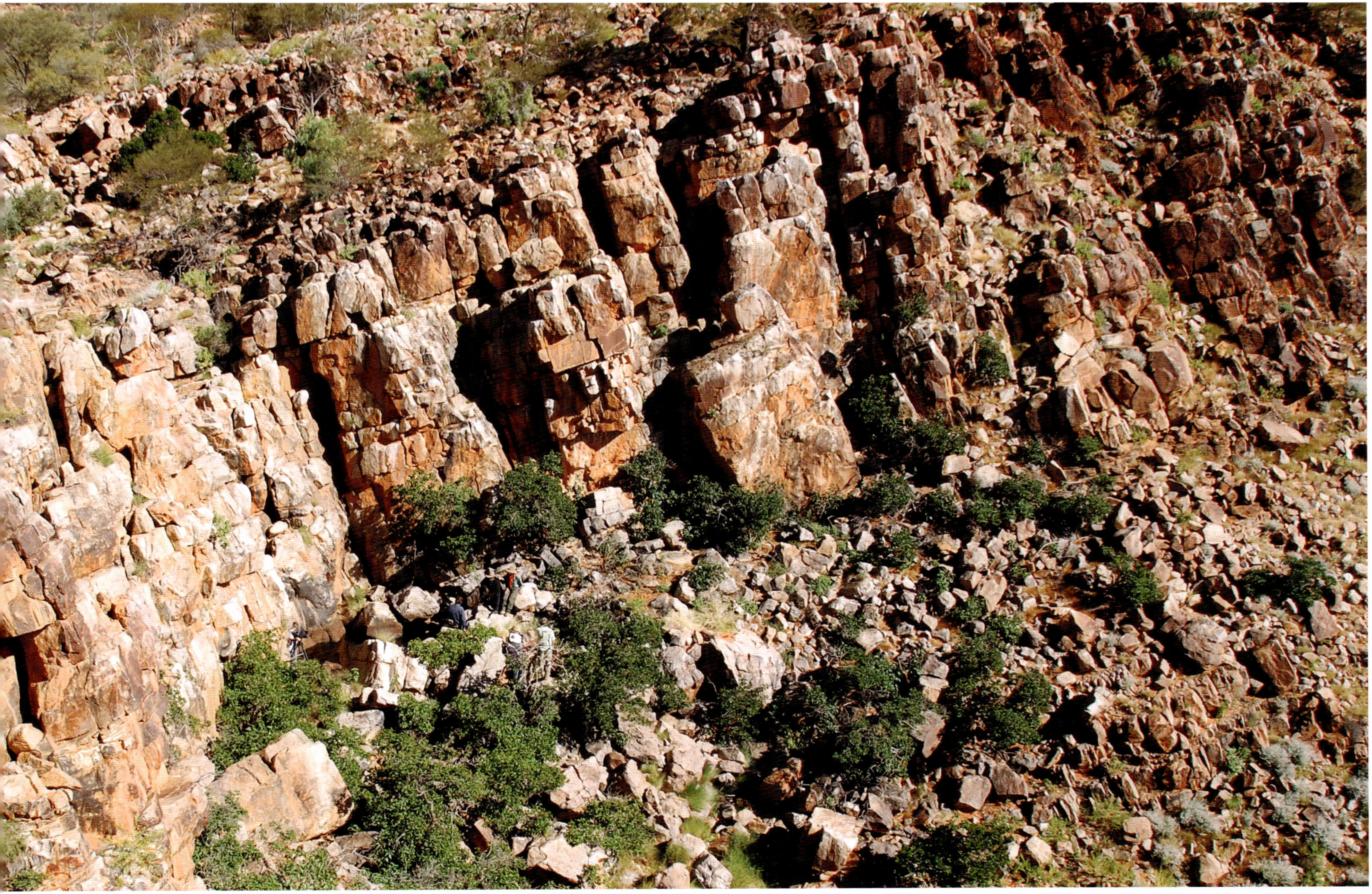

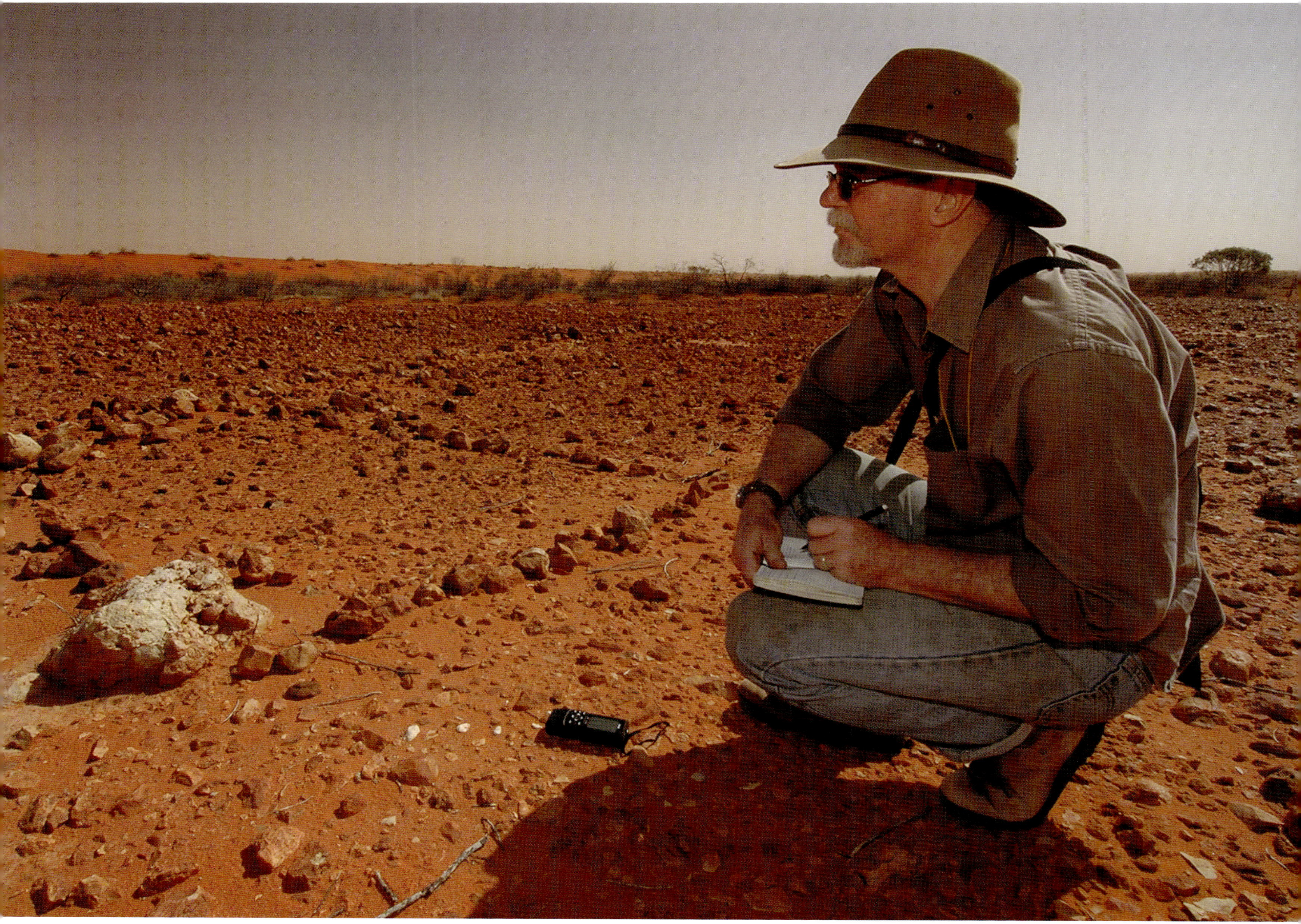

Dr Mike Smith, here in the Simpson Desert, believes that parts of Central Australia were occupied 35,000 years ago.

people came into the desert later than other areas, around 10,000 years ago. But Dr Smith's groundbreaking investigations have now dated the occupation of some parts of Central Australia as far back as 35,000 years. But that's just a starting point for his work: 'To establish a history you need to work on the details, because of course the Aboriginal history of the desert is as richly nuanced and finely textured as European history.'

It's the great unknowns about the human history of the desert that most intrigue him; for example, when he spots archaeological deposits — stone artefacts among other things — where erosion has cut through a weathered section of rocky debris, with fine stone chips that fan out across the base of a gully. There he identified white specks as food remains; others as animal tooth fragments and flakes from the manufacture of stone knives.

Right around Lake Eyre the landscape bears the scars of millions of years of weathering. To the south-west of the lake are the Painted Hills on Anna Creek Station: heavily eroded sandstone hills in stunning shades of ochre red and mustard yellow. And south of the lake is the most dominant feature of all — the unfolding peaks of the Flinders Ranges rising out of the plains. Nature has sculpted the ridges and gullies of the Flinders to form intriguing patterns and forms. There's a soft, inviting finish to this mountain range that has made it a magnet for tourists and artists alike. But in the early days of white settlement it was considered to be part of the hostile inland. It wasn't until 1926, when artist Hans Heysen ventured from Adelaide to the Flinders Ranges to paint his famous landscapes of the region, that the outback began to be portrayed in a softer light. The highest peaks in the Flinders rise majestically to over 1000 metres, providing dramatic vantage points to view the ancient surrounds. History dwarfs you here. To the west, on a clear day, Lake Torrens can be seen glittering on the horizon; and to the north, the flat countryside sweeps away in a heat haze towards Lake Eyre — dusty rocky plains, once a sea bed but now one of the driest places on the globe. Lake Eyre sits at the heart of one of the biggest internal drainage systems in the world. Rivers flow to the lake from a catchment

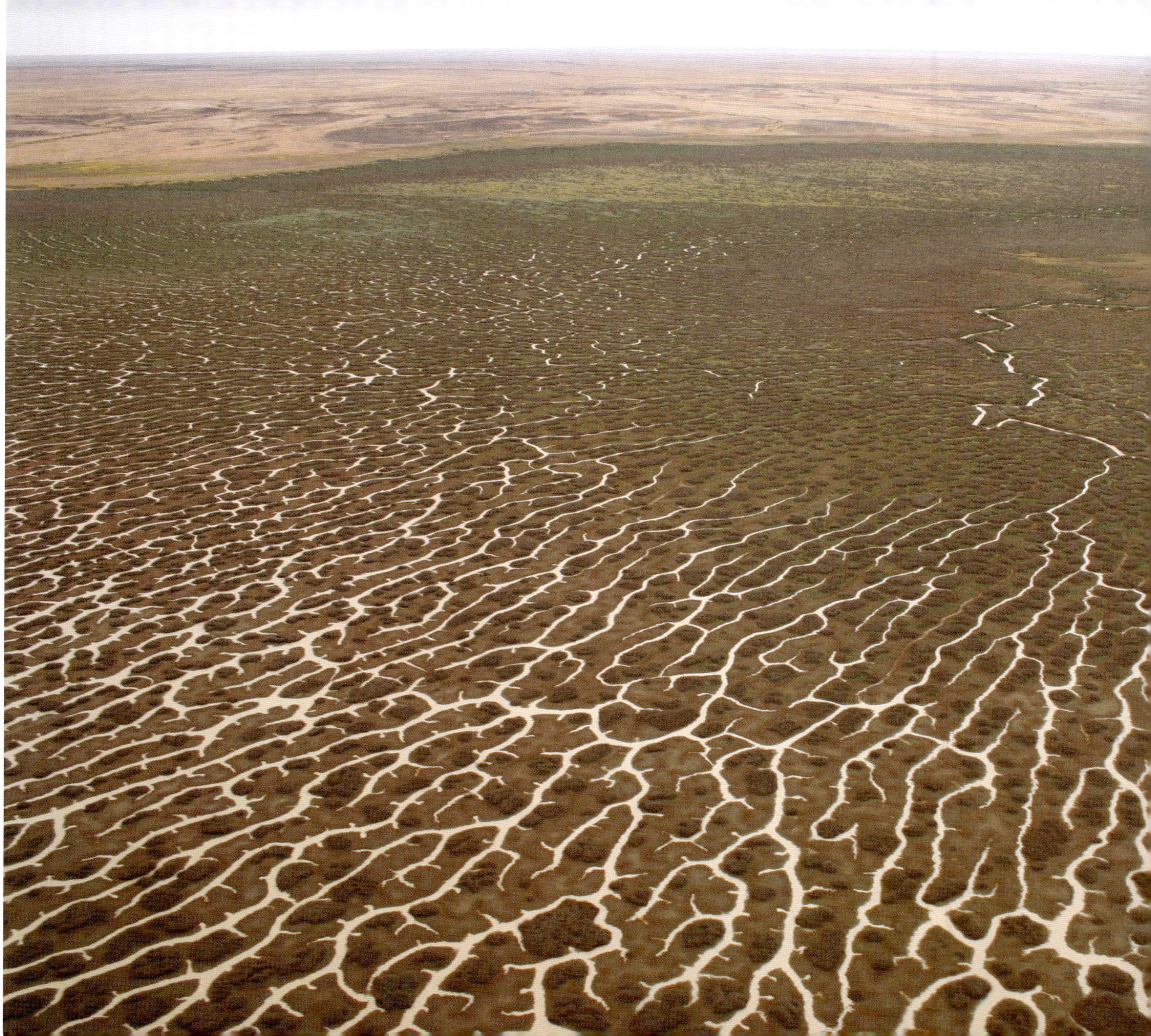

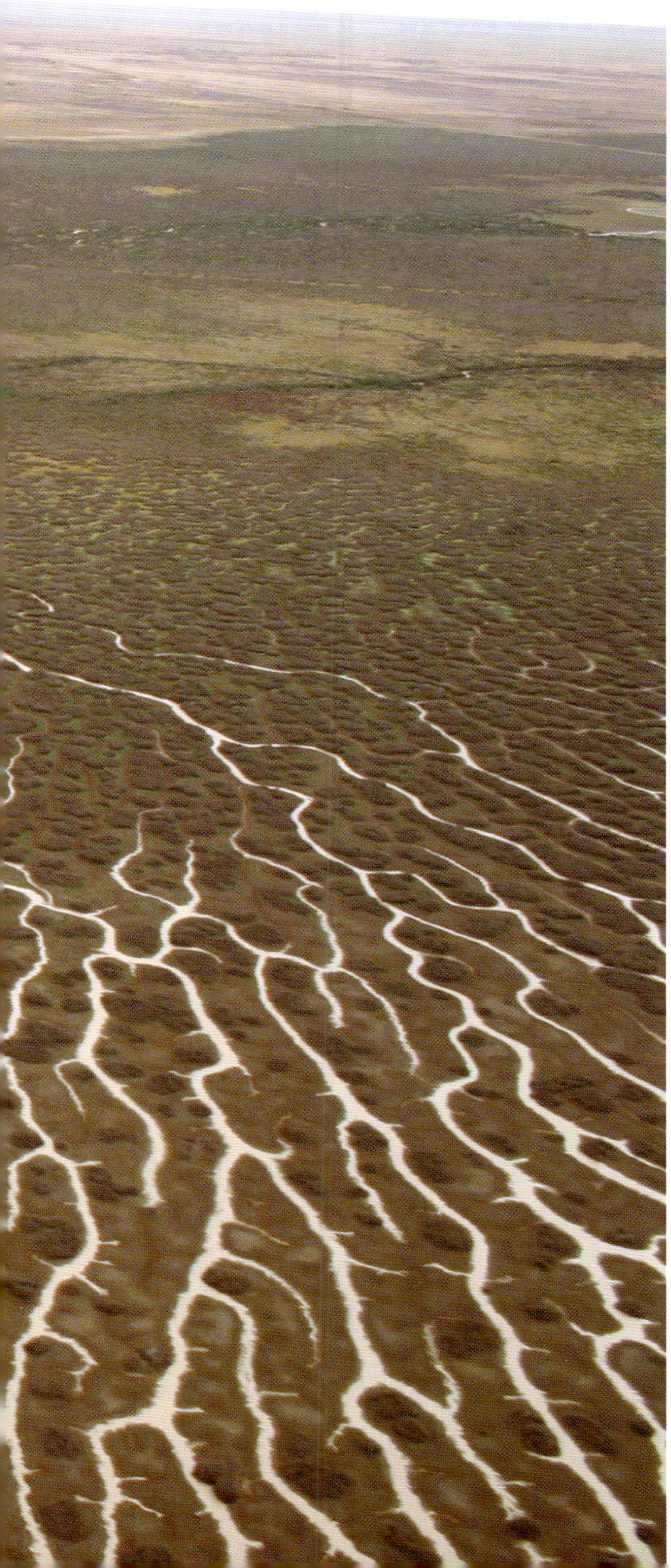

Covering one seventh of Australia, the Lake Eyre Basin is one of the largest endoheric — internal drainage — systems in the world, with a catchment area spreading over four states.
Overleaf: Cloud patterns form over the channels of Warburton Creek and Goyder's Lagoon

area that stretches wide across South Australia, New South Wales, Queensland and the Northern Territory. It forms what's called the Lake Eyre Basin, stretching over more than 1.2 million square kilometres and covering one seventh of the continent. It's like a huge saucer in the middle of Australia with Lake Eyre at the centre — big enough to contain Italy, Germany and France combined.

Scientists marvel at the massive system, which has largely escaped development. 'There are very few river systems in the world,' say Richard Kingsford of the Universtity of New South Wales, 'that haven't been dammed or had water taken out of them, so this is one of the great natural river systems of world.'

Professor Kingsford is an environmental scientist who has spent much of his life studying the outback wetlands and the waterbirds that rely on these habitats. He believes the Lake Eyre Basin is one of Australia's great environmental jewels: 'People can always come out here and see how these river systems have been operating for thousands of years.'

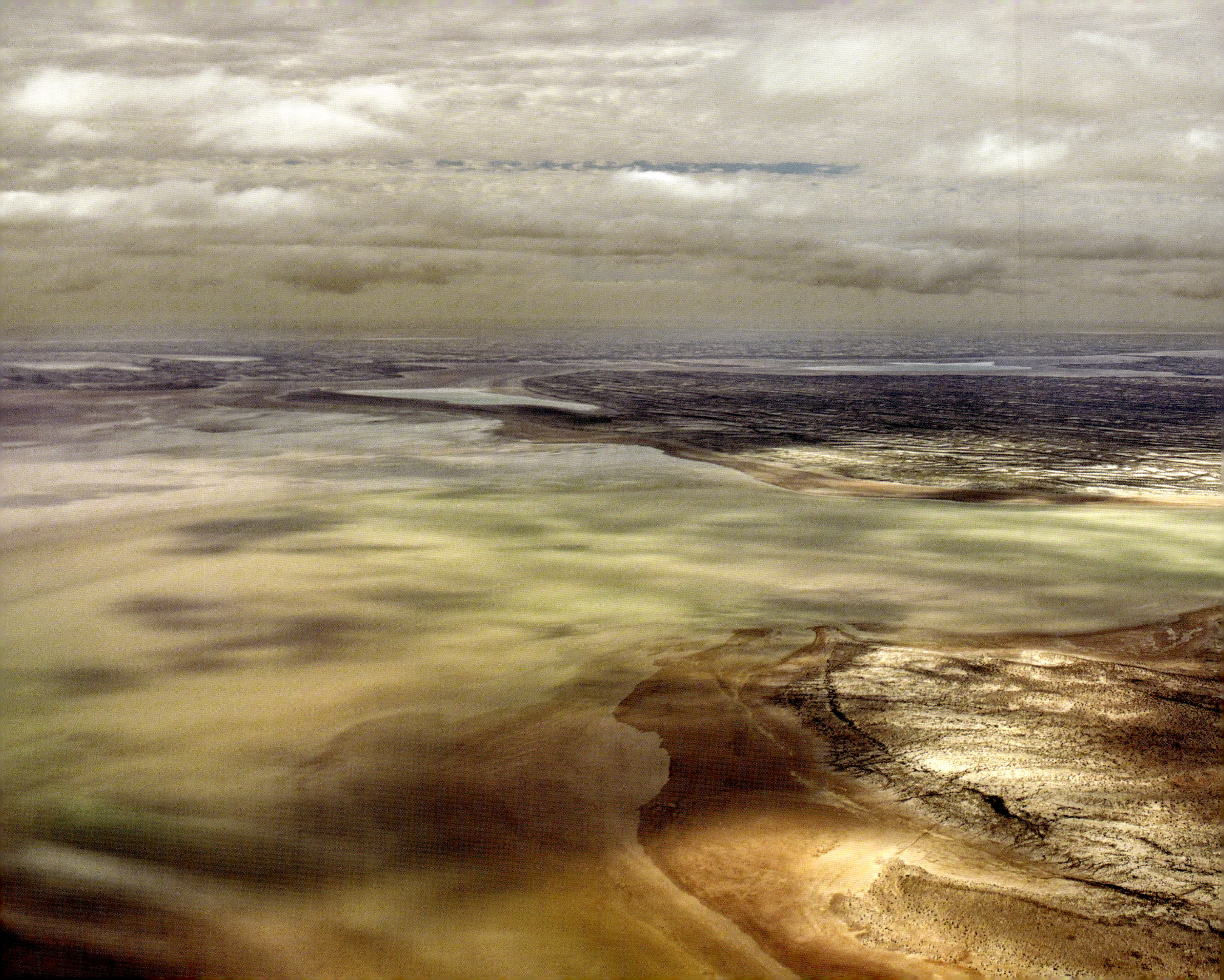

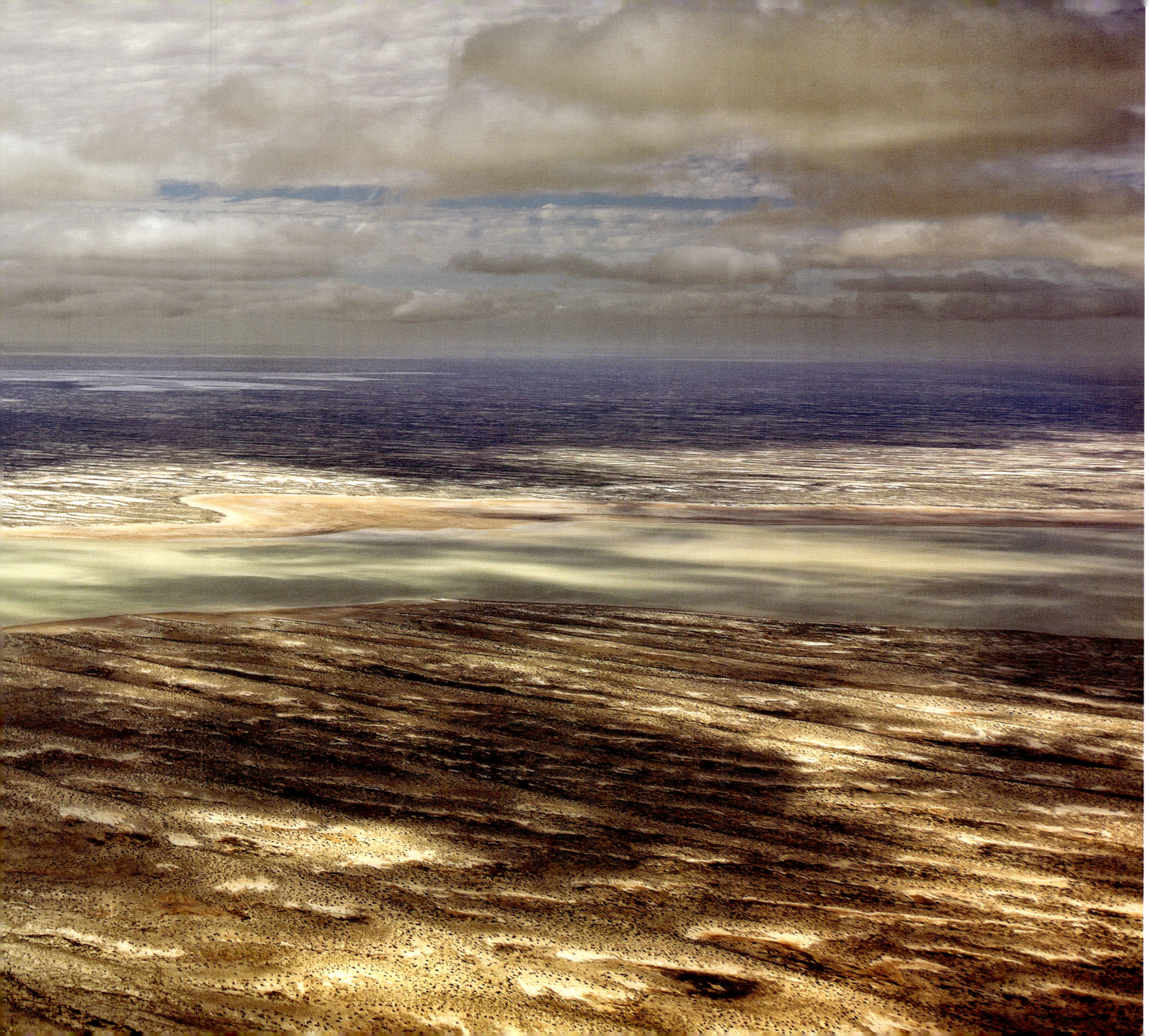

Outback wetlands, such as this one at Eyre Creek, depend on the uninterrupted flow of their rivers to underpin the survival of wildlife species.

But the rivers of the Lake Eyre Basin are usually little more than a string of boggy waterholes; scars running across a barren landscape waiting for the next rain. In the long dry years between the floods only the hardiest of desert creatures survive in the harsh environment around Lake Eyre, including one that makes its home on the salt pan — the Lake Eyre dragon. This tiny reptile has developed a high tolerance to heat and has even adapted eyelashes to keep out the glare from the sun and the salt. The little lizard survives on a diet of harvester ants — tiny ants that gather seeds and build their nests in the salt — and other insects. The Lake Eyre dragon escapes the worst of the heat by burrowing into the moist sediment beneath the salt crust. Few animals in the world live in such an inhospitable environment. But what is even more astounding is that there is also life to be found in the dry, cracked mud of the floodplains around Lake Eyre. The building blocks of the future are locked away in the baked earth — too small for the eye to see.

In the crevices crisscrossing the cracked landscape of Lake Eyre's vast floodplain life exists in the dried mud. Professor Kingsford explains: 'If we take a clod of dirt and put it into a container of water you would have hundreds of small crustaceans and things hatching out of that. Not only that, you'll get lots of aquatic plants. In the wet times this would have been brimming with life. Right down in those cracks there will be hundreds of eggs and seeds of plants that have been left behind. They'll go from egg to adult stage in about three weeks, and not only that but the numbers of different species are also increasing at the same time,

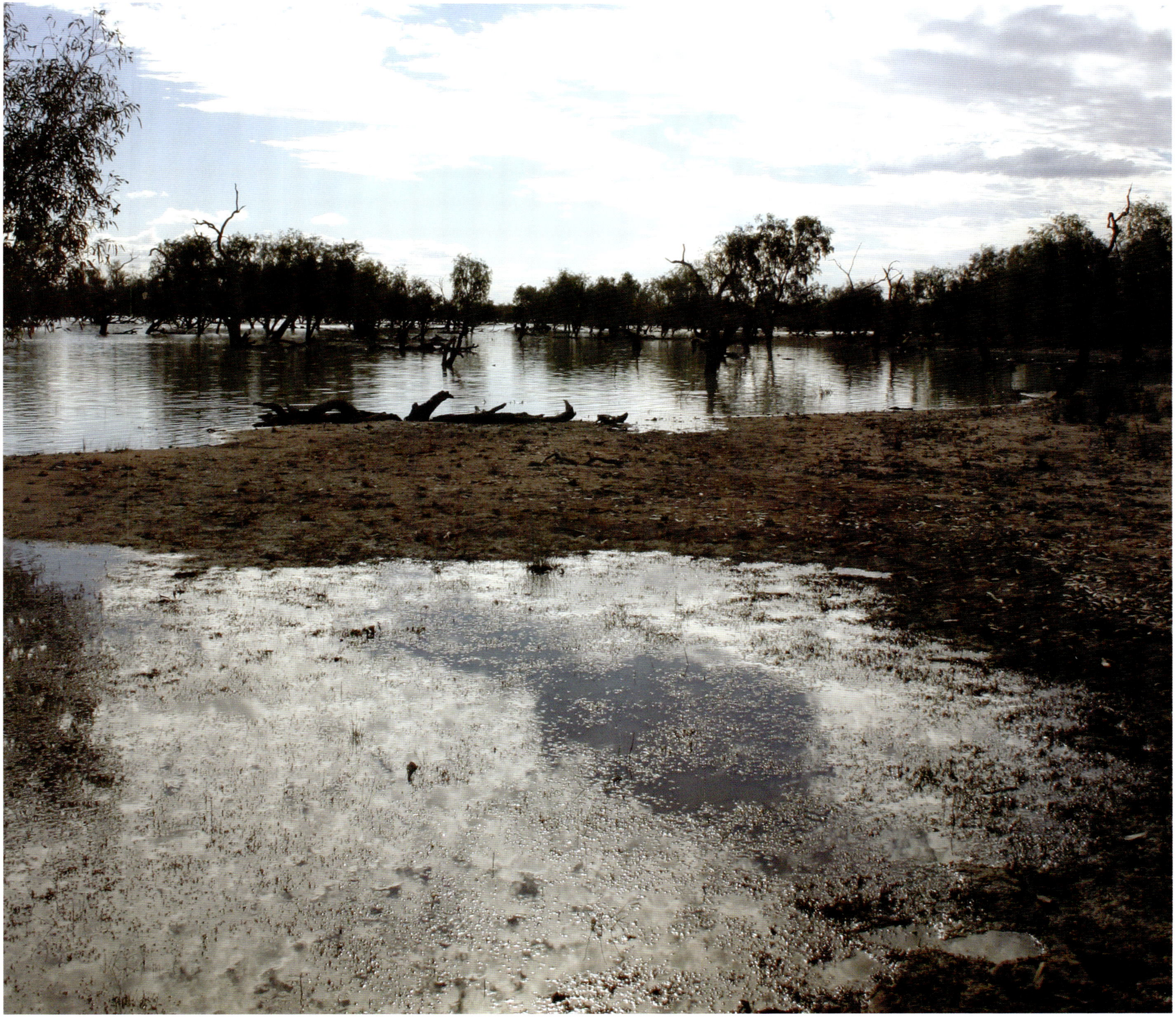

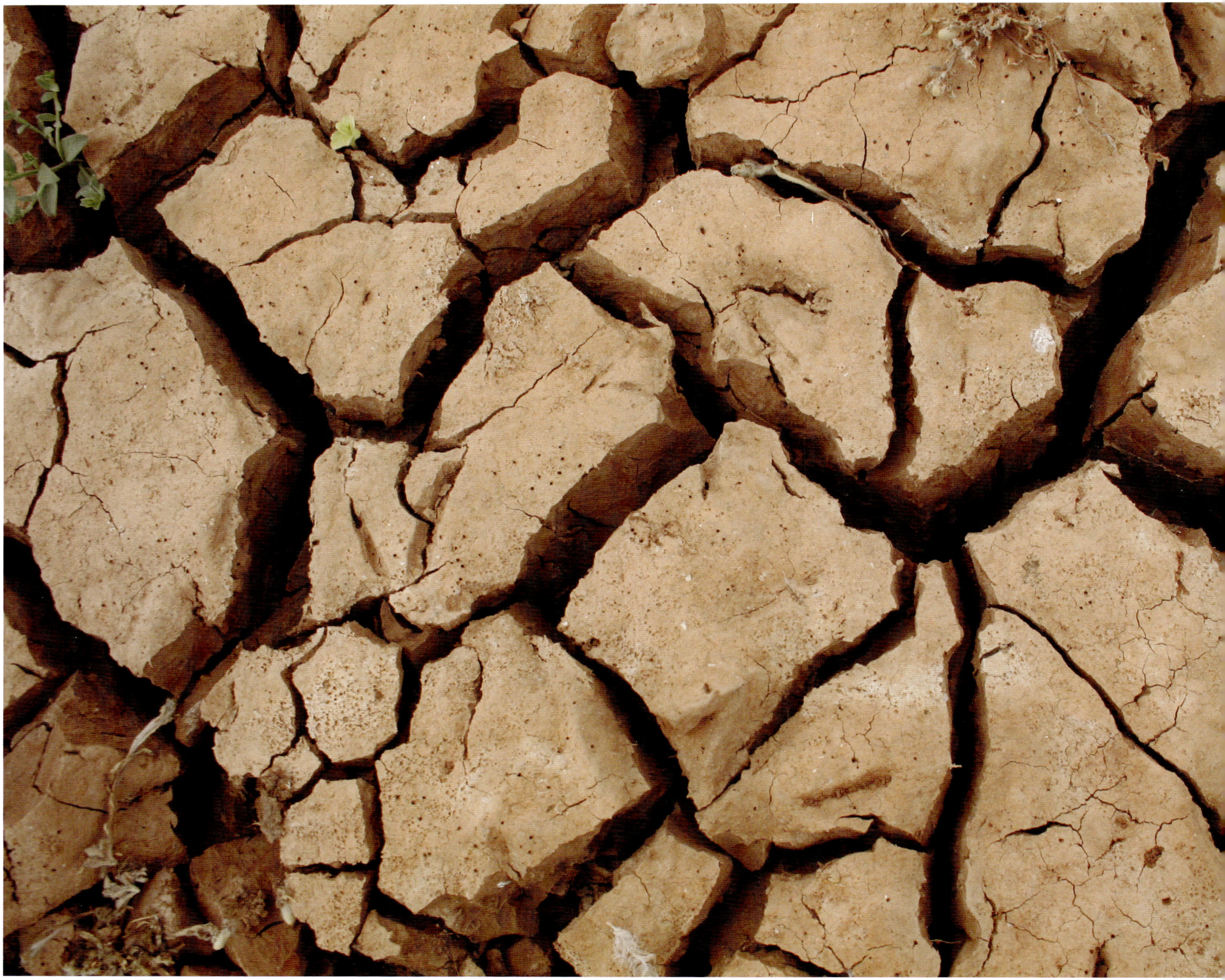

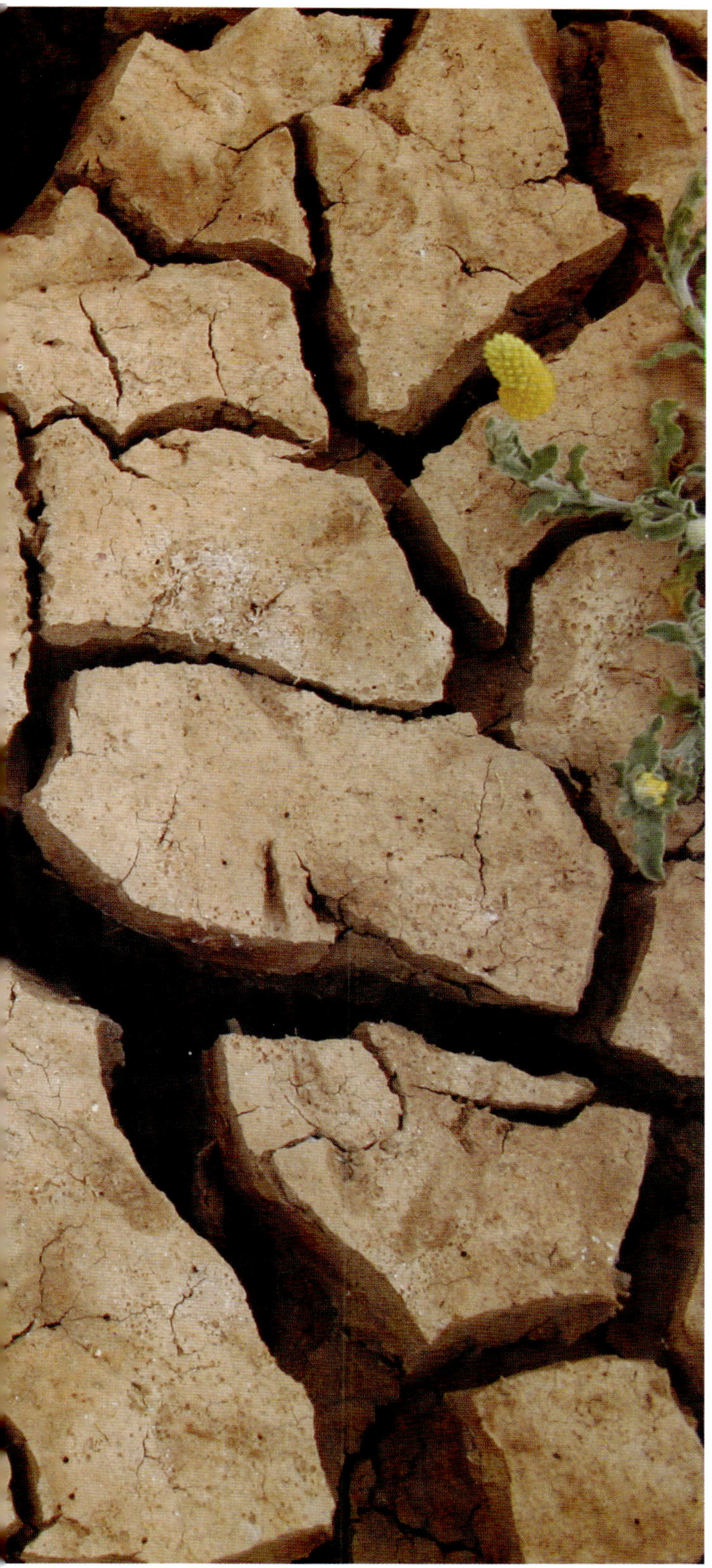

Despite appearances, life exists in the dry, cracked mud of the floodplains of Lake Eyre. When water arrives, the floodplains soon teem with life from the tiniest microorganisms to flowering plants, frogs, reptiles, birds and mammals.

so you've got this incredible exponential increase in biology when the water arrives.' Nature has learned to be very patient.

Archaeologists have established that people first reached Australia at least 50,000 years ago. DNA studies suggest it was part of the global diaspora of humans from Africa across the rest of the world. They would have faced a major sea journey from South-East Asia — a story that is still possibly being told through contemporary Aboriginal Dreaming traditions.

Movement from the tropical north into the arid heart of the continent would have been the real challenge but archaeology has shown that people had reached the northern and southern margins of the desert by 45,000 years ago and were well established in Central Australia up to 35,000 years ago. Lake Eyre had already dried out by then and the flows in the rivers that ran to the lake had declined. After they settled into the area, Aboriginal societies formed a long engagement with the land around Lake Eyre. By the time the first white explorers pressed inland in the 1800s the lands around the lake was held by a number of tribal groups, including the Arabana, Wangkangurru, Dhirari and Dieri, and the land was interlaced with their myths and songlines about the ancestral beings that had given it shape.

The version told by the Arabana tribe, whose homelands stretch south-west from Lake Eyre, describes how a kangaroo was hunted down after a long chase by a young boy who decided to rest before cooking the animal. But while he slept an old man took the kangaroo and began cooking it himself. The boy tracked him down and told the old man he could keep the meat but must return the skin. Spirits had told the boy that the skin was magic and, once he had recovered it, a bird guided him to a spot in the desert where he placed it over the sand. The skin began expanding and water poured in to form the body of the lake. This story in various forms has been passed down by the Aboriginal tribes of Central Australia over thousands of years — as have the fears held for the area. This barren place of mud, blinding white salt and ghostly mirages was to be avoided. A number of terrifying ancestral beings are believed to exist in the muddy wasteland, including a terrifying, ghostly white spirit the Arabana call Warrenar, and Kuddimukra, a giant serpent with the head of a kangaroo. They are believed to be the protectors of Lake Eyre, lying in wait for the unwary traveller.

Many of the white explorers who attempted to cross Central Australia were daunted by the endless sandy ridges they found there. Aboriginal tribal groups, including the Arabana and the Dieri, however, had a long engagement with the land around the lake and its inflowing rivers. This 1846 watercolour by S. T. Gill was taken from a sketch by explorer Charles Sturt.

Overleaf: Miles of eerily empty expanses of salt characterise the lake during the region's long dry spells

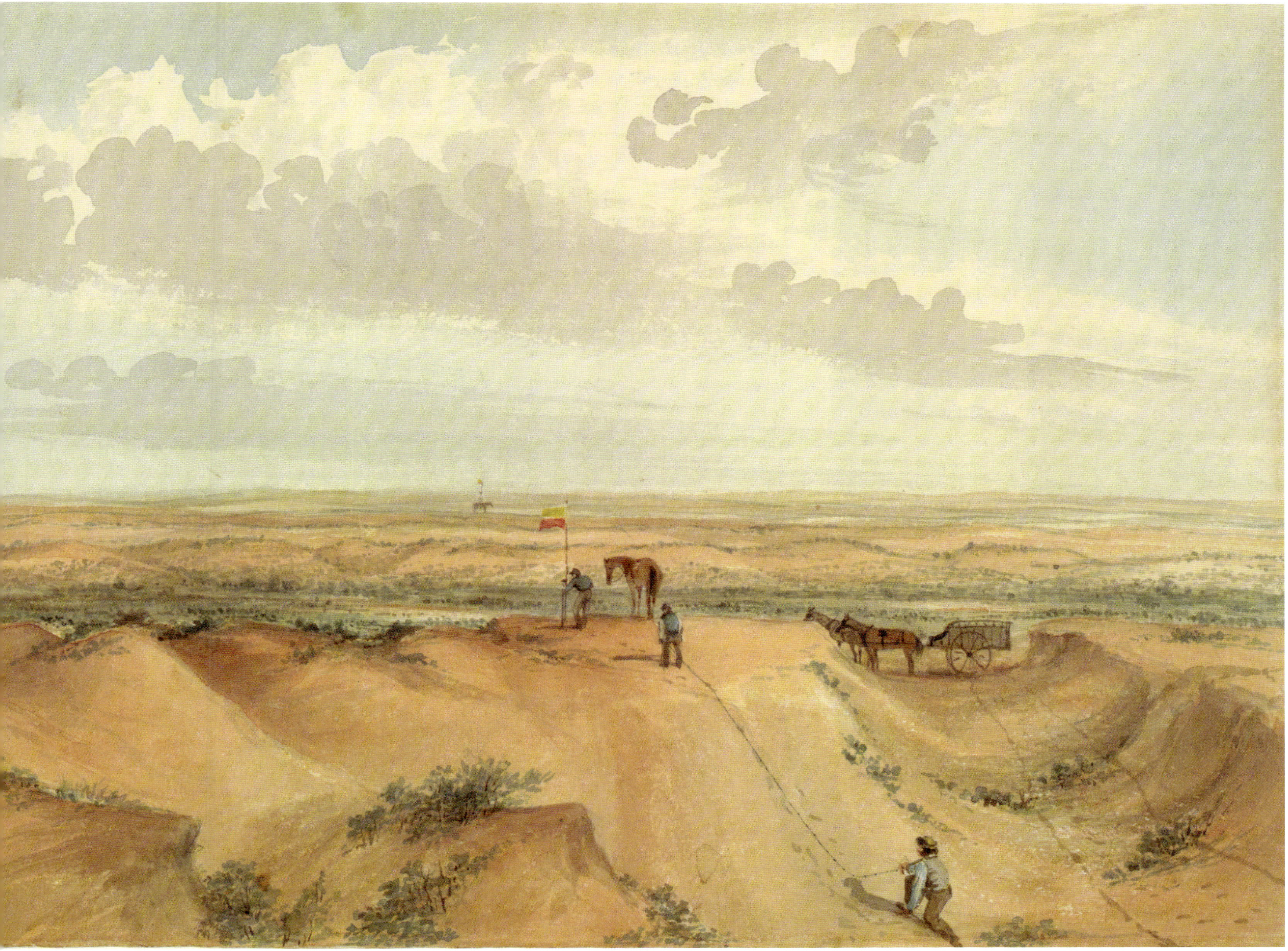

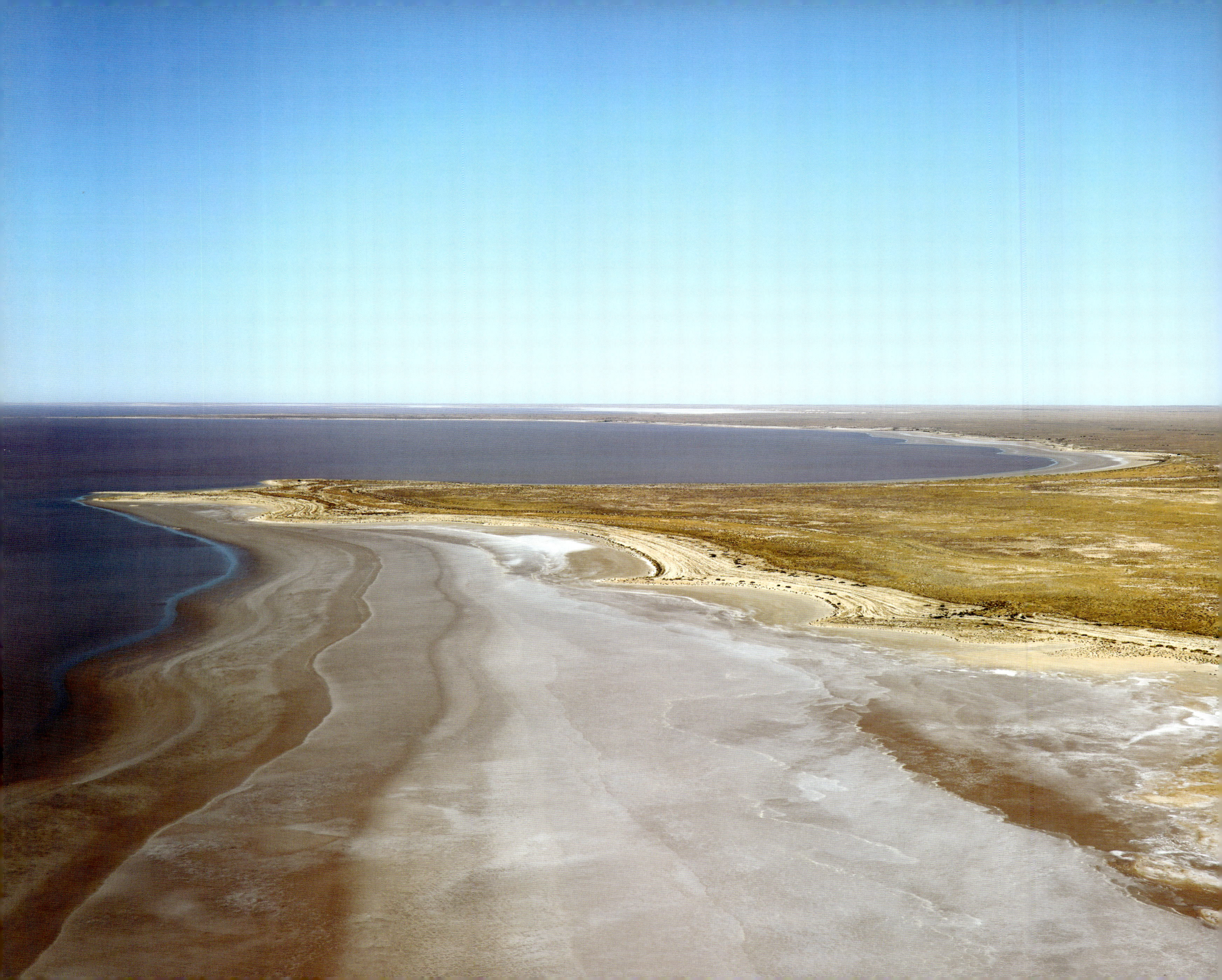

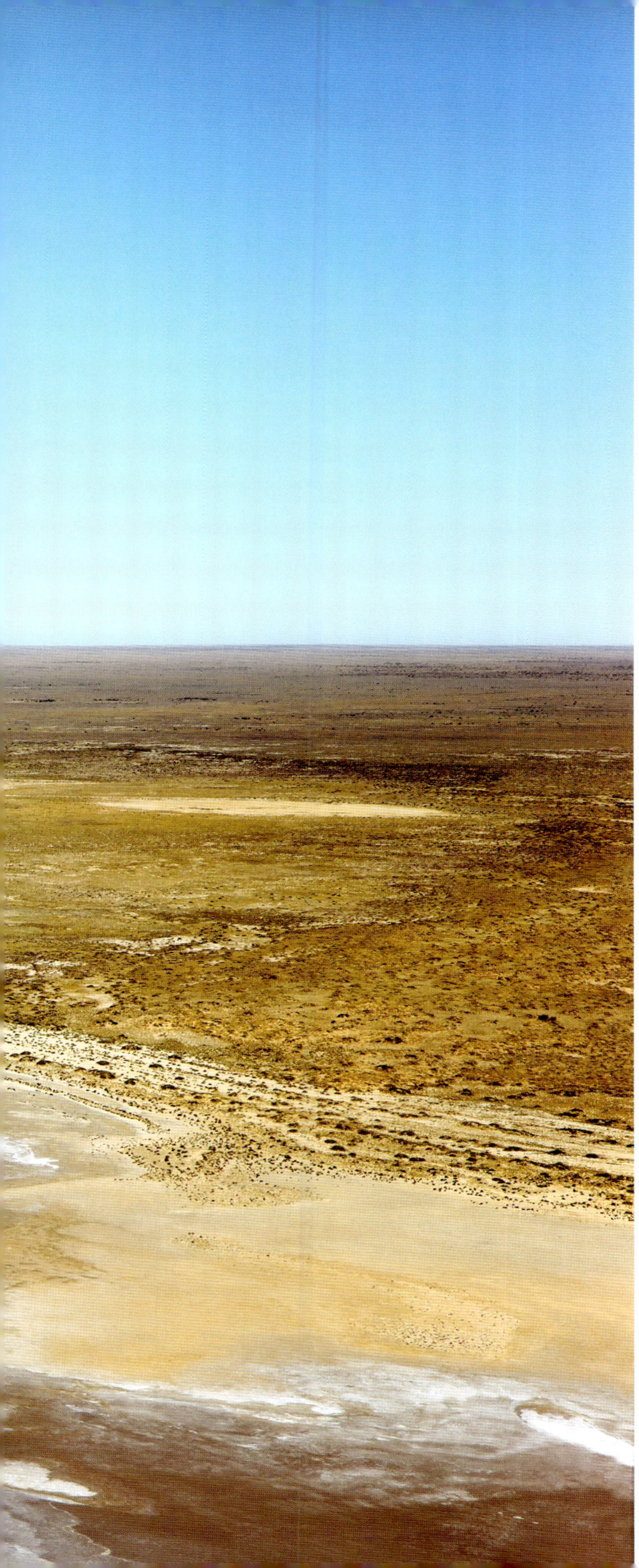

The paradox of Lake Eyre

Professor Richard Kingsford

THE BRITISH GEOLOGIST JOHN GREGORY WASN'T PARTICULARLY impressed when he visited a dry Lake Eyre — 'the dead heart of Australia' — at the turn of the twentieth century. If he had explored it during a flood year, on the other hand, he would have been able to enthuse about a spectacular inland sea, brimming with life.

Lake Eyre is a paradox — often desolate and lifeless but occasionally full of aquatic life. It is the largest natural lake in Australia and one of the largest lakes in the world. Its ecology is defined by salt — about 400 million tonnes worth. Few animals can tolerate Lake Eyre's extremely high salinities, which sometimes exceed those of seawater. Aquatic life can only boom when enough fresh water reaches the lake from intermittently flowing rivers to overcome the salt levels, a phenomenon that only involves the whole lake during particularly large floods. Even after the two years of flooding in 1974 and 1975 had filled the lake and dissolved the salt, the water still tasted salty.

The heart-shaped lake is made up of two parts: Lake Eyre North and the smaller Lake Eyre South, which are connected during large floods by the salt-filled, 15-kilometre-long Goyder Channel. Lake Eyre North is about 120 kilometres long by 60 kilometres wide, while Lake Eyre South is about 60 kilometres long and 25 kilometres at its widest. The lake lies 15 metres below sea level at its deepest point in Belt Bay.

Salt lines — resembling waves breaking on a shore — on the western coast of Madigan Gulf

When it is dry, the blinding salt expanse stretches as far as the eye can see but varies in its thickness across the lake, a reflection of the lake's flooding patterns. In the south, the salt is hard-baked, but in the north the crust is thin where the rivers flow in. Soft black mud lies beneath

Cooper Creek entering Lake Eyre from the east in the1950s. On average the river only makes it to the lake every thirteen years, prior to the 2010 floods, it hadn't reached Lake Eyre since 1990.

this crust. Lake Eyre is always changing across its extent and over time because its nature is totally dependent on its rivers.

About 100,000 years ago, the lake into which these rivers constantly poured water was fresh, deep and big. The version of the lake about 35,000 years ago was also very big and is referred to by another name — Lake Dieri, after the Aboriginal people living to the east of that great expanse of water. Then, the lake was about three times the size it is today, and its ecology was very different, as the fossils of the time reveal. It is hard to imagine, but the lake's shores were probably surrounded by thick vegetation, which supported many of Australia's extinct megafauna. The lakes and rivers were home to an even more astonishing range of aquatic animals. There were platypus, dolphins and even four species of flamingos. These died out as the climate became drier and the rivers and their lakes dried out, about 20,000 years ago.

Today the rivers still flow but not nearly as often as they once did, and this has promulgated myths about how often the lake fills.

Many people think that Lake Eyre fills only once a lifetime. Perhaps this is why it is so fascinating to so many people. Of course, the lake actually starts to fill every time water flows into it from any of its rivers — about every two years based on analysis by Vincent Kotwicki. Much of the surface area of the lake is often covered by only a shallow veneer of water. In 2009 and 2010, probably more than half the surface area of the lake was flooded. A full lake of more than 4 metres deep, however, is rare. The last time was during the big floods of the 1970s, and before that the floods of the 1950s. The 1974 flood reached levels higher than they had been for a hundred years. We might currently be in a new wet phase, since Lake Eyre had filled for three years, from 2009 to 2011.

Since 1979, water has flowed into the lake in twenty-three of those thirty-three years, meaning there were more years that it received water than years that it did not. The Lake Eyre Yacht Club, with an eye clearly on their hobby, has identified that the depth reaches 1.8 metres in Jackboot Bay at the bottom of

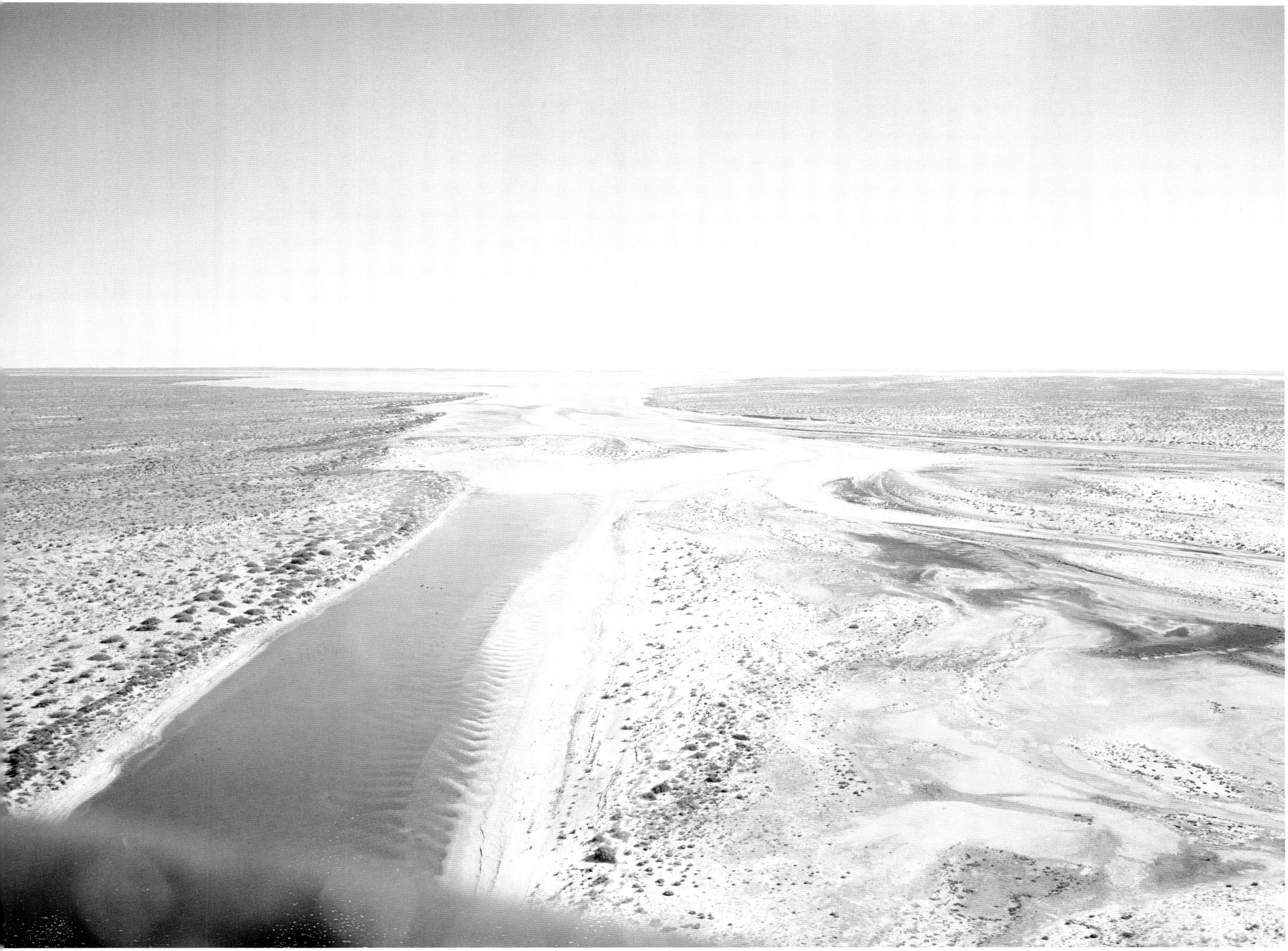

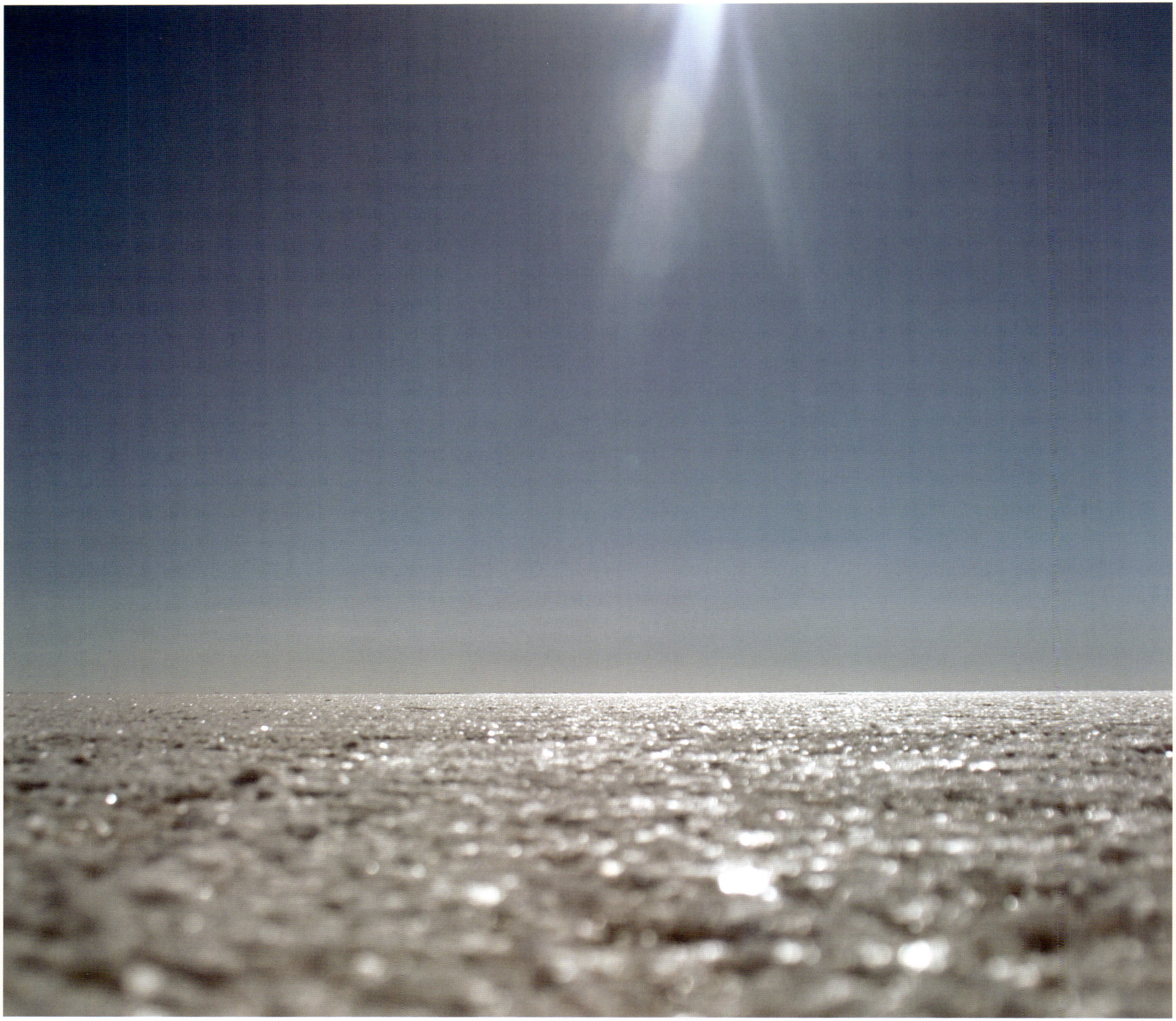

Few animals can tolerate the high salinity levels of Lake Eyre — there are around 400 million tonnes of salt in the lake.

Lake Eyre North about every three years. And if the lake fills, it can hold water for four to five years as it did in the mid 1970s.

The flooding cycles of the giant circulatory system that centres on Lake Eyre depends on rain that falls more than 1000 kilometres away. Tropical cyclones and deep rain depressions dump their loads into the top of the Lake Eyre catchment, running the rivers.

The rivers that flow through the Lake Eyre Basin are the world's most variable — the size of their floods, their frequency and duration, even where the water flows, is more unpredictable than in any other part of the globe. If you were a doctor listening to their rhythm, you would be worried by the arrhythmia.

Lake Eyre's rivers oscillate between boom and bust extremes and it is this that defines the ecology of this huge connected system. Only one maxim holds: every drought will be broken by a flood. But *when* that flood will come and how long it will last remains guesswork.

Outback conversations and even people's moods inevitably oscillate between the depressive effects of drought and the optimism of the floods. Good times are always followed by dry times. The flooding of the Lake Eyre Basin brings life to the environment and boosts livestock production across vast cattle stations. Outback floods also capture the public imagination on an unprecedented scale and the money pours in through tourism.

Understanding the behaviour or rhythm of the rivers governs it all. Thankfully, water planners installed river gauges on Lake Eyre's major rivers more than thirty years ago, and these have given us a great understanding of the flooding. It is clear that no two floods are the same since there is always some level of chaotic behaviour involved. Slow, inexorably spreading floodwaters can be diverted from a previous flood path by anything from a newly grown lignum bush to a change in a channel. Flood behaviour is also dependent on which of the many tributaries run and the timing of the flooding as they contribute their flow to the Georgina–Diamantina catchment, which

Normally a series of disconnected waterholes, the Diamantina River in western Queensland eventually flows into Lake Eyre when flooding rains fall.

gives Lake Eyre about 64 per cent of its water, and the Cooper, which accounts for about 17 per cent.

Along the way, the rivers fill channels, floodplains, waterholes and lakes. Their roles in the ecology of the system vary, reflecting diverse filling and drying patterns. There are, for example, more than 100 shallow freshwater lakes on the Lower Cooper that differ enormously in how long they retain water. Lake Hope, for example, holds water for more than four years, while nearby Lake Kopperamanna dries in about half that time. Further upstream, some lakes in the Coongie Lakes system are hardly ever dry.

Inevitably after a flood, the amount of water contracts to only a few of these permanent lakes and the waterholes. For animals that have to live in water — fish, turtles and even some water birds — these become refuges and boltholes during the long, hard droughts. Between the dry channels and the lakes, deep gashes in the floodplain mark distinctive waterholes. These are the most dependable and widespread areas of water in the desert, sometimes extending a few kilometres in length but seldom reaching more than about 50 metres in width. The network of branching creeks, rivers and floodplains is more often than not dry, with only rare boom years flooding the entire system, usually over a sequence of flood years.

When the rivers do flow, however, they sustain an amazing network of wetlands on their way to Lake Eyre, each with its own ecology. They include some of the largest floodplains in Australia, such as the one surounding Cooper Creek. As well, there are many freshwater lakes, including Coongie Lakes on Cooper Creek, Lake Blanche supplied by Strzelecki Creek, and the lakes supplied by Eyre Creek and the Mulligan River. Scattered among these freshwater lakes are other salt lakes, which hold water less often and are considerably smaller than Lake Eyre. And even the freshwater lakes become salty as they dry out since evaporation concentrates the salts.

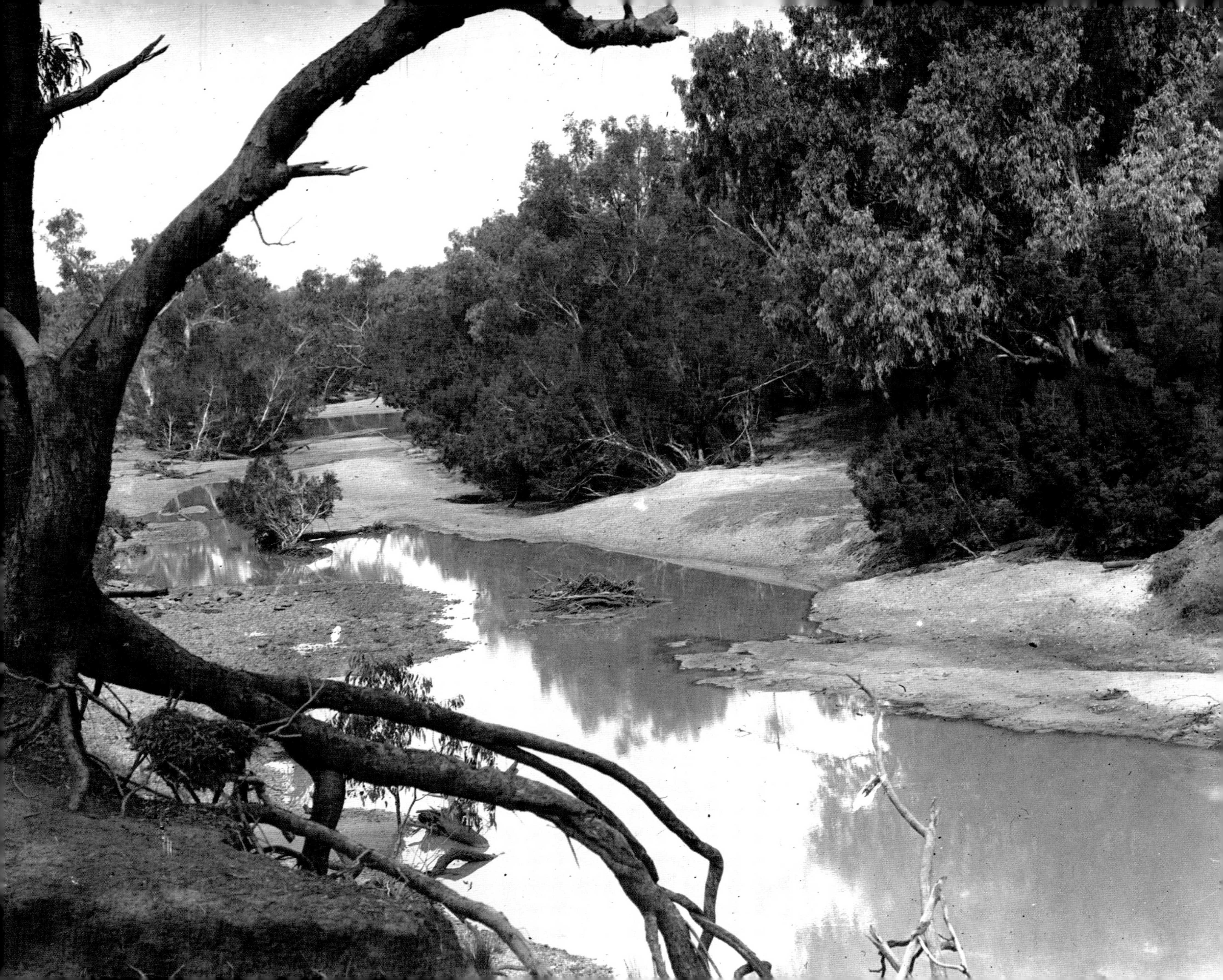

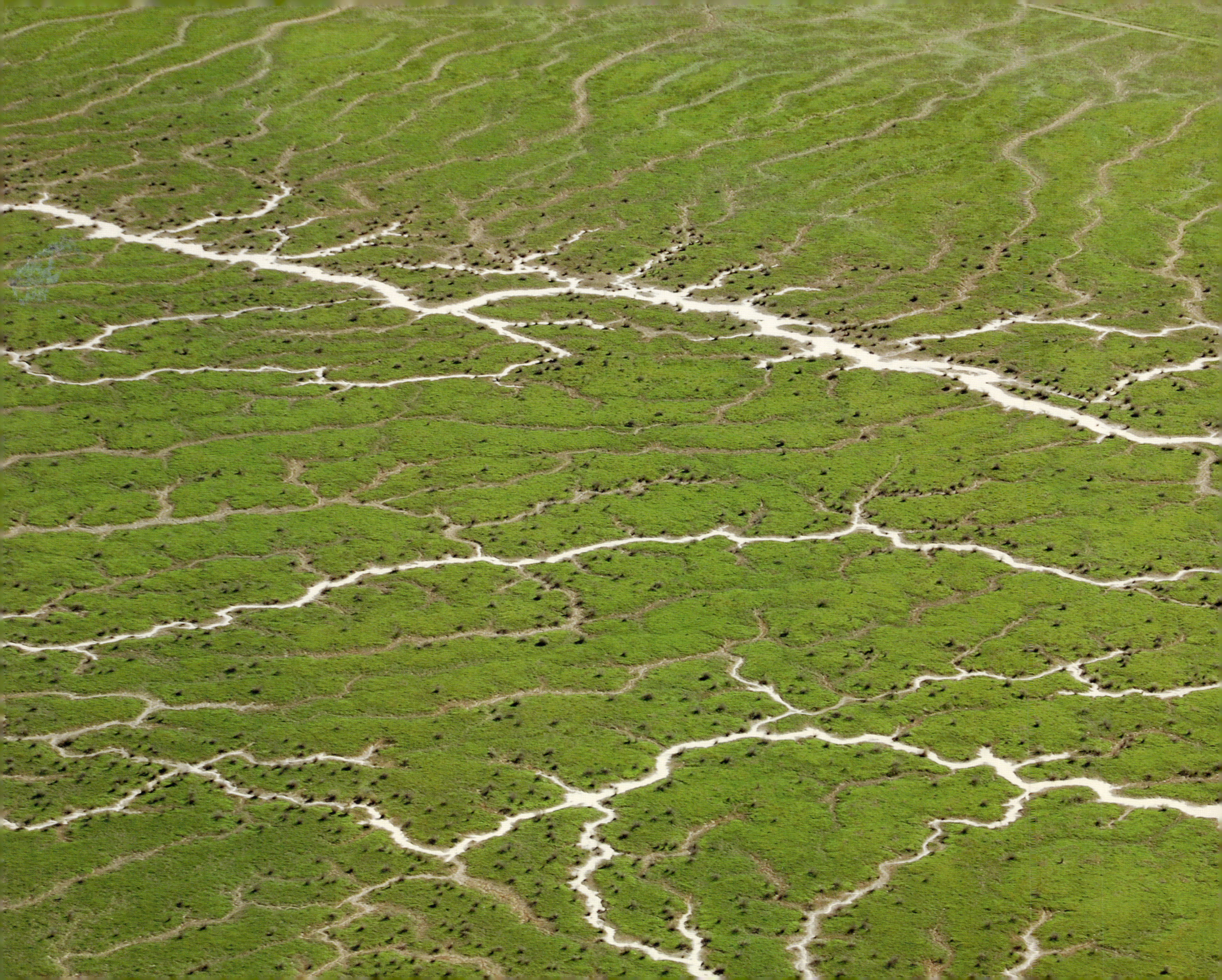

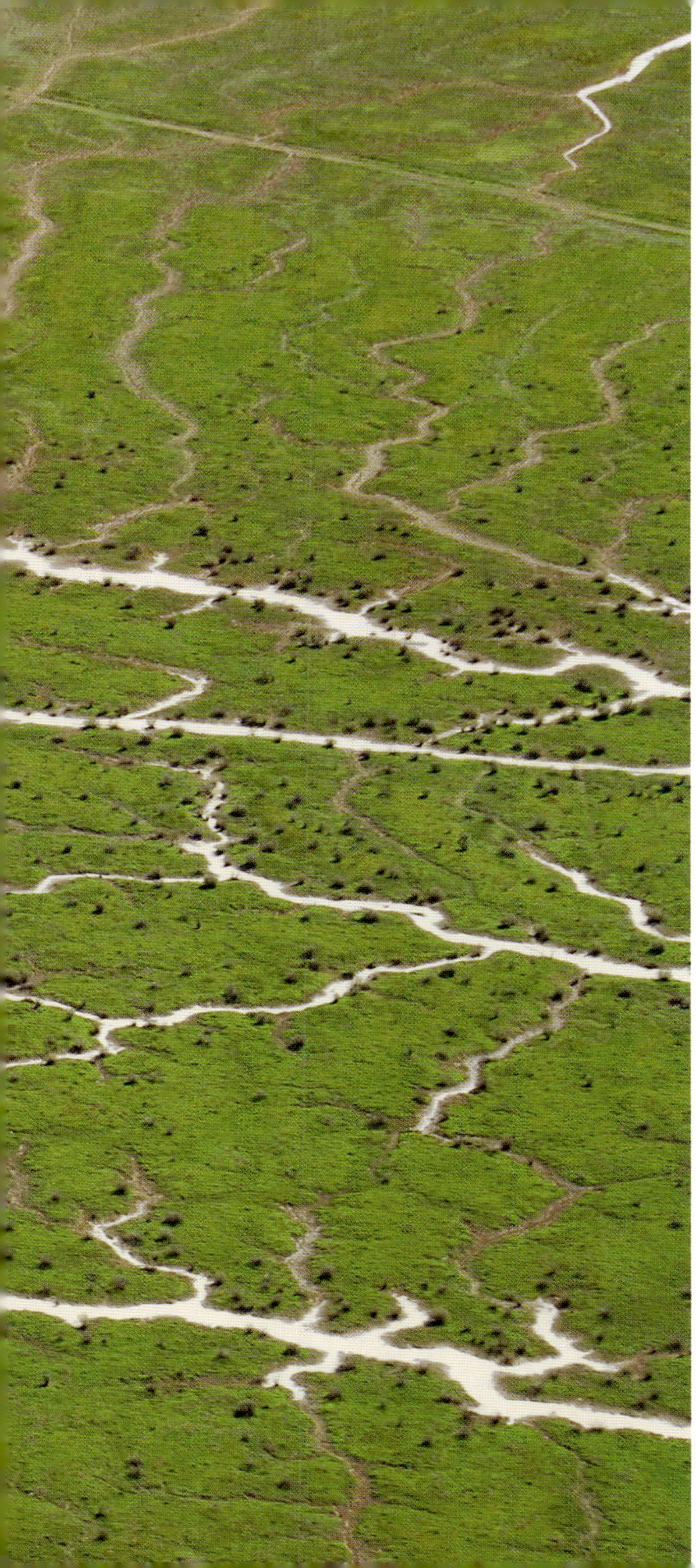

The floods course down the many small, finger-like connected channels across the floodplain of Eyre Creek, before spreading out and forming a sheet of water which lasts only weeks or months before drying back to leave a carpet of green vegetation.
Overleaf: Madigan Gulf on Lake Eyre North

The Lake Eyre Basin extends over a catchment through which rivers from all directions of the compass flow into Lake Eyre. From the north, the Warburton River, sometimes called Warburton Creek, brings water from the Georgina–Diamantina catchment into Lake Eyre. This vast river network extends north all the way to the Queensland mining town of Mount Isa and then north-east to Winton. Two mighty rivers join to form the Warburton: the Diamantina River from the north-east and the Georgina River from the north. In its upper reaches, the Diamantina forms a series of disconnected waterholes across a broad floodplain. It was here that the legendary swagman was immortalised by Banjo Paterson in Australia's most famous bush ballad, 'Waltzing Matilda'.

When the rains come, the waterholes are linked by a braided network of channels, forming a shallow sheet of water across the floodplain. The Diamantina makes its way south past the town of Birdsville in Queensland before disgorging its floodwaters into the huge expanse of Goyder's Lagoon where it meets the waters of the Georgina. This river starts south of Mount Isa and is joined by the Burke River. The Georgina River then merges with the Hamilton River to form Eyre Creek, named in 1845 by the explorer Charles Sturt, who had a propensity for identifying Australia's large desert rivers as creeks because he couldn't believe that such shallow channel systems deserved the status of river.

Eyre Creek is, however, a mighty river system with an extensive network of lakes and channels. Joined by the waters of the Georgina, Hamilton and Mulligan rivers, the far-reaching floodplain of Eyre Creek works west before narrowing as it meanders through the dunes of the

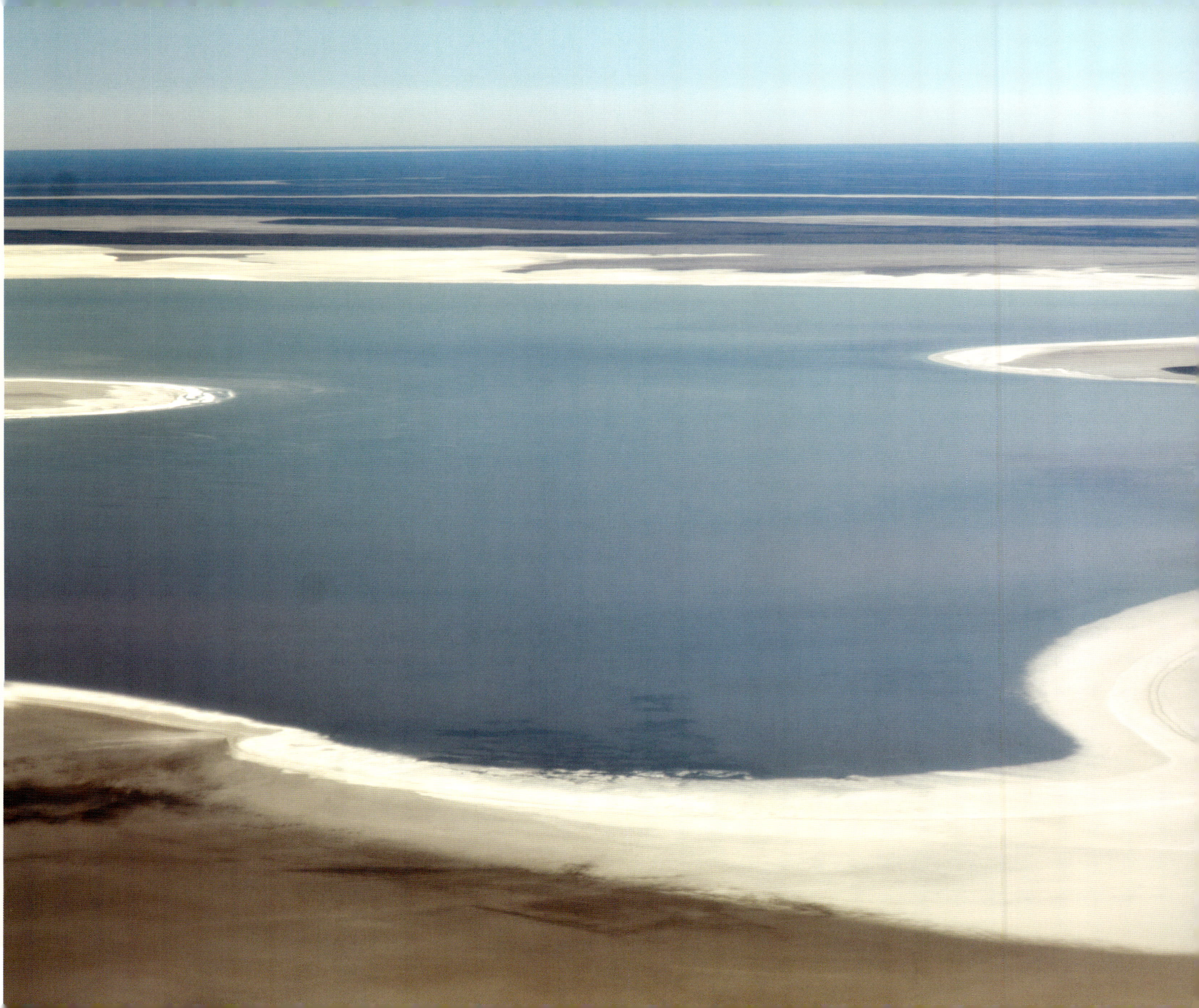

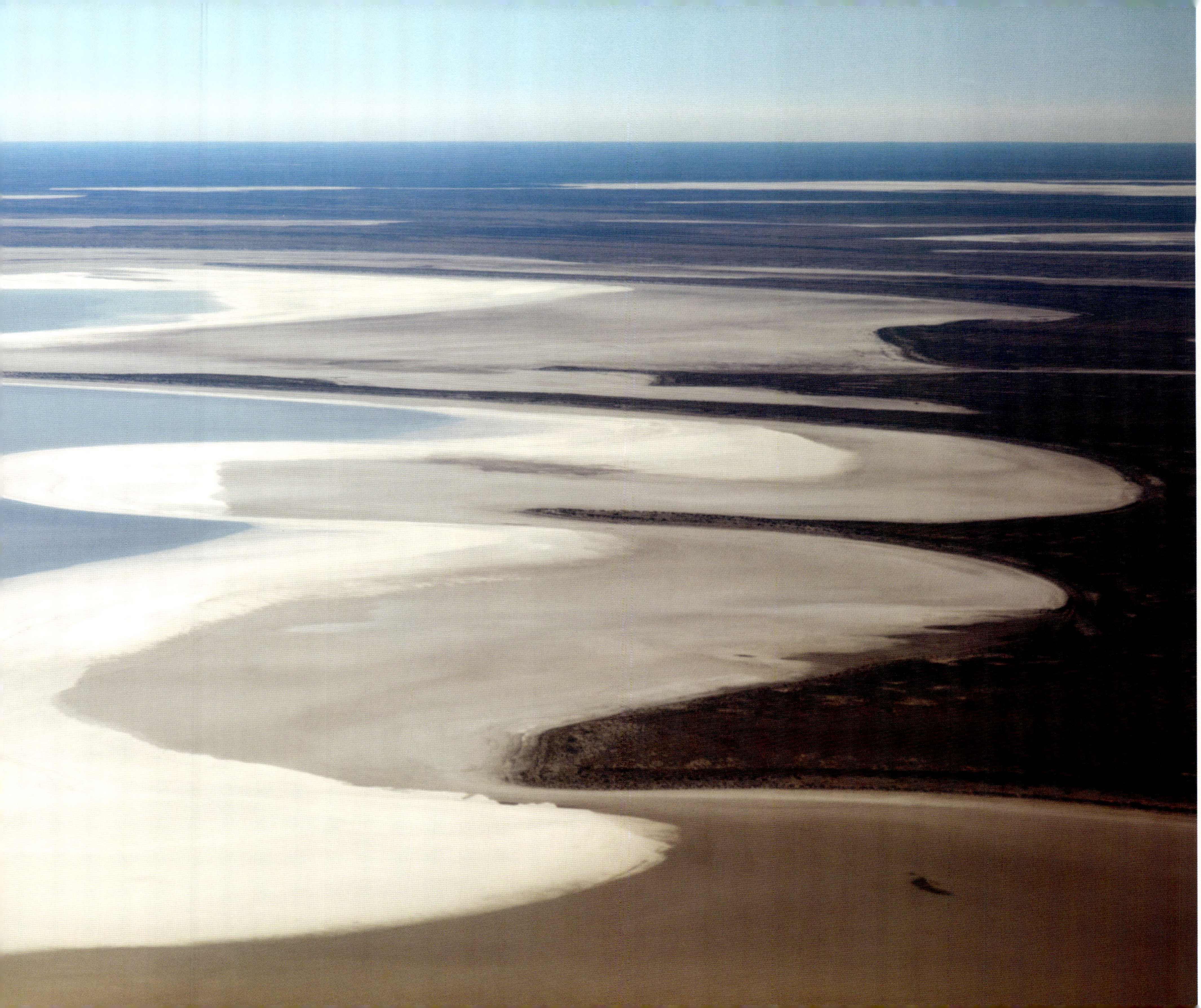

Simpson Desert and eventually pours into Goyder's Lagoon. This massive floodplain extends about 120 kilometres on its long axis by 30 kilometres on its short axis. A lot of water needs to fill this ecological sponge before the river can continue to flow south to Lake Eyre. This is the way with many of Australia's rivers — enough water has to reach a destination before another river can come to life. In this case, when enough water emerges from Goyder's Lagoon, the river that is reborn is the Warburton. This river and its tributories are the most dependable source of water for Lake Eyre.

The next most important source is Cooper Creek, which comes in from the east but has to make a long journey to deliver its waters; most of the time it fails, petering out somewhere upstream. Cooper Creek, named by the explorer Charles Sturt after the Chief Justice of South Australia, originates in the Great Dividing Range, west of Rockhampton in Queensland. It has two main tributaries: the Thomson River, draining the north-eastern part of the catchment, and the Barcoo River, draining the eastern catchment. The Thomson flows through Longreach, the hub of rural life in central Queensland, while the Barcoo flows through the town of Blackall. Unlike most other outback rivers, which bear names drawn from the European heritage, the Barcoo has an Aboriginal name. Explorer Edmund Kennedy chose to rename it after Surveyor-General Thomas Mitchell originally called it Victoria Stream, after the queen.

The junction of the two rivers, near the small town of Jundah in Queensland, lies in the middle of the Channel Country of the Cooper Creek floodplain, which spreads to about 60 kilometres wide downstream of the outback town of Windorah. On the way south, the Cooper fills the freshwater Lake Yamma Yamma, a key breeding site for Australian pelicans, before narrowing and continuing on to the South Australian town of Innamincka. In a large flood, the water continues flowing west but also cuts to the south, forming Strzelecki Creek, which eventually runs into lakes Callabonna, Blanche and Gregory on the northern edge of the ancient Flinders Ranges. The Strzelecki only makes it to Lake Blanche every ten to fifteen years. The lakes also fill from local rainfall — Lake Callabonna last filled this way in 1971.

About 25 kilometres west of Innamincka, the Cooper splits into two branches. The north-west branch takes most of the water in the river and flows into the magnificent Coongie Lakes, an oasis of water that almost never dries up and is well recognised for its biodiversity. About 2 million hectares of the floodplain is protected under the Innamincka Regional Reserve, which includes Coongie Lakes National Park. In 1987, the importance of the area was recognised under the Ramsar Convention, an international treaty to conserve significant wetlands around the world. Once through this maze of lakes, the Cooper flows south and is joined by the main branch of the river, going on to fill the Lower Cooper lakes, including Lake Hope.

The green Eyre Creek floodplain and water-filled channels are a contrast to the surrounding brown desert. In the dry times, when little other water exists, the thin waterholes provide essential refuges for many animals including turtles and fish.

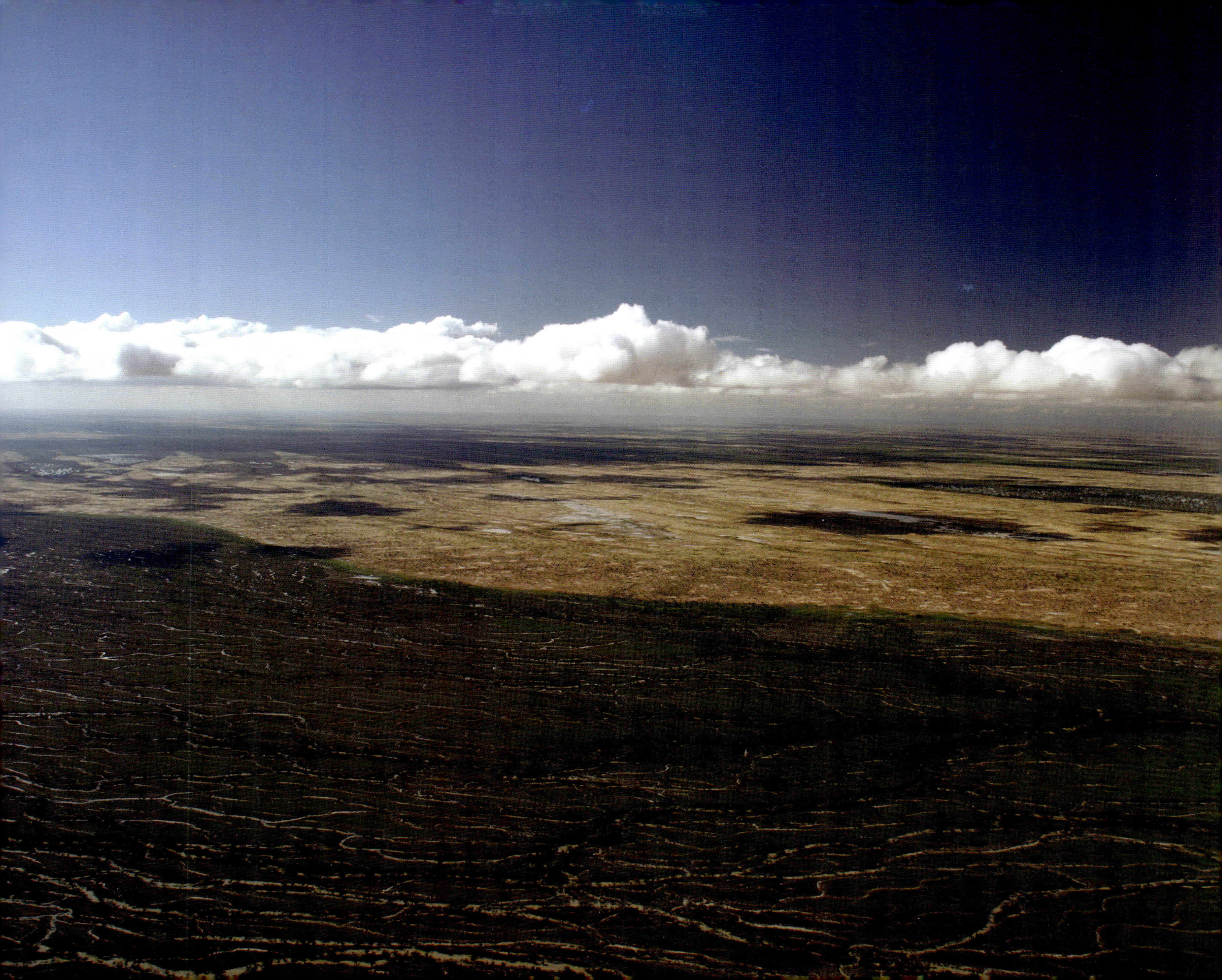

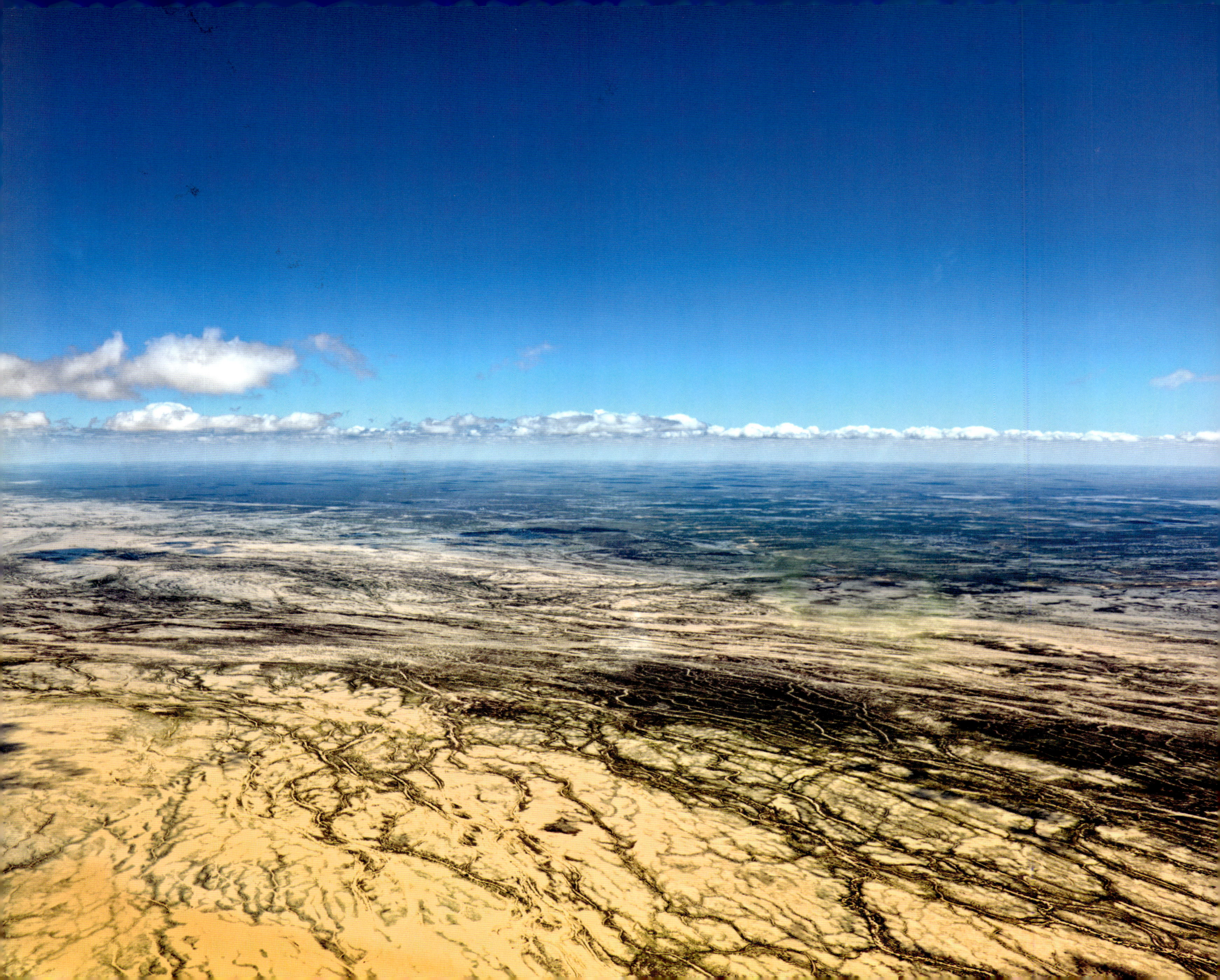

When the floods come, Goyder's Lagoon swells and flows with brown water on the way down to the lake.

Here floods can cut the Birdsville Track, one of the main roads through the outback. The river only reaches this far about every four years and only then will it continue on to reach Lake Eyre. Even in the Lower Cooper, there are lakes and swamps everywhere. Each one must be filled before the water can move on, pushing through the sand dunes east of Lake Eyre. On average, the river only makes it to Lake Eyre roughly every thirteen years — but averages in this part of the world aren't particularly useful. The Cooper just made it into the lake in 2010 but the time before that was in 1990.

The other river and creek systems that flow into Lake Eyre from the west and south are much less reliable and also considerably smaller than the two major river systems. These include the Neales and Macumba rivers, which only rarely flow in from the north-west. Frome River or Creek flows into the south-eastern part of Lake Eyre from the Flinders Ranges. In 1984 and 2011, it virtually filled the southern part of the lake. Finally, the Warriner and Margaret creeks flow into Lake Eyre from the Stuart Range.

Together, this network of rivers and creeks can flood Lake Eyre but, given how far the water has to travel, it is not surprising that it is considerably difficult to predict how much the lake will fill.

Lake-filling floods come along every twenty years or so and are well known in the outback. Records abound of the size and impact of the large floods of the 1950s, 1970s, 1990s, and most recently from 2009 to 2011. There are marks on trees and on buildings in towns throughout the outback showing the height of these floods. Two or three years of flooding primes the floodplains, lakes and waterhole, and the sequencing of the flooding is almost as important as the size of the flood. The outback rivers will only reach Lake Eyre when the floodplain, channel, waterhole and lake sponges are thoroughly saturated.

EXPLORERS & PIONEERS

Search for an inland sea

The sense of foreboding Lake Eyre can generate was shared by some of the early white explorers. Edward John Eyre, after whom the lake was named, did nothing to hide his disappointment when he first ventured into the region in 1839. Like the other explorers, Eyre was drawn by a sense of adventure and perhaps the lure of the place in history his discoveries might earn him. Settlers were pressing further and further inland and Eyre hoped to find rich grazing lands and reliable water supplies north of Adelaide. But he, like his fellow explorers, was anxious to finally provide an answer to the intriguing question being widely debated at the time — what was in the deep interior of the huge continent?

For settlers accustomed to the geography of the great river systems of Europe, it was popularly thought that there must be similar waterways to be found in the centre of Australia, perhaps even running to an inland sea. But the further Eyre and his party pressed into the north, the drier the country became. They travelled as far as the Flinders Ranges, discovering the salty wasteland of Lake Torrens, to the south of Lake Eyre, before they were forced to turn back because of lack of water, as Eyre despondently recorded in his journal:

> *Nowhere could we see the least sign of grass or water; the hills before me were high, barren and rocky, and there was no gum trees or other indications of water emanating from them to be seen anywhere — the whole was barren and arid-looking in the extreme, and as I gazed on the dismal scene before me I felt assured I had approached the vast and dreary desert of the interior, or, it might be, was verging on the confines of some inland water, whose sterile and desolate shores seem to forbid the traveller's approach.*

But Eyre still held hope that there might be better country much further north and returned the following year determined to strike out beyond Lake Torrens towards a low range of hills north of the Flinders Ranges which he thought could be the watershed of a

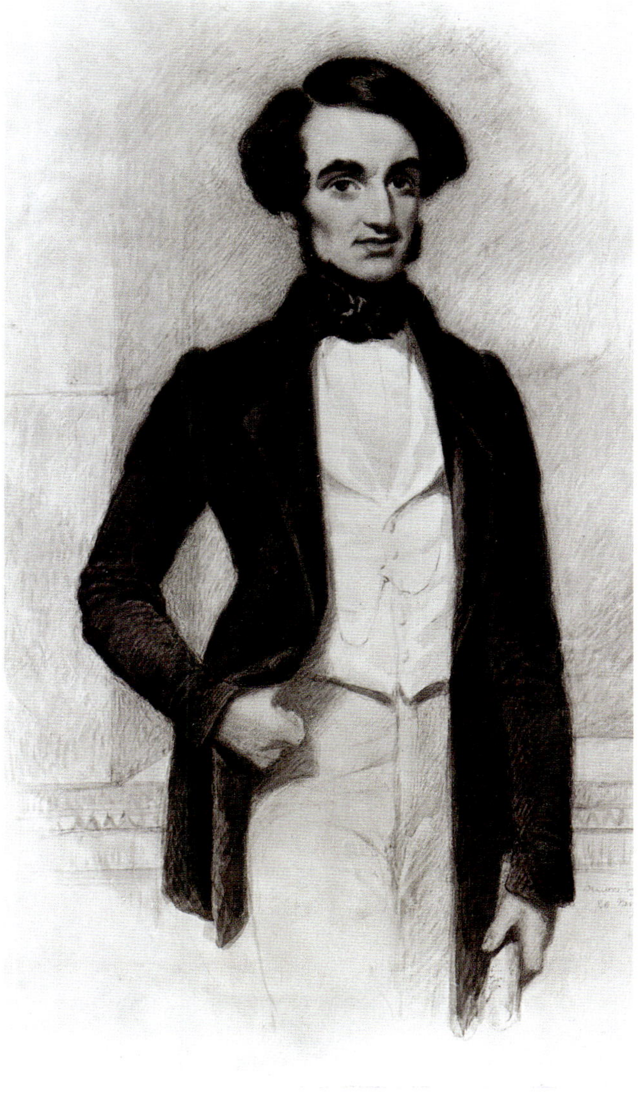

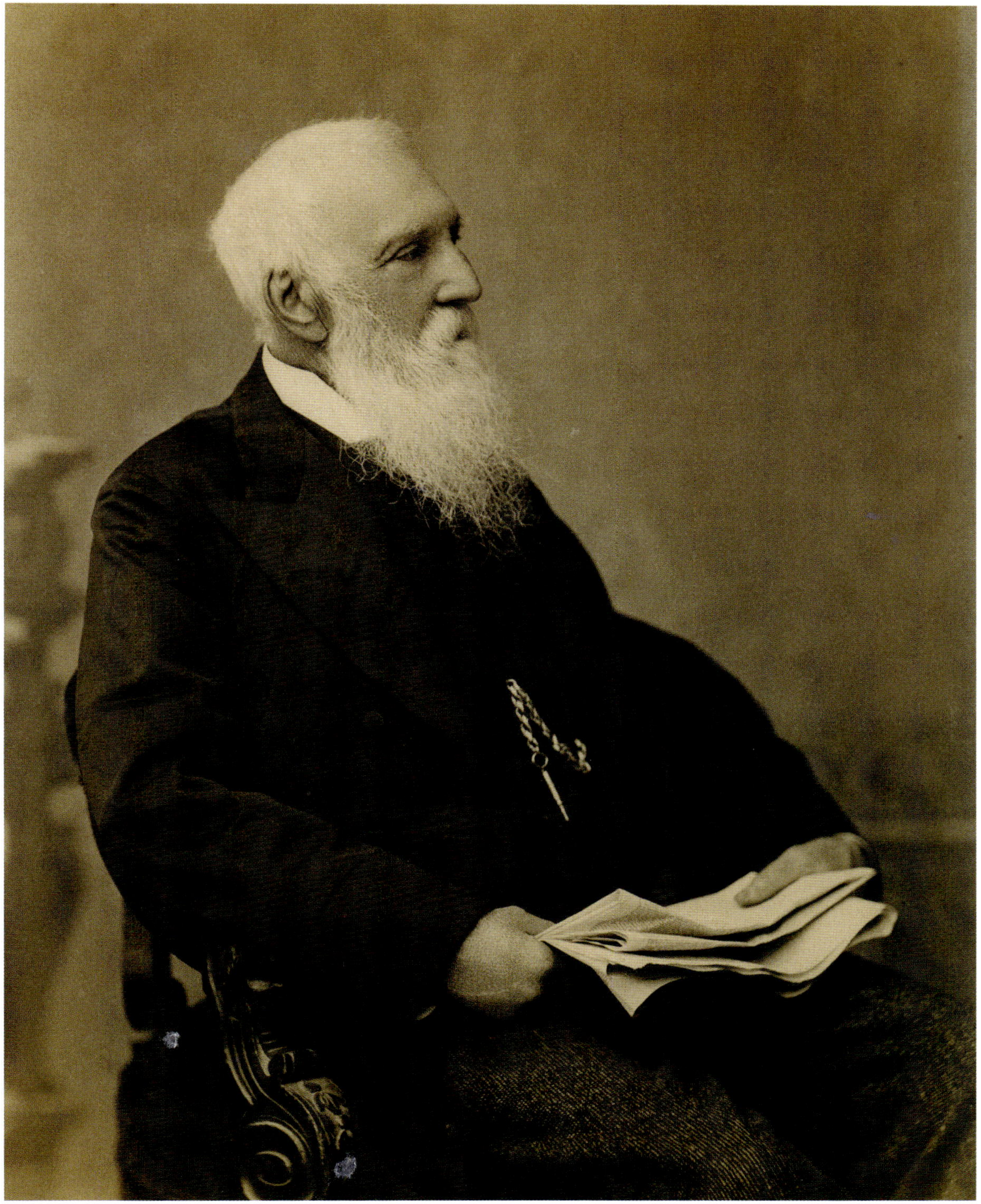

Edward John Eyre (above and right), after whom Lake Eyre is named. Still a teenager when he arrived in Sydney from England, he was just twenty-two when he set out on his first exploration — to complete the overland route from Sydney to Adelaide.

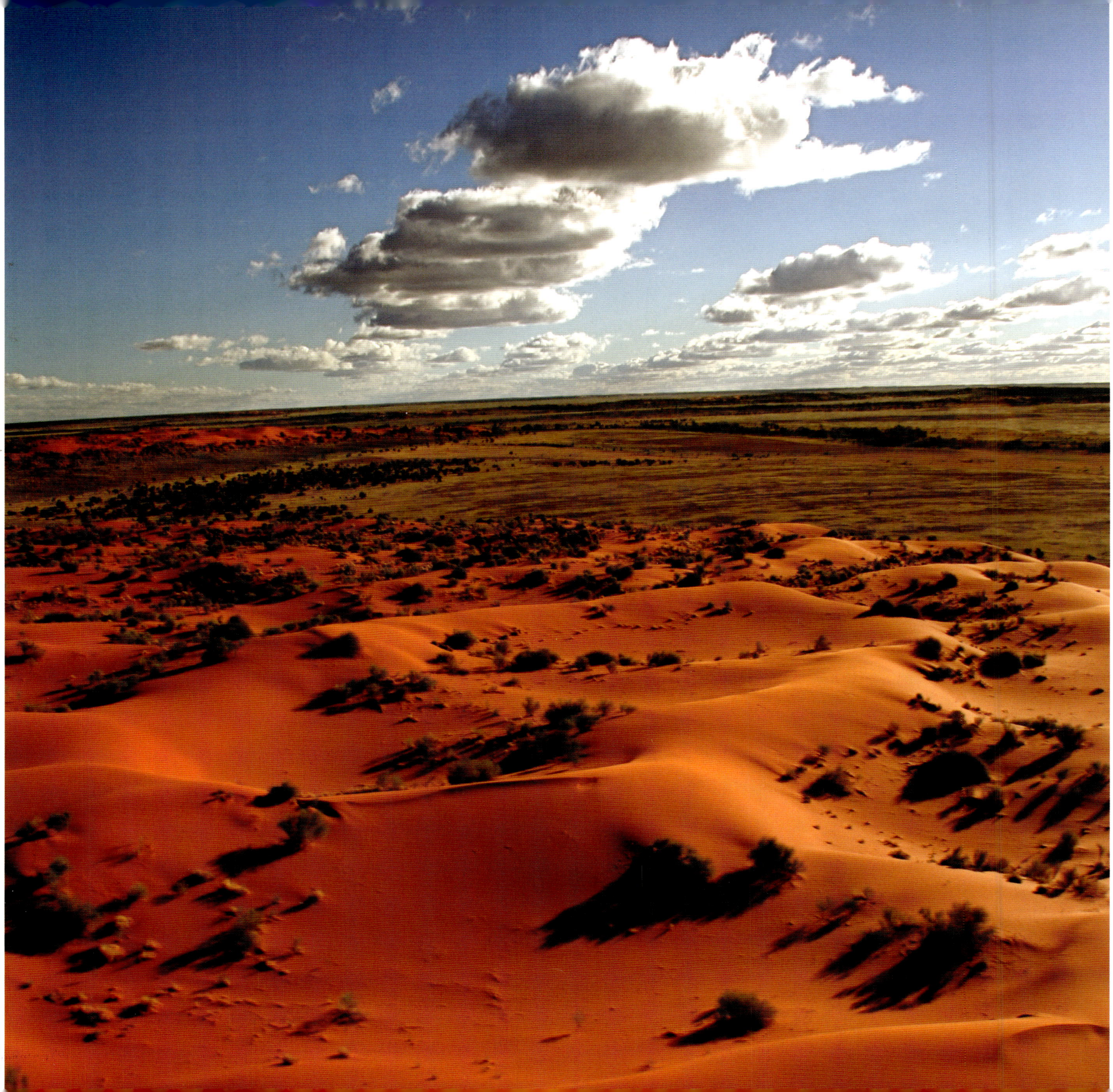

big water source. But there was no change in the countryside: '... all was uncertainty and conjecture in this region of magic,' he wrote. Eyre was again confronted by a stretch of salt lake. On 14 August 1840, he recorded that he had arrived at 'a winding arm of the Torrens'. He thought the way north was barred by a huge horseshoe lake but he was mistaken. He had missed a land passage dividing Lake Torrens from a lake to the north, where he had ended up. He had no idea but the lake he now surveyed would famously come to bear his name. He stood on the shores of Lake Eyre.

As he peered out over the expanse he noticed a glimmer of water and thought he had finally discovered some fresh supplies — but it proved to be as salty as the sea. His efforts to journey further inland were blocked at every turn. He was now too far north to see the land passage between the lakes. Eyre climbed hill after hill to try to find a way through but was confronted every time with the same depressing view of shimmering salt. In a downcast mood he named one peak Mount Deception, and another Mount Hopeless. This expedition, like the first, ended in despair, as Eyre's log records: 'Our toils and labours and privations had all been endured to no purpose; and the only alternative left would be to return, disappointed and baffled.'

Eyre's probe into Central Australia was followed by the irrepressible John McDouall Stuart, who mounted an incredible six expeditions into the South Australian interior between 1858 and 1862. Stuart, who had emigrated from Scotland to work as a surveyor in the new colony of South Australia, was renowned for his drive and determination — and for his hard drinking. But away from the taverns of Adelaide he came

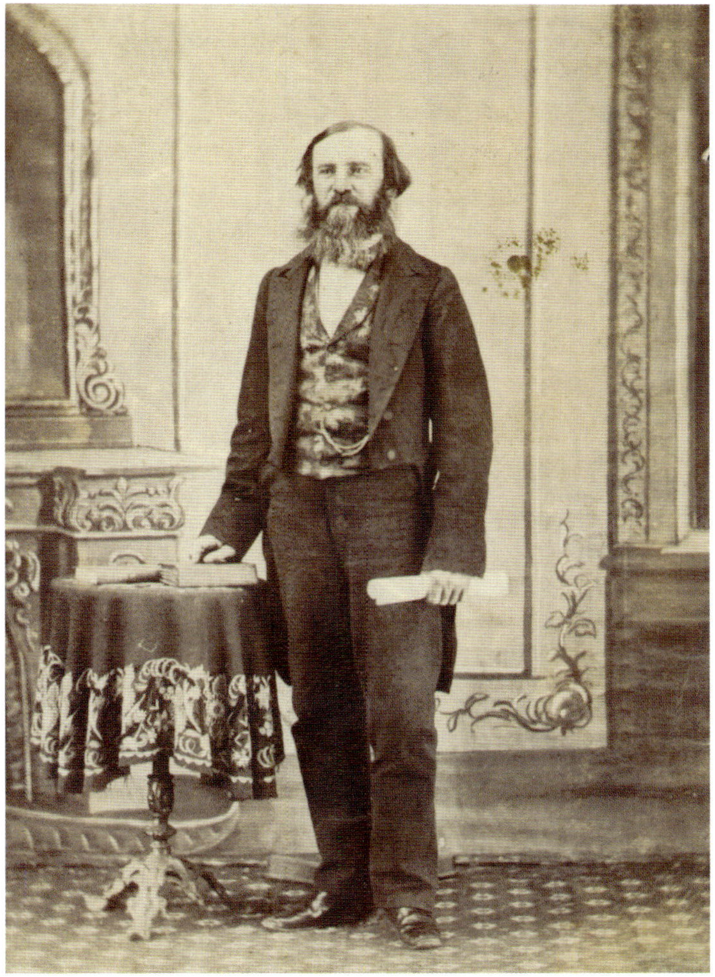

Opposite: 'It's probably one of the world's largest dune fields,' says Mike Smith of the endless line of red dunes running through the Simpson Desert

Above: John Macdouall Stuart would push to make the crossing from the south of the continent to the north. He eventually succeeded in his final expedition, which left Adelaide in October 1861. Stuart and the remnants of his party reached the Indian Ocean near the site of present day Darwin in July 1862 and struggled back into Adelaide in December that year.

into his own. He professed a love for the quiet of the bush and proved to be one of Australia's most tenacious explorers. Despite continuing poor health, Stuart saddled up again and again to take on some of the toughest and most dangerous expeditions attempted thus far in the new continent.

He made his first foray into the outback with Charles Sturt, on Sturt's expedition beyond the Darling River in 1844. Sturt had watched flocks of birds heading to the inland and believed that they must be heading to water there — a theory that was enhanced when his expedition discovered Cooper Creek and other muddy watercourses running towards the middle of the continent.

But later, when Stuart took control of his own expedition and headed out from Adelaide in 1858 to search for the fabled inland sea, he was only able to confirm Eyre's pessimistic assessment of a salty wasteland. 'Very disheartening,' he wrote in his log. 'A fearful country.' The huge salt pans that confronted him reminded him of glittering snowfields. But businessmen in Adelaide, still anxious to find grazing lands and mineral deposits — especially gold — in the South Australian outback, financed Stuart to continue the search. So he was the first to discover artesian springs bubbling from deep in the ground in the middle of the desert south-west of Lake Eyre, offering further incentive for pastoral settlement. Later, in the 1880s, the South Australian Government would sink a chain of wells along the outback routes around Lake Eyre to provide crucial watering spots for travelling stock.

Stuart pushed himself to near death on several expeditions, He would return to Adelaide only to regather his strength and put together fresh teams to head out again. But the theory of a huge horseshoe lake north of Adelaide forming a barrier against travel to the inland was debunked by others.

Benjamin Herschel Babbage, who was commissioned by the South Australian Government to explore and survey land south-west of Lake Eyre for possible settlement, speculated that a land passage existed north of Lake Torrens but he didn't get time to prove his theory. The government fumed at Babbage's slow progress in his exploration work, in comparison with Stuart's frenetic adventures, and decided to recall him. Major Peter Egerton Warburton was dispatched from Adelaide to deliver the news to Babbage and take over his expedition. Babbage insisted that he was on the point of exploring the area where he believed land divided Lake Torrens from Lake Eyre, but to no avail. He was ordered home, leaving Warburton to test the theory. Warburton found the gap and became the first to ride through it, opening up a crucial passage for fellow explorers and, later, for road, rail and telegraph links to run through Central Australia.

John McDouall Stuart made the most of the new land passage to press ever further north in his explorations of the inland, but on the way he lingered at Lake Eyre. The sheer size of this newly discovered lake stretching out through Central Australia captured his imagination. He spent days riding around it, astonished by its

Benjamin Herschel Babbage, a meticulous surveyor, mapped part of the shore of southern Lake Eyre during his 1858 expedition, but his methods were too slow for the South Australian Government, and he was replaced by Major Warburton.

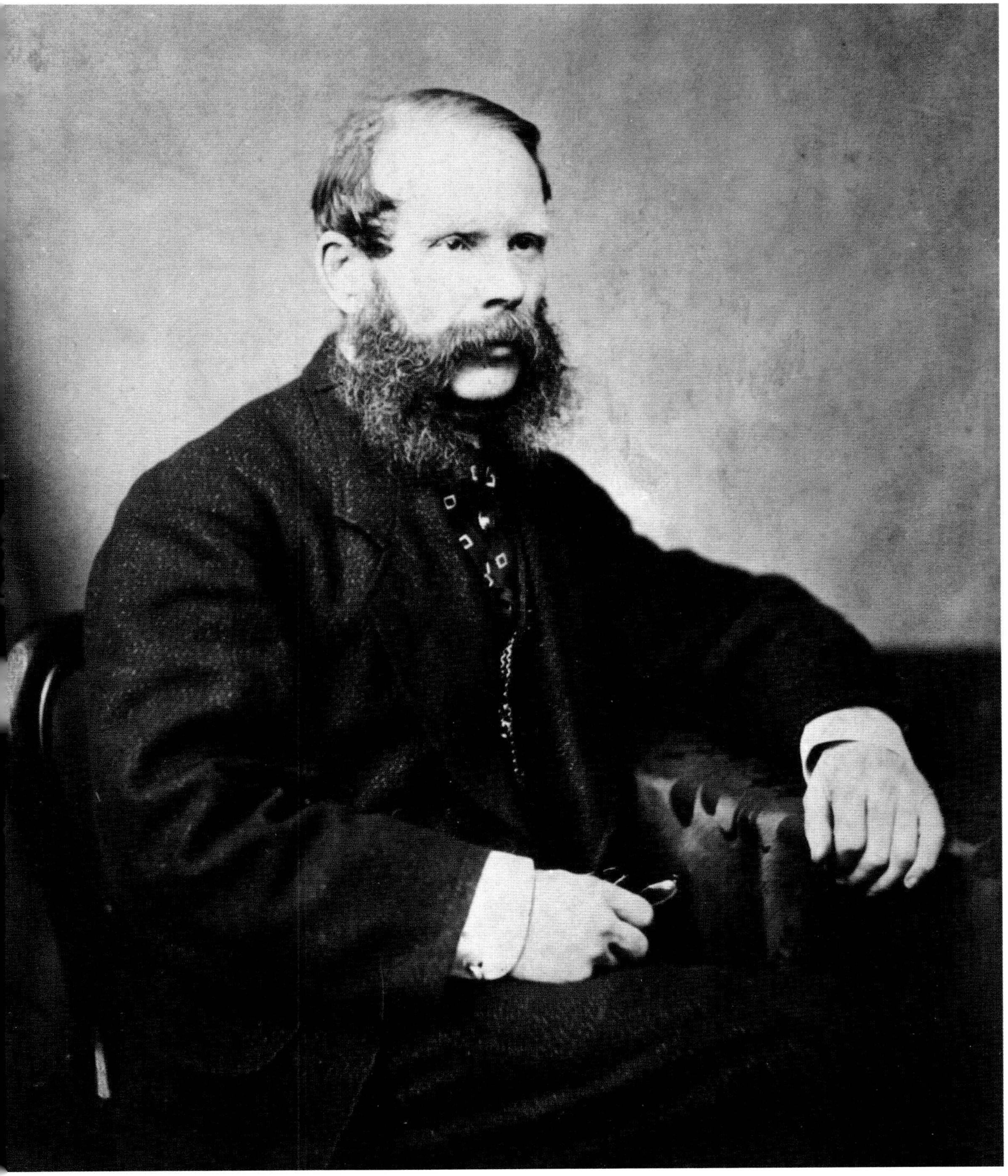

seemingly endless shoreline. He recorded the discovery of dead fish near a muddy shoreline in one area, which led him to believe that the now-dry river beds he had found leading into the lake must have delivered a recent life-giving flow, but he couldn't understand what had then happened to the supplies. 'Where can all this water drain to?' he asked in his log. 'It is a mystery.'

His puzzlement about Lake Eyre was shared by a string of other explorers. In 1866, Major Warburton made a search for water sources and grazing country north of the lake, only to report:

> *Lake Eyre was dry — terrible in its death-like stillness and the vast expanse of its unbroken sterility. The weary wanderer, who, when in want of water, should unexpectedly reach its shores, might turn away with a shudder from a scene which shut out all hope — he could hide his head in the sand hills and meet his fate with calmness and resignation; but to set foot on Lake Eyre would be like cutting himself off from the common lot of human beings.*

The many mysteries surrounding Lake Eyre, and the inland rivers that fed it, would persist for years. Little wonder. The enormous scale of Lake Eyre wasn't established until it was mapped in 1897 when it was found to be almost 80 kilometres long and 40 kilometres wide. It covers 9690 square kilometres, making

John McDouall Stuart raises the flag to celebrate finding what he believed was the dead centre of Australia — Central Mount Stuart in the Northern Territory.

it Australia's biggest lake and the fifth largest terminal lake — one that has no outward flow — in the world.

After Stuart found his way past Lake Eyre he headed deep into the desert, claiming to be the first to find the centre of the continent. By his reckonings, using a sextant and prismatic compass, he pinpointed a spot a little over 200 kilometres north of present day Alice Springs.

On 23 April 1860 he and his party clambered up a nearby rocky hill, which they named Central Mount Stuart, to raise the flag and leave a message in a bottle, buried in a pile of stones, outlining their feat. As Stuart's log recorded: 'We then gave three hearty cheers for the flag, the emblem of civil and religious liberty, and may it be a sign to the natives that the dawn of liberty, civilisation and Christianity is about to break on them.'

While Stuart was marking out new frontiers for the colony of South Australia, there were rumblings of competition building in Victoria. The broad outlines of the continent were now known but no one had yet crossed the continent from south to north. History beckoned, and in Melbourne, amid great fanfare, an expedition was assembled to strike out for the Gulf of Carpentaria led by Robert O'Hara Burke, a local police officer, and William John Wills, who worked at the Melbourne observatory and joined the party as a meteorologist, astronomer and surveyor.

The South Australian Government retaliated by offering £2000 to the explorer who could race Burke and Willis to the Top End. There was enormous colonial pride at stake. South Australia championed its hero, John McDouall Stuart, but Burke and Wills got a head start. They left Melbourne in August 1860, a huge party of nineteen men, twenty-three horses, twenty-six camels and six wagons. Stuart had a much smaller party, relying on horses and fast travel, but his initial attempts to get through the Northern Territory to the coast failed, not least because his party came under attack from an Aboriginal tribe near Tennant Creek.

But the Victorian expedition was to face a much worse fate. Dogged by problems at every turn, Burke and Wills eventually led a small, bedraggled team to the mangrove mud flats

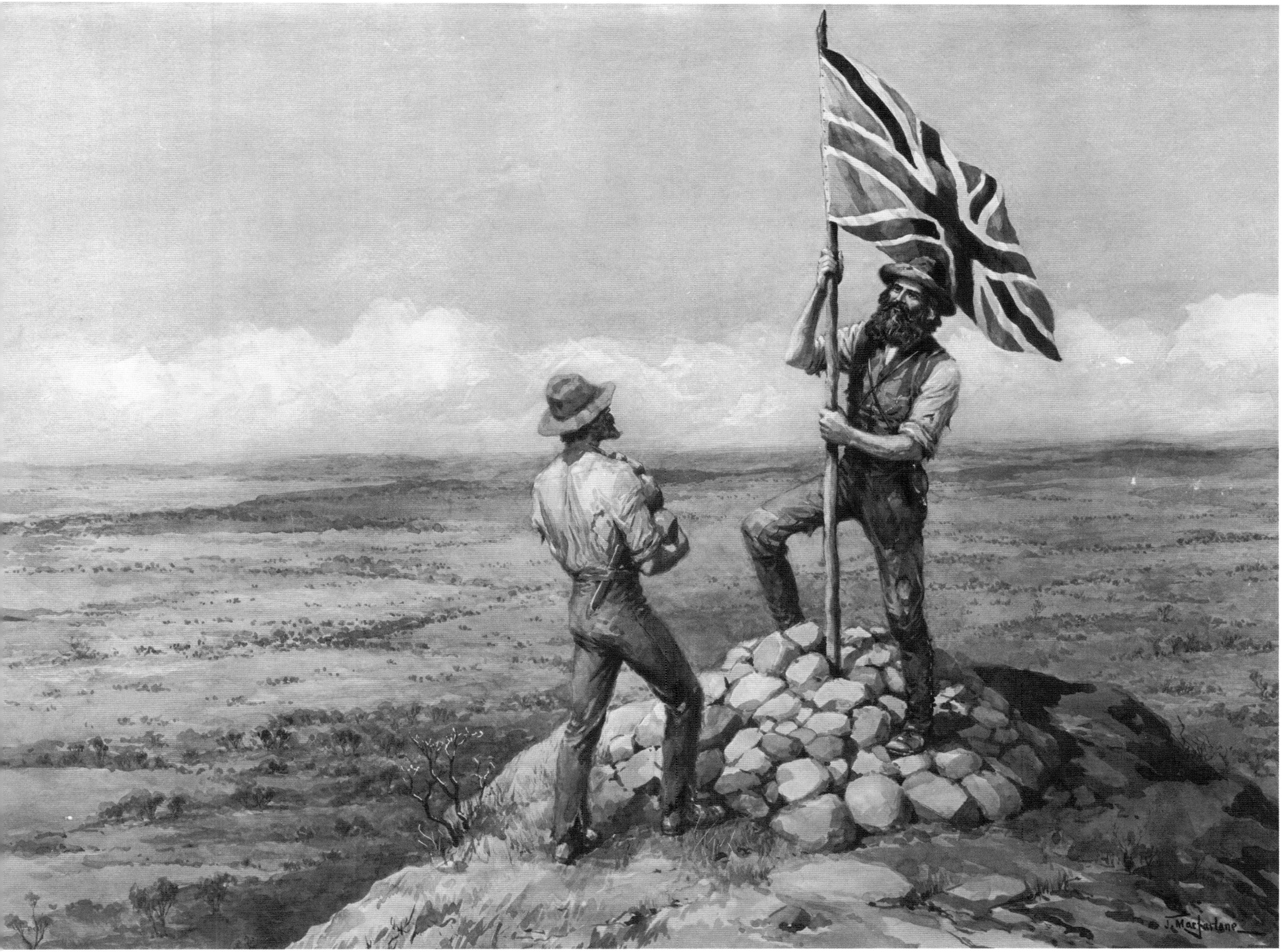
J. Macfarlane

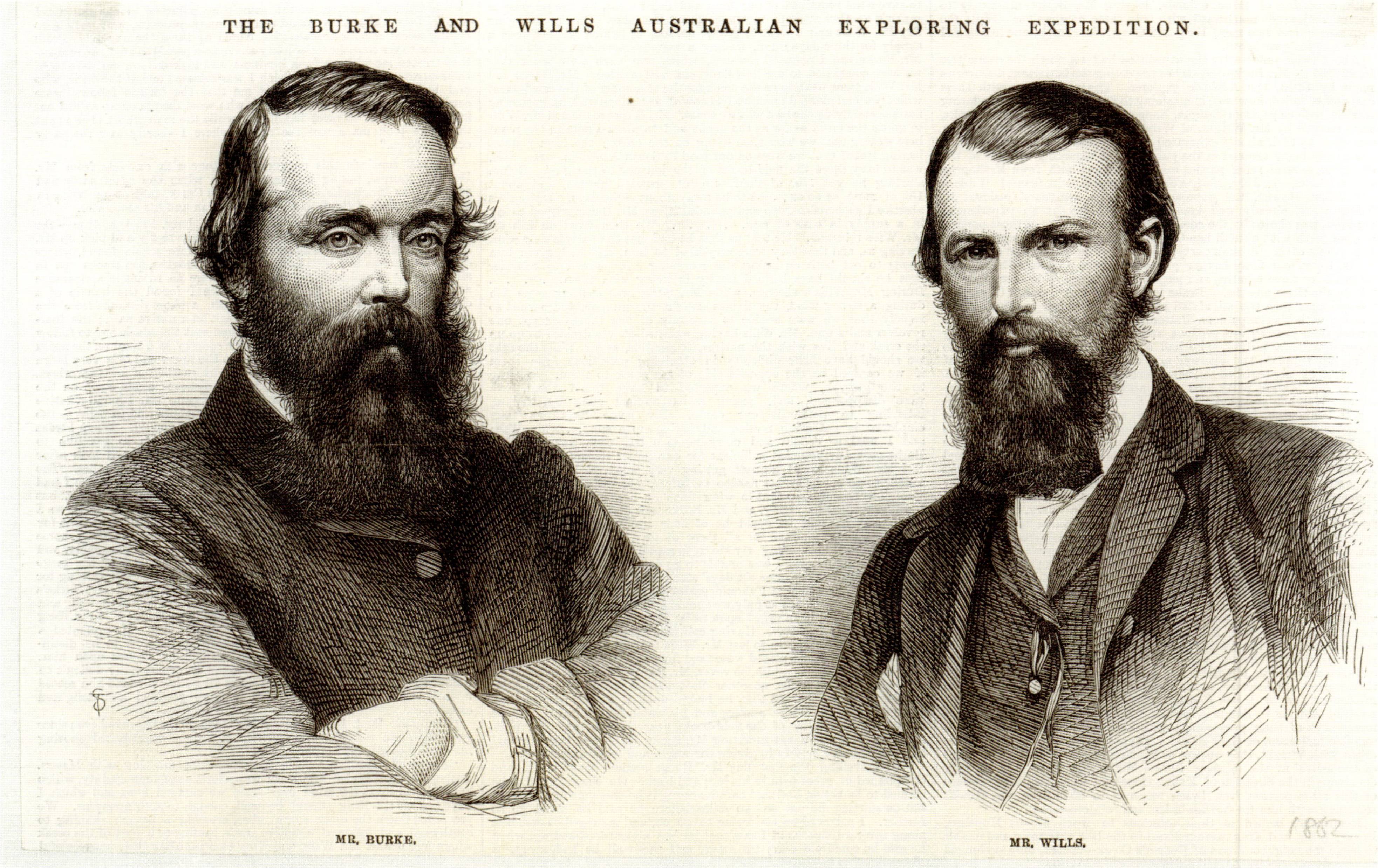

Robert O'Hara Burke was a police officer and William John Wills worked at the Melbourne observatory. Despite this lack of experience, the pair led the largest, most expensive expedition ever mounted in Victoria in the race to cross the continent. Opposite: A likeness of Burke's face carved in 1899 into a tree next to Cooper Creek, a little downstream from the famous Dig Tree.

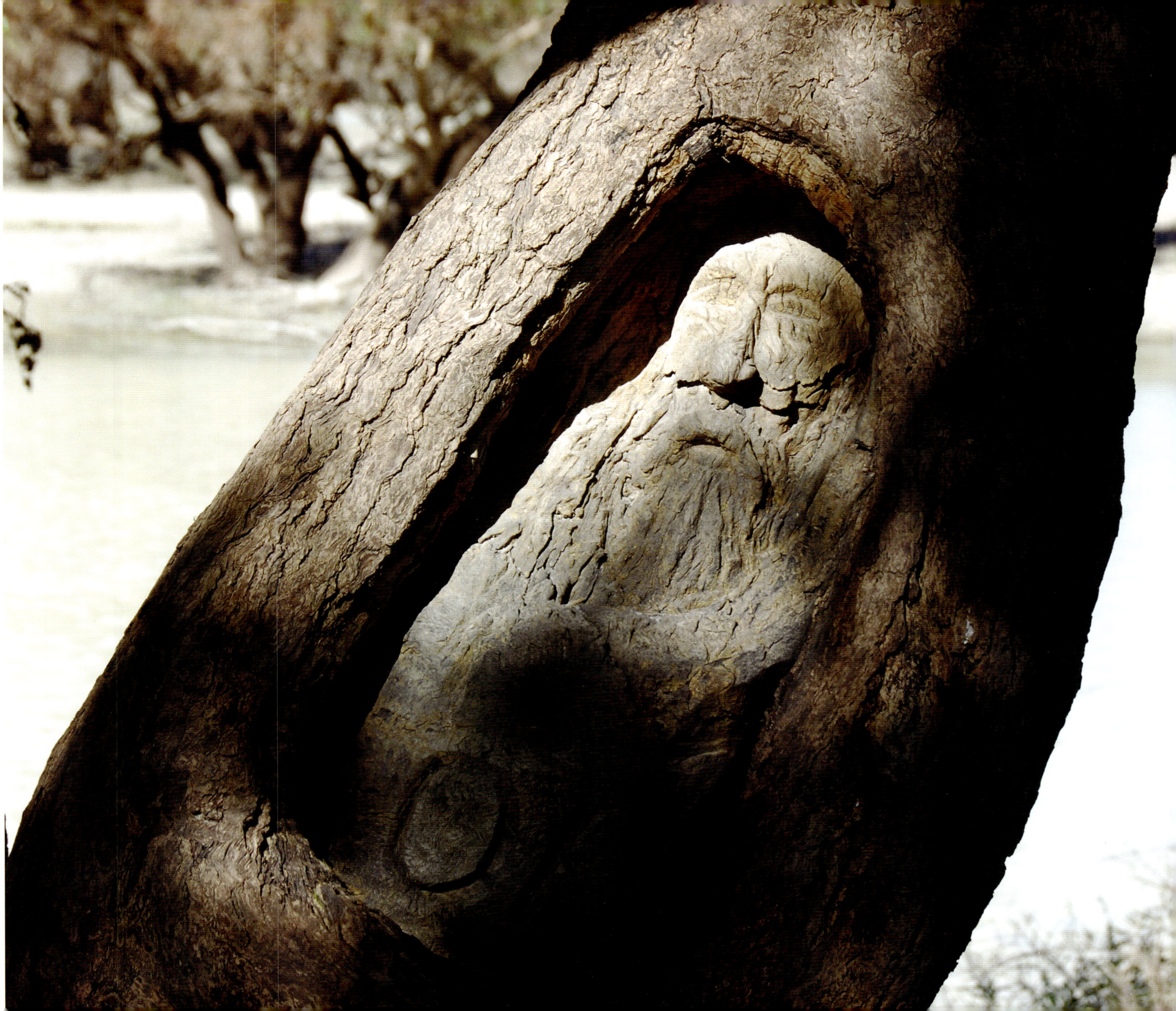

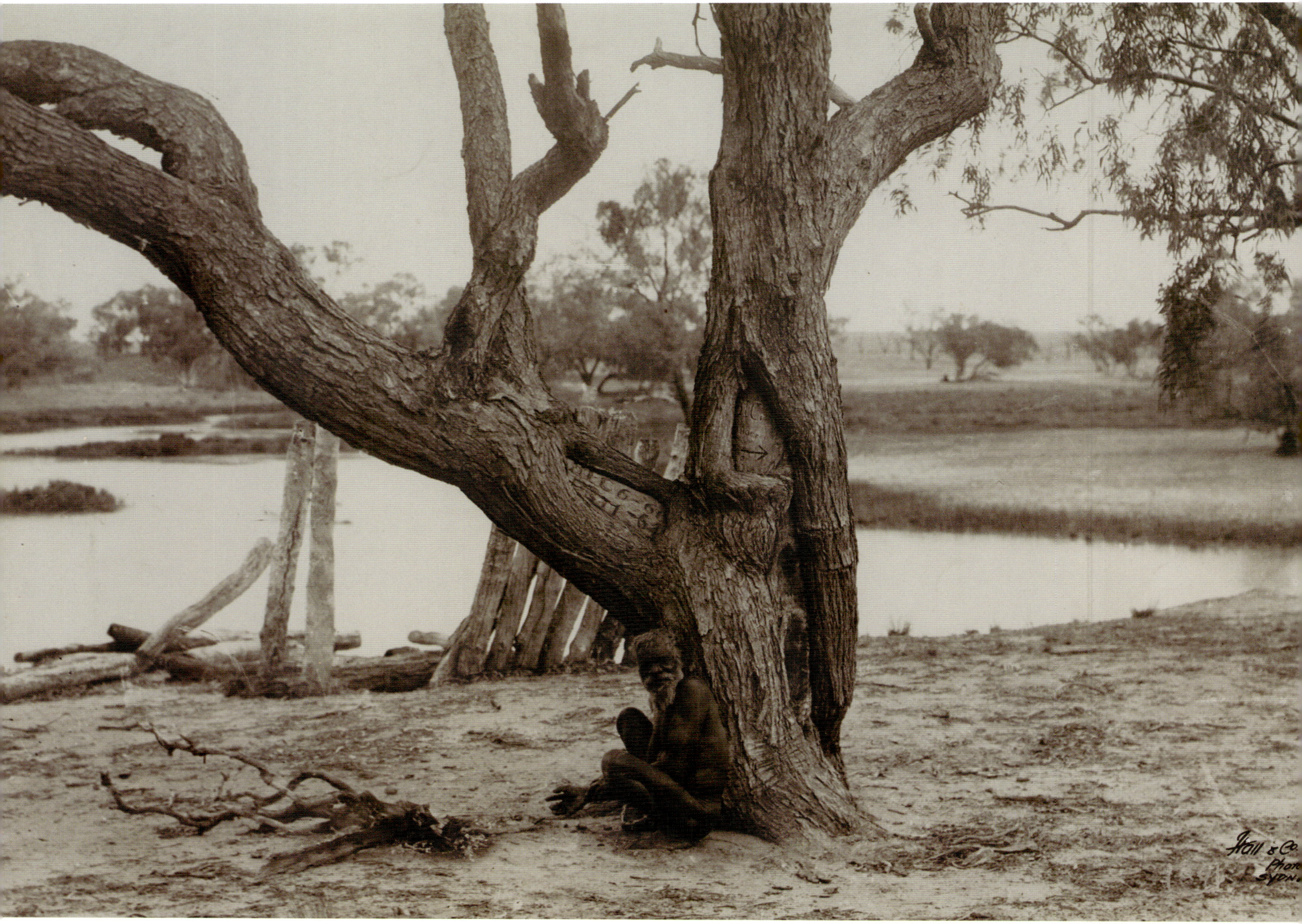
Hall & Co.
Photo
Sydney

on the edge of the Gulf of Carpentaria in Queensland on 9 February 1861, before turning back to try to struggle home. Their story is best remembered for the ill fortune that they encountered on their return to their depot on Cooper Creek, near the Queensland–South Australian border.

Dehydrated, starving and ill after their long trek back from north Queensland, they discovered to their horror that a support party had abandoned the campsite just nine hours earlier, believing that they had perished. A carving on the trunk of a coolibah directed the distraught men to supplies buried near the tree. Despite this, both Burke and Wills eventually died of starvation. The coolibah, which came to be known as the Dig Tree, has survived through drought and flood ever since — standing as a memorial to misadventure in the harsh outback.

Stuart heard that Burke and Wills and members of their party were missing and volunteered to join in the search but it was already well underway. He was still determined to blaze a trail across the continent and his sheer persistence finally won through on his third attempt, when he reached the northern Australian coast, east of Darwin on 24 July 1862. He opened up a route that would eventually be followed by the Overland Telegraph and later by railway and road. Today the Stuart Highway stands as a memorial to one of Australia's greatest explorers.

Whether you drive or fly over the stony desert country surrounding Lake Eyre, you can't help but wonder at the thoughts that would have passed through the minds of those early explorers, pressing on into the unknown. No sooner would they have scrambled to the top of one sharp, rocky ridge but there would be another, and another, floating on the horizon in a shimmering heat haze. Worse still, where was the water? As the explorers discovered to their cost, the dry years rule in Central Australia and as they ventured into one of the most arid areas on earth they were left to search desperately for springs and muddy waterholes. Even today, most international news about Central Australia is generated by the tragedies or misfortunes of travellers who become lost or stranded in the vast, unforgiving environment.

The Dig Tree — An exhausted Burke and Wills made their way back to the campsite on Cooper Creek only to find it abandoned. Carvings on the coolibah directed them to supplies buried nearby, but it was too little too late and they died of starvation in 1861.

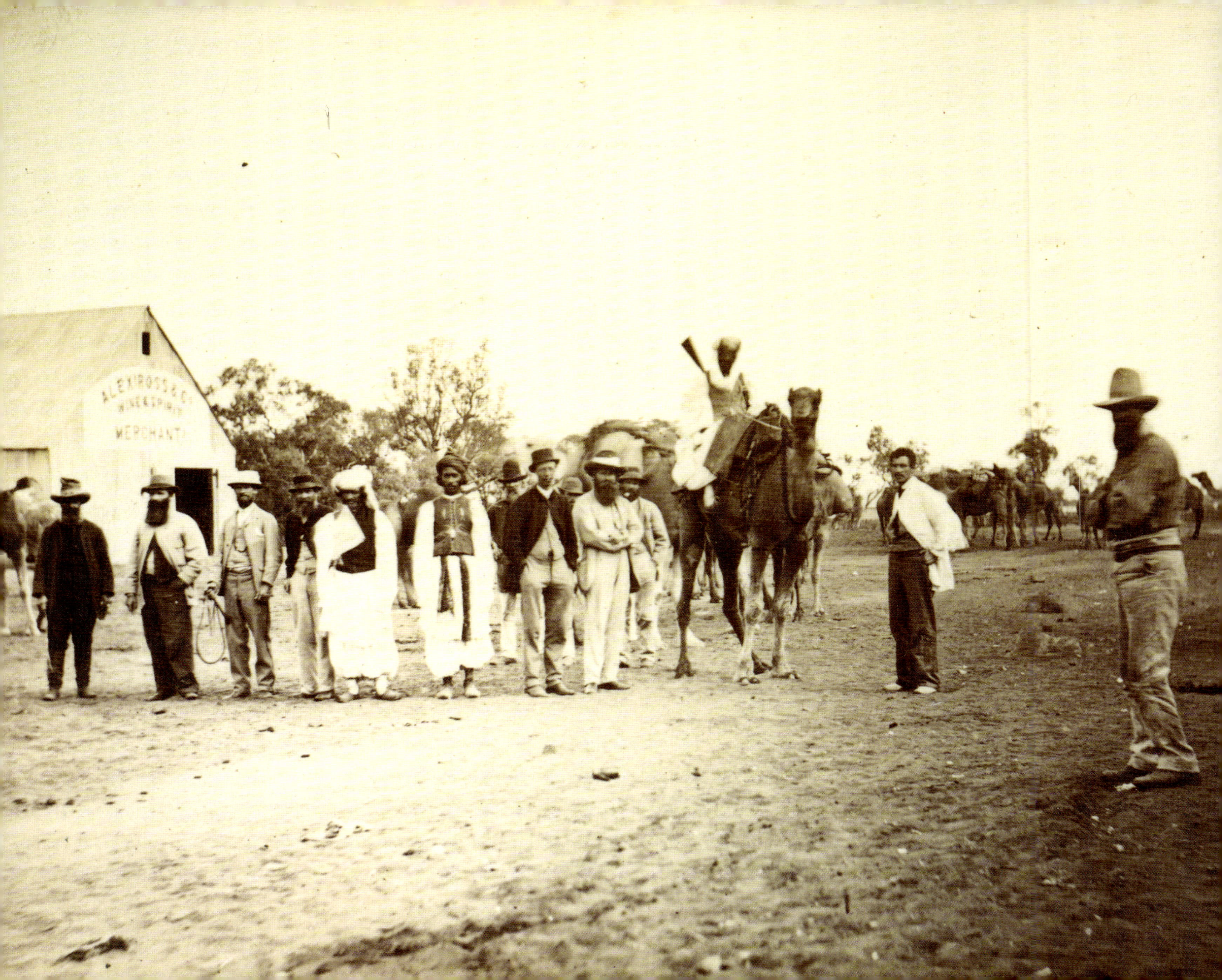
ALEX ROSS & Co
MERCHANT

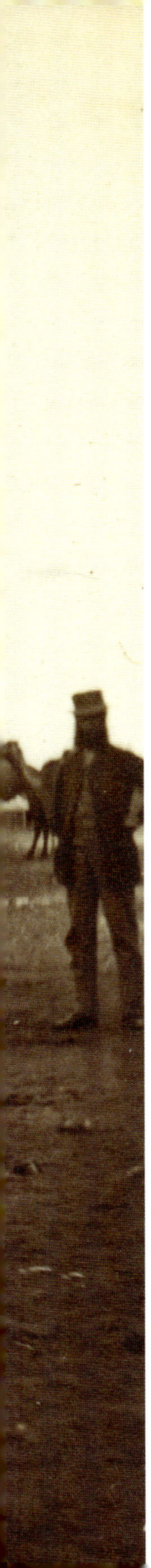

The pioneers of Lake Eyre

Thomas Elder, a South Australian pastoralist, was one of the first to recognise the value of camels in the harsh Australian desert — and he imported more than 120 animals and their handlers in 1865. Here they bring supplies to Wilcannia, NSW, from Burra Burra in South Australia in 1869.

Burke and Wills left a significant legacy — the camel. The first major shipment of camels for outback transport was organised for their expedition. Even though it ended in tragedy, the stamina and endurance of the camels that were used on the long trek through the outback impressed many, including South Australian pastoralist Thomas Elder. In 1865 he organised a shipment of more than 120 camels and thirty-one handlers from the sub continent. They carted wool from his sheep stations dotted through the colony. Soon other major camel shipments were organised and between 1870 and 1920 about 20,000 camels and 2000 handlers were brought to Australia to help open up the outback.

The cameleers became loosely known as Afghans and while many had originated from the hills of Afghanistan, others came from what is now Pakistan and north-western India. They had earned a reputation as reliable and tireless handlers with camel teams on the harsh and rugged trade routes of Central Asia, and quickly adapted to the deserts of Central Australia, establishing tracks to remote communities and properties and helping build the rail and telegraph lines that would connect them. The camel teams handled the most awkward and heavy loads, living alongside the telegraph and railway lines as they pushed further into the interior. But not everyone welcomed them. Bullocks and horses had traditionally been used to haul freight in the outback and the bullockies and teamsters railed against the new competition. Unlike horses and bullocks, camels could go without water for long periods and easily weathered the intense heat of Central Australia. Tensions led to brawls in some outback areas but there was no stopping the spread of the cameleers. With their assistance,

An early photograph of the railhead at the small town of Marree, south of Lake Eyre, which was established in 1884. Marree is also the southern end of the Birdsville Track. Opposite: More than a million wild camels, descendants of those brought to the desert by Afghan cameleers, now roam wild across much of Central Australia, well adapted to a life in Australian deserts.

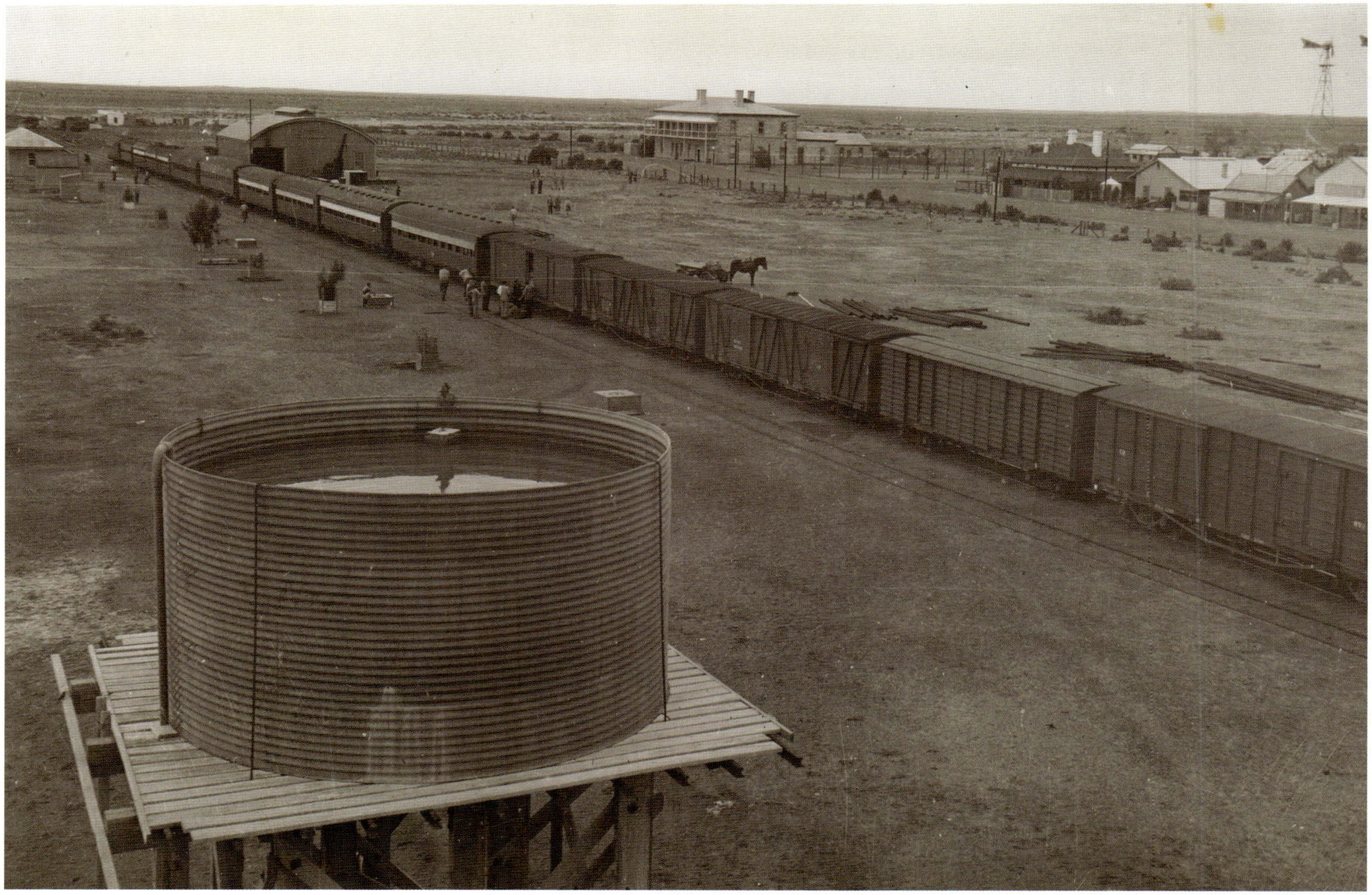

the railway line reached Marree, south of Lake Eyre, in 1884. Some cameleers settled there to provide transport and haulage to the railhead from the developing properties and settlements around Lake Eyre. The camels had no problems with the hot, dry conditions or the desert terrain, carting goods as far as Birdsville, 500 kilometres north of Marree, in far western Queensland.

Birdsville was established as a supply depot in the early 1880s for the emerging cattle industry. It quickly became a thriving town with a customs post, where Queensland duty was levied on the mobs of cattle that crossed into South Australia to be walked south to market in Adelaide. The drovers found a route through the desert, running from Birdsville, east of Lake Eyre, to Marree. The camel teams padded along the same path, carting everything from food, clothing and medical supplies to bulky building material. They became a lifeline for remote stations and communities, creating an historic outback trail — the Birdsville Track.

Despite the pessimistic findings of the early explorers, hopeful pioneers still took their chances in Central Australia, establishing vast

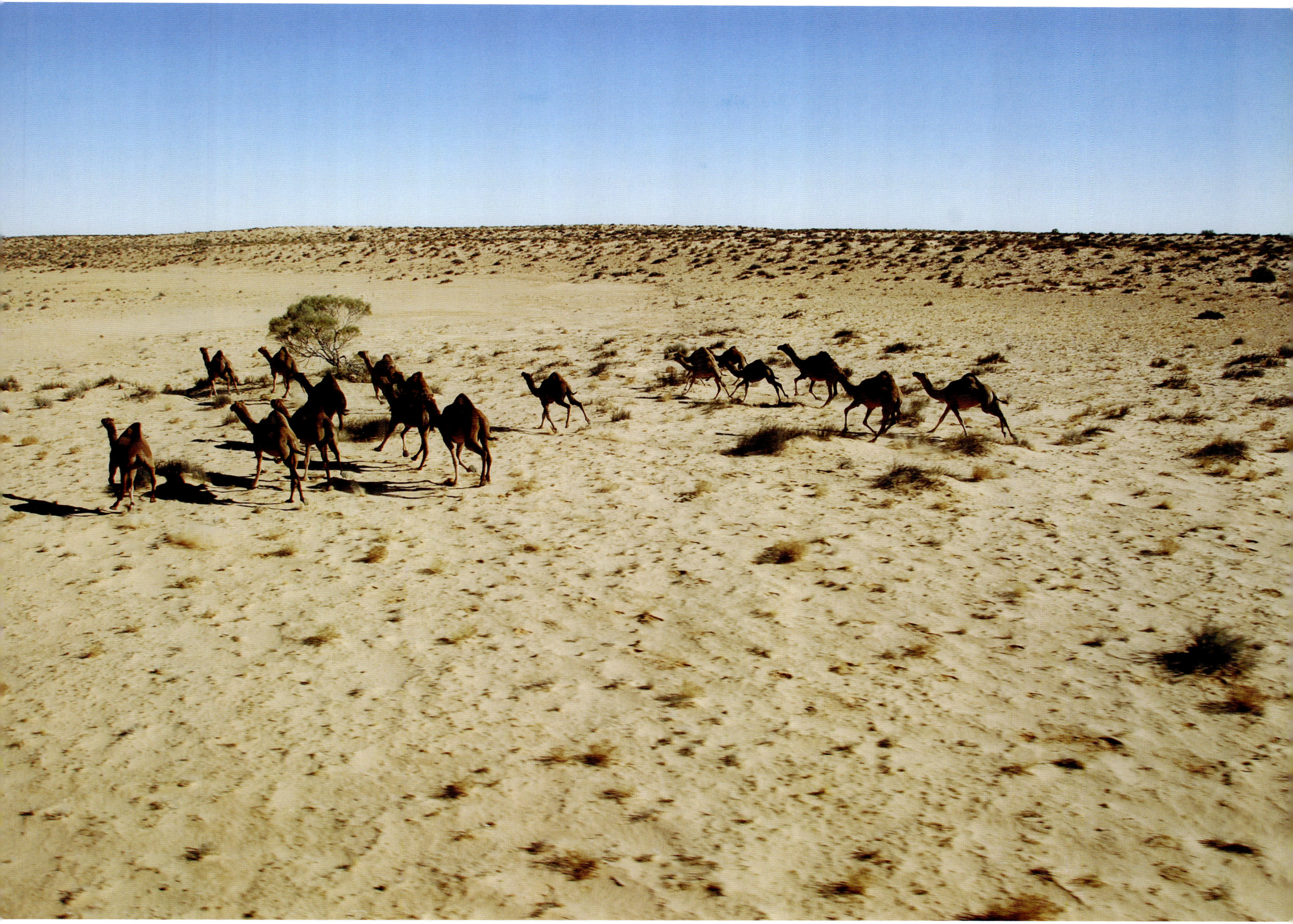

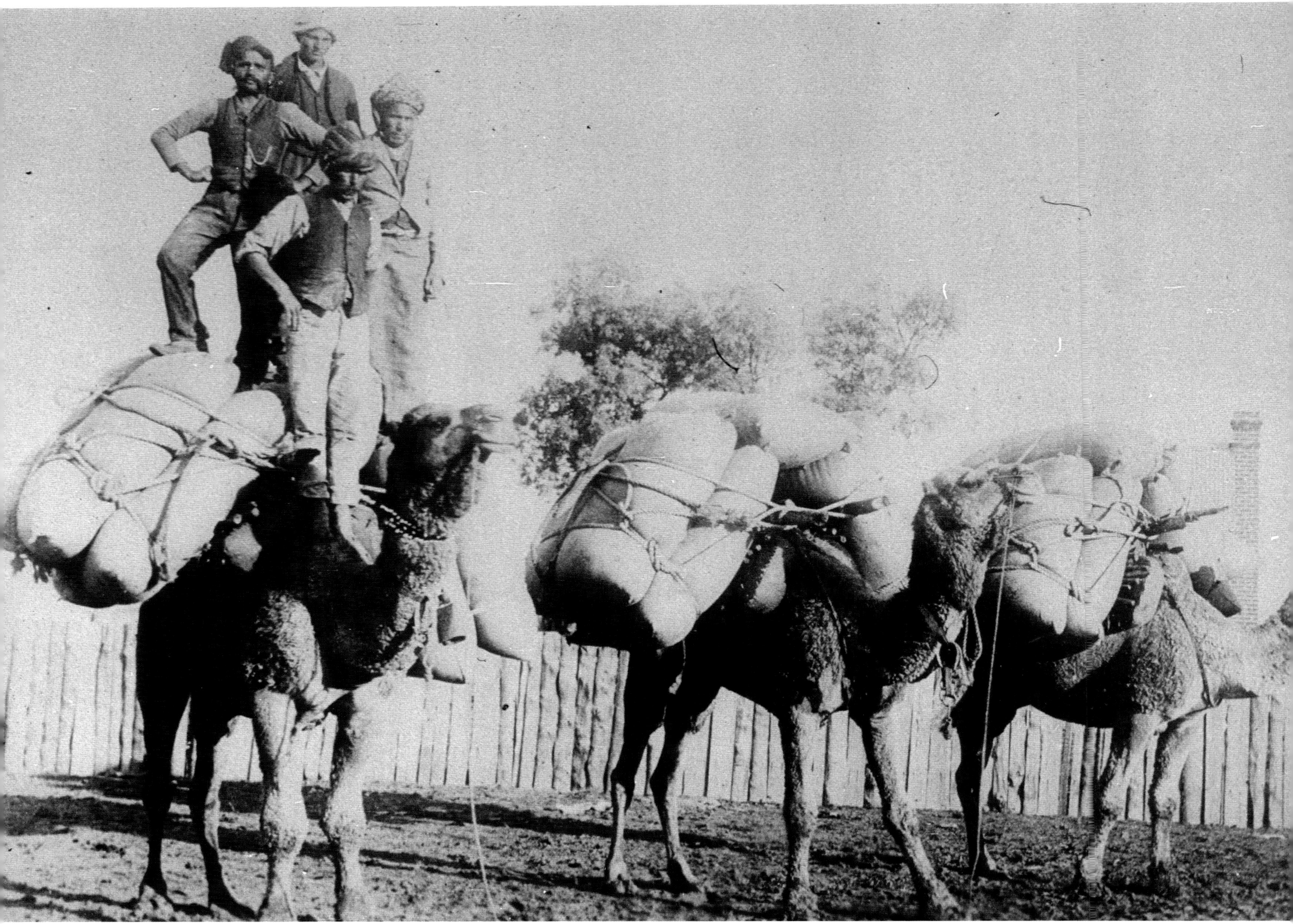

Eight Afghan drivers with twenty-four camels were brought to Australia in 1860 for the ill-fated Burke and Wills expedition. They soon established a reputation as useful outback transport, carrying loads such as these wool bales in Western Queensland, circa 1895.
Overleaf: A camel train with sixty-eight camels moves along the Birdsville Track across the Sturt Stony Desert in Queensland, circa 1930.

sheep and cattle stations around Lake Eyre. They were encouraged, in part, by the exploits of a cattle rustler!

In 1870, Harry Redford stole 1000 cattle from Bowen Downs, a station in western Queensland, planning to walk them all the way to Adelaide, a distance of about 1600 kilometres. This was less than a decade after Burke and Wills had perished in the same country. Redford was heading into little known territory, gambling on finding water and feed. He didn't reach Adelaide, but nursed the mob to Lake Blanche, south-east of Lake Eyre, where he sold the cattle to an unsuspecting buyer. In the eyes of many pioneers, Redford's droving achievement far outweighed his crime and his story was celebrated in stock camps across the outback.

The law finally caught up with Redford in 1873, assembling what it believed to be an ironclad case against him for cattle stealing. But it made the mistake of taking him to trial in the Queensland beef town of Roma where Redford's cattle droving feat had won him many admirers. Community sentiment was firmly with Redford and the jury acquitted him, much to the irritation of the Queensland Supreme Court, which then suspended further trials in Roma for the next two years.

Redford's cattle trek had shown that the outback could be conquered.

The early settlers had been particularly drawn to far south-west Queensland, around Cooper Creek. There the river fans out over a huge area of the outback that the pioneers called the Channel Country. Here a maze of channels runs off the Cooper to streams and waterholes, crisscrossing flat, stony desert areas, known as gibber plains, and through extensive dune fields. The Cooper runs from the town of Windorah, more than 1000 kilometres west of Brisbane, all the way through desert country to Lake Eyre, a distance of 1300 kilometres. In the long dry times, the Channel Country has a desperate appearance to outsiders — but not to those born and bred in the area. When the big floods occasionally come, they transform the region. It becomes ideal cattle-fattening country, with sweet pastures

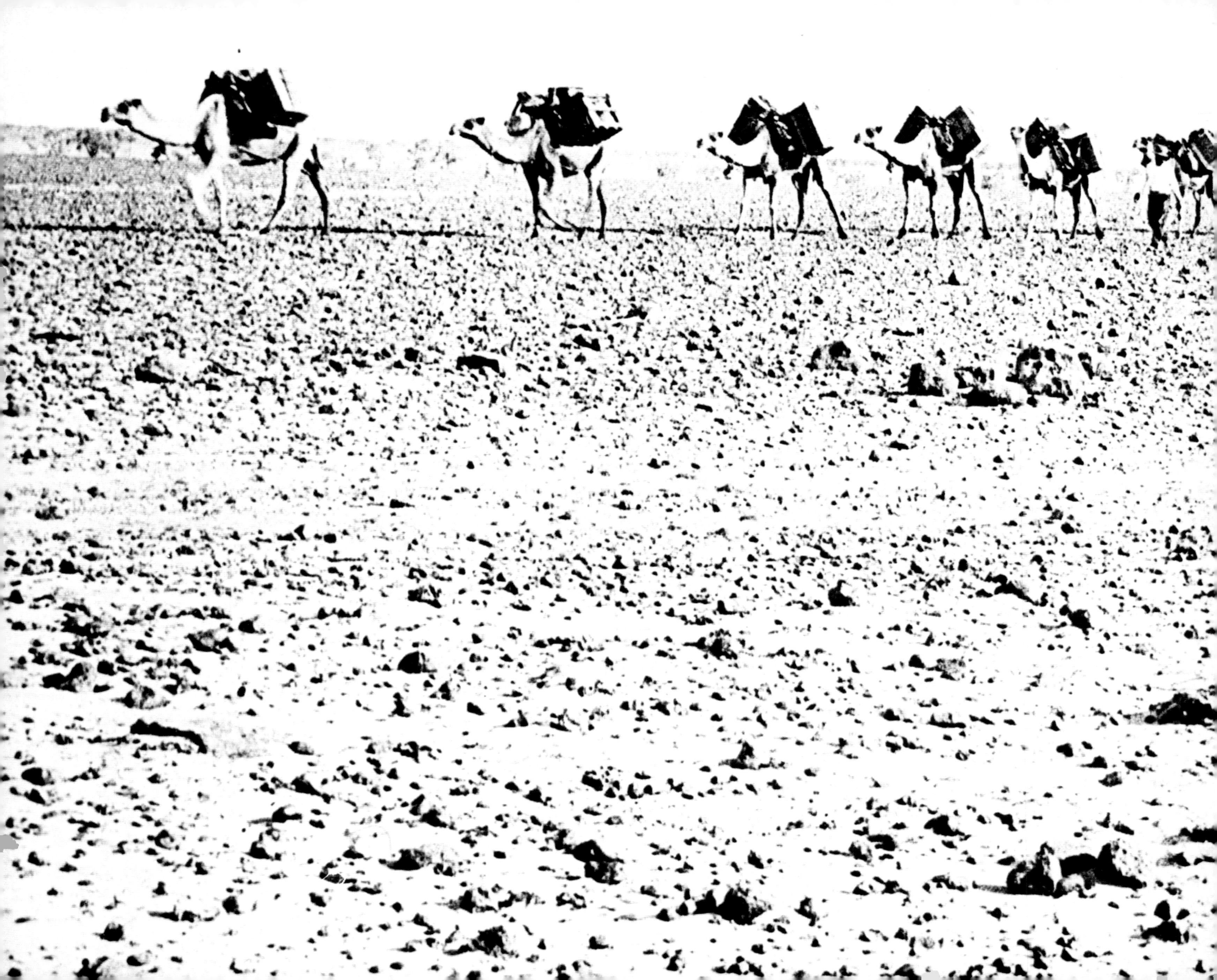

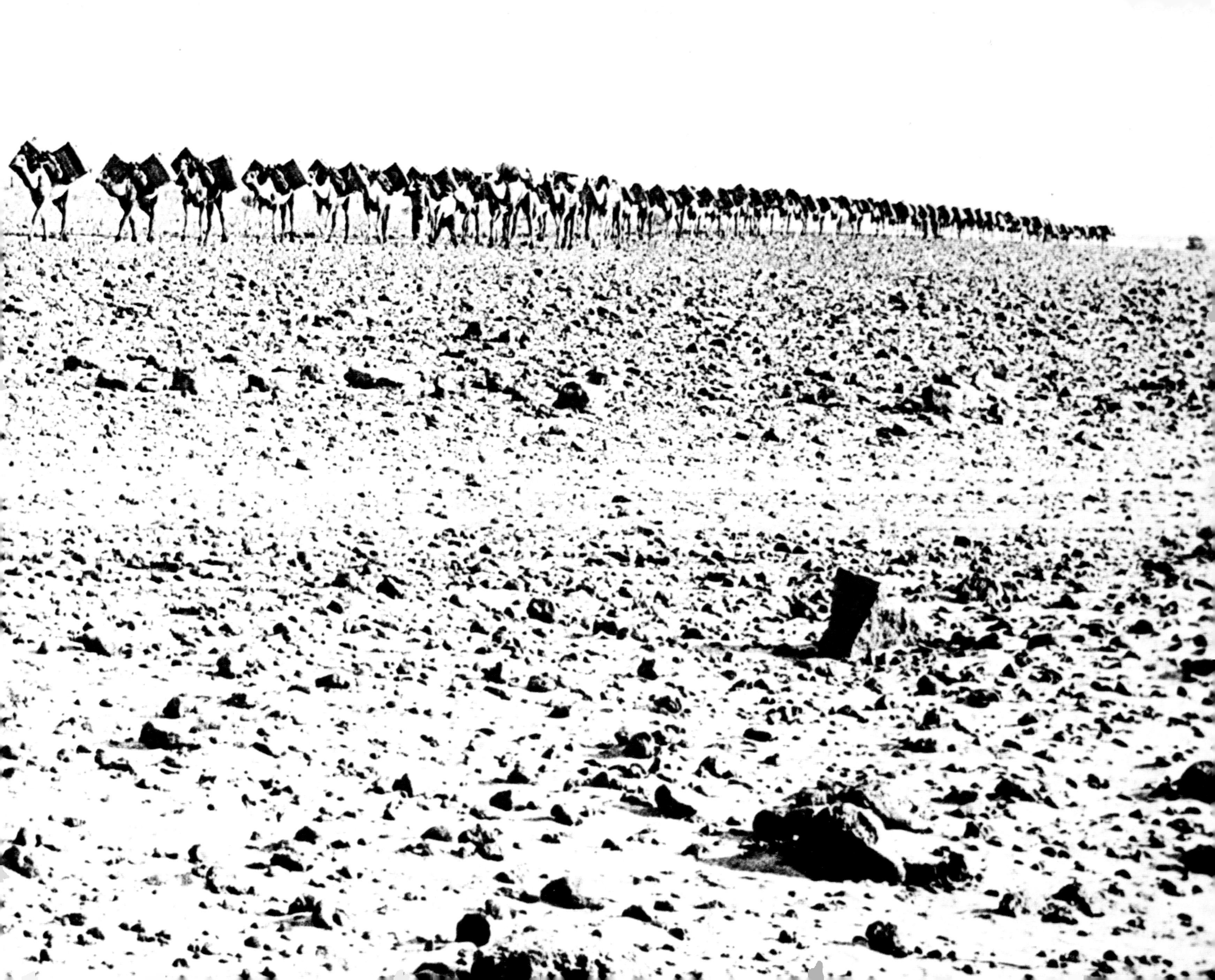

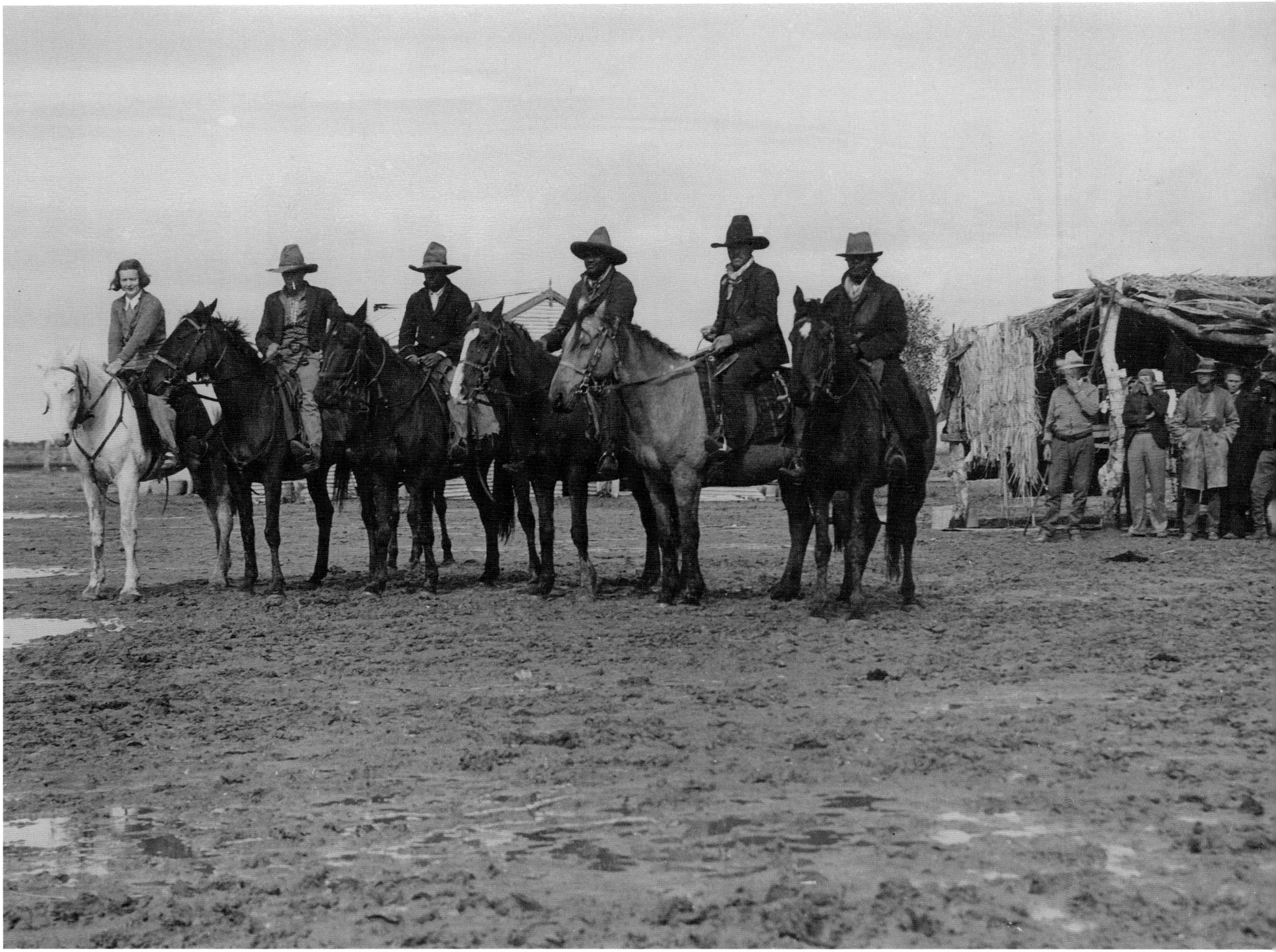

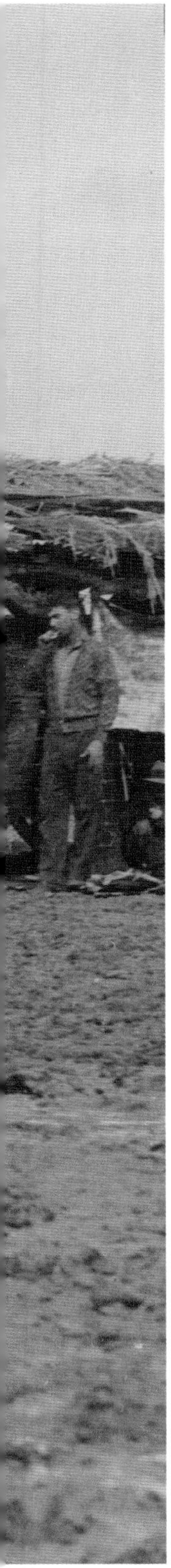

and reliable water supplies. Drovers shifting cattle through the inland had been astounded to discover these rich grazing areas on the edge of the desert.

Harry Redford's cattle-rustling exploits had shown that as remote as these areas were, cattle could still be walked to distant markets. It provided further encouragement to would-be settlers and the Channel Country was quickly taken up. But the long dry spells, the summer heat, and the choking dust storms constantly tested the resolve of the early settlers around Lake Eyre. And it was to get much worse. A drought began to take hold in the mid 1890s. Scant reserves of water dried up and stock began to die in big numbers. Some properties were simply deserted. Huge sand storms covered the abandoned homesteads. Drover Jack Clark was caught in a dust storm with a mob of 500 bullocks east of the Birdsville Track. His graphic account is told in *Kidman — The Forgotten King*:

> *A cool breeze blew up as if coming off rain. The bullocks had their heads up and sniffing. Five minutes later we were smothered in dust. Horses, cattle and all turned their backs to the dust, huddled together in a heap. You couldn't see your hand before you. When we looked at our watches we had to put calico around them and strike a match to see what time it was.*
>
> *Three hours later it showed no sign of breaking. We'd hobbled our horses where they stood and dropped the packs at their feet. Some of the packs were never found. They were buried in the sand. About sundown the dust slackened a little so we had to try to get the cattle to move. Seventy were smothered. The ones that lay down were smothered too. Then we got them to face the dust. Some would horn others that were struggling and dying.*
>
> *Their eyes were like balls of fire in the dust. They walked well for a couple of miles and then the dust came up as thick as ever and we were wound up in a knot again. We were all knocked up.*

Even big operators like Sir Sidney Kidman, the cattle king of the era, with his huge spread of stations, were unable to escape the drought and suffered huge stock losses.

Birdsville Track drovers at Cannuwalkalanna Creek on the Birdsville Track, circa 1930. Early settlers took the risk of establishing large sheep and cattle stations in Central Australia, and drovers moved the beasts in large mobs along stock routes to find feed and water when the land was afflicted by drought.

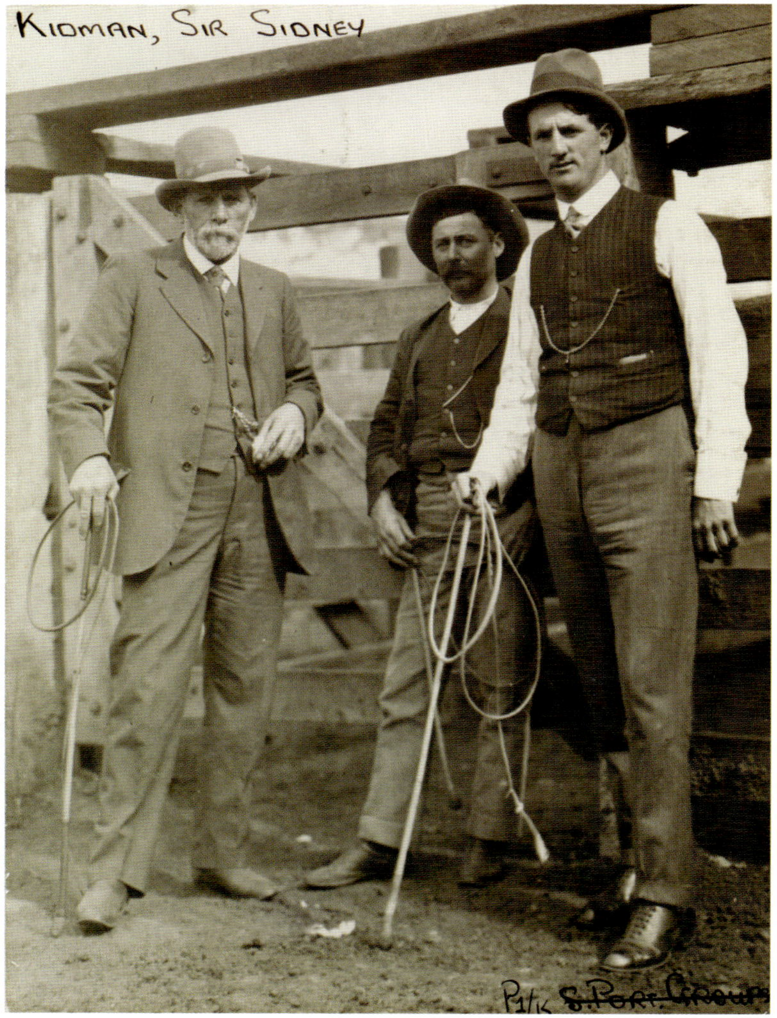

Capitalising on the boom and bust nature of the environment, pastoralist Sir Sidney Kidman (left) cannily established chains of properties that ran almost from the Gulf of Carpentaria in Queensland through New South Wales to South Australia, near Adelaide. He was then able to move his stock more easily to better pastures and better markets.
Opposite: Despite the standard of the 'roads', by the 1920s motorised transport began to replace camels along the old inland camel train and droving tracks.

Only the resolute saw it through. David Brook, a third-generation beef producer based at Birdsville, grew up with tales of the big droughts and recently witnessed some of the worst times himself:

> *I've had parents and grandparents and great-grandparents living on these river systems from way back in the 1880s and 1890s. I've read the dramas they've had in droughts. It slows you down and shortens your step but you don't have any choice but to try to ride it out.*

By 1900, the desert was in full control around Lake Eyre, leaving the pioneers scattered across the desert at the mercy of the brutal weather.

Muloorina Station, a sheep and cattle property on the southern shores of Lake Eyre, was abandoned and taken by the South Australian Government as a camel depot in 1902. But the camel's days were numbered. By the 1920s, motorised transport began to push into the outback along the trails fashioned by the drovers and the camel trains. Many camels were turned loose to breed in the wild. They adapted perfectly to Australian conditions and now roam the deserts of Central Australia in disturbing numbers. Motorised transport even replaced camels on the Birdsville Track — but it was no easy ride ...

On a scorching New Year's Day in 1936 a young man started up a six-wheel truck and headed out of Marree for Birdsville — bound for a place in history. It was the first mail run being made with Tom Kruse at the wheel. Harry Ding, who ran a transport business, had won the Marree

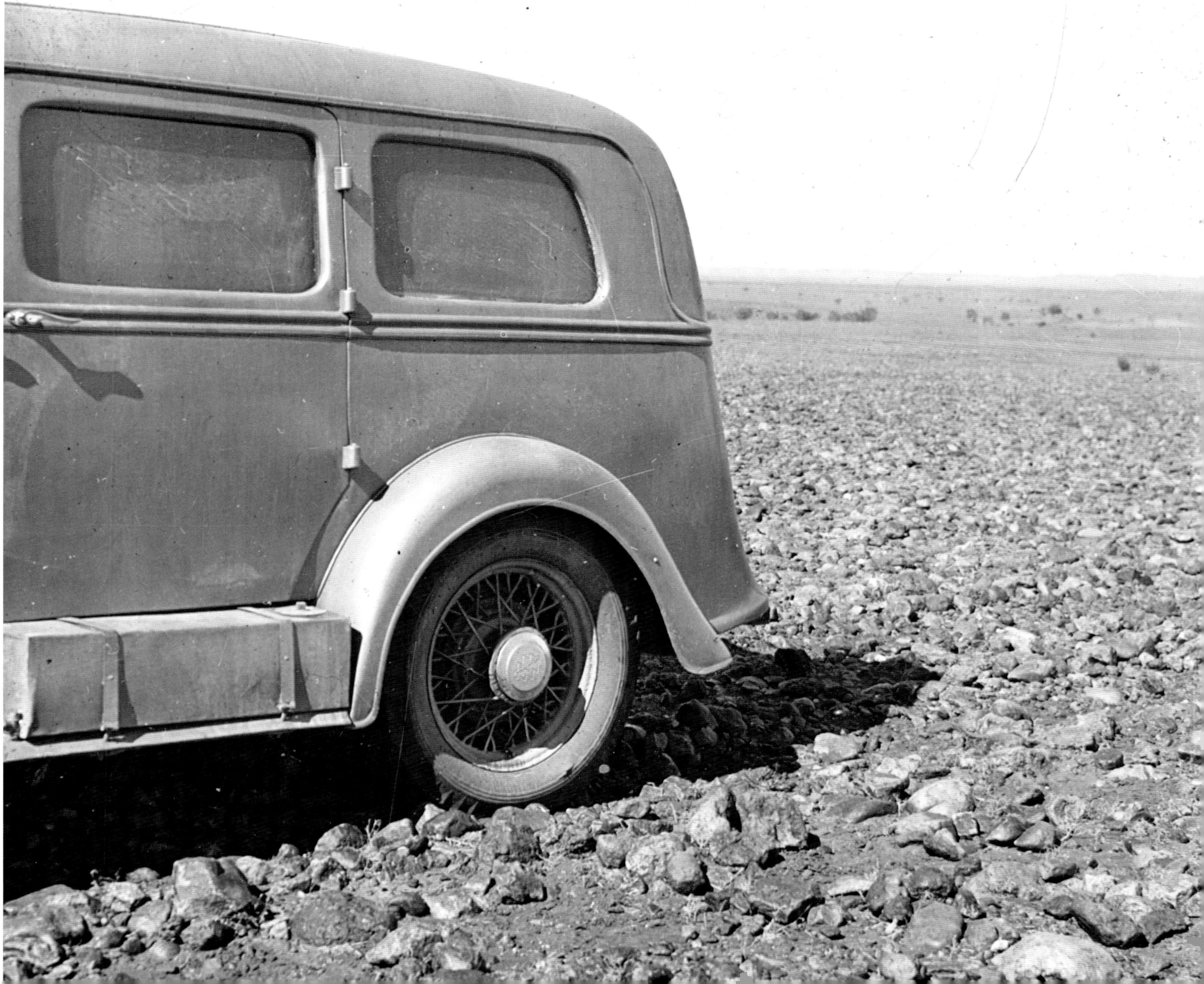

Mailman Tom Kruse, Marree – Birdsville Mail. Sandhills north of the Cooper.

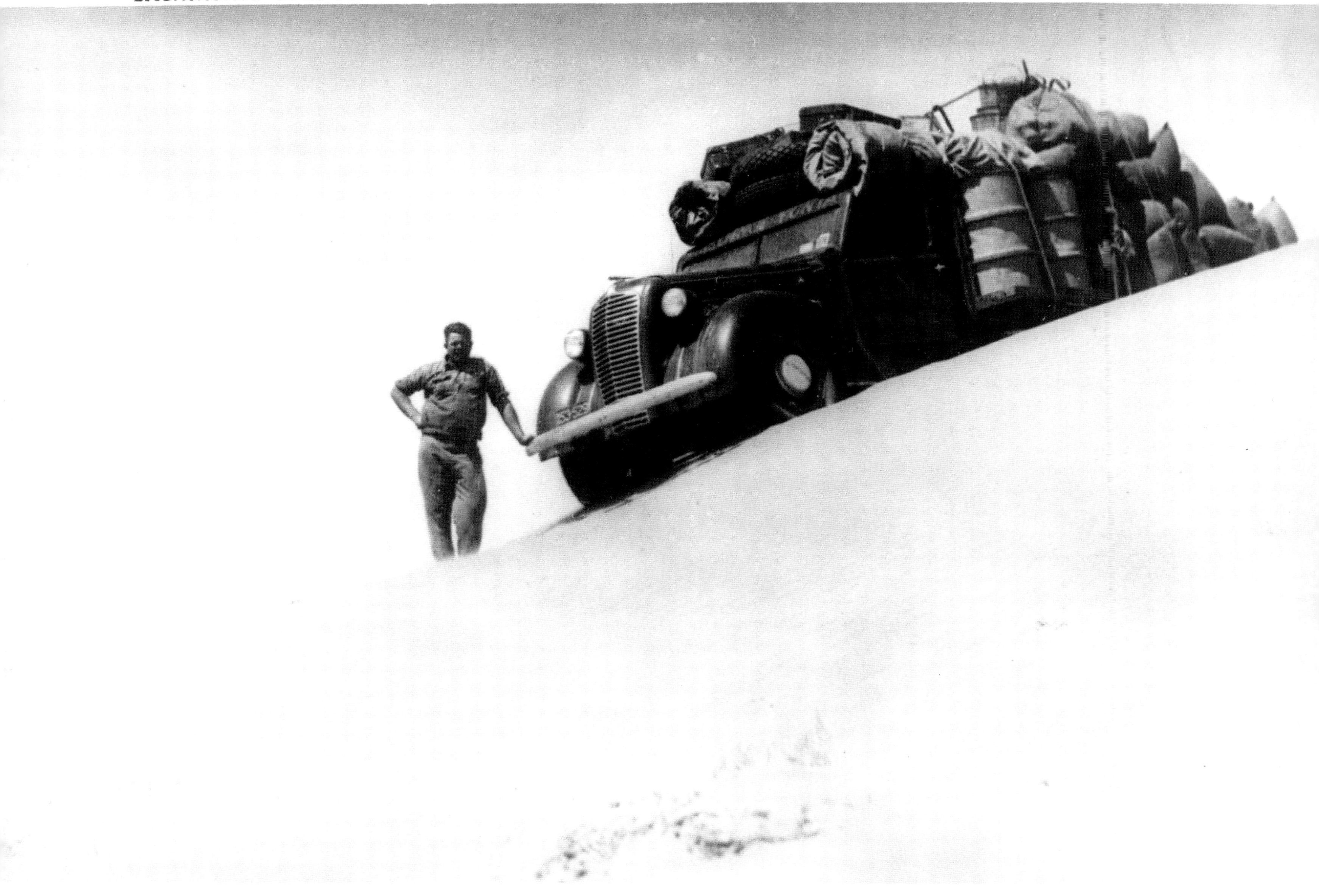

to Birdsville mail contract, agreeing to make deliveries once a fortnight. Twenty-one-year-old Kruse was his chosen driver. For more than twenty years, through drought and flood, Kruse would coax his trucks along one of the most formidable tracks in Australia, to get the mail through. He followed the rough desert trail the drovers and the cameleers had fashioned from bore hole to bore hole, but when the sandstorms came and the desert shifted he had to find new ways through.

The challenges were enormous but he became a master of mechanical improvisation and of survival. In the early years before radio communications Kruse would sometimes find himself stranded for days until his non-appearance would spark a search. On one trip with an offsider he became bogged after a downpour in Goyder's Lagoon, north of Lake Eyre. Kruse decided it was better to stay put and wait for the track to dry out, rather than waste fuel trying to get out of the bog. Fortunately there were some crates of potatoes aboard, as Tom Kruse explained in *The Mailman of the Birdsville Track*: 'Look, it's amazing how you can cook potatoes ... you can have 'em grilled, baked, chips, raw ...' It was two weeks before a rescue vehicle reached them.

He took adversity in his stride to become a legend of the outback, his tough life captured in a 1952 documentary, *Back of Beyond*, which played to audiences in cinemas around Australia and at film festivals overseas. Tom Kruse provided much more than a mail delivery. He carried goods of all kinds on his heavily laden truck and became a crucial point of contact for the people who lived on the remote stations all the way along the Birdsville Track. Whenever he made it to the end of his journey in Birdsville there was great excitement. David Brook, who was a schoolboy in the early 1950s, vividly recalled the scene for ABC TV's *Australian Story* in 1996:

> *It was a very big day. It was the big event of the fortnight for everyone in town. The kids would all run out of school when Tom came into town in his truck. I reckon one of the things that kept Tom going was the fact that everyone up the track was dependant on him for their provisions and if he didn't get through they wouldn't get a feed for a week.*

From 1936 until 1957 Tom Kruse made a regular mail run from Birdsville to Marree along the Birdsville Track, a 500-kilometre round trip over difficult terrain. He not only carried the post to remote properties but also essential supplies. Stoic and enterprising, Kruse became a legendary outback figure.

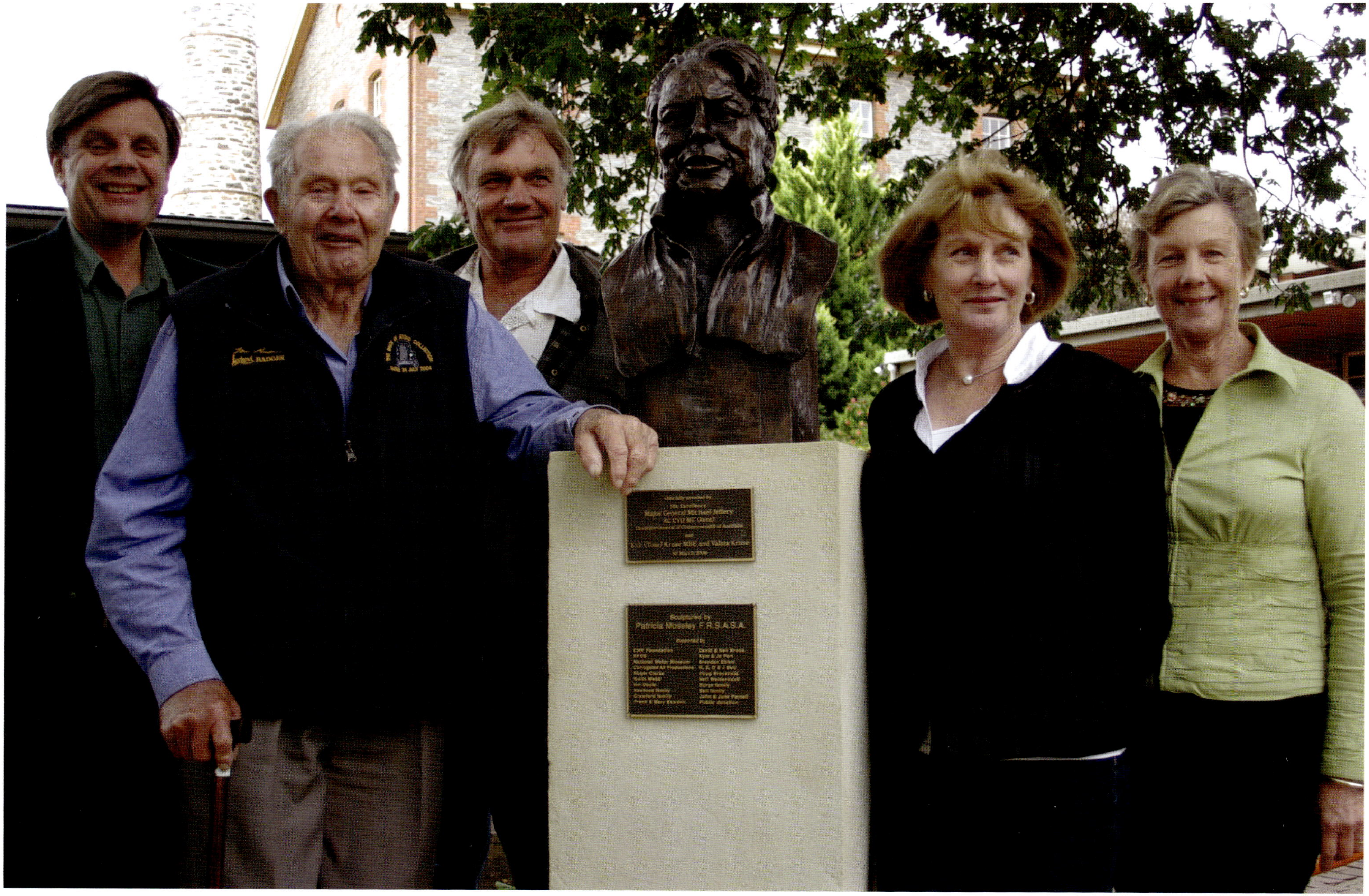

Tom Kruse was appointed MBE in 1955 but missed the ceremony because of outback flooding. He was inducted into the National Transport Hall of Fame in 2000, recognised as an Outback Legend in 2003, and in 2008 bronze busts (above) of this Australian icon were erected in Marree and Birdsville in celebration of his extraordinary contribution to outback life. Back of Beyond, *a documentary recreating one of his mail runs, was filmed in 1954. Opposite: Scenes from filming the documentary.*

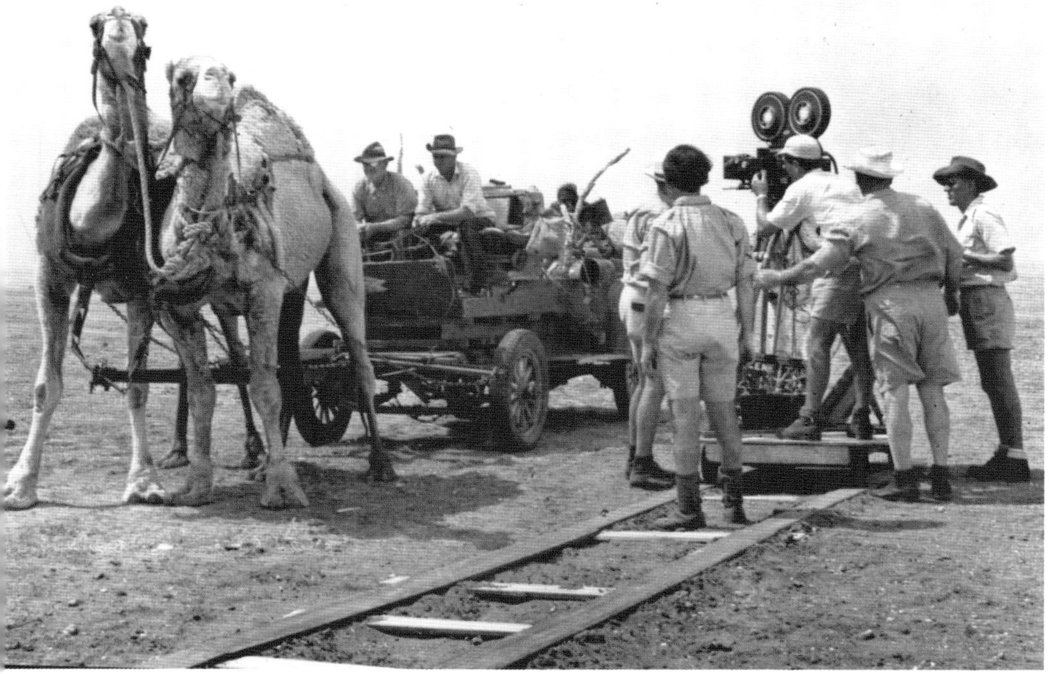

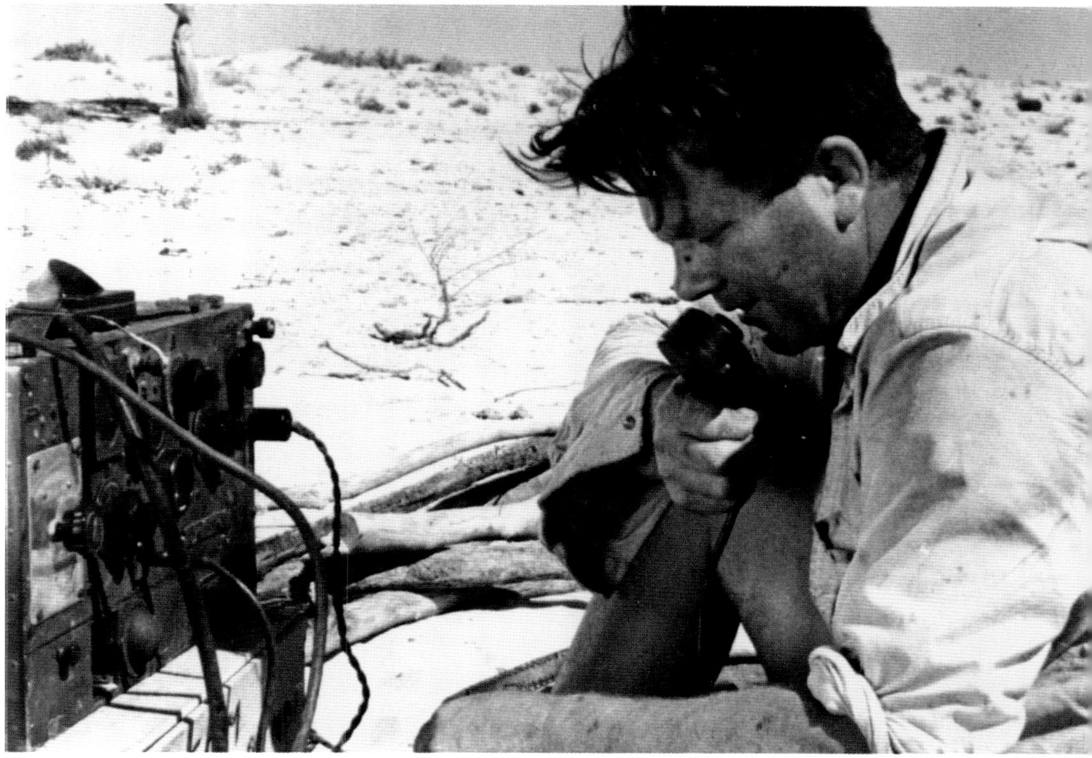

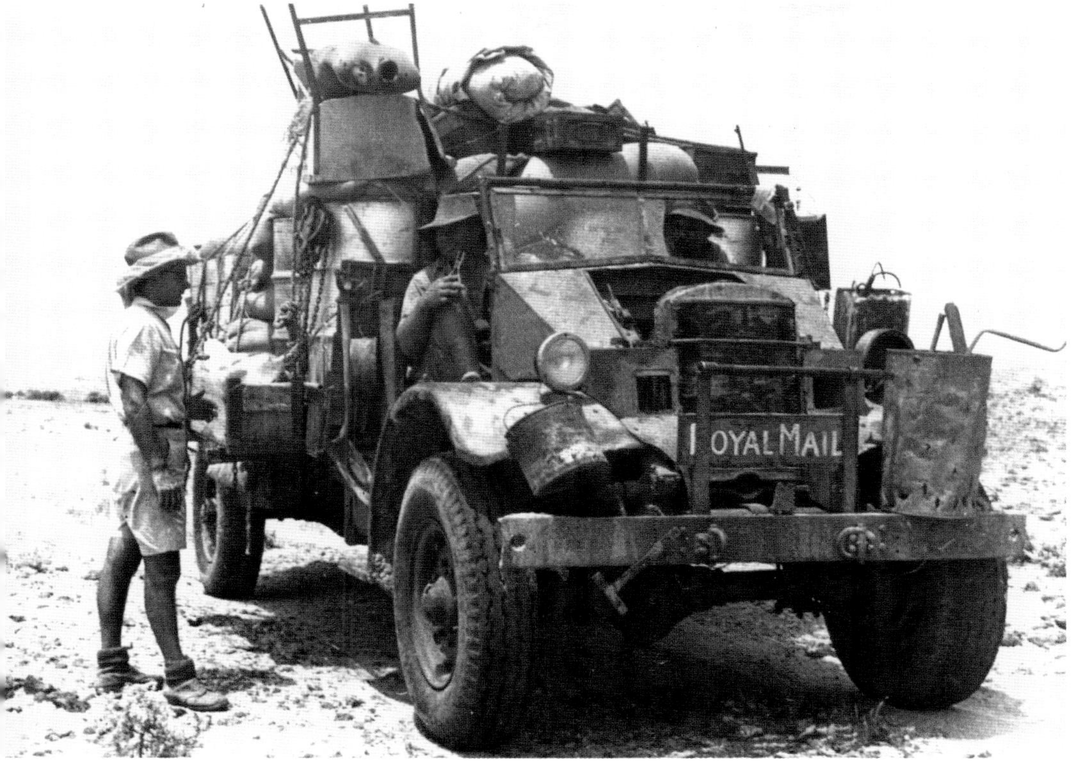
ROYAL MAIL

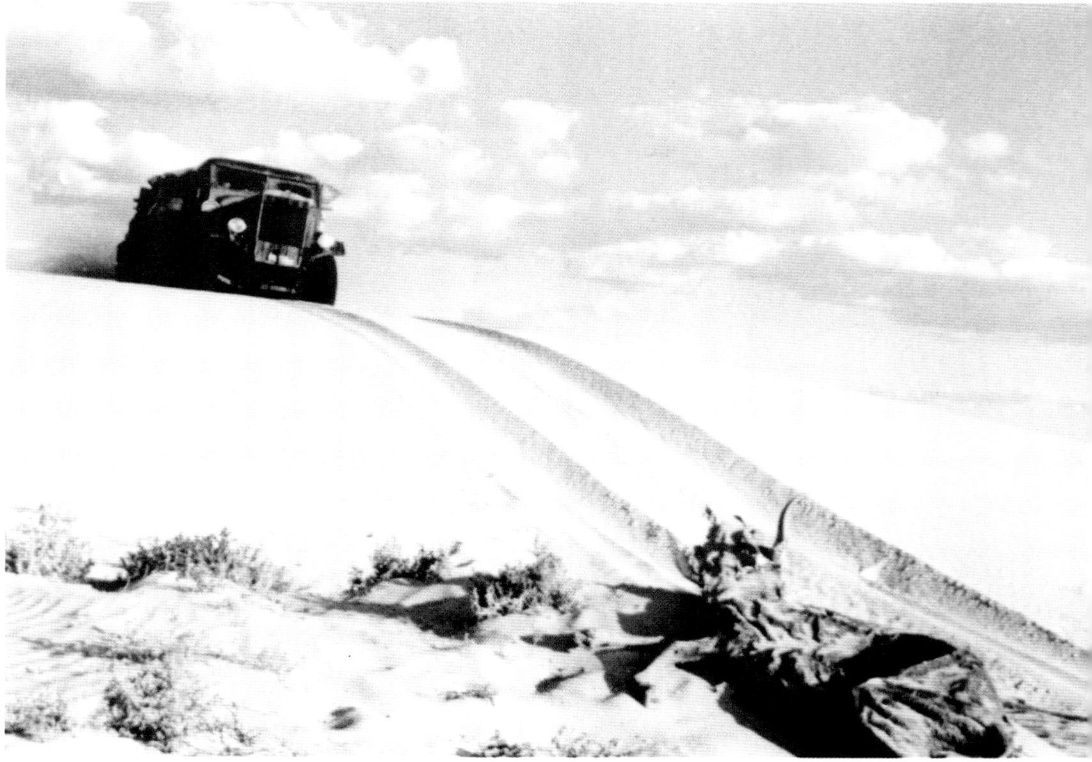

Although relatively thin in some parts of Lake Eyre, the salt crust can reach thicknesses of up to forty-five centimetres; here a slab of crust cut from the surface of the lake at Madigan Gulf near Muloorina Station shows what lies beneath.

Opposite: Sheep were introduced soon after exploration opened up the land, requiring bales of wool to be transported long distances. Carting wool in the International truck in 1936. Third from the left is Tom Kruse.

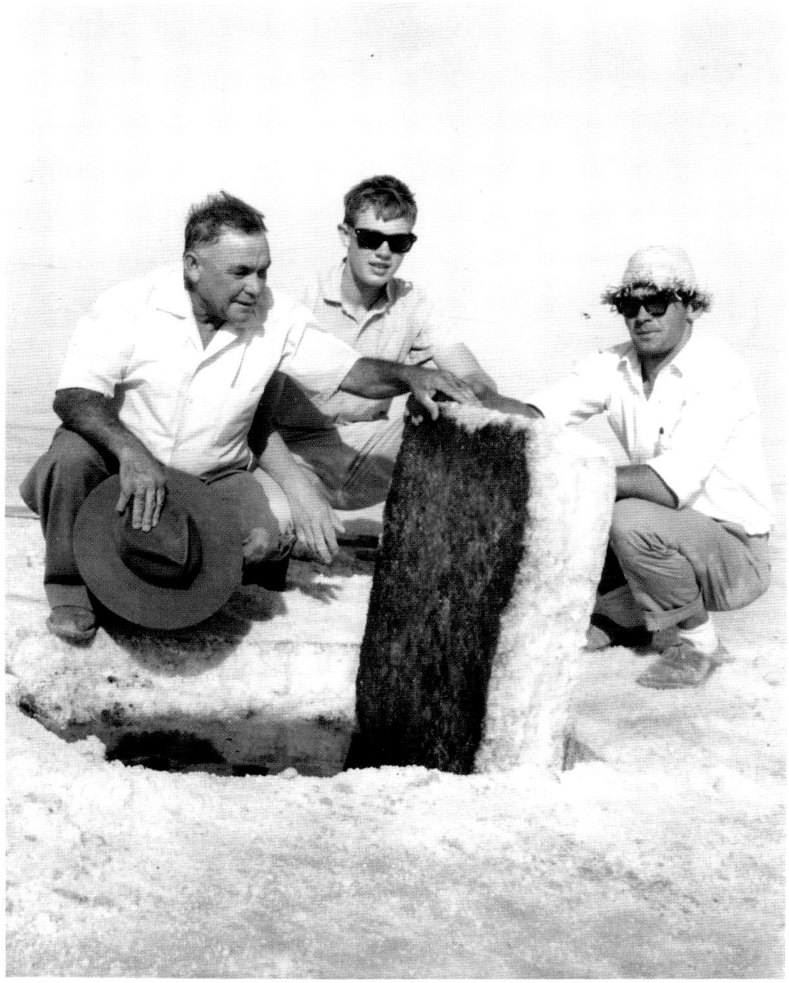

In 1955 Tom Kruse was awarded an MBE for his services to the outback. The citation read:

> *In all weathers Mr Kruse makes a fortnightly journey between Marree and Birdsville, calling at all properties adjacent to the track, delivering mail, provisions and supplies for the families scattered through this remote area. Tom Kruse is not only a romantic figure but something of an institution, having earned the love and respect of all residents of the outback. He has risked his life on many occasions in carrying out this service.*

After Edward John Eyre first went in fruitless search of an inland sea in 1839, there was no reason for early settlers to believe that Lake Eyre was anything but a vast dry salt pan. But that notion changed dramatically in 1949 and 1950 when heavy rain started the desert rivers flowing, producing the first recorded flooding of the lake since European settlement.

Locals knew that even small falls of rain could make a big difference to water supplies and pastures in the desert country, but here at last was a boom and the promise of a string of good seasons to come. By this time Muloorina Station, stretching over more than 4000 square kilometres on the south-eastern shores of Lake Eyre, had reverted from being a camel depot to a sheep and cattle property. Times were good but aside from the exploits of mailman Tom Kruse, the world seldom took notice of remote Central Australia. But that changed in 1963 when Muloorina, little more than a dot in the outback, suddenly found itself at the centre of the biggest international story ever to break at Lake Eyre — a world speed record attempt by Donald Campbell. The lure for the British speedster was the flat, hard-baked salt surface of Lake Eyre.

Here was a near-perfect racetrack created by nature, stretching for kilometres, with little or no chance of rain intervening.

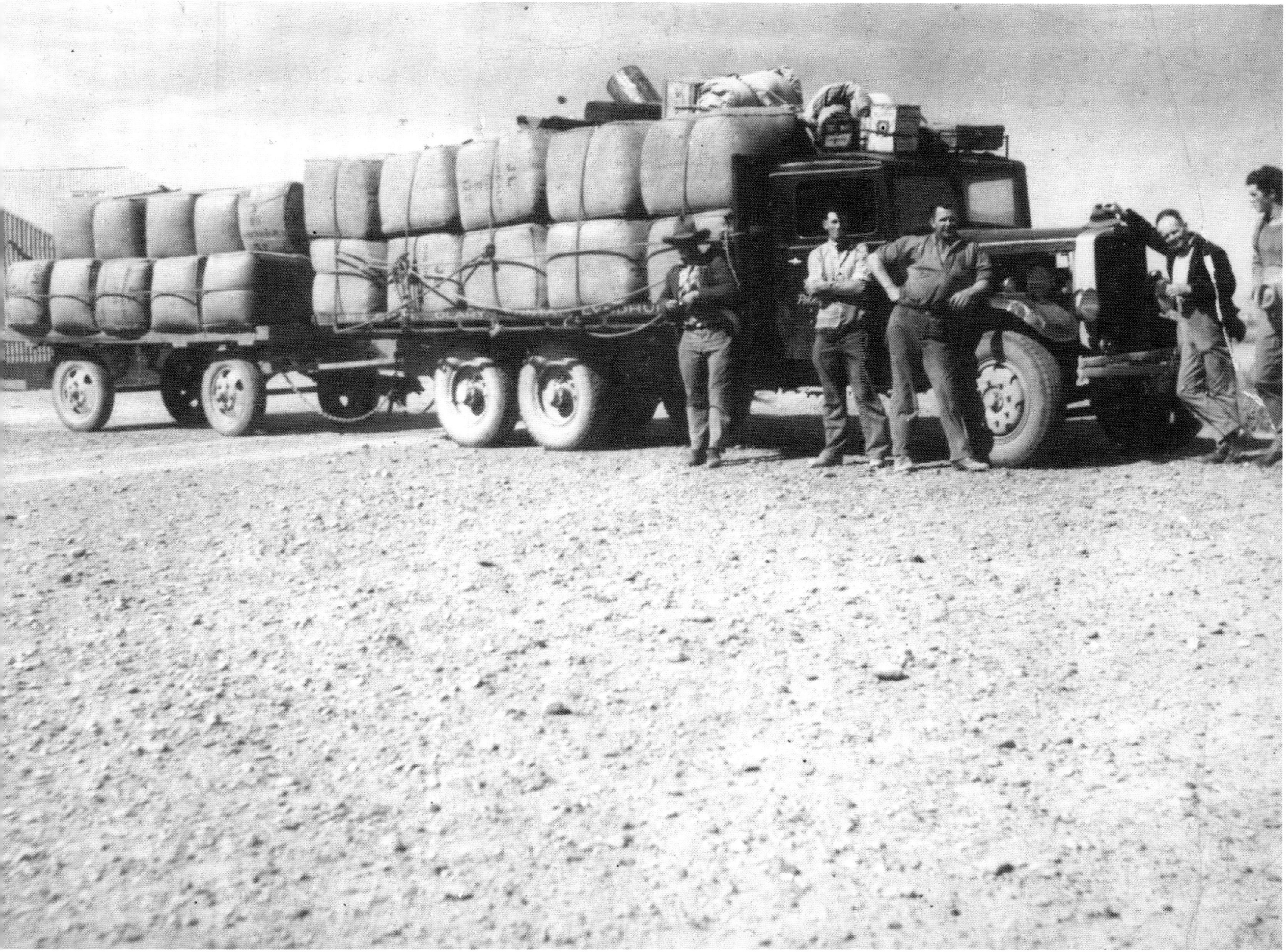

The bluebird of Lake Eyre

In the 1960s, the intense race to set new land and water speed records made world headlines. And Donald Campbell, following a family obsession, was at the forefront of the often-dangerous efforts to push back the barriers. His father, Sir Malcolm Campbell, famously set thirteen world speed records in cars and boats in the 1920s and 1930s. It seemed that the son was determined to emulate, if not eclipse, his father's proud performances.

Donald Campbell started his racing career in the early 1950s in one of his father's old speed boats, the Bluebird K4, but in one of his earliest record attempts — on Lake Coniston in England's Lakes District in 1951 — the vessel hit a submerged log and was so extensively damaged that it had to be scrapped. Campbell was lucky to escape injury. Undeterred, he built his own speed machine — the Bluebird K7 — a jet-propelled hydroplane launched in 1954 in which he set a new water speed record on Ullswater — also in the Lakes District — the following year of 202.15 miles an hour (324 kilometres per hour).

He set another six water speed records in the K7 over the following nine years, bettering the world mark more often than anyone in history. Those performances earned him international acclaim but it wasn't enough for the restless Campbell. He also had an eye on the land speed record, and from 1955 he worked on plans for a revolutionary car constructed like the body of an aircraft and capable of speeds more than 400 miles an hour (644 kilometres per hour). He traded on the fame of his water speed records to raise support in Britain for his new car, winning the backing of seventy leading companies. It was finally unveiled in 1960. The Bluebird-Proteus

British racing driver Donald Campbell with his car, Bluebird. His attempts to break the land speed record on Lake Eyre were initially foiled by heavy rains.

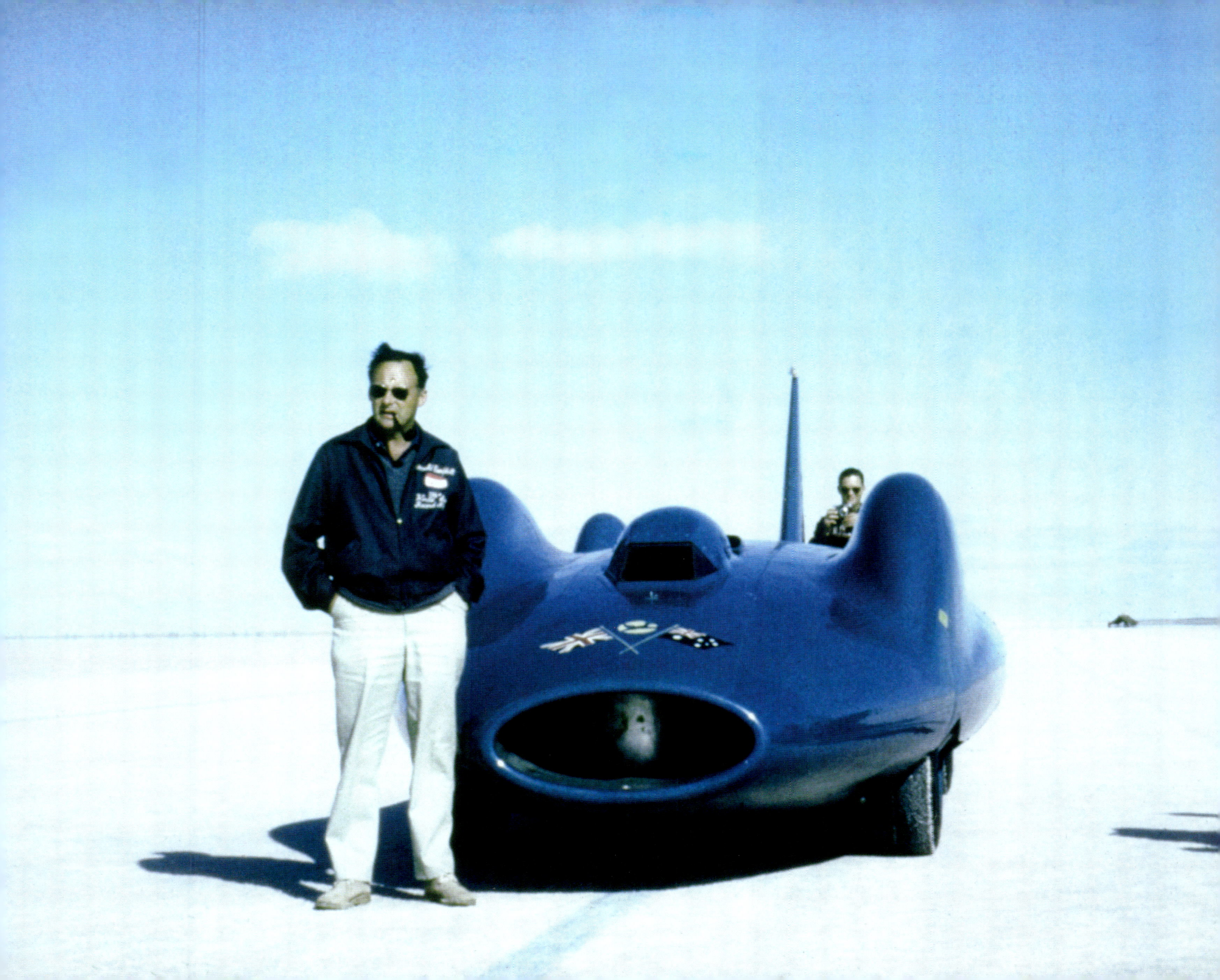

Television cameramen film Campbell during his world speed attempt on Lake Eyre in 1964. The surface of the lake was ideal, 'like concrete … and it seemed to go on for ever'.

CN7 was powered by a Bristol Siddeley Proteus free-turbine engine, capable of speeds up to 500 miles an hour (800 kilometres per hour). In the same year, Campbell took the vehicle to one of the world's most famous test tracks, the Bonneville Salt Flats in Utah, where his father had set a land speed record in 1935, a feat his son had been there to witness. But for Campbell, his attempt would end in disaster.

On 16 September 1960, Bluebird veered wildly off course in a high-speed crash that left Campbell with a number of injuries, including a fractured skull. From his hospital bed in Salt Lake City three weeks later he simply dismissed the injuries and the frightening crash as part of the risk and vowed to try again.

His stoic display won more admirers in Britain and he gathered even wider corporate support to rebuild Bluebird. It was through one of his backers, the oil company BP, that Campbell was told about a possible new racetrack — Down Under. Campbell didn't want to return to Utah, complaining that the course of a little over 16 kilometres was too short and was often left dangerously slick from the oil left by other vehicles. He wanted another site that offered a longer, more reliable speed track and fewer people. Lake Eyre offered all he required — a near perfect track created by nature and stretching for miles into the Australian wilderness.

Late in 1961 Campbell flew to Australia to assess the site for himself and was delighted by what he discovered. 'I could hardly believe it,' he later said. 'The surface was like concrete. It was flat, it was smooth and it seemed to go on for ever.' Back in Adelaide he enthusiastically told the South Australian Premier, Sir Thomas Playford, that if he succeeded in his speed attempt there was no reason why Lake Eyre couldn't replace Bonneville and Daytona in the United States as the world's new record-breaking speed track. A headline in the *Australian Women's Weekly* in November 1961 declared, 'Speed could make a town called Eyre', with Campbell suggesting that a thriving community could emerge around an international speed track carved out of the lake in one of Australia's most desolate areas.

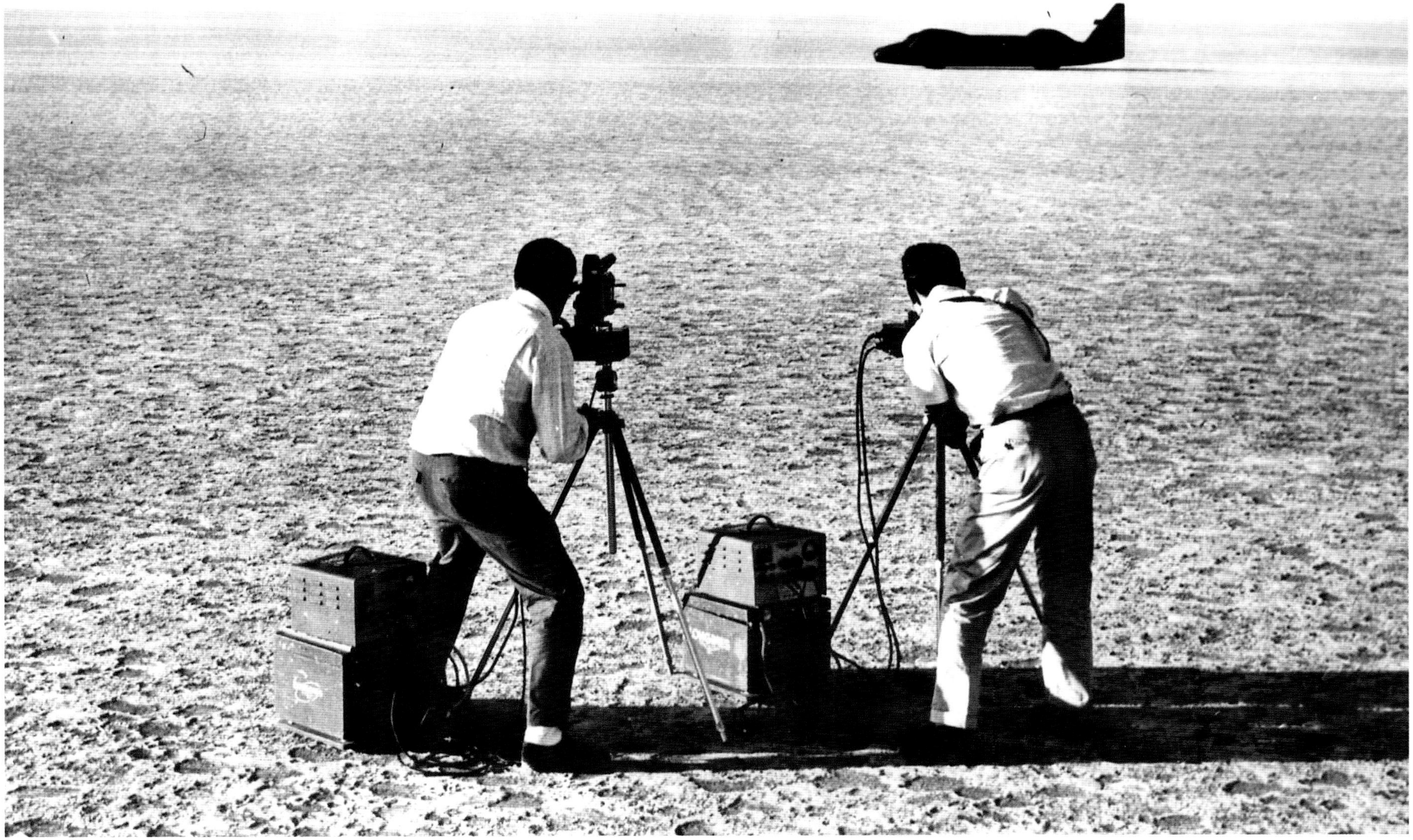

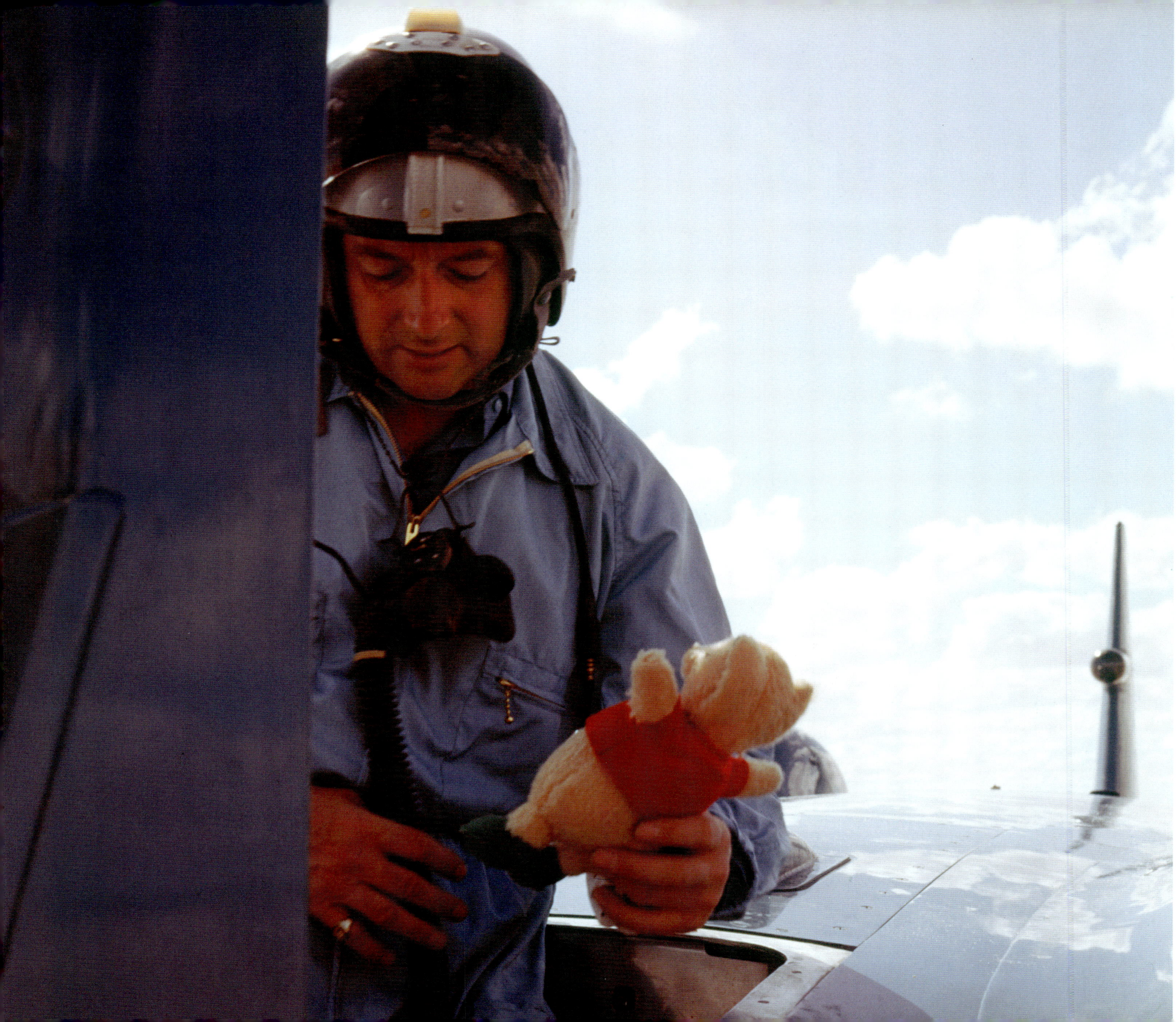

Donald Campbell and his mascot, Mr Woppit, pose before climbing into the cockpit of Bluebird.

Bluebird was rebuilt and sent to Australia at the end of 1962 for a planned speed attempt on Lake Eyre the following year. There was great excitement Down Under at the prospect of Australia becoming part of a history-making event. But despite the bravado, Campbell feared that bad luck was stalking him — fears that had intensified since his crash in Utah in 1960. He admitted to being superstitious, as was his wife, Belgian singer Tonia Bern-Campbell. When they journeyed to the dead heart of Australia in March 1963 they were quickly given cause to believe that bad luck was indeed following them. Light rain started falling as they arrived at Muloorina Station to establish their base camp with an army of support staff and a big press contingent.

For three months the rain persisted — the first heavy falls in the region for years. Out on the salt there was chaos as Campbell's team had to rescue Bluebird, which was in danger of floating away. 'Bluebird of Unhappiness' declared the *Adelaide Advertiser* in a headline in May 1963, above an aerial photograph of Bluebird almost submerged in Lake Eyre.

A pall was cast over the speed attempt and it had to be abandoned.

Their bad luck unnerved the Campbells, who had heard of the Aboriginal legends associated with Lake Eyre, and it was with a sense of unease that they returned in 1964 for a second attempt with Bluebird. The South Australian Government was backing the speed record attempt and the Australian Army was providing logistical support but the people of the outback were, typically, unfazed by all the fuss, particularly Elliot Price, who owned Muloorina Station: 'The Campbells fitted in real nice. They got the same treatment as anyone else — can't afford to waste time on fools in the outback!'

Campbell and his wife, Belgian singer Tonia Bern-Campbell, admire a model of Bluebird. Bern-Campbell used cabaret performance to lift what she believed was the curse of the lake.

But rain intervened again in 1964, softening the rock-hard track. There were weeks of frustration, waiting at Muloorina for the lake to dry. After yet one more muddy and dangerous run, Campbell was on the point of giving it away, as related in *Bluebird and the Dead Lake*:

> *Look at it. What a hope we've got. Forget it. Let's all forget the whole silly damned business. This course will never get dry. There's a jinx on it. It's this lake, this bloody lake. It's out to get me and this morning it nearly succeeded.*

His wife Tonia rode every emotion of Campbell's speed attempt on the salt. She shared her husband's fears that the lake was jinxed and decided to use her talents as a cabaret performer to counter the curse of the lake, as she explained to George Negus on ABC Television in 2003:

> *When we arrived we were told about the legend that two young Aboriginals had been killed on the lake and a witch doctor cursed the lake — anyone coming on to the lake would be swallowed up again and again. So eventually, when we went there the second time, I went to Marree and I did a show for the Aboriginals.*

Tonia Bern-Campbell hoped that by staging a concert in Marree and raising money from the performance to donate to the Aboriginal community it might help to assuage the negative spirits of Lake Eyre.

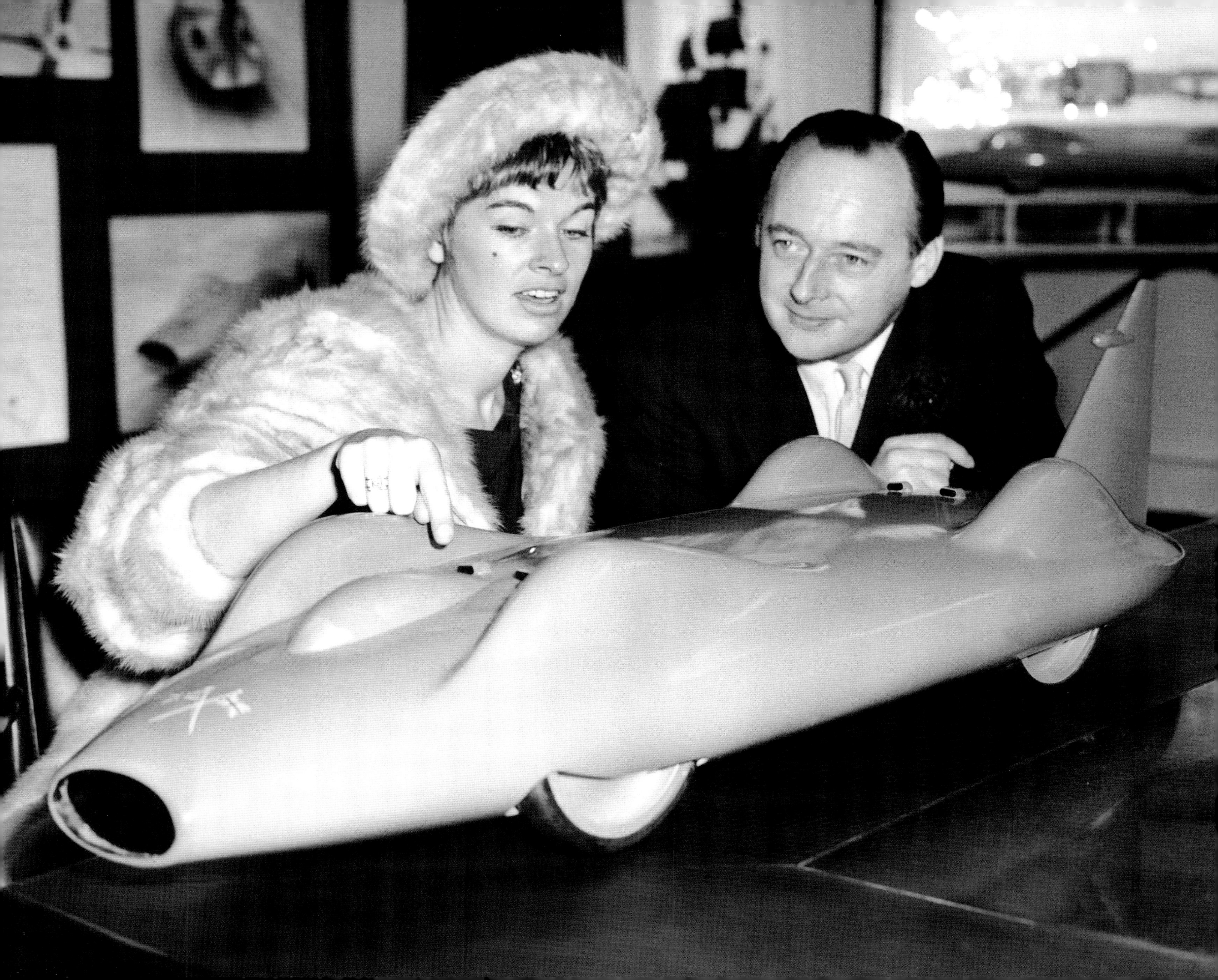

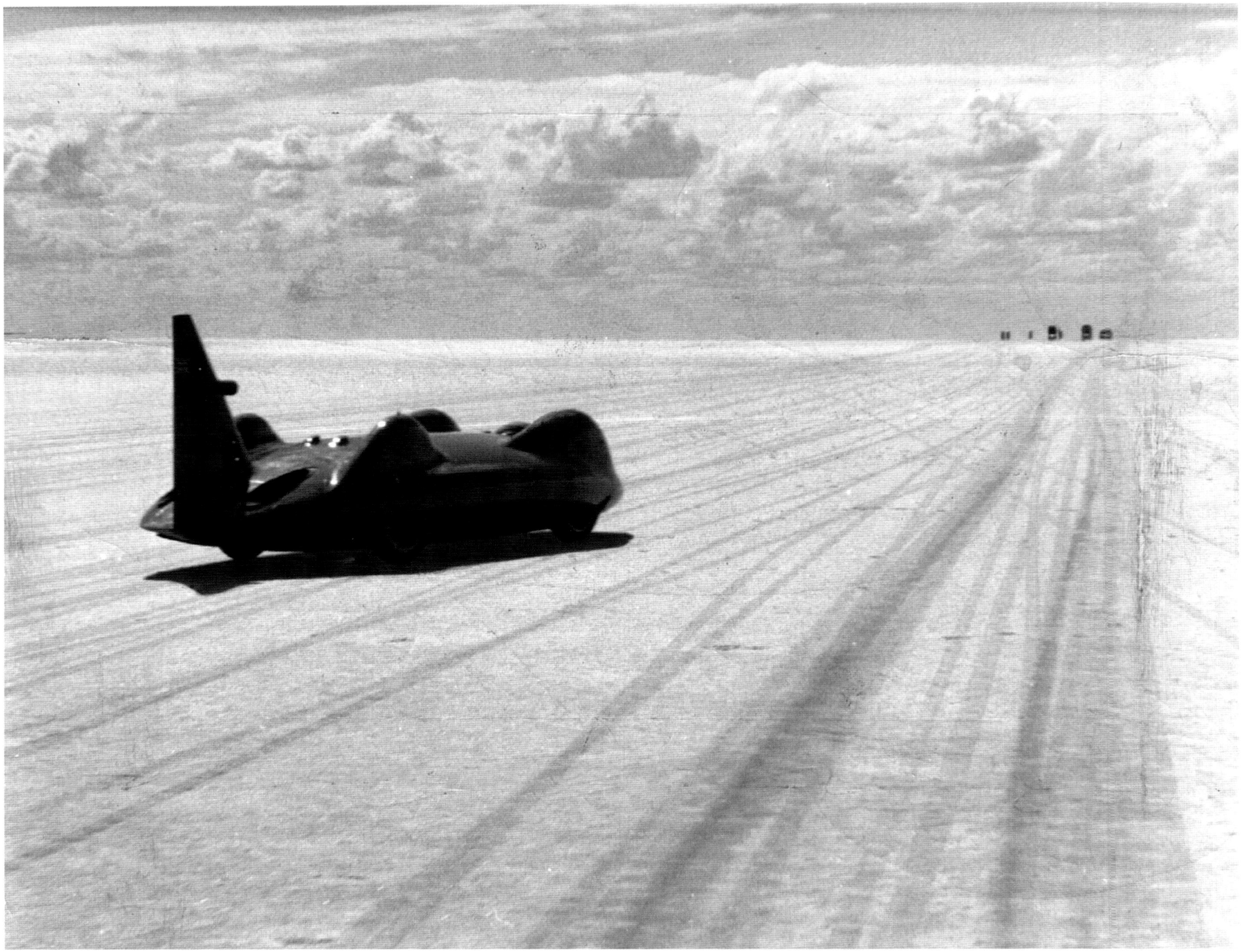

If a big kindness was shown towards the Aboriginals, the curse might be broken. So I did a show for them. I sang songs to them, then took them back to Lake Eyre for a picnic. And two days later, we broke the record — fact or fiction!

The moment of triumph finally came on 17 July 1964. Bluebird screamed across the salt pan, under more than 4000 horsepower, to set a record of 403.10 miles an hour (648.73 kilometres per hour) for a four-wheeled vehicle. Donald Campbell had hoped to get closer to the 500 miles an hour mark, but given the many difficulties he had encountered he was relieved to leave Lake Eyre behind. Yet he had some unfinished business in Australia — on the water. Campbell wanted to become the first person to break the world land and water speed records in the same year. He left it until the very last minute to achieve his aim, breaking the water speed record on Western Australia's Lake Dumbleyung on New Year's Eve 1964.

Campbell's luck was finally to run out two and half years later when he was killed attempting another world water speed record on Coniston Water in England's Lakes District.

Lake Eyre quickly faded from the news after Campbell's achievement in 1964. It was to be ten years before the region would again excite wider attention. That was the year that floodwaters on a scale never witnessed before began coursing towards the dead heart.

Donald Campbell returns Bluebird to the start to commence his land speed record attempt on the vast salt plain of Lake Eyre.

FLOODS & THE LAKE

The surprising centre

The flooding of Lake Eyre in 1974 astounded locals and created great excitement amongst scientists and adventurers alike. For the first time in recorded history water lapped at the shoreline, triggering an influx of birdlife and setting the desert to bloom.

The wonders of Lake Eyre were finally on display.

Entranced by it all was Rex Ellis. As a young man Ellis worked as a jackeroo on cattle stations around Lake Eyre and was fascinated by the desert country around him, especially by the hardy flora and fauna that managed to survive in the arid terrain. In 1971 he led the first party of tourists across the Simpson Desert — a four-wheel-drive convoy taking on a thousand sand dunes. Ellis has been taking tours through Central Australia ever since; camel treks across the deserts and boat trips down the outback waterways when they occasionally flow — there's little that he hasn't attempted in his expeditions through Central Australia. Every trip has been a journey of discovery for Ellis: 'Our deserts are special. I mean they haven't been buggered up like the old world deserts. We go there chasing rare wildlife and rare birdlife — there's nowhere in the world that you can really do that to the same extent.' Birds are his great love and he'll excitedly rattle off the sightings he's made on his most recent adventures. In May 2011, for example, a pair of northern pintails, a European duck species rarely found south of the equator, were spotted by a group of birdwatchers he was taking down Warburton Creek. One of the great lures is his search for the rare night parrot, a bird he's certain he'll spot some day on one of his treks across the desert.

In 1974, flooding caused Lake Eyre to fill for the first time since records had been kept, bringing fish and the novel opportunity to sail.

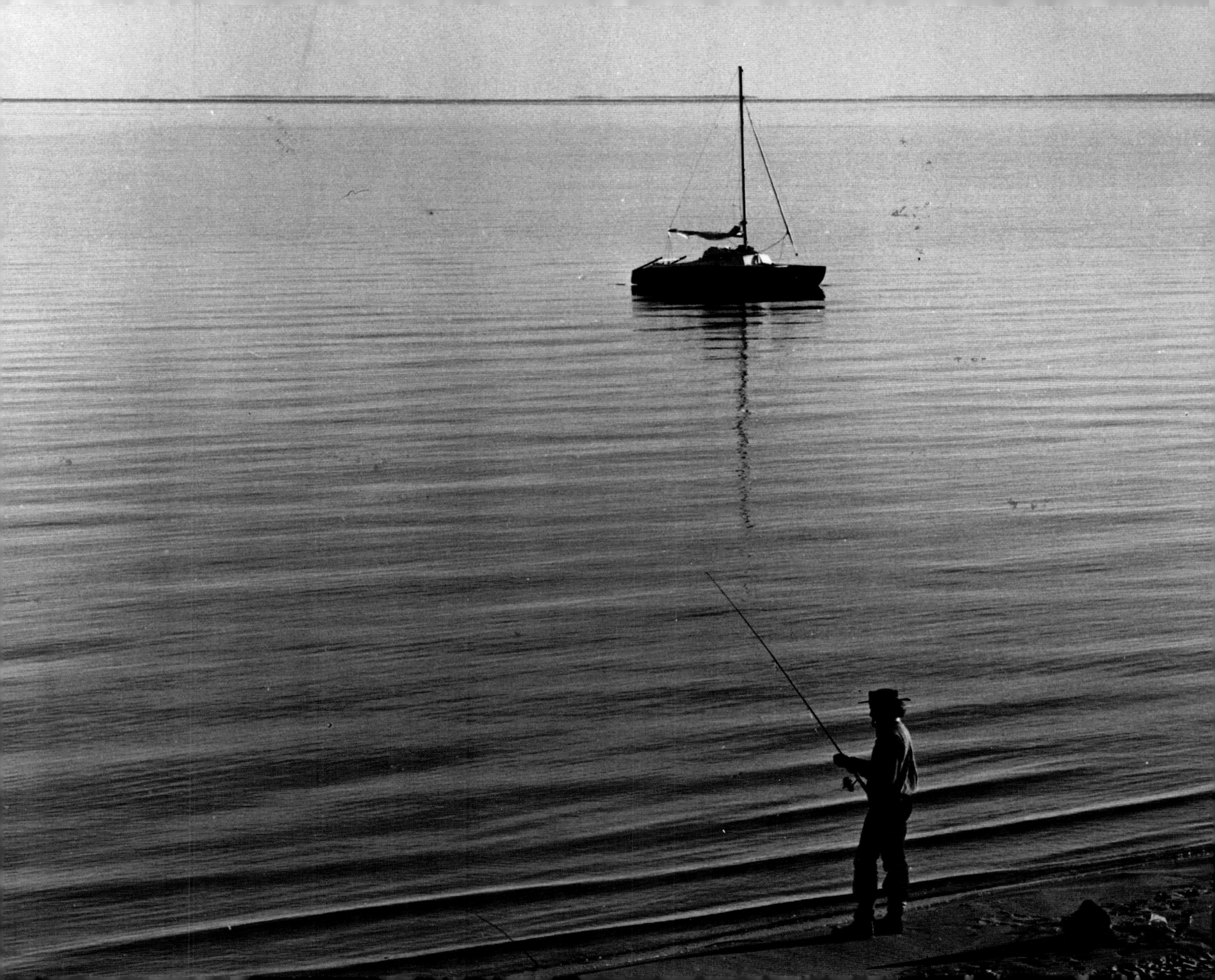

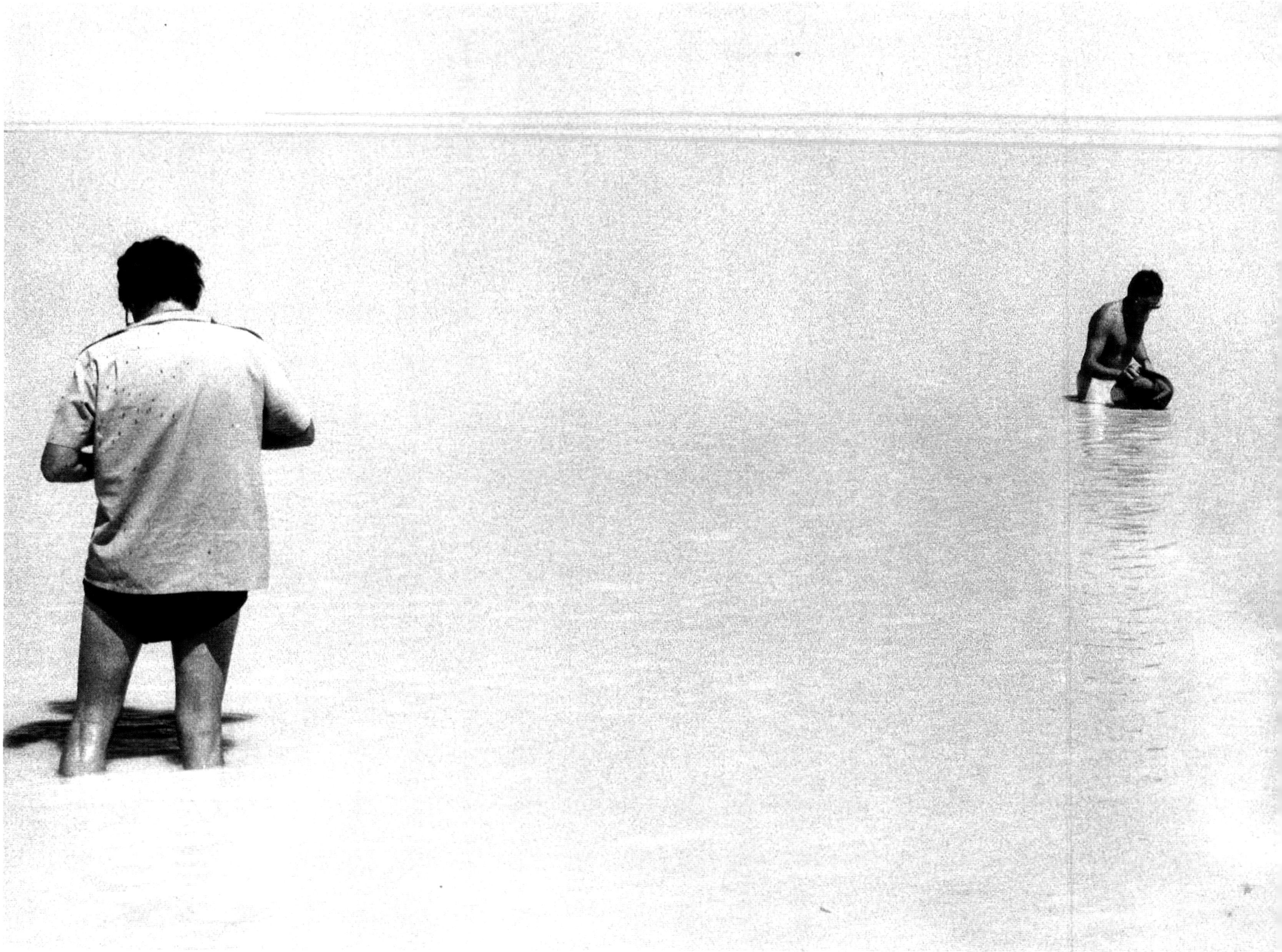

Rex Ellis, who has taken tours through Central Australia since 1971, and noted environmentalist and film-maker Vincent Serventy documenting the flooding of 1974. Despite the calm appearance, the floodwaters could turn rough as they discovered when they tried swimming across.

When Lake Eyre flooded in 1974, Rex Ellis had a grand plan — to become the first to cross it by boat. He invited Vincent Serventy, a noted environmentalist, author and filmmaker, to join him and three others on the trip. Just getting to the lake was an adventure in itself, as Ellis describes in one of his many books, *Boats in the Desert*. On their way up the Birdsville Track from Adelaide in March 1974, the party was confronted by the swollen Cooper Creek, running into Lake Eyre from the east. The small vehicular ferry that had been pressed into service in the middle of the desert by the South Australian Government was on the other side of the fast-flowing Cooper, about 100 metres away. There was no one in attendance to bring the ferry over, so Ellis and one of his companions, Gerald Day, decided to swim across and bring it back. They were swept away in the muddy water and the flood debris before they could finally struggle to the bank 300 metres downstream. As Rex Ellis put it, 'We weren't sorry to crawl out the other side.' The pair started the ferry up, got the four-wheel-drive truck, heavily loaded with boats and supplies, across the Cooper, and then headed north, intending to get to Lake Eyre by riding the massive flood flow streaming down from Queensland. Their objective was Warburton Creek, which funnels most of the water from the north into the top of Lake Eyre.

Ellis turned off the Birdsville Track to head west towards Kalamurina Station, which stretches across the northern shore of the lake. He nursed the truck over towering sand dunes, up to 30 metres high, before reaching the floodwaters spreading out from Warburton Creek. There, among the desert dunes, two aluminium flat-bottomed punts were loaded up for the voyage. Along with the food and fuel, Rex Ellis records that there was also six flagons of red and white wine and several cartons of beer. Gerry Day was left to drive the truck south, with luck to rendezvous with the adventurers six days later at the bottom of Lake Eyre. The boats still had some distance to travel through the floodwaters stretching out between the dunes on Kalamurina Station to reach the Warburton channel. They discovered that the station homestead — which had never been threatened by flood before — had gone under, and the manager, Jim Dunn, and his wife, Joan, had been forced to make camp on the crest of a nearby sand dune. As they passed by, the adventurers delivered fresh vegetables and stayed for lunch. The Dunns reassured their visitors that they were well prepared to sit out the flood — they just had to keep a constant lookout for snakes keen to share their sanctuary with them.

After the boats eventually found their way through the flood waters to the main channel of Warburton Creek it took another three days for the party to meander their way down to the top of Lake Eyre. There the Warburton streams into the lake, spreading wide across the salt pan. Rex Ellis, who had lived with years of drought, was enthralled by what he witnessed:

> *All we could see was the most sterile and desolate part of Australia at its all-time best; instead of the white glare of salt, sand hills and parched watercourse there was a vast lake with white caps breaking the surface. There were gently rolling hills covered in green herbage and wildflowers, and through the mouth came life-giving fresh water at the rate of hundreds of millions of litres per hour.*

There was growing excitement in the group about the history-making lake crossing they would now attempt, but their enthusiasm became tempered by unfavourable weather. A stiff breeze was whipping up the waves and there were fears that the heavily laden boats could be capsized. Rex Ellis suggested that it was better to start at night, when the wind had eased and they could navigate by the stars, so they set off at dusk and made good progress. But then the wind came up and they were forced to drop anchor in about 2 metres of water, more than 10 kilometres from shore. The waves continued to drive water into the boats and they were forced to bail out furiously, right through the night.

The expedition eventually struggled back to shore and regrouped for a second attempt.

They again set off at dusk, when the wind dropped, and everything went smoothly as they journeyed through the dark. But in the middle of the next day, a sudden burst of wind whipped up a big wave, which swamped the boat carrying Ellis and Serventy, flipping it over. They were

Fresh water flows into Lake Eyre from rivers such as Eyre Creek (taken here from the eastern Simpson Desert), slowly dissolving the salt until the water is fresh enough for invertebrates, fish and waterbirds to thrive.

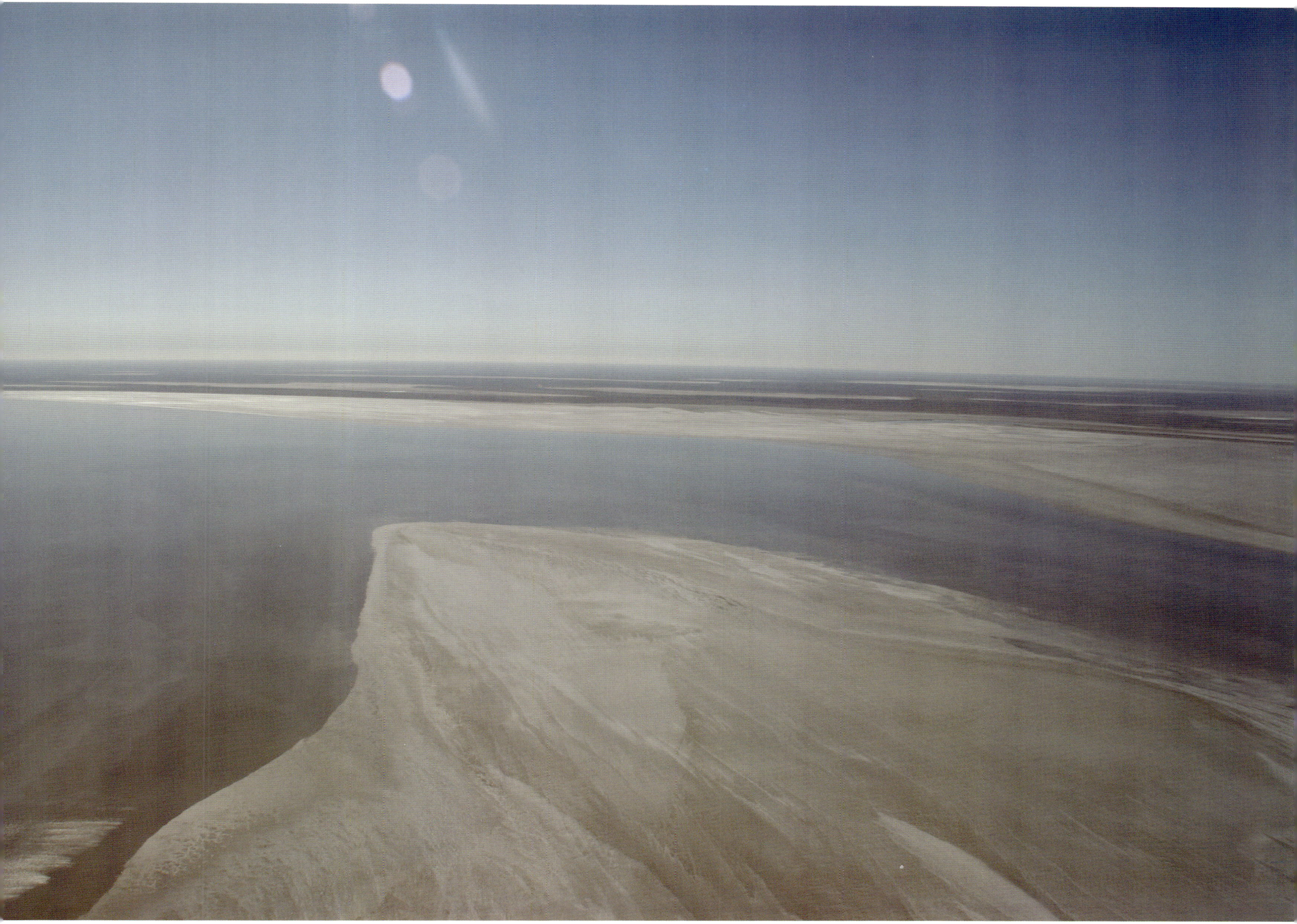

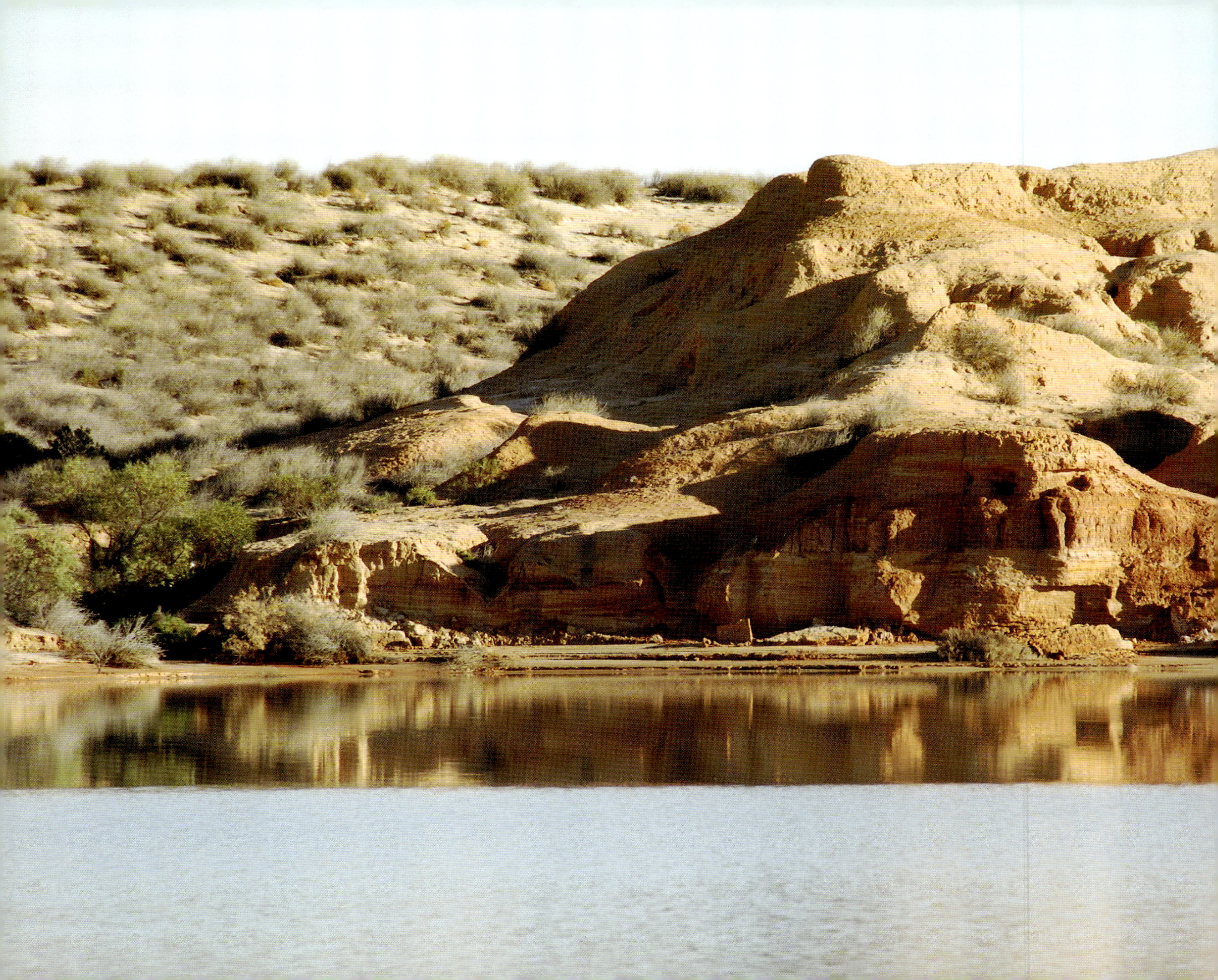

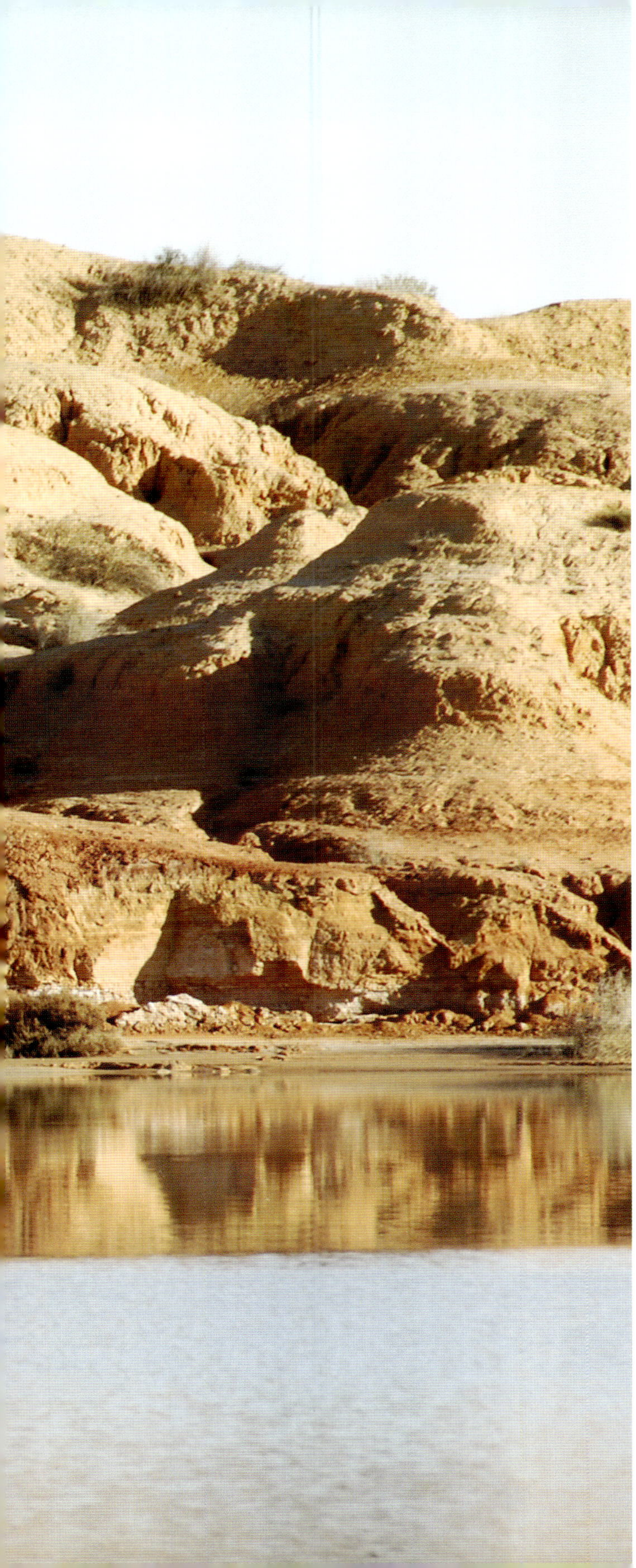

'The dead heart, but it just comes to life every now and then,' says Rex Ellis of the region. *Overleaf:* The southern end of the lake after the floods.

left to cling to their overturned punt, watching as much of their equipment — their clothes and notebooks, painting and camera gear — drifted away or sank. It was a bedraggled group that completed the historic crossing of Lake Eyre.

In his own book, *The Desert Sea*, Serventy summed it up: 'With no camera it was a frustrating time for me during the next few days as pelicans, black swans and mountain ducks came to examine the convoy, before flying off as though impatient with our slow progress.' When he looks back on the escapade, Rex Ellis is struck by the great irony of it all — being capsized in the middle of the desert.

The flooding in 1974 was just the start of a wet cycle in Central Australia that was to last for three years — much like the flooding that took place between 2009 and 2011.

But in the mid 1970s no one had ever witnessed such sustained flooding of Lake Eyre. Rex Ellis and Vincent Serventy were determined to make the most of it. Despite the disasters they had encountered on their first lake voyage, they planned another boating expedition — to try to circumnavigate Lake Eyre. When the artist John Olsen heard about their planned adventure he was keen to join them, excited by the possibilities it presented for his landscape work. The party gathered at Muloorina Station, as Donald Campbell and his support team had almost ten years before. But they didn't get far before trouble struck.

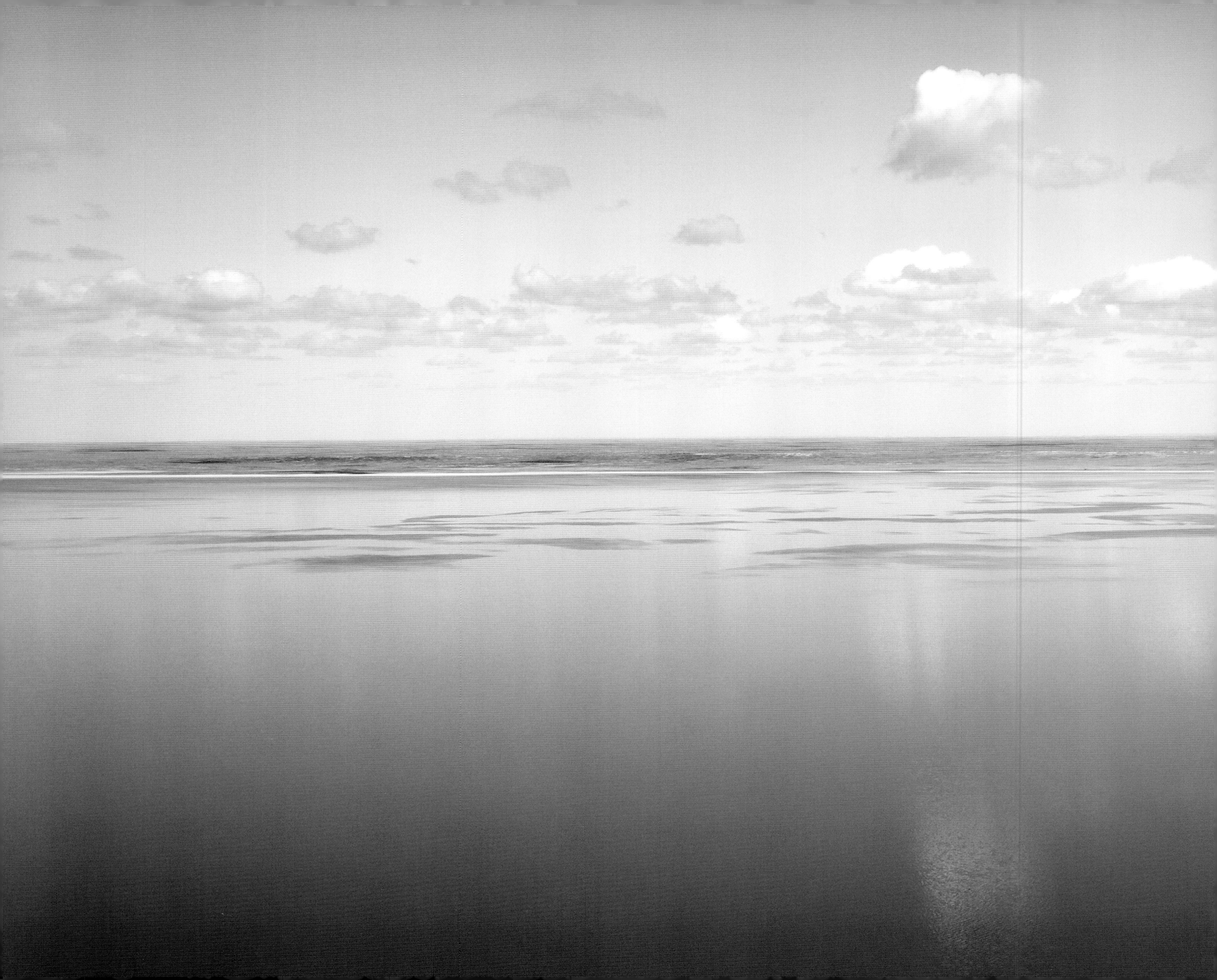

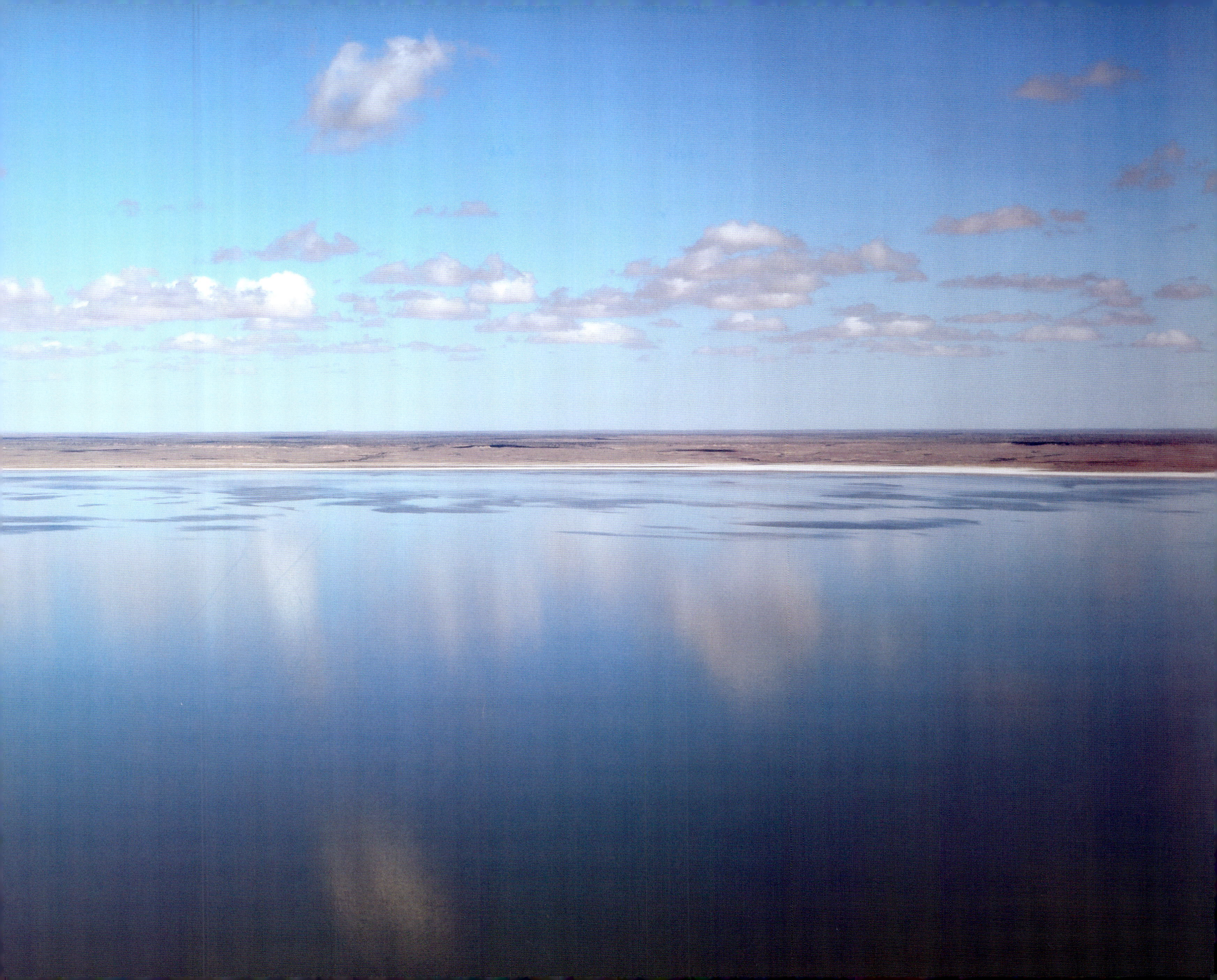

As they happily cruised along the southern shore, a westerly suddenly swept in, whipping up waves on the tranquil lake and capsizing the boat carrying John Olsen and Vincent Serventy.

In *The Desert Sea*, Serventy wrote: 'After the initial shock of finding ourselves in the water, surrounded by the drifting flotsam of food, paintings and camera gear, we had time to worry.' John Olsen recalls watching his straw hat, slices of bread and his prized camelhair brushes float away. The second boat, with Rex Ellis at the helm, was still afloat but struggling to make its way through the rough water to reach the travellers bobbing in their life jackets. Eventually Serventy and Olsen were able to get to a rubber dinghy they had been towing and waited there for the support boat to arrive. They salvaged what gear they could from the water and then made landfall on a desolate part of the southern coast of the lake, warming themselves before a driftwood fire. John Olsen's clothes had sunk to the bottom of the lake and Vince Serventy, whose clothes had been kept dry in the second boat, shared his wardrobe with the artist so they could continue their Lake Eyre trip. They decided, however, that a circumnavigation of the lake might now be a little ambitious. Instead the group decided to simply edge their way along.

They continued along the southern shore — in and out of the bays and inlets — never too far out in case the weather should turn nasty again. John Olsen had retrieved enough of his art supplies to sketch and paint the first of his many works on Lake Eyre. Recording his thoughts from that time in his book, *Drawn from Life*, Olsen wrote:

> *I draw studies of insects, animals and birds, that will eventually be realised as prints and watercolours. My devotion to Chinese art and philosophy finds a fulfillment in this experience. Nothing too small or too strange should escape my attention — an insect's wing, the leap of a frog, the flight patterns of dragonflies. They all induce poetic rapture.*

It was an experience that was to have a profound impact on Olsen and his work for decades to come. He was brought further and

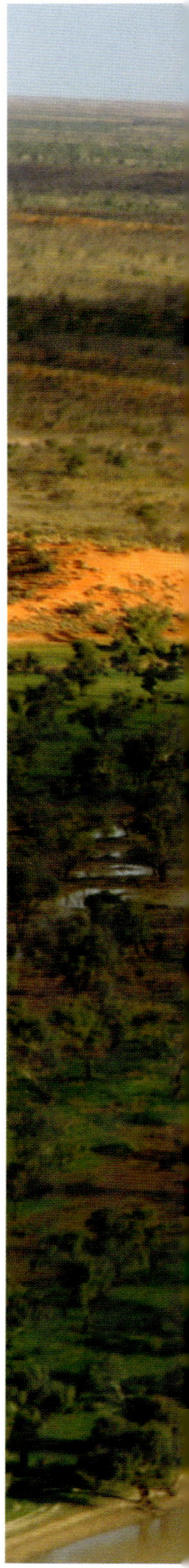

Water finds the well-worn paths down the main channels, such as Eyre Creek, that course through the Simpson Desert, and then inexorably spreads out onto the floodplains, bringing life to the system.

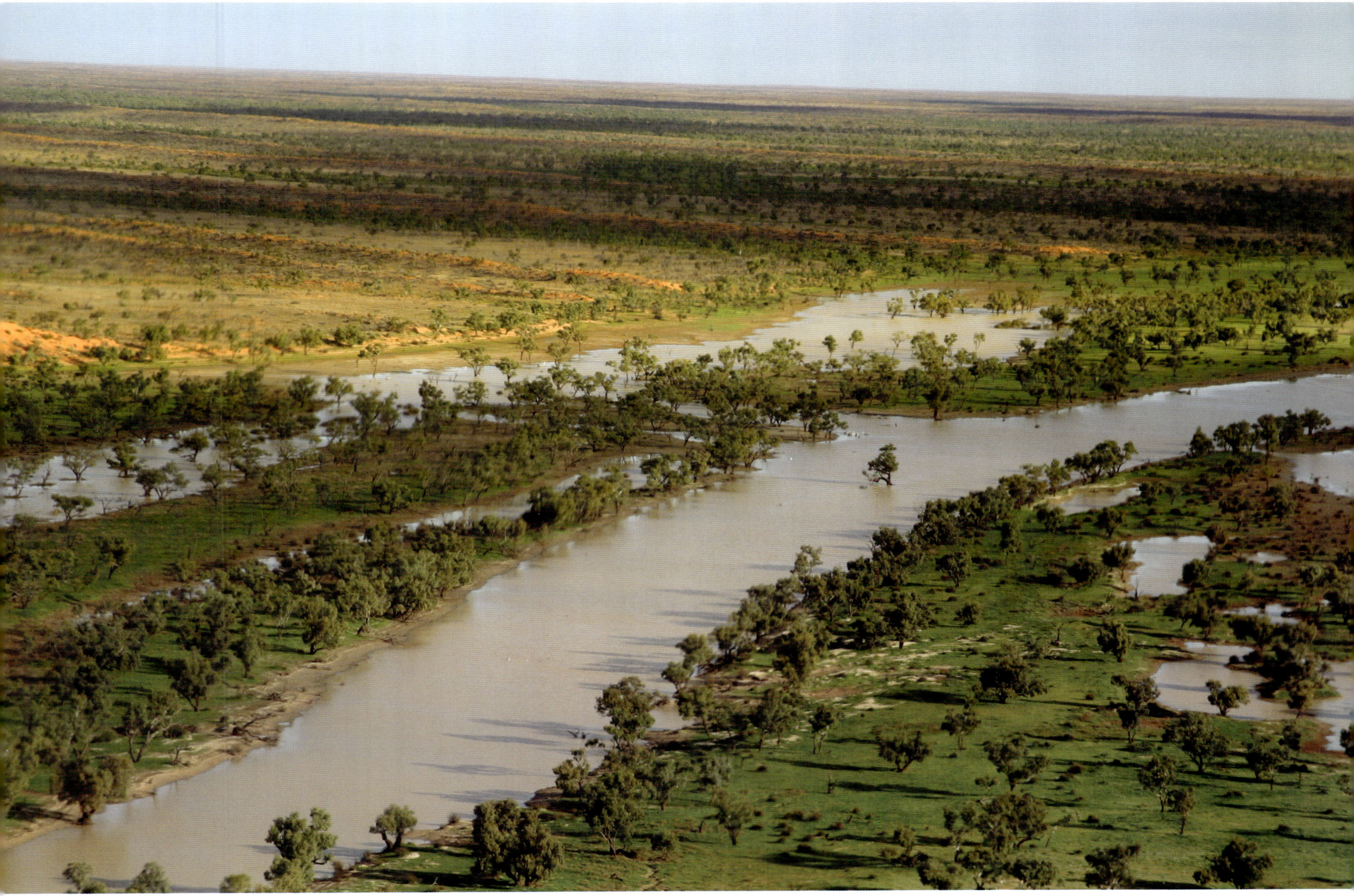

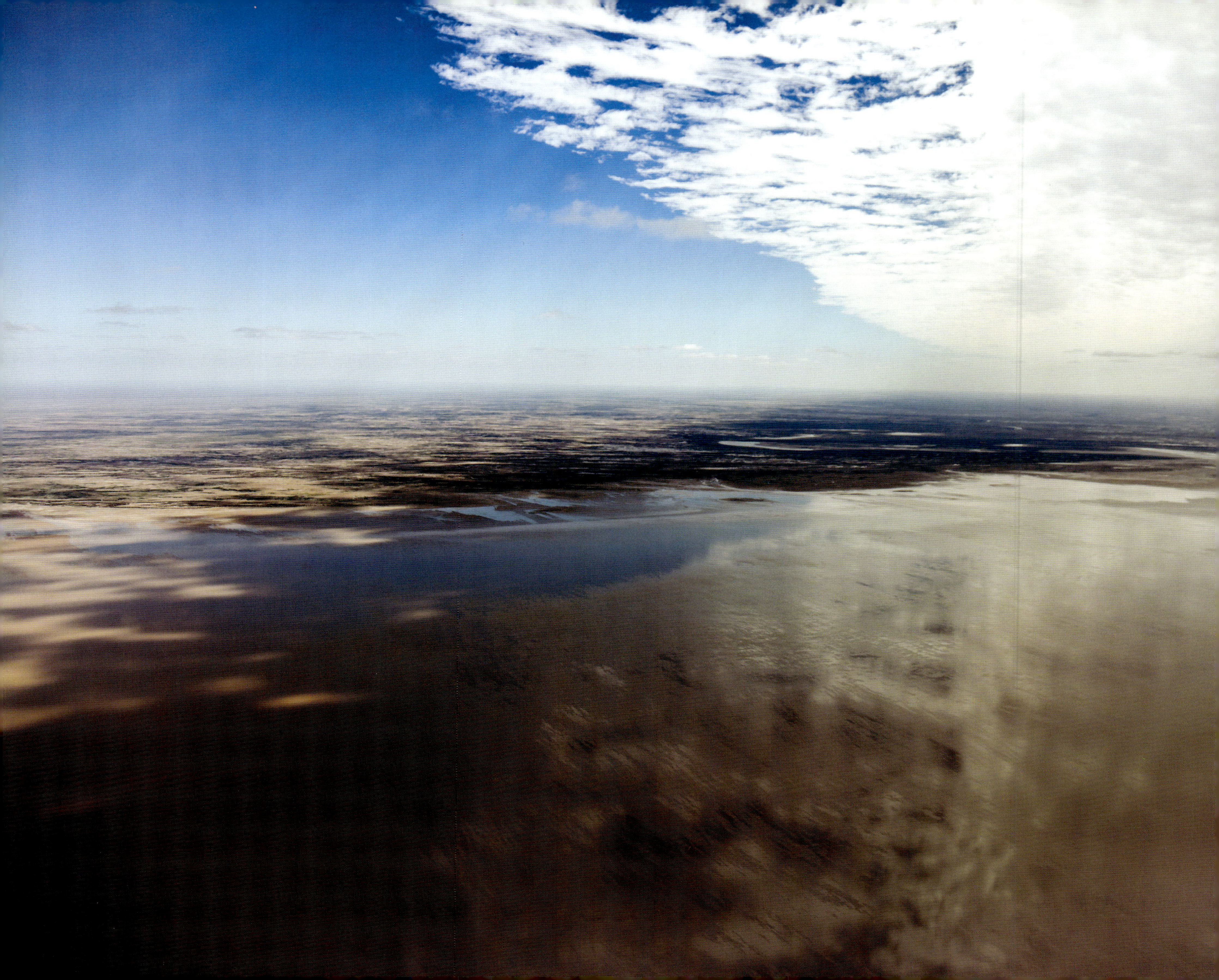

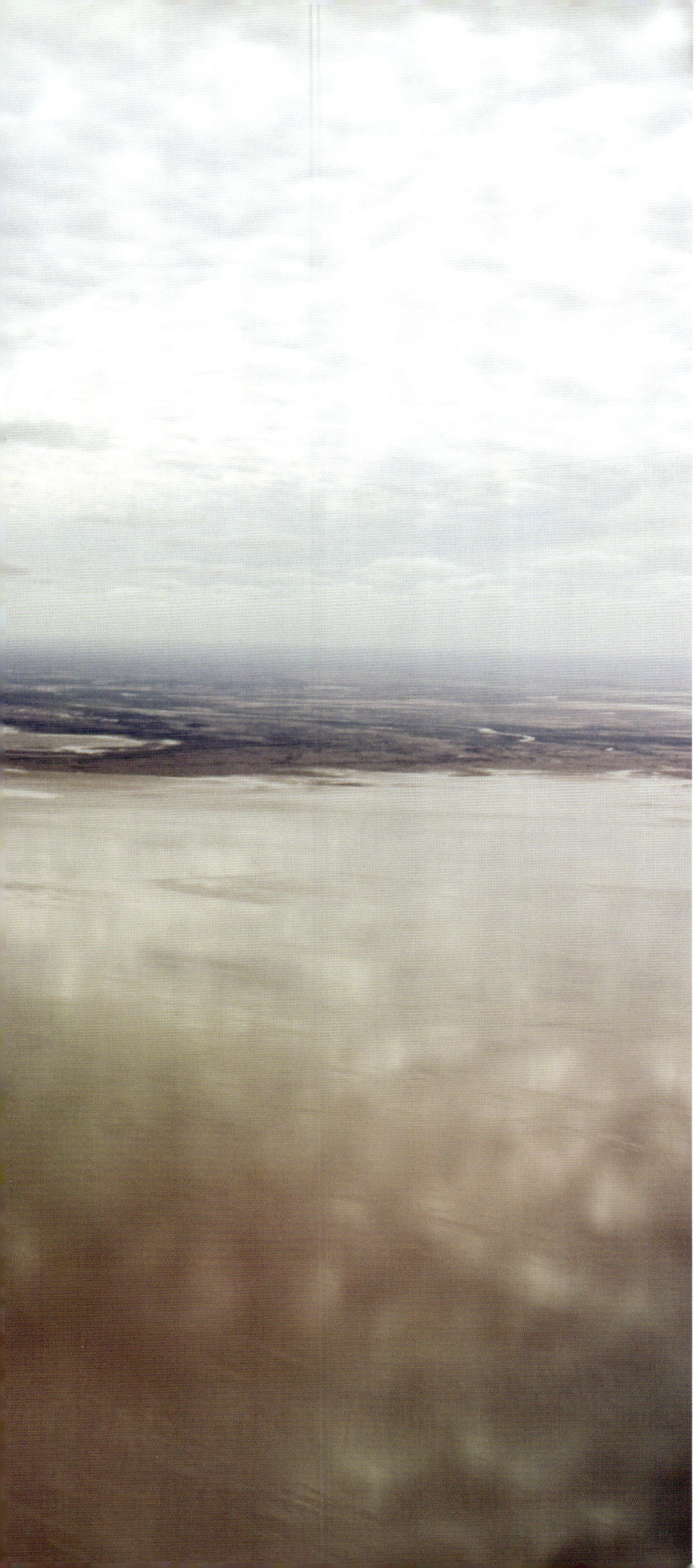

Extraordinary reflections of clouds on the now-filled lake

further under the spell of Lake Eyre as the journey continued in 1974. 'Lake Eyre is shaped like Salvador Dali's melting watches,' he wrote, 'and is set in a surreal emptiness. It is the plughole, the lowest point in Australia. Like the Tao, it's the lowest place into which everything flows back.' Vincent Serventy gathered important material on the trip to Lake Eyre for his scientific research, books and films — and Rex Ellis put it all down to experience. Ellis had happily linked his life to the outback and had now seen Lake Eyre in all its moods:

> *It's the sump of Australia, that's what I call it ... the sump of Australia and the dead heart, but it just comes to life every now and then — [it] just needs water. We've had lots of dramas out there, [and] you remember all those things ... but when it's dry it's just 4000 miles of bugger all ... it's [still] fascinating you know. There's nothing else like it in the world, so that has a different appeal as well.*

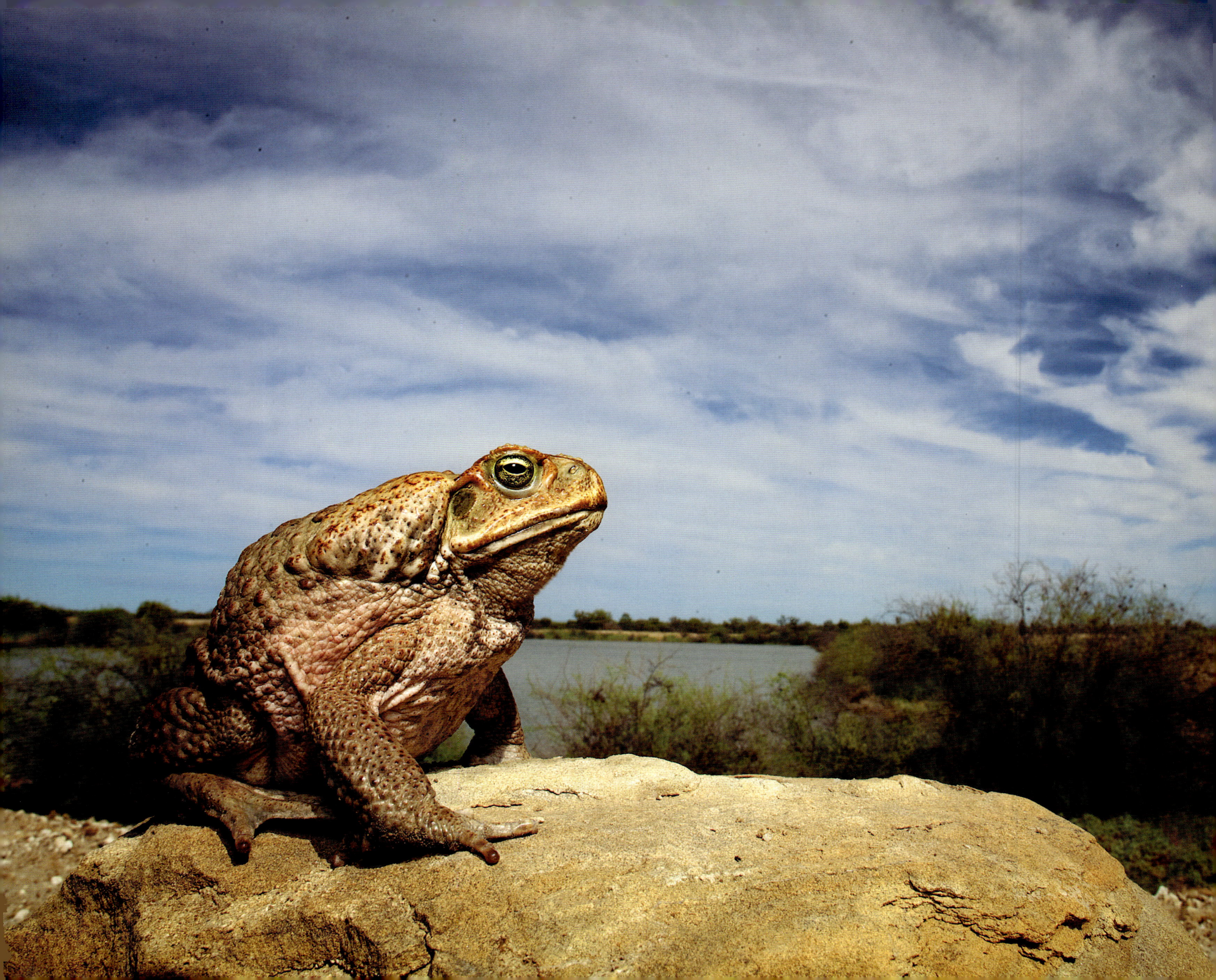

The boom and bust

Professor Richard Kingsford

*The ubiquitous and destructive invader, the cane toad (*Bufo marinus*), has reached the top of the Lake Eyre catchment in the upper reaches of Cooper Creek in its relentless march through Australia.*

IT IS HARD FOR US TO IMAGINE HOW OTHER SPECIES COPE with the extremes of Lake Eyre's environment, given our reliance on water. Many people live in the Lake Eyre Basin but usually near permanent water and with easy access to essential supplies. Aboriginal people have, of course, for millennia understood the country's vicissitudes, which reflect its flooding and food resources. Their movements and trade routes indicate a deep understanding of how long water lasts in the dry landscape. Likewise, many species of plants, invertebrates, frogs, fish, reptiles and mammals have evolved to cope with the boom and bust cycles, and we are just beginning to understand their astounding array of strategies.

When heavy rain falls in the top of the catchment, devastating flash floods run the creeks. But by the time the water reaches the floodplains of the Cooper, much of its ferocity has abated. Here, it slowly and inexorably spreads across the parched cracked floodplain soils. These soils resemble crazy paving with unfilled, gaping cracks forming abysses that provide homes for the innumerable terrestrial animals that colonised the floodplain after the previous flood, including slaters, spiders, centipedes and scorpions. Even small native rodents, such as hopping mice, and small marsupials, such as fat-tailed dunnarts, may shelter here from the blazing sun. But the floods turn this dry world upside down. Land animals either drown or are forced to escape — this is an aquatic world now. The floodwaters carry debris, one of the vital ingredients for the boom times since bacteria form biofilms that smear across flood-deposited leaves, bark and other dead matter, allowing decomposition to start in earnest. At the

The floods do not just benefit aquatic life but also more terrestrial wildlife, such as enormous numbers of flock pigeons (Phaps histrionica), *which will gather to graze and breed on the herbage of outback rivers after floods.*

same time, algae grow prolifically around the edges of waterholes and out on the floodplains. These are the powerhouses for the food web, making food for other animals to eat, from tiny invertebrates right up to pelicans.

As the flood arrives, it kicks off growth spurts in the majestic eucalypts, river red gums, coolibah and yapunyah that line the main channels of the rivers and creeks; they have been largely dormant to conserve water and energy during the long Dry. The floods also bring on flowering and seed production, which of course provides food even for animals we don't usually associate with water, such as honeyeaters. As the water recedes, the grasses on the floodplain suddenly burst forth. This makes this country some of the most productive in Australia for beef cattle. These grasses also support huge flocks of budgerigars. With a synchronous coordination similar to a school of fish, they rise when startled from the grass plains almost as a single organism, and then whirl and wheel, presumably as one or other individual communicates the need to change direction.

The water also stimulates germination of many purely aquatic plants. Some of these, such as water milfoil, germinate and grow, changing the shape of their leaves and stems to cope with rising floodwaters. The lignum bush, an iconic plant of the Australian floodplains, forms a mass of tangled green stems, often the only indication of life during the Dry. Water transforms the bush, which quickly sprouts and then flowers. Other plants, such as grasses and forbs (broad-leaved plants that grow in fields), germinate from dormant seeds when the flood arrives. Such seeds can exist for up to a decade or more without water, but are abruptly switched into life's next phase by a flood. Since floods are not predictable, some aquatic plants hedge their bets by varying the 'flood switches' of their seeds — not all of a plant's seeds germinate with one flood. This strategy ensures that long-term mistakes are avoided and that not all of a plant's seeds will germinate on a flood that may not be large enough or long enough to sustain the plant's full life cycle from germination to growth and seed setting. The length of the life cycle of plants

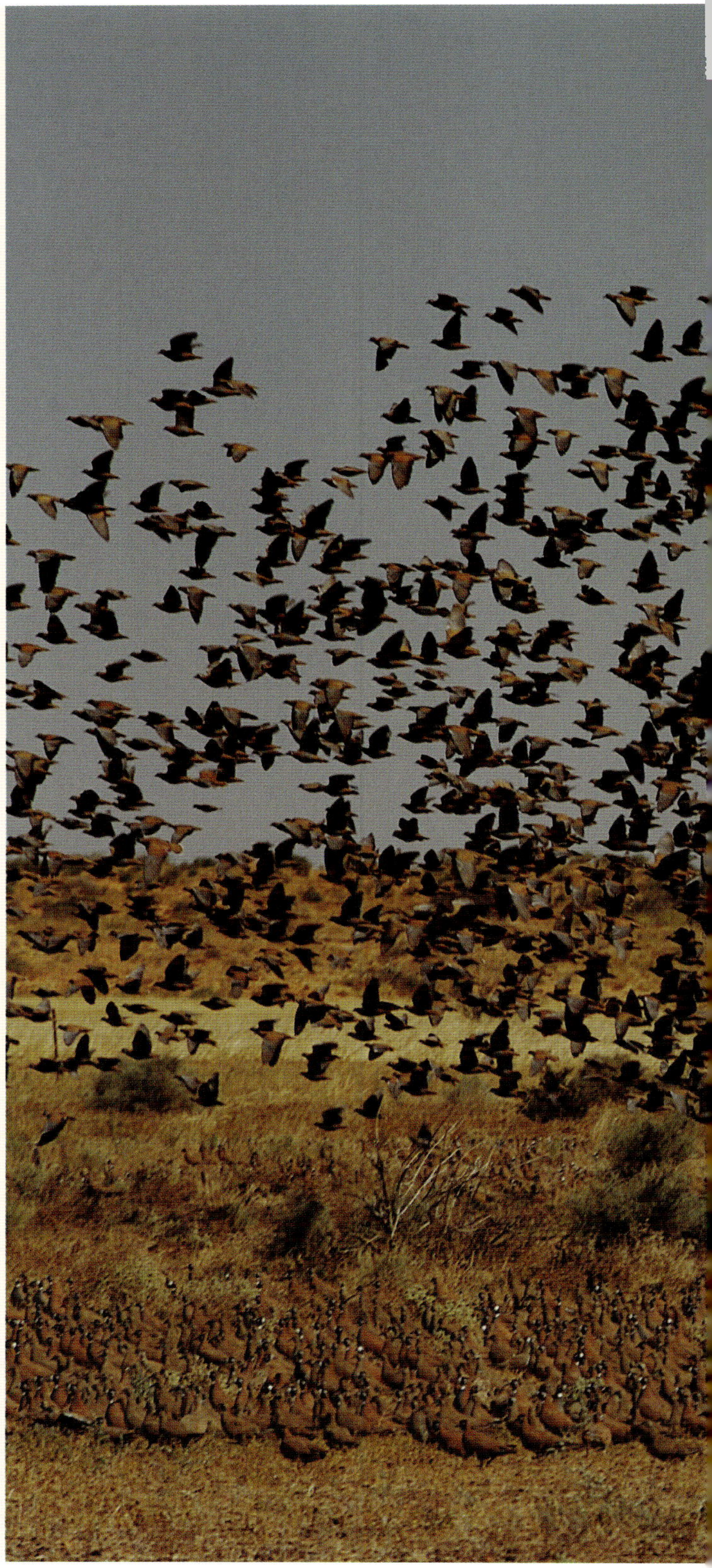

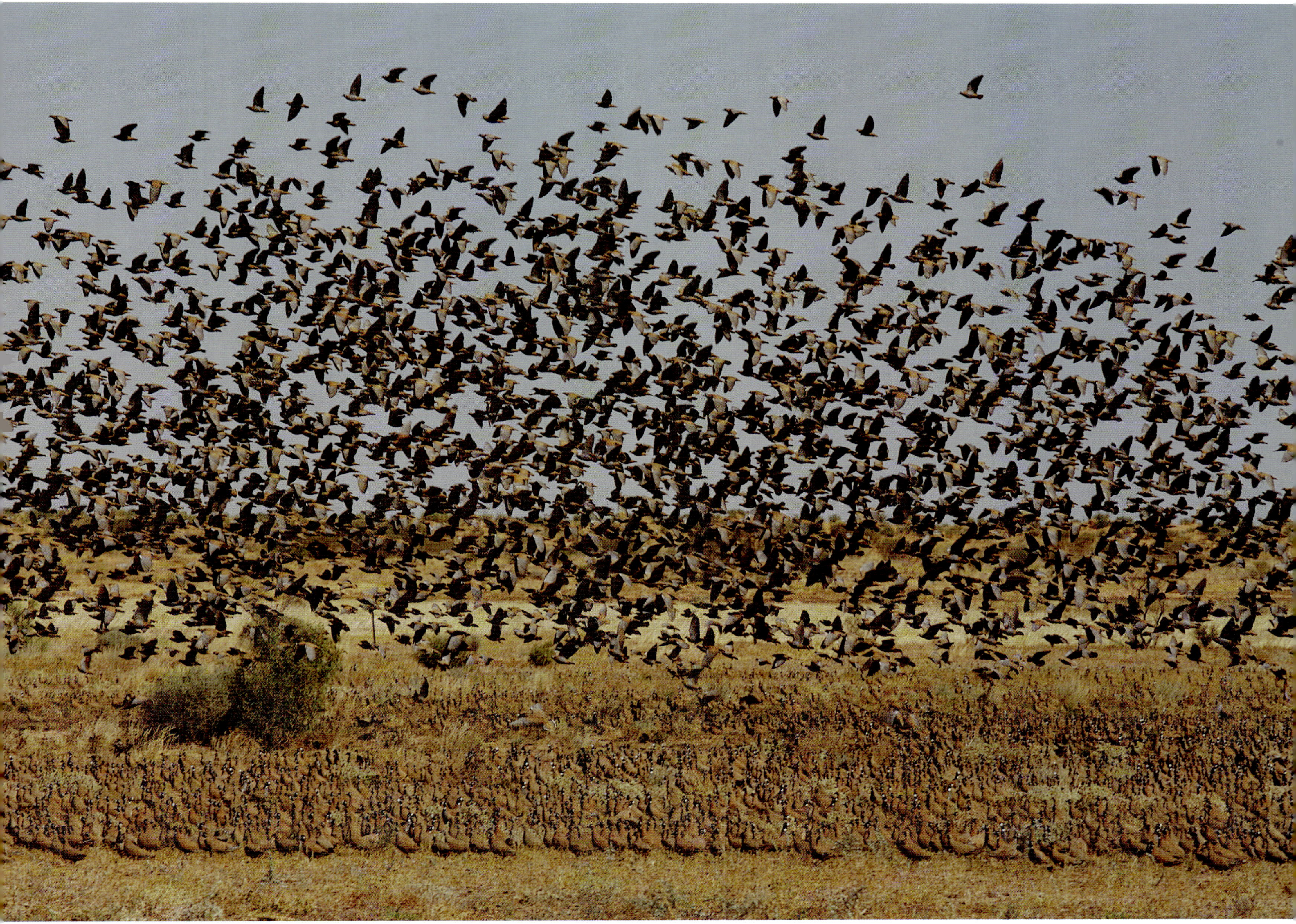

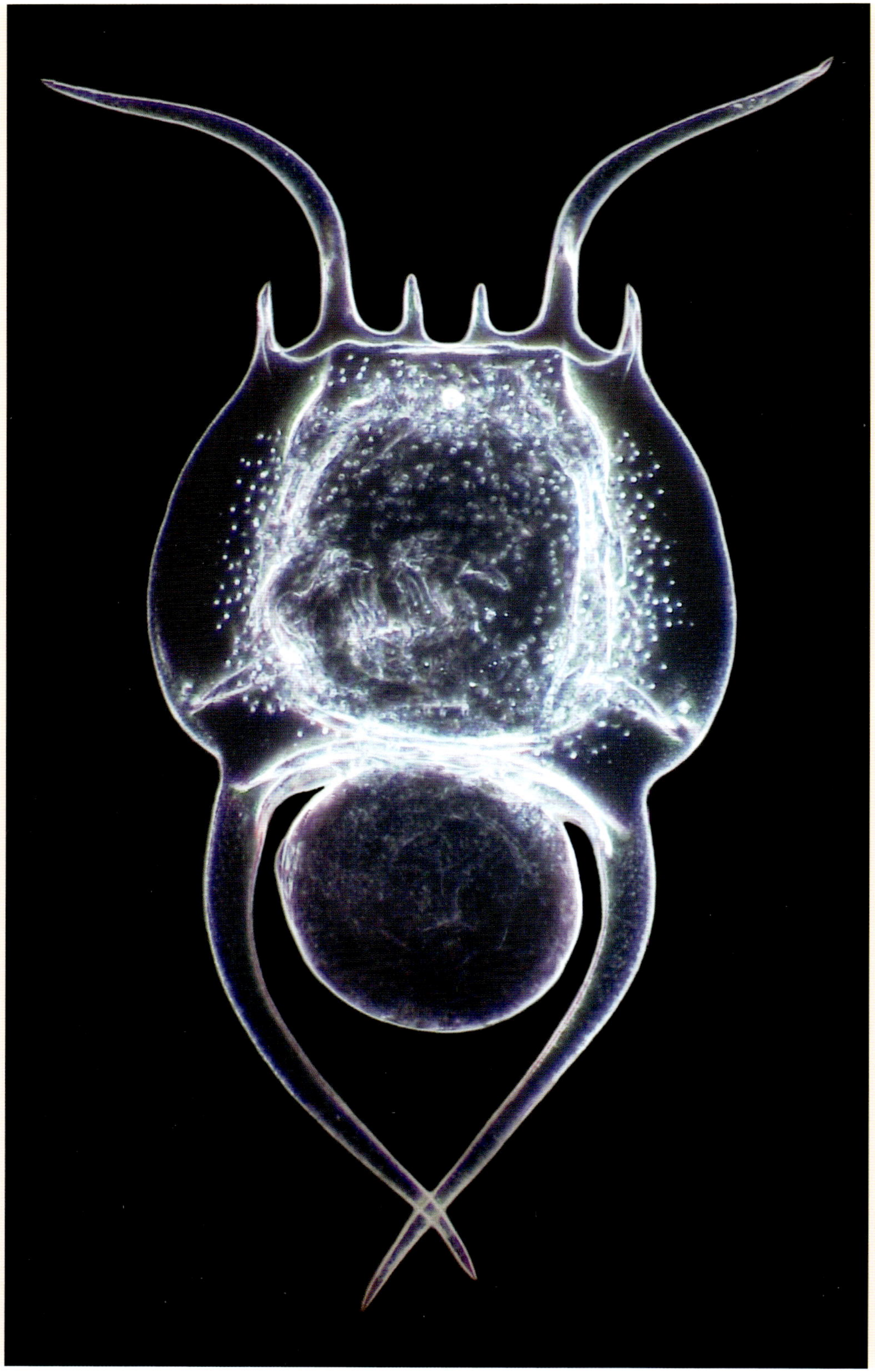

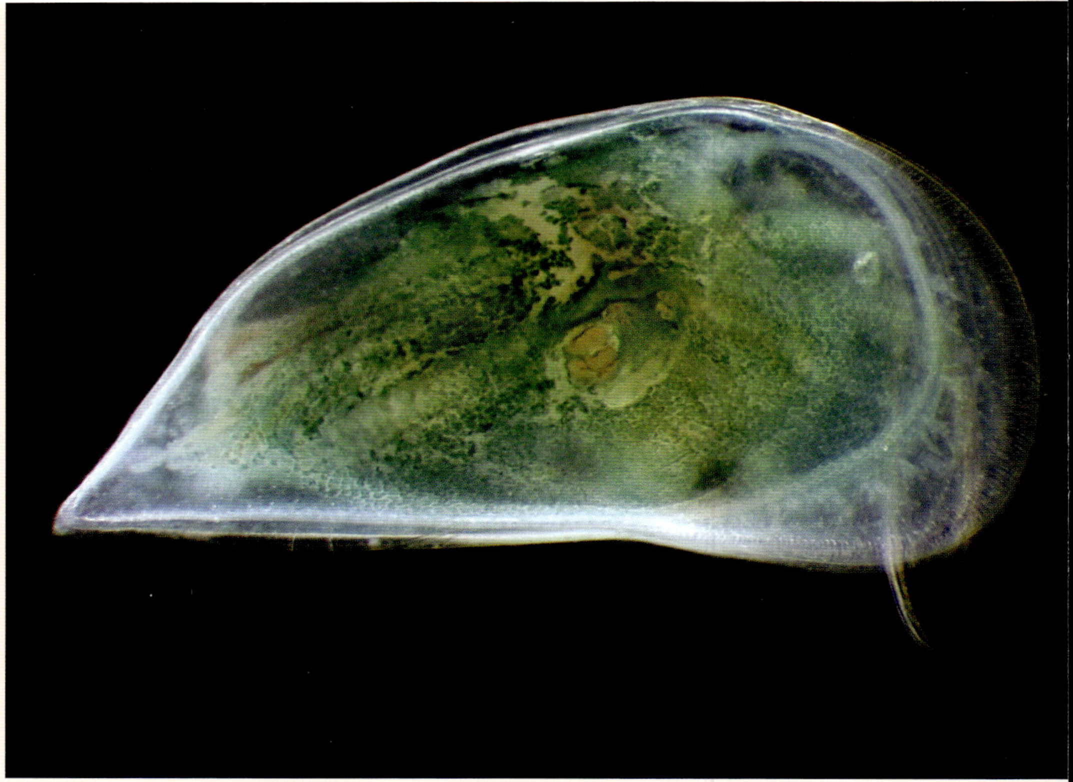

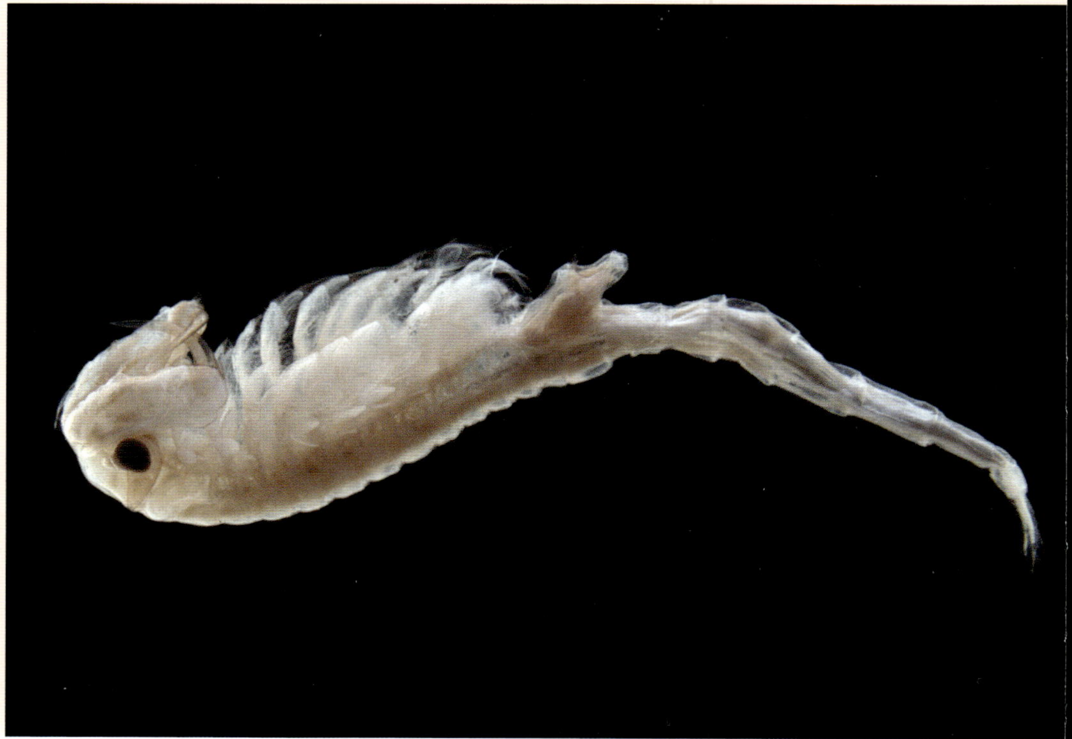

Just add water and the cracked soil comes to life with microscopic organisms that form part of the food web of Lake Eyre's floodplains and lakes. Typical invertebrates include: (far left) a salt lake rotifer, Brachionus falcatus*; (top right)* Mytilocypris mytilodes*, a salt lake ostracod; and (bottom right) a male* Pratemia minuta.

vary too. Aquatic plants will flower and seed before the water begins to dry back, while other plants wait for the land to begin drying, and then spring up, spurred into life by the moisture in the soils and producing vivid red and yellow carpets of flowers across the floodplain.

The ubiquitous nardoo, a perennial fern, grows like a clover across the floodplain as floodwaters recede. Its reproduction produces spores, encased in sporocarps. These cases detach and release the spores into the soil to germinate with the next flood. Roasted spore cases are nutritious, and have sustained Aboriginal communities along the rivers of the Lake Eyre Basin for tens of thousands of years. Roasting them is believed to remove the enzyme thiaminase, which is not good for our wellbeing as it breaks down vitamin B1. Burke and Wills apparently did not understand this critical step, which contributed to their death from beriberi on the banks of the Cooper in 1861, even though they ate 2 to 3 kilograms of nardoo each day.

Out of our sight, the water also kicks off countless microscopic animal lives. Just adding water triggers the emergence of tiny animals, including crustaceans and insects, which hatch from dormant eggs in the dry floodplain soils. Eggs can remain viable for decades, although the number that will actually hatch drops over time. The oldest recorded specimen of a viable egg is more than three hundred years old. Within just days and weeks, these tiny animals reach adulthood and breed. Bizarre microscopic wheel animals — or rotifers — appear in countless numbers, with their earwig tails and bristle-circled mouths, feeding on bacteria, detritus, algae and other smaller animals called protozoans. Small crustaceans also appear everywhere, among them various species of water fleas, seed and clam shrimps, and copepod crustaceans, which move around the floodwaters grazing and preying on smaller animals and plants.

Then there are the insects. Huge water beetles and dragonfly nymphs are the voracious predators of this underwater world. Dragonfly larvae ambush their prey, pouncing on it with giant jaws, while water beetles move with incredible speed, feeding on crustaceans and other insects and their

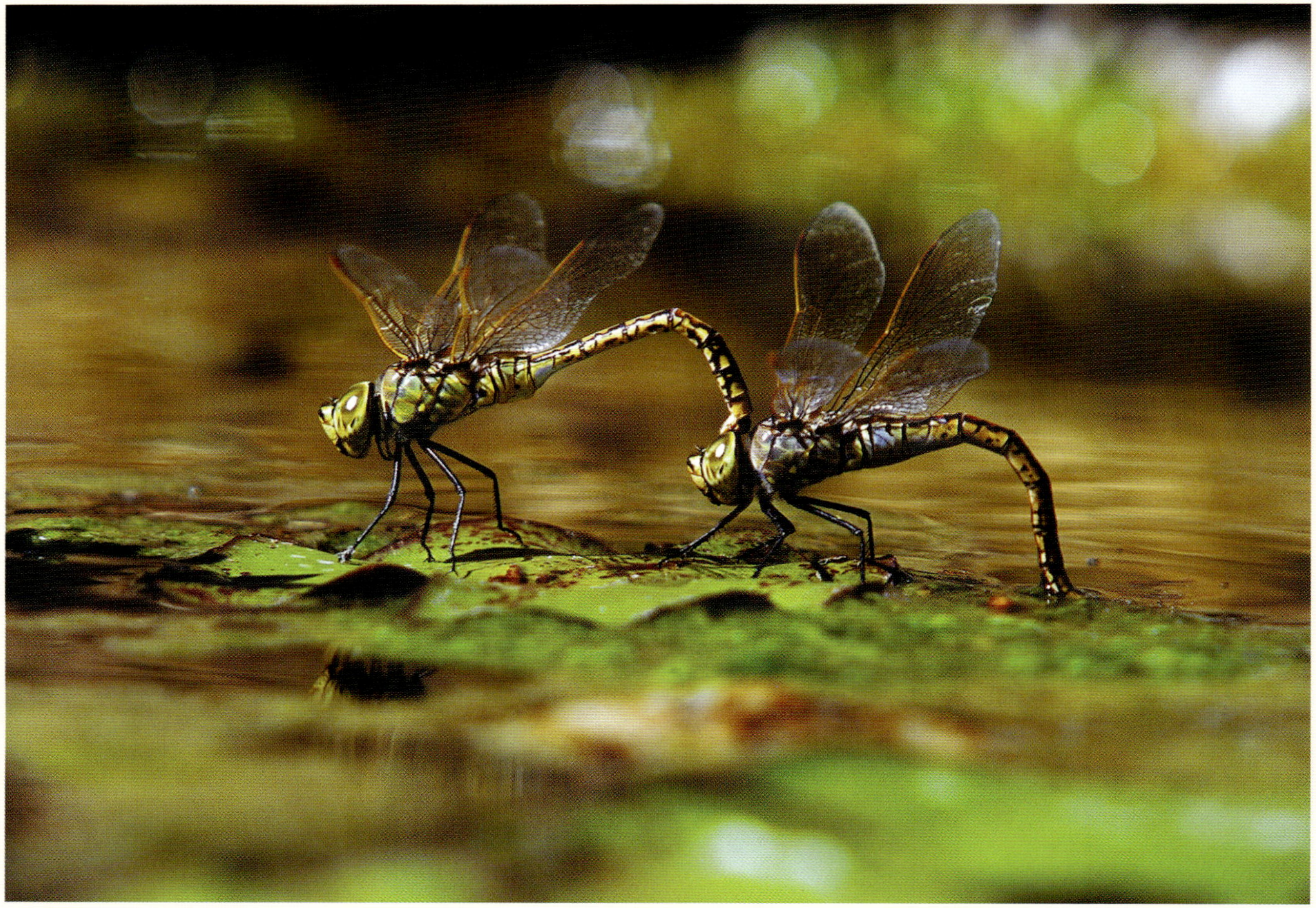

Dragonflies and their nymphs (left) are part of the frenzied eruption of life after flooding, providing plenty of food for fish, turtles, frogs and waterbirds. And (right) freshwater yabbies are ubiquitous, proliferating with the floods.

larvae. These include the worm-like larvae of mosquitoes and closely related midges, which all begin life in the water. Adult midges form dense mating swarms and, like most things during flood times, their life cycle is rapid, lasting less than a month.

Large invertebrates also build up in big numbers during floods. Included in this group are delicate fairy shrimps, sometimes over 2 centimetres in length, which swims upside down through the water filtering particles of food. Shield shrimps, freshwater shrimps, freshwater mussels, snails and even freshwater crabs all capitalise on the boom in food that comes with the flood. And of course freshwater yabbies are ubiquitious. Like the other animals, flood periods force a race against time to make sure that each animal gets a chance to produce the future generation. Most of the invertebrates will die leaving drought-resistant eggs in the soil for the next flood. Some, such as mussels and freshwater crabs, are longer lived and tend to remain where the water is more permanent. Freshwater crabs can lose more than 40 per cent of their water and still recover; they shut down their system by up to 70 per cent to achieve this. Floodwaters are an invertebrate soup, brimming with life, with up to 10,000 tiny animals in every litre of floodwater.

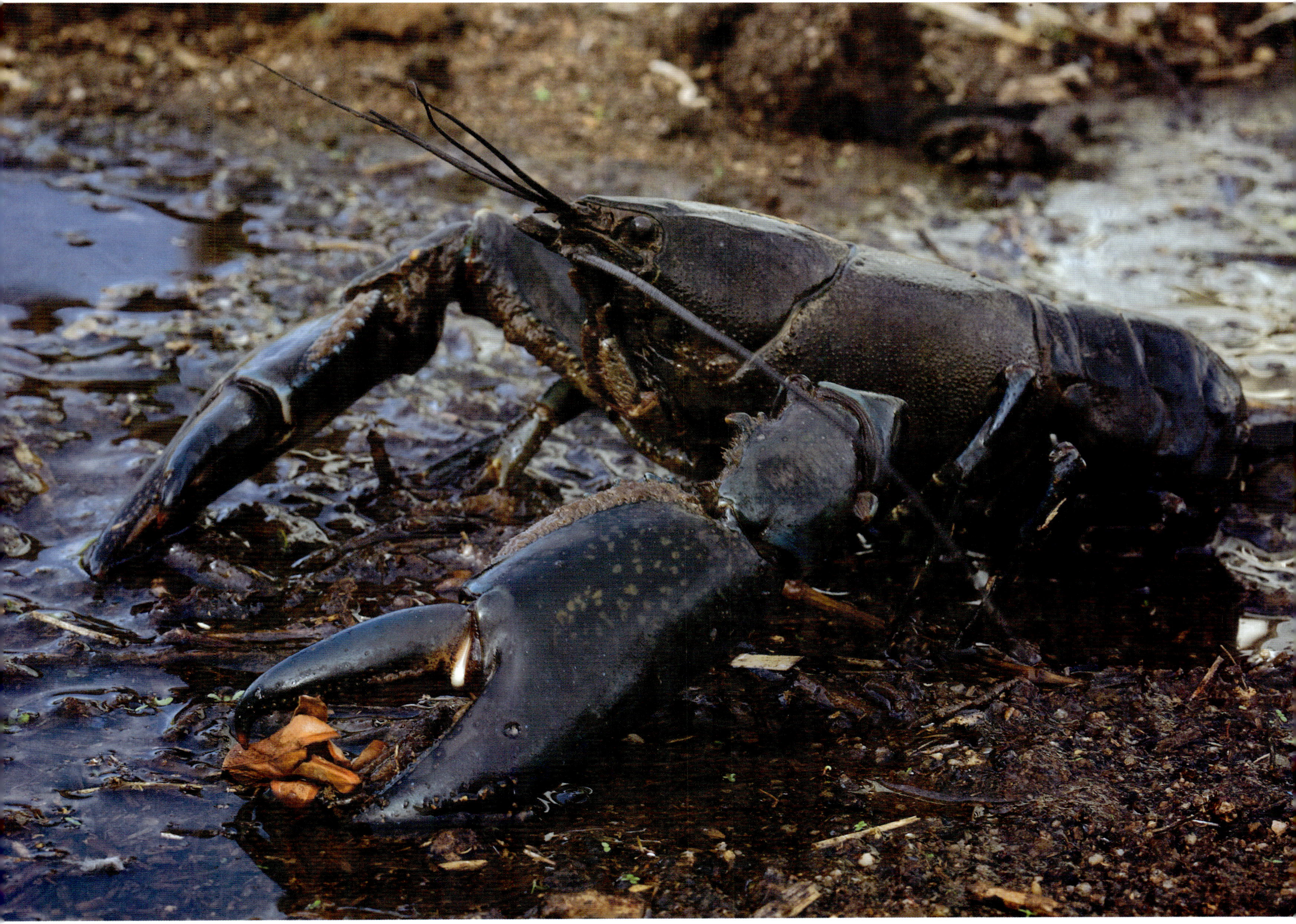

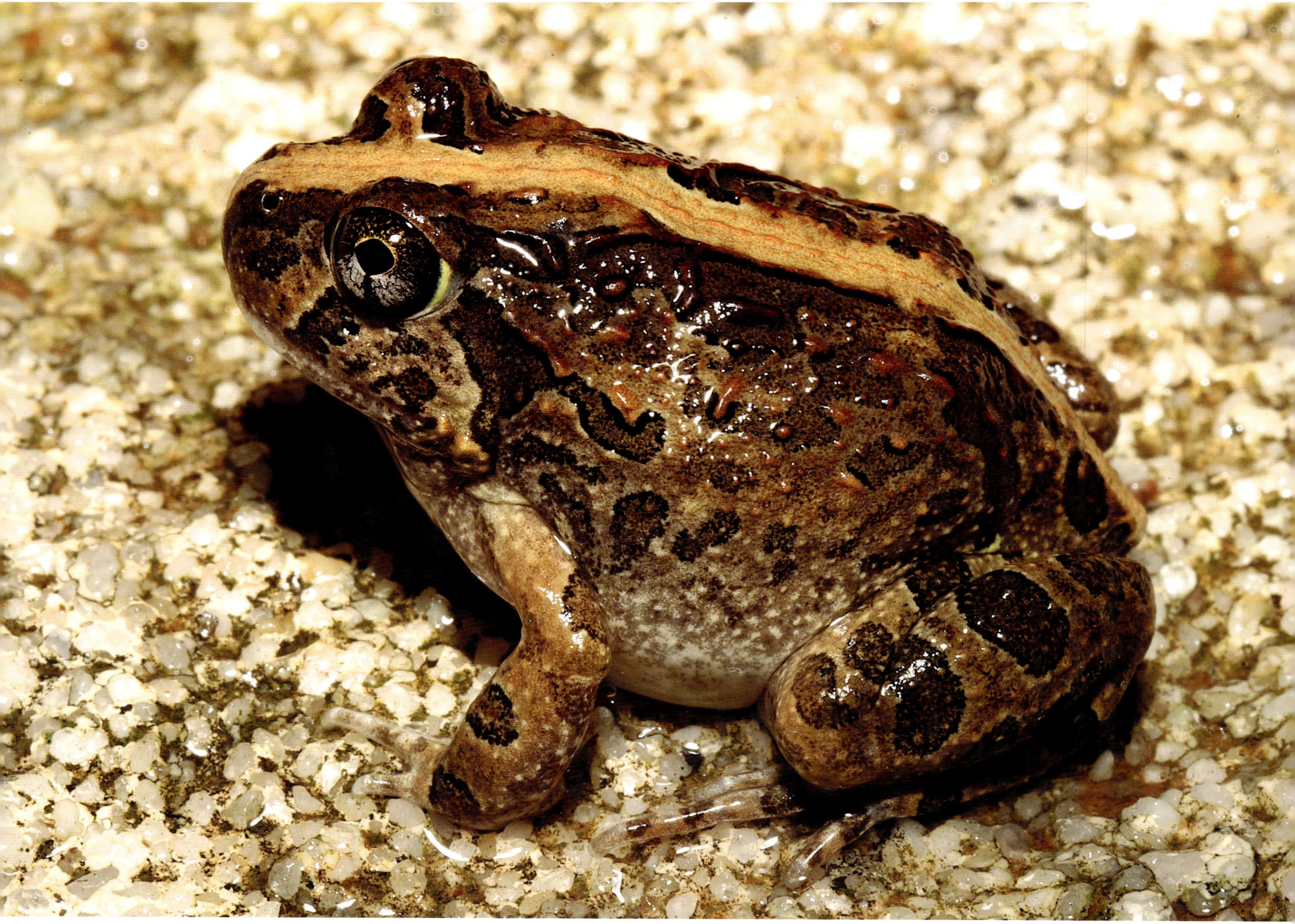

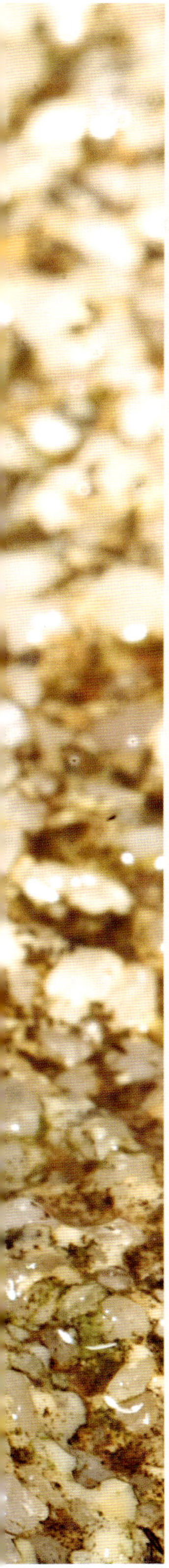

Burrowing frogs, such as this Spencer's frog (Platyplectrum spenceri), *bury themselves underground during drought in protective cocoons made of discarded skin. They emerge during rains and flooding.*

This incredible diversity of minute and large invertebrates and plants provides a smorgasbord for bigger creatures such as fish, frogs, turtles and other reptiles, which are ready to capitalise on the boom in food resources. Floodwaters release a habitat valve for fish and turtles that are forced to live cheek-by-jowl in the waterholes, the only permanent water remaining during long dry periods. All of a sudden, these animals can spread far and wide. It is time to move and procreate. The Cooper Creek turtle usually lurks in waterholes, feeding on plants, invertebrates and probably dead fish, but during times of rain or high water they move out across the floodplain.

Rain in the outback is also a catalyst for an explosion in the number of frogs. Burrowing frogs, in particular, are among the most remarkable animals in the outback. During dry times they bury themselves in water-filled cocoons, shutting down their bodies, sometimes for years. But when the rains come, there is a frenzy of activity in the world of the desert frogs, as they fight for food and mates. Tadpoles become young frogs in only a month. Adult Australian water-holding frog may even eat its own tadpoles and other small frogs that venture too close.

Obtaining as many resources as quickly as possible is the driving force of nature in these circumstances. This is one reason that fish species will invade anywhere there is a skerrick of water. Stories of raining fish in the outback are probably a reflection of the prodigious ability of fish to move when a flood is on. Spangled perch, for example, reportedly swam 16 kilometres over a six-hour period, travelling via water-filled wheel ruts.

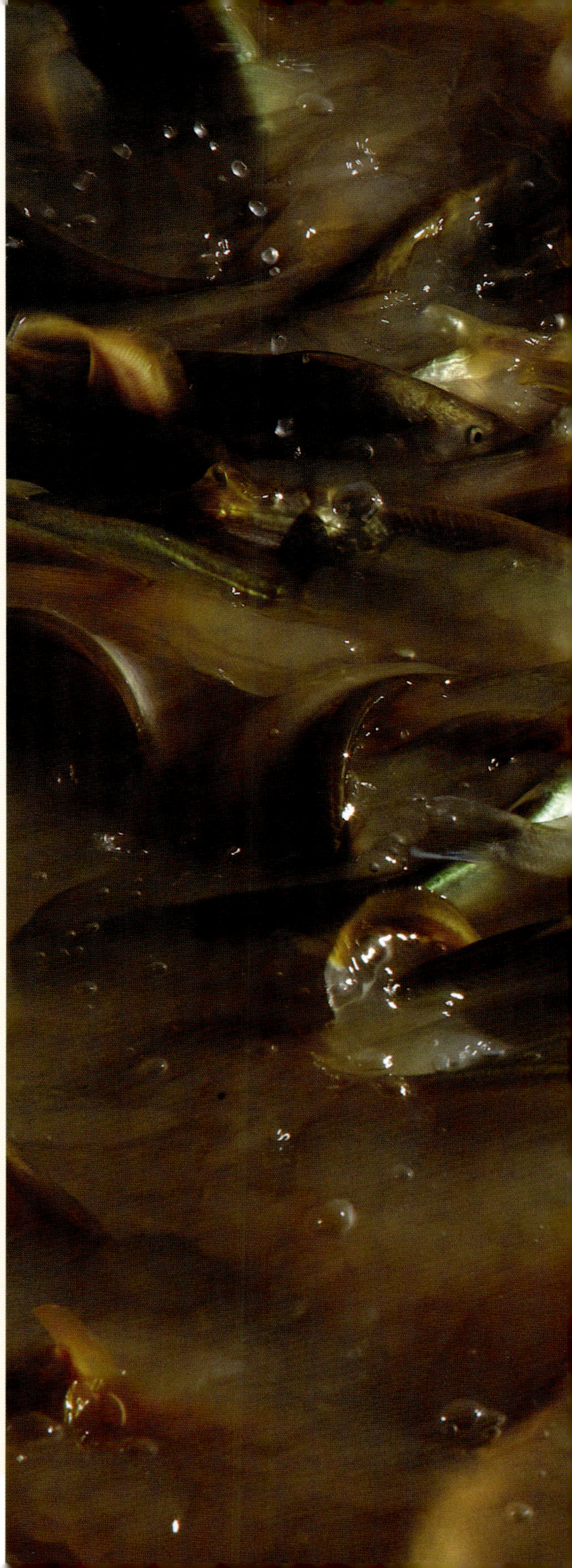

The driving force to survive is one reason that fish species will invade wherever there is a skerrick of water. They have been known to travel via water-filled wheel ruts. Here, a tumult of fish, primarily silver tandan (Porochilus argenteus), *at a crossing over the Thomson River.*

Once they are filled, many of the dry lakes provide huge areas for catfish, spangled perch and bony bream to invade and feed. Fish pour into Lake Eyre with the large floods and build up to extraordinary numbers. Inevitably, though, the system dries and increases in salinity, catching many fish before they can escape upstream to freshwater. It was estimated that after the large floods of the 1970s, there were about 40 million dead fish lying in contours around the edge of Lake Eyre, including equal numbers of bony bream and Lake Eyre hardyhead. Death follows life on a grand scale in the Lake Eyre Basin.

There are few more pleasurable experiences than sitting beside one of the rivers of the Lake Eyre Basin, watching the waterbird traffic. The rivers are freeways for cormorants and pelicans hunting fish, particularly when the waters are running. At such times, there is a feeding frenzy not just of the pelicans and cormorants, but also herons, ibis and even some of the ducks such as the hardheads. This particular species usually eats small snails but during floods will switch to fish migrating down the rivers.

It seems a paradox that Australia's deserts would be home to hundreds of thousands — perhaps even millions — of waterbirds, but the rivers running through the outback create a vast expanse of waterbird habitat. Of course, should these rivers eventually flow into Lake Eyre, a habitat of such immense size is created that it can rival that of the Kakadu wetlands

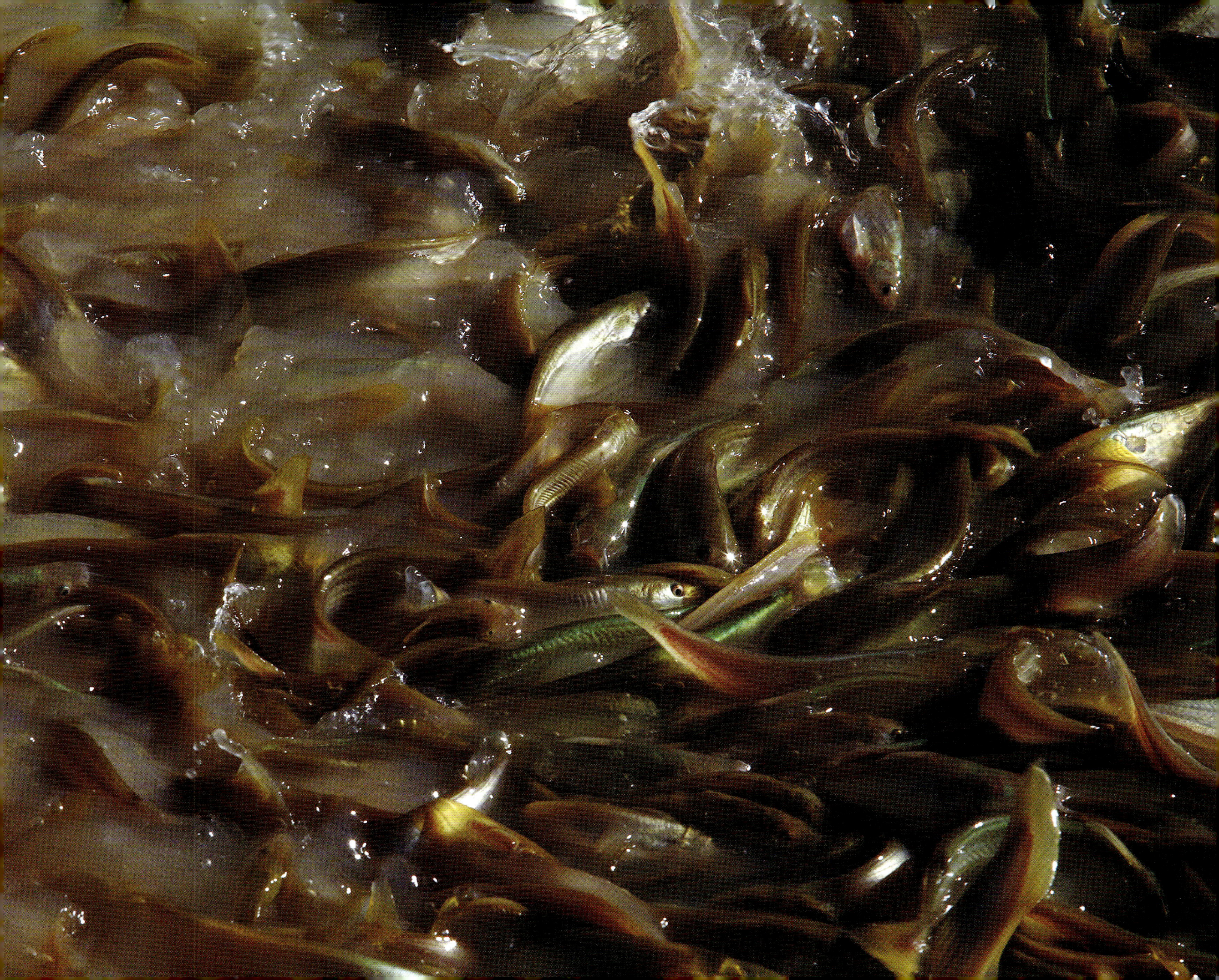

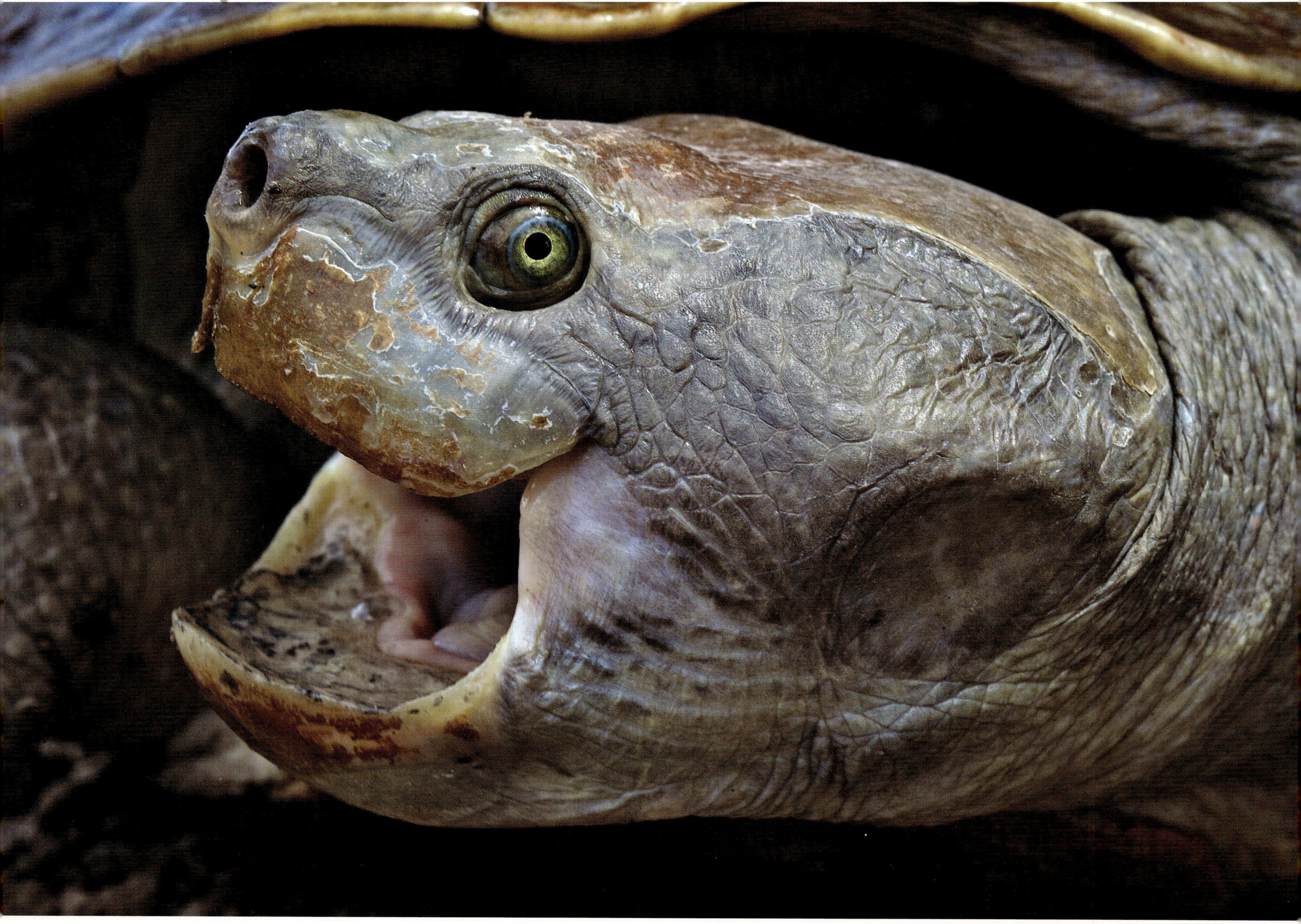

Cooper Creek turtles (Emydura macquarii emmotti) *live for up to eighty years in the large waterholes of the Lake Eyre Basin, capitalising on the boom flood years when there is plenty of food available.*

as one of the most productive habitats for waterbirds in Australia. In the 1990 flood that made it to Lake Eyre, there were probably more than half a million waterbirds on the relatively small section where Cooper Creek flowed into the lake.

Over fifty different waterbird species follow these inland floods, all keyed into the boom in their particular food. Different bills, feet and behaviour have evolved to allow a wide range of species to exploit the different foods on offer. Fish specialists include pelicans, cormorants and darters, with herons, spoonbills and ibis switching between fish, shrimps, yabbies and frogs. The different duck species feed on the spectrum of available food, ranging from herbivores to invertebrate and even fish feeders. Some, such as the Australian wood duck and the beautiful plumed whistling-duck, with extravagant, oversized cream feathers on its flank, graze on the herbage that grows during and after the floods. Extraordinarily large flocks of more than 10,000 plumed whistling-ducks collect on these outback rivers, emitting their characteristic whistle when they fly. Herbivorous black swans prefer to feed on grasses and algae that grow underwater, but sometimes they will waddle far afield in search of nutritious herbage. The bizarre-looking pink-eared duck with the tiny patch of pink feathers behind its eye and its spatulate bill is an inland specialist. It feeds on the microscopic invertebrates that are so plentiful in the warm outback waters, sieving them from the water with the fine hairs on its bill.

There are also many small wading waterbirds, often seen pecking at invertebrates on the edge of a wetland or river. These include the stilts, sandpipers and red-necked avocets. Amazingly some of these birds breed in Russia and China, returning to Australia in our spring. Normally they would fly over the dry rivers and wetlands of Lake Eyre but the floods and their rich food supply of invertebrates are sufficiently enticing to attract them down from their transcontinental flight path. Here then they will remain for the summer, building up their energy before setting off in autumn for their epic flight back to their breeding grounds in the northern hemisphere.

As floodwater moves out across the floodplains, species that have been crammed together in drying waterholes have room to spread out and breed. A juvenile Cooper Creek turtle (Emydura macquarii emmotti) *hitches a ride on a goldfish carp* (Carassius auratus)*, an introduced species.*

In and out of the vegetation, crakes and rails move quietly and secretively, only appearing fleetingly even to keen observers.

At the top of this food chain are the raptors or birds of prey. The huge numbers of waterbirds, fish, frogs, reptiles and small mammals that proliferate with the floods offer a wide range of foods for whistling kites, letter-winged kites, wedge-tailed eagles and even the occasional majestic sea eagle, a long way from the sea.

Pelicans are particularly indicative of how waterbirds capitalise on the boom and bust cycles of Lake Eyre's dynamic river system and its wetlands. The key, as for all animals, is the food supply. Pelican behaviour is inextricably linked to what the fish are doing. Many people think of pelicans as a seaside bird but, paradoxically, there may be more inland pelicans cruising along outback rivers, herding fish into the shallows of the lakes, than on the coast where most people see them. Lake Eyre can be a magnet for pelicans when the fishing is good, which only happens when there is enough fresh water for small crustaceans and insects — fish food — to thrive. The fish follow, streaming down the rivers into the lake. Where there is food, there is life and procreation, and the pelicans follow the fish trail down the rivers, all the way to Lake Eyre.

Like all birds, pelicans are adapted through evolution to breed when short-term and long-term conditions are most likely to produce a surviving next generation. There has to be enough food for female pelicans to be

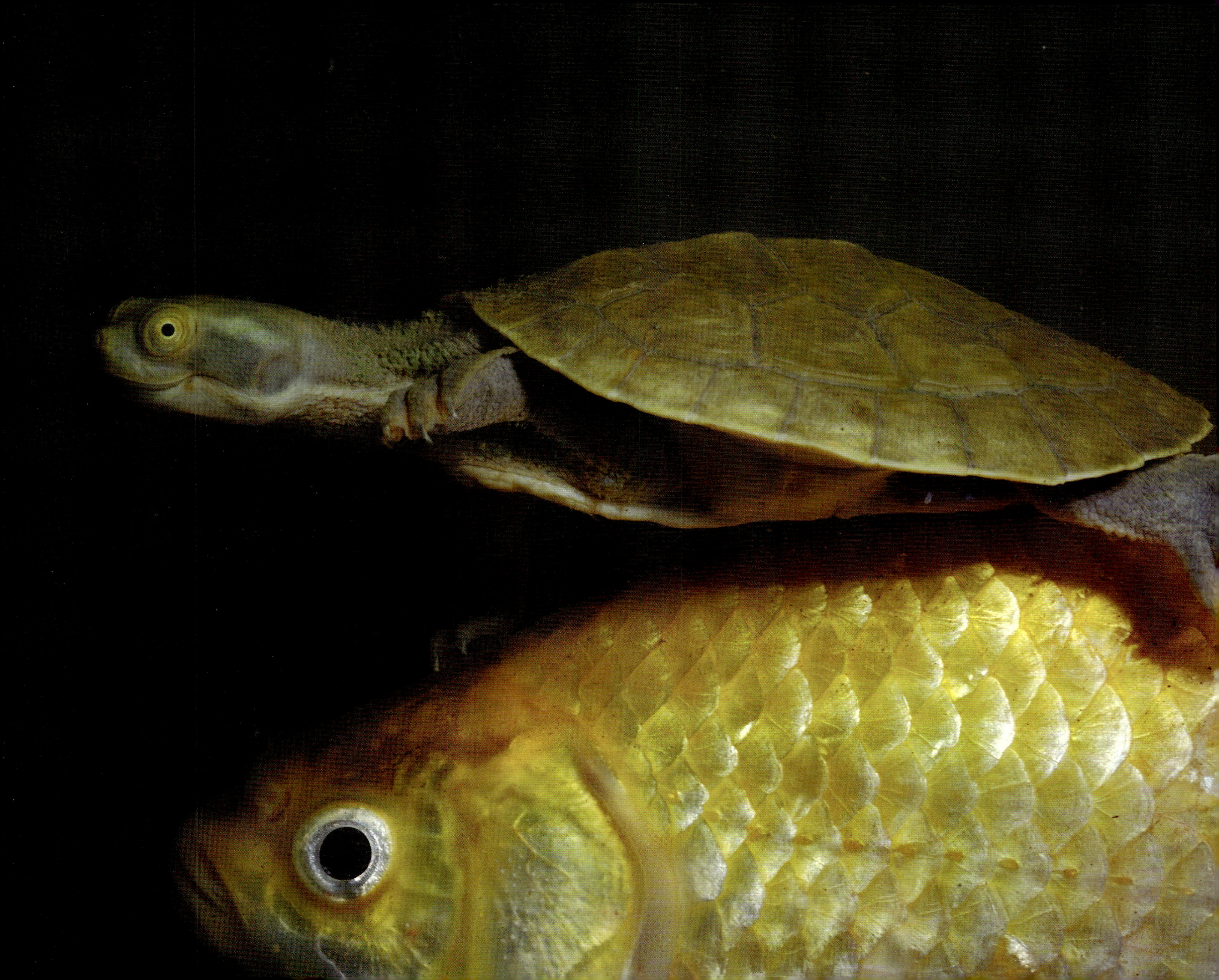

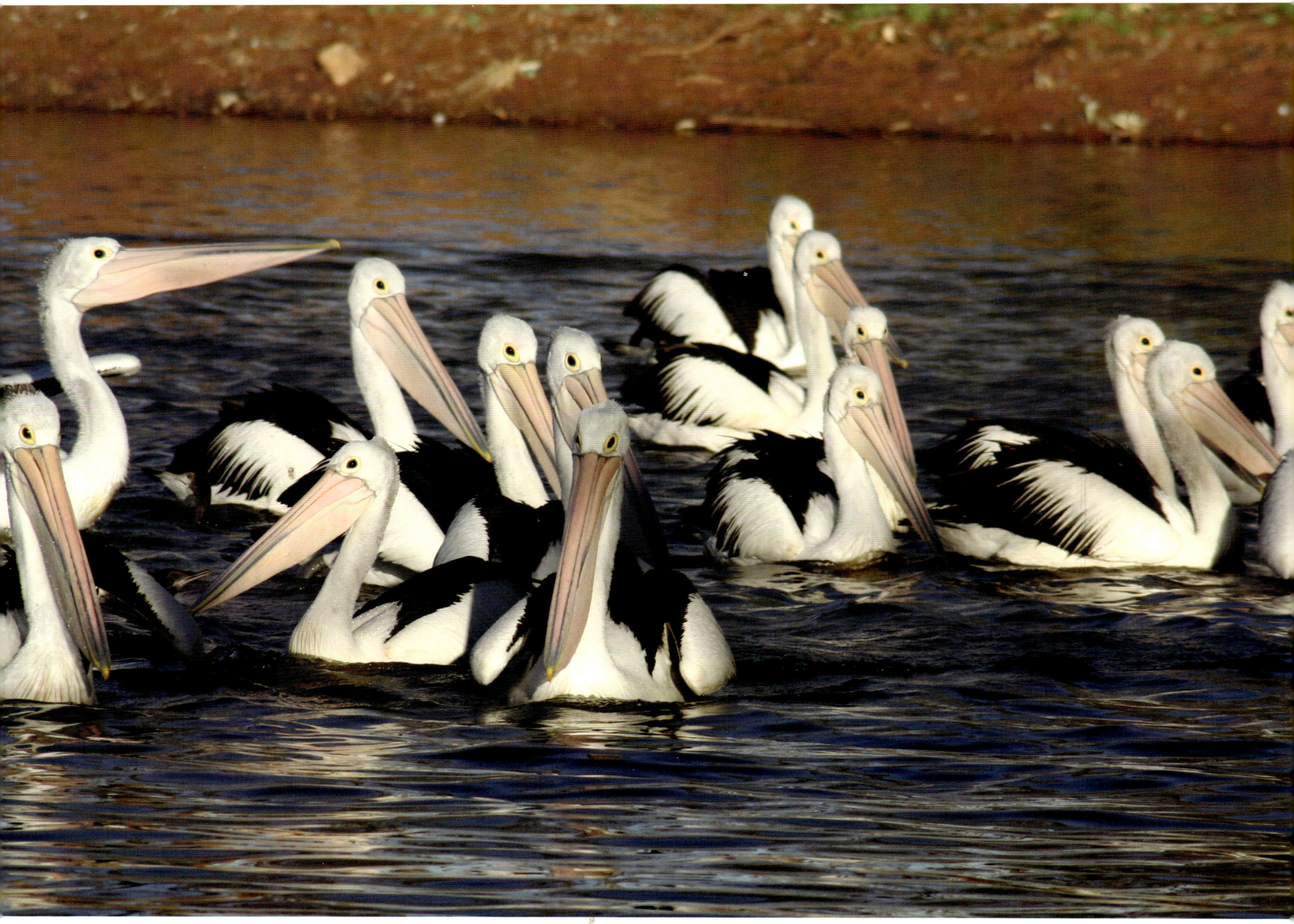

More Australian pelicans cruise the country's inland waterways than can be found on the coast. Their numbers are indicative of the boom and bust cycle in the river systems of the Lake Eyre Basin. Here they gather to feed on a waterhole on the Burke River near Boulia, western Queensland.

healthy enough to make and lay eggs. Then they incubate their one to three eggs for about a month. Once hatched, young, pink, naked chicks need to be fed by their parents until they are old enough to fend for themselves. Eggs in the one nest hatch at different times and so one chick will be slightly older and bigger by a couple of days than the others. Even here, there is an evolutionary adaptation to this boom-and-bust world. If food is short, the older chick will kill its smaller and weaker siblings to make sure it gets as much food as is available from the parents. In evolutionary terms, this ensures that at least one chick will survive. There needs to be a constant supply of food and lots of it for parents to successfully raise more than one young since the fledging period is as long as three months. The whole window of opportunity for breeding, from courtship to independent young, is probably a minimum of about five months.

When Lake Eyre fills, it supports Australia's largest breeding colonies of pelicans. In 1990, 100,000 pelicans raised an estimated 90,000 chicks on Lake Eyre. This incredible productivity was well known to Aboriginal people who also lived with the boom-and-bust cycles of this river system: moving in during times of plenty and then away to dependable water supplies during dry times. One of the more remarkable stories is of how the Aboriginal Yandruwandha people on Cooper Creek 'farmed' pelicans while they were breeding. Pelican chicks form crèches after they have grown feathers and are old enough to move away from the nest. When this happened, Yandrawandha people put the larger chicks into a yard, confining them while the parents fed them up until they were large enough to eat.

Across all waterbird species, there is a race against time to build up enough condition to breed and successfully raise offspring. The floods are the magnet for productive breeding and feeding but how waterbirds can detect the flood signal from a river or wetland thousands of kilometres away and know when this will

Nankeen night-herons (Nycticorax caledonicus)*, such as this juvenile, feed on fish and frogs that build up in large numbers on the rivers and floodplains of the Lake Eyre Basin.*

happen is an enduring mystery. Clearly, the dividends are enormous for individuals that make the journey — lots of food and a chance to breed successfully. The science attempting to uncover this mystery of waterbird movements has progressed slowly, since such movements are unpredictable, sometimes taking decades, and don't lend themselves well to scientific funding and planned investigations.

In contrast, much is known of most waterbird movements in the northern hemisphere where there are remarkably similar species, including pelicans, herons and ducks. In the northern latitudes, the seasons rule waterbird movements as they do most natural things. For a long time, migration remained a mystery, beautifully exemplified by the story of the barnacle goose. These geese fly from Britain each summer to breed in the Arctic, returning in autumn — a mystery in medieval times. This is where the goose barnacle comes in and how the barnacle goose gets its name. The goose barnacle is a crustacean related to prawns, which attaches to hard surfaces including driftwood. To the fertile imagination of the twelfth-century Welsh cleric Giraldus Cambrensis, goose barnacles that washed up on the shores of Britain had the shape and colour of a goose and must therefore be the source of barnacle geese 'hatched' from their shells. It wasn't long after that bird migration was understood with clear seasonal patterns of coming and going for most waterbirds.

In Australia, though, the seasons are poorly defined, particularly in the inland, and so our understanding of waterbird movements remains in its infancy. We know, of course, that floods are the key, and there is considerable research documenting the 'disappearance' of coastal waterbirds when the inland rivers are in flood. For example, there was an exodus of waterbirds such as banded stilts from the Coorong and the Lower Lakes in South Australia when the rivers ran into Lake Eyre in 2010. These stilts are inland specialists, relying on the large floods and islands in places such as Lake Eyre for their breeding, tied to high concentrations of their food, which is almost exclusively brine shrimp.

Recently, our knowledge of waterbird movements in Australia has improved through the use of satellite transmitters attached to individual birds. This new technology is revolutionising our understanding of animal movements around the world, from polar bears to the small migratory shorebirds that move between Australia and the Arctic Circle. Dr David Roshier from Deakin University leads the field in Australia, with exciting findings from our waterbirds, particularly for the small inland duck, the grey teal. The story emerging is complex. Waterbirds probably use the full repertoire of sensory and experiential information available to them. We know they can navigate using the earth's magnetic field, the stars, the sun and even the earth's contours and shapes, such as rivers and mountains. They may even be able to detect weather systems.

One of the intriguing observations to have emerged is of 'reconnaissance' flights. When the rivers of the Murray–Darling system were recently in drought, one grey teal flew 600 kilometres west and returned via southern Queensland over a period of ten days, an

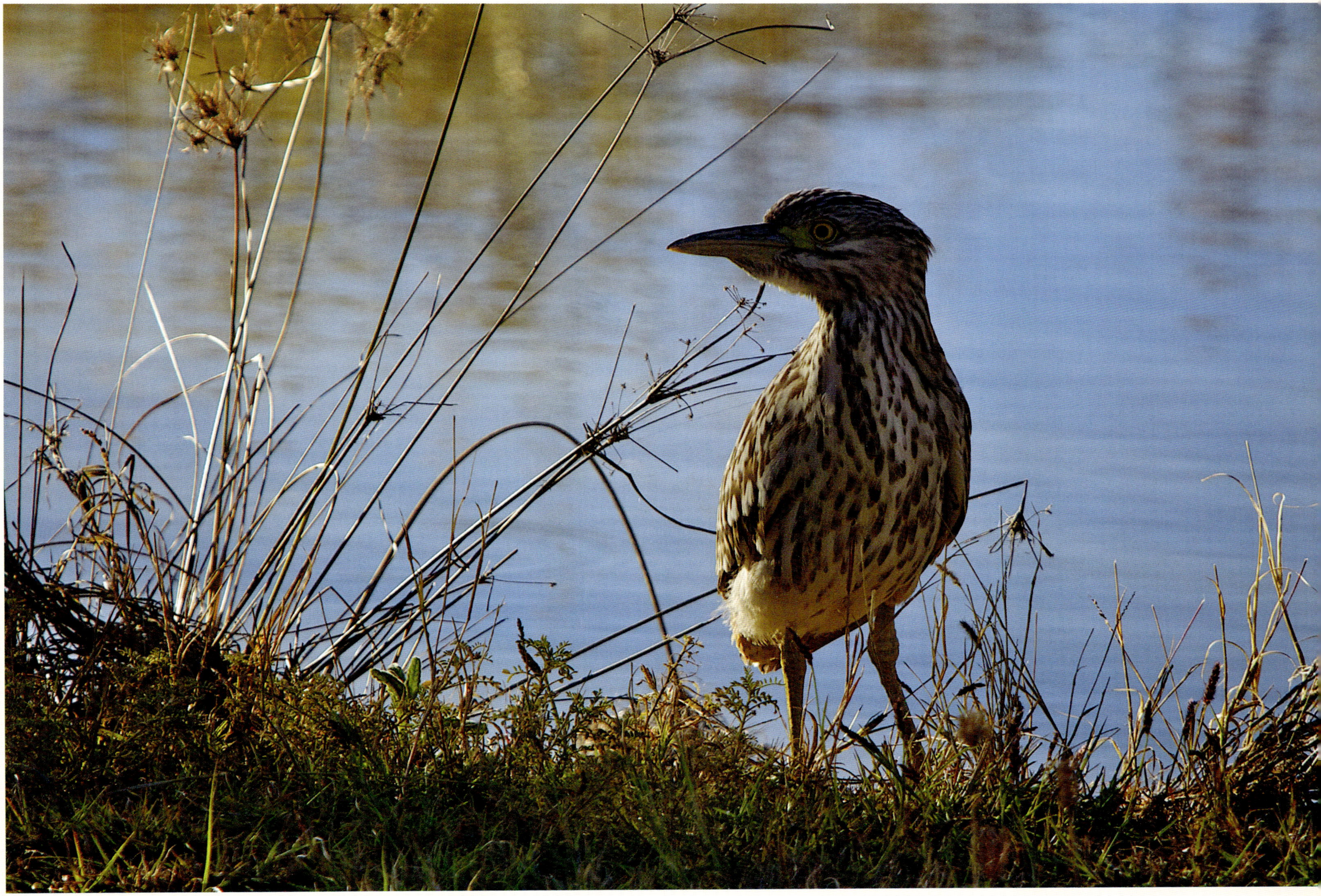

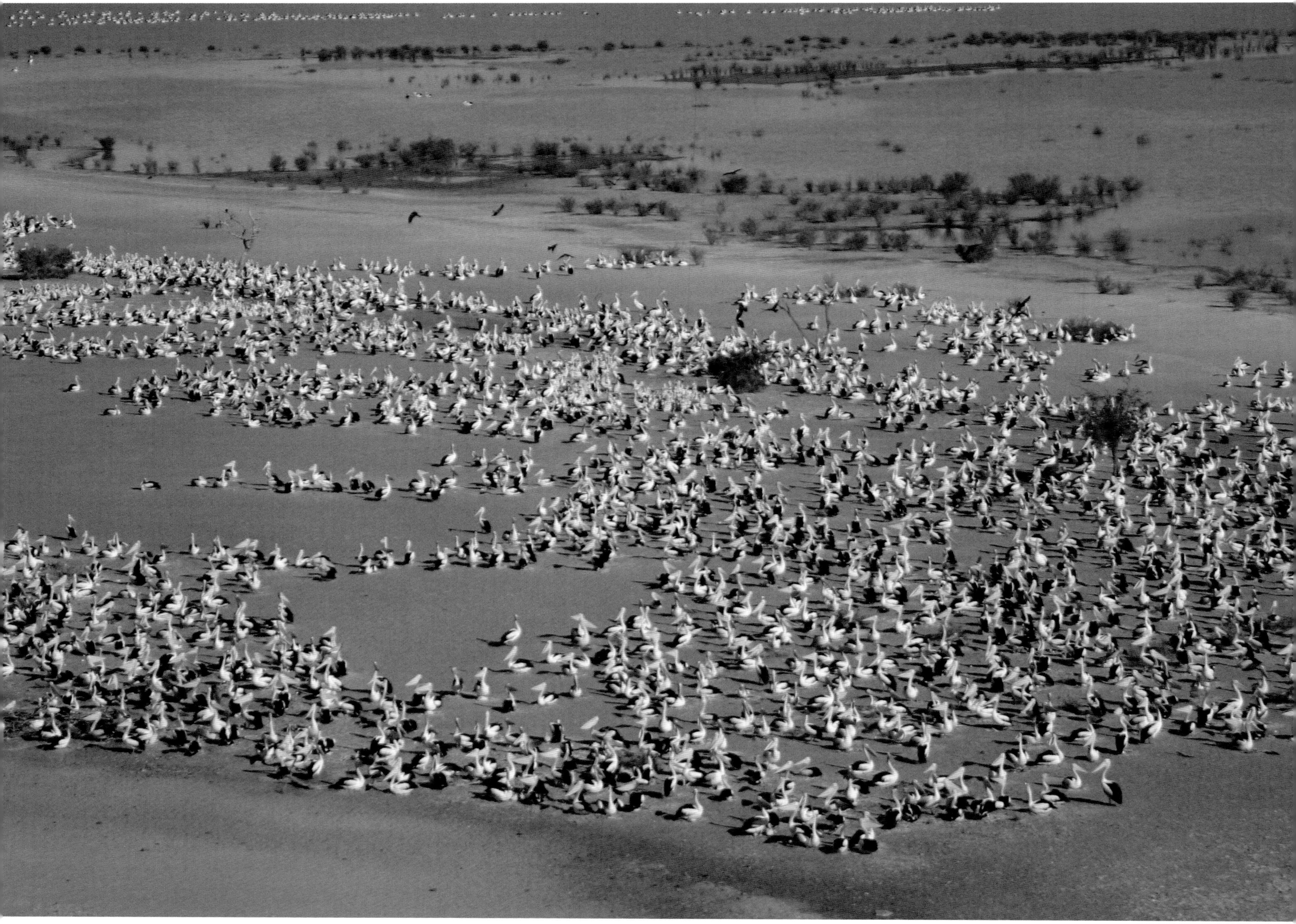

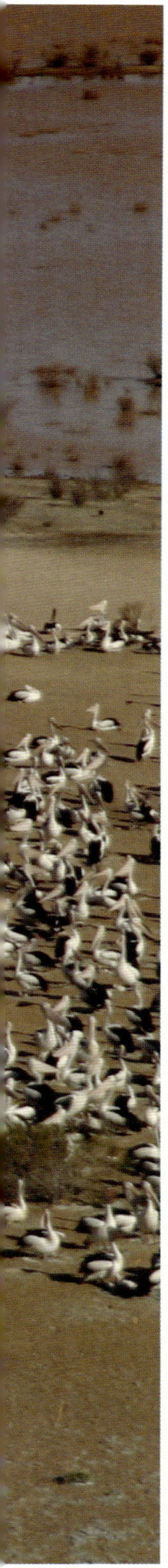

Pelicans travel huge distances to the flooded lakes and rivers of the outback, where large breeding colonies of up to 100,000 birds can nest, usually on islands. Here they gather on a large lake of Eyre Creek. Overleaf: A flock of plumed whistling ducks in flight over the Eyre Creek floodplain.

amazing round trip of more than 1200 kilometres. Potentially, the bird was investigating the floods. Incredibly, it flew more than 500 kilometres in the first six and a half hours, averaging nearly 100 kilometres an hour for more than three hours. Over a year, this bird travelled an impressive distance of more than 4800 kilometres, mostly at night.

Ecologist Julian Reid suggests that the extraordinary ability of pelicans to traverse huge distances, helped by their experience of the rivers and wetlands of the continent, allows them to 'find' the lakes and rivers of the outback, something akin to finding a needle in a haystack. Pelicans often travel during the day, capitalising on thermals to gain height and allowing them to save energy by gliding large distances, but they also probably fly at night, like most waterbirds. It is quite likely that pelicans use a similar range of behaviours to grey teal to get out to Lake Eyre when it floods and then to escape when it dries. After the 1974 to 1976 floods, pelicans hatched and banded on Lake Eyre scattered to the winds when the lake dried; some even made it as far as Palau, Christmas Island and New Zealand.

The bust part of the flood cycle has a polar opposite effect on waterbird life cycles and movements. As the rivers stop flwowing, their precious fresh water no longer reaches Lake Eyre. Temperatures, sometimes more than 50° Celsius, drive evaporation — water almost disappears as you watch, particularly through the summer. For all animals, including waterbirds, this is a dangerous time. They must move before it is too late and there is not enough food to provide them with the energy for escape. Inevitably, some waterbirds get it wrong and delay too long.

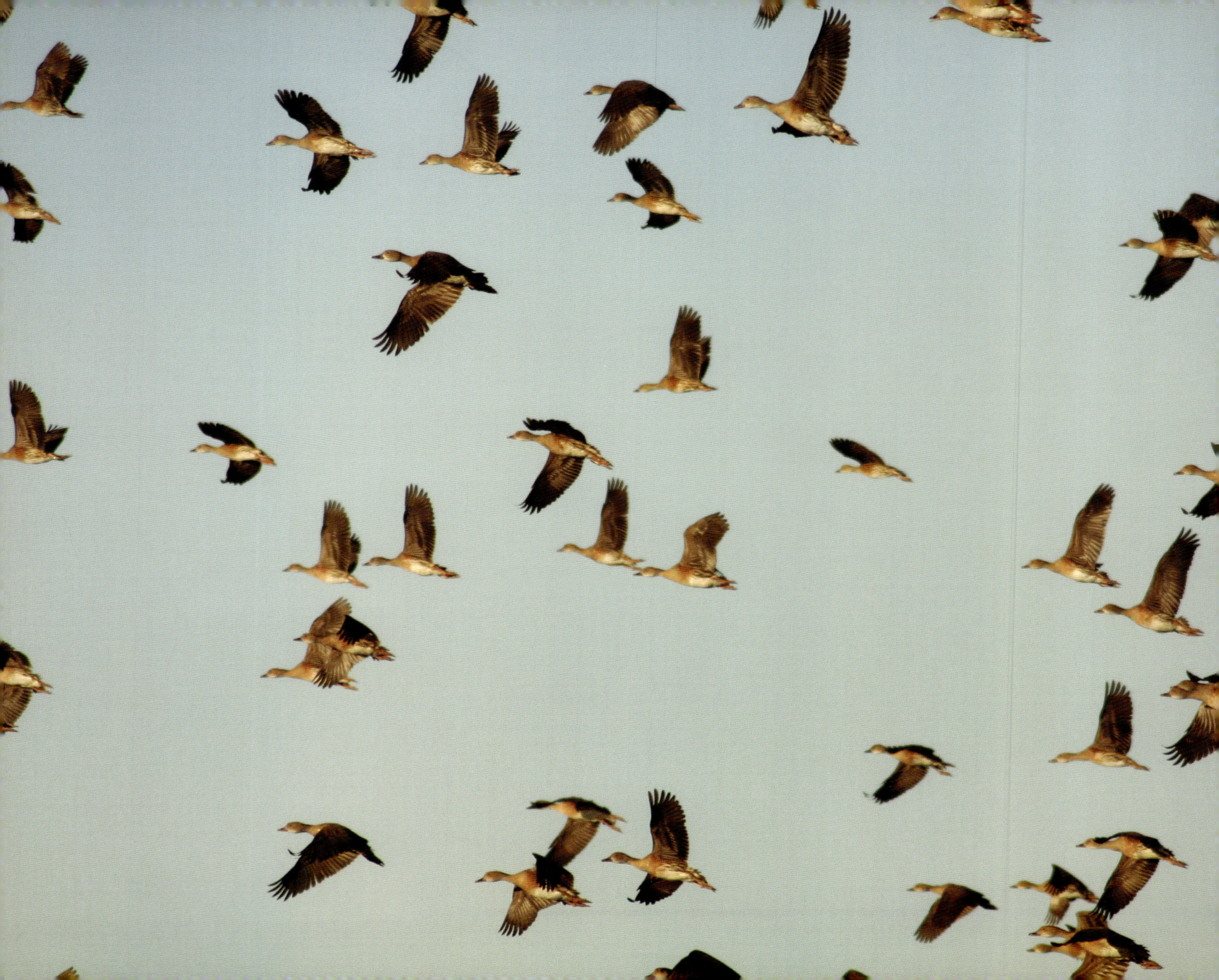

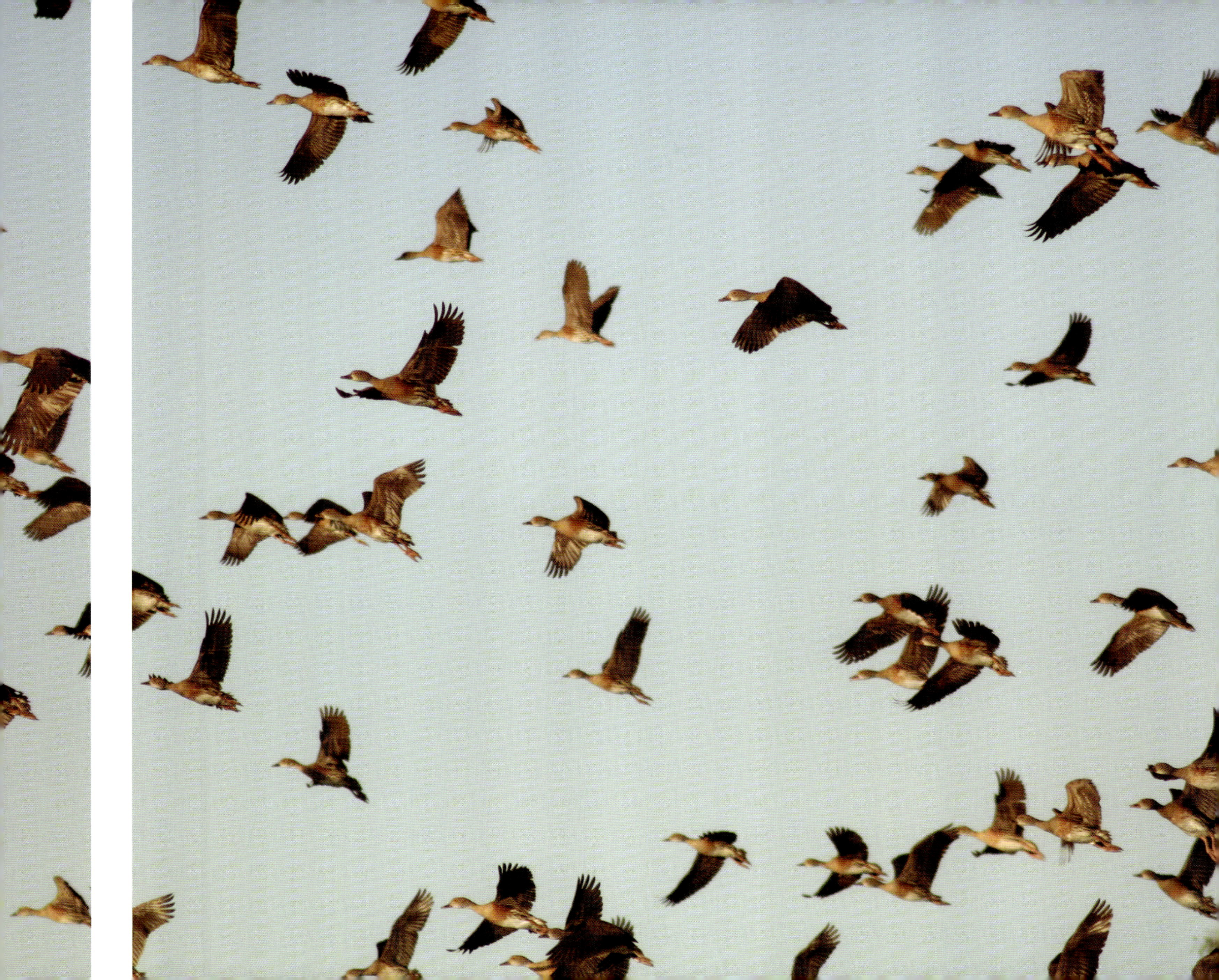

Birds of prey such as kites, eagles and this brown falcon (Falco berigora) *occupy the top of the food chain, feeding on the animals that proliferate during the floods.*

The wetland, with its abundant resources of plants, invertebrates and fish, collapses as the water dries back. For latecomers to a pelican colony, the timing is all wrong; their five-month breeding window closes before their young fledge. These are probably young, inexperienced parents that arrive late and then still need to take time to build up their energy for courtship, egg laying and chick rearing. When their food supply crashes, they need to escape before it is too late. Often, they will abandon eggs and even chicks that are almost fully grown. With no parent, these chicks cannot fend for themselves and die, sometimes in their hundreds. Sometimes adult birds make the wrong decision, fatally reaping the consequences of the sudden depletion of their staple food. For example, one inland lake supported a carpet of aquatic plants and more than 1000 swans, but slowly the plants began to die off as they went through their bust cycle. Many of the swans left before it was too late but a number did not. About a 180 swans died. Rigor mortis even preserved some in their feeding position, floating on the water with their heads submerged.

Sometimes waterbirds manage to get away, but not sufficiently far to build up their energy. For example, after the big floods of Lake Eyre in the mid 1970s, 1000 cormorants jammed into a nearby concrete tank with only 30 centimetres of water and died. Also, there were pelicans purportedly found along the roads of the dry Mallee in outback Victoria after the same floods, probably mistaking the glistening bitumen as water during their nocturnal escape.

Most waterbirds experience this race against time in such an unforgiving environment — but when it hits depends on the cycling of their food. Different foods can be at different phases of their life cycles or even out of phase with each other. Times that are right for fish may not be when most aquatic plants are growing. So the breeding cycle of the fish-eating pelican may not coincide with that of the herbivorous black swan. This was graphically illustrated on one inland lake. Pelicans experienced a crash in their fish supply and parents abandoned dead and dying young on the nesting island. At the same time, seagrasses growing on the bottom

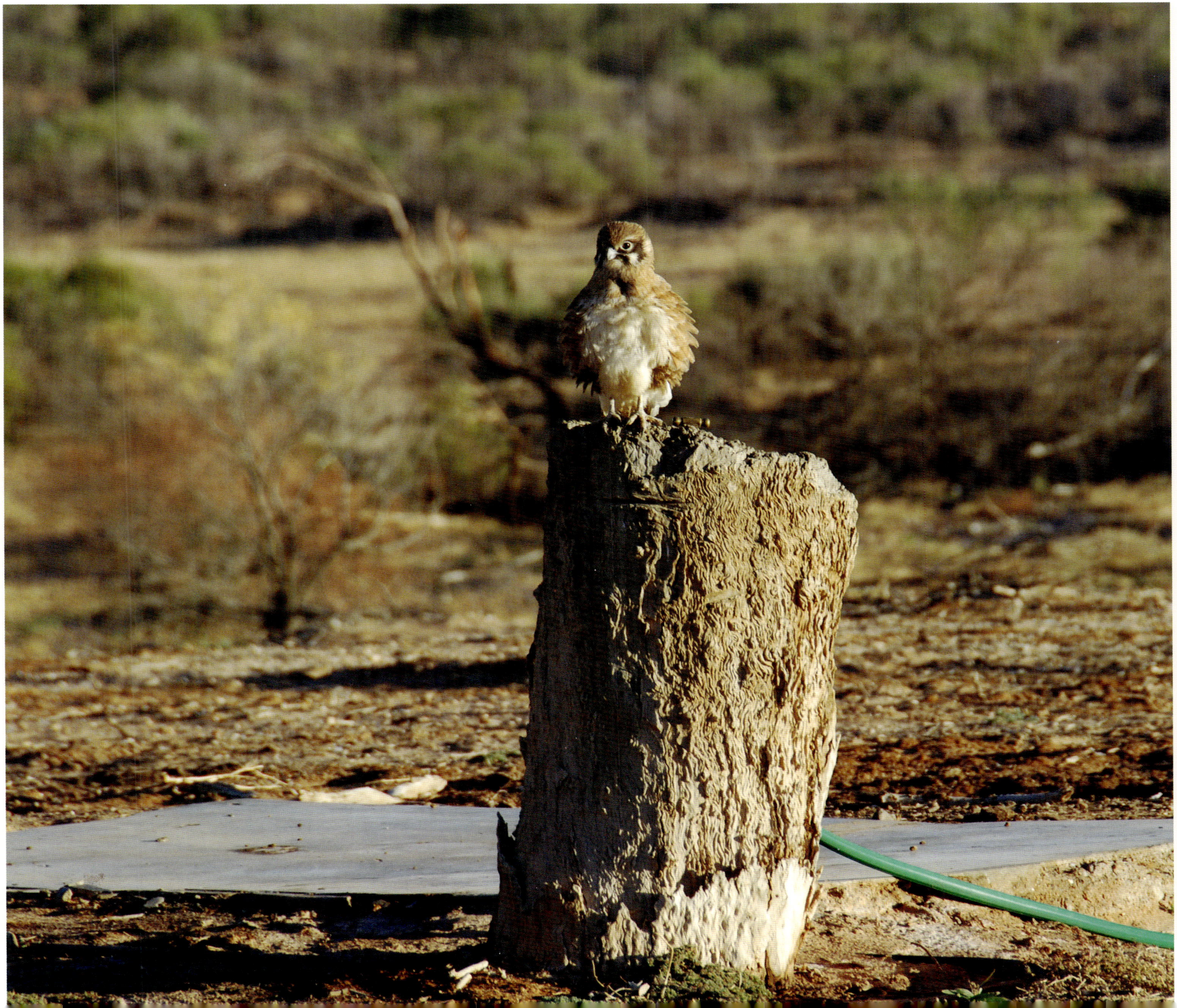

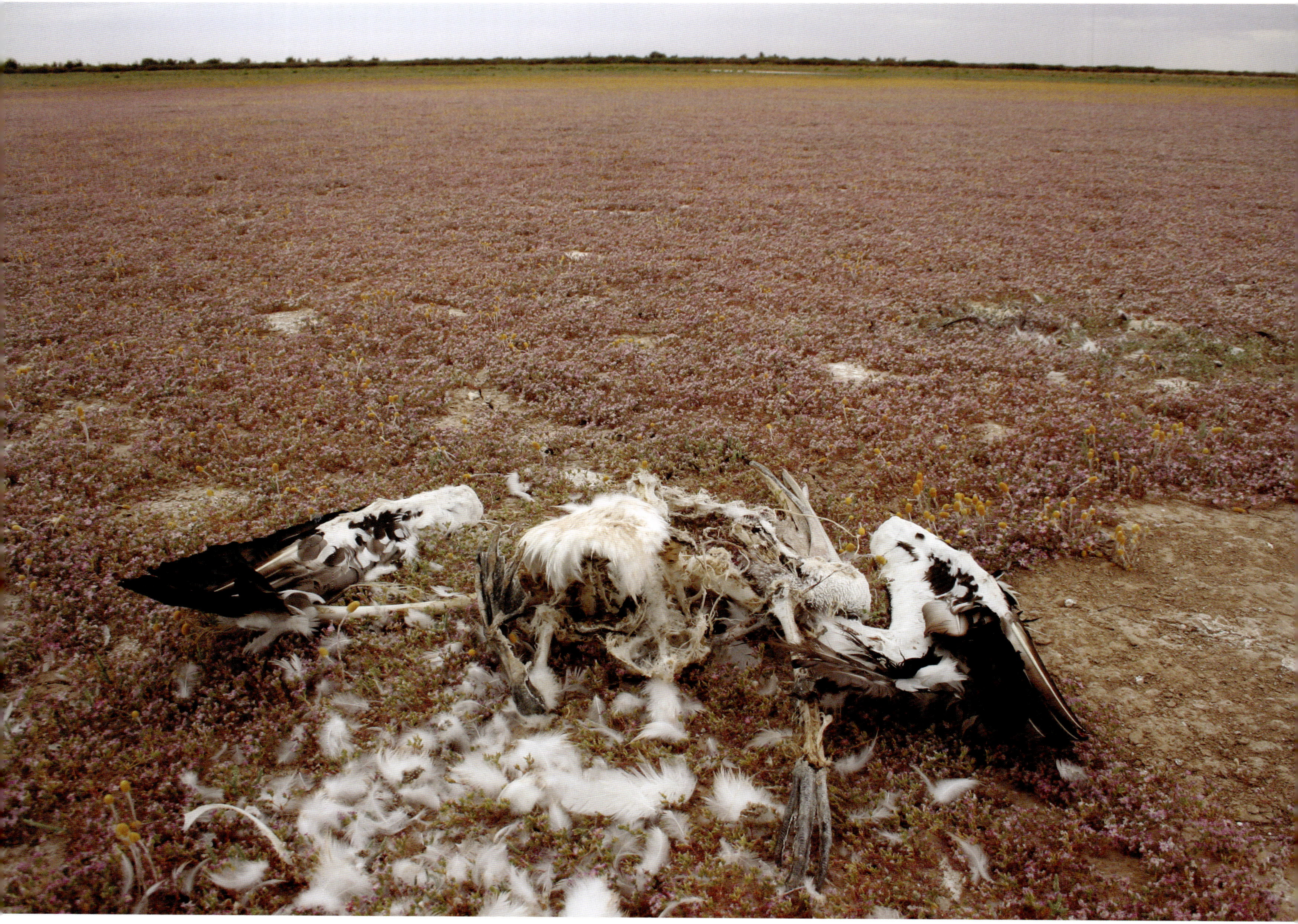

of the lake flourished, stimulating swans to breed on the same island. Dead and dying pelican chicks were scattered among the large nests of black swans, which glistened with clutches of up to ten eggs. Black swans usually heap up vegetation to provide a soft platform for their clutch. On this particular island, they substituted their traditional plant nesting material with the most appropriate nesting material to hand — dead pelican chicks. Their platform nests consisted of layers of feathers and pelican carcases.

The inevitable drying is the ticking clock that determines whether each species of waterbird will have enough time and energy to breed and then escape the big Dry. Most of them get it right — tens of thousands of years of selective evolutionary pressure have ensured this — but some fail and pay the price. These two ends of the climate spectrum, flooding rains and harsh droughts, drive the waterbird cycles of this arid landscape.

Lake Eyre and its rivers are examples of a natural global phenomenon epitomised by the incredible contrast of drought and flood, taking the landscape from parched desert to water-filled wetlands overflowing with life. These rivers have the world's most extreme boom-and-bust cycles, driven by unpredictable rainfall patterns such as cyclones. Added to this, they are among very few remaining large rivers around the world that have continued to flow they way have for millennia. The flows of the Cooper and the Georgina–Diamantina rivers are hardly hindered by dams or diversions. Elsewhere across the globe, people have interrupted the natural flows of most rivers with dams, often changing the way the rivers flow to generate hydroelectricity, and also by removing substantial amounts of water to supply towns and cities and irrigation areas. This has devastated the rivers, and in particular their downstream floodplains and wetlands. The microbes, plants and animals — including many subsistence human societies — have suffered as the rivers have dried up.

The earth's most devastating ecological disasters have almost always been caused by human interference with rivers. Three examples stand out.

Sometimes waterbird species don't time their departure before the inevitable drying. Many — particularly chicks — can die as their food supplies run out.

The fish in the rivers that run into Lake Eyre, such as this catfish (Neosiluroides cooperensis) *from Cooper Creek, build up quickly into vast numbers with the floods.*

The Aral Sea, once a massive freshwater lake lying between Kazakhstan and Uzbekistan, has shrunk because its two main supply rivers, the Amu-Dar'ya and Syr-Dar'ya, have had much of their flow diverted for irrigation of rice and cotton. A once-thriving fishing industry that produced nearly 50,000 tonnes of fish a year collapsed when sixteen of its twenty fish species became extinct as the lake dried. Rusting fishing boats now lie abandoned, some as far as 80 kilometres from the edge of what remains of the lake. Driven by the collapse in the ecology of the lake and pollution coming down the rivers from irrigation areas, cancer rates in local fishing villages increased and life expectancy decreased by as much as 20 per cent.

The second ecological disaster is the Mesopotamian Marshlands lying in Iraq at the end of the Tigris and Euphrates rivers, and sometimes referred to as the cradle of civilisation. Like Lake Eyre, most of these wetlands form at the end of river systems, and are critically dependent on life-giving flows. The amazing Mesopotamian Marshlands, with its three distinct marsh areas, each more than 3000 square kilometres, is now only about a tenth of its original size, most of its life squeezed out by upstream dams in Turkey, Syria, Iraq, and Iran, and channels built by the dictator Saddam Hussein in the 1990s. He built a destructive system of canals, dykes and sluices, originally designed by British engineers in the 1950s, cutting off the flows to this garden of Eden, so that he could take revenge on the the Madan or Marsh Arabs who lived in the wetland, and who had risen up against him after the first Gulf War.

Nearer to home, the Murray–Darling Basin and its rivers are plagued by declining flows that affect the wetlands and their environments and the people that rely on the river. The recent drought saw unprecedented high levels of salinity as well as the exposure of large areas of lake bed in the lower lakes of the Murray–Darling, which, when exposed to the air as they dried, produced sulfuric acid. River scientists have progressively documented such ecological and often social disasters along many of the world's rivers, caused by changing the natural patterns

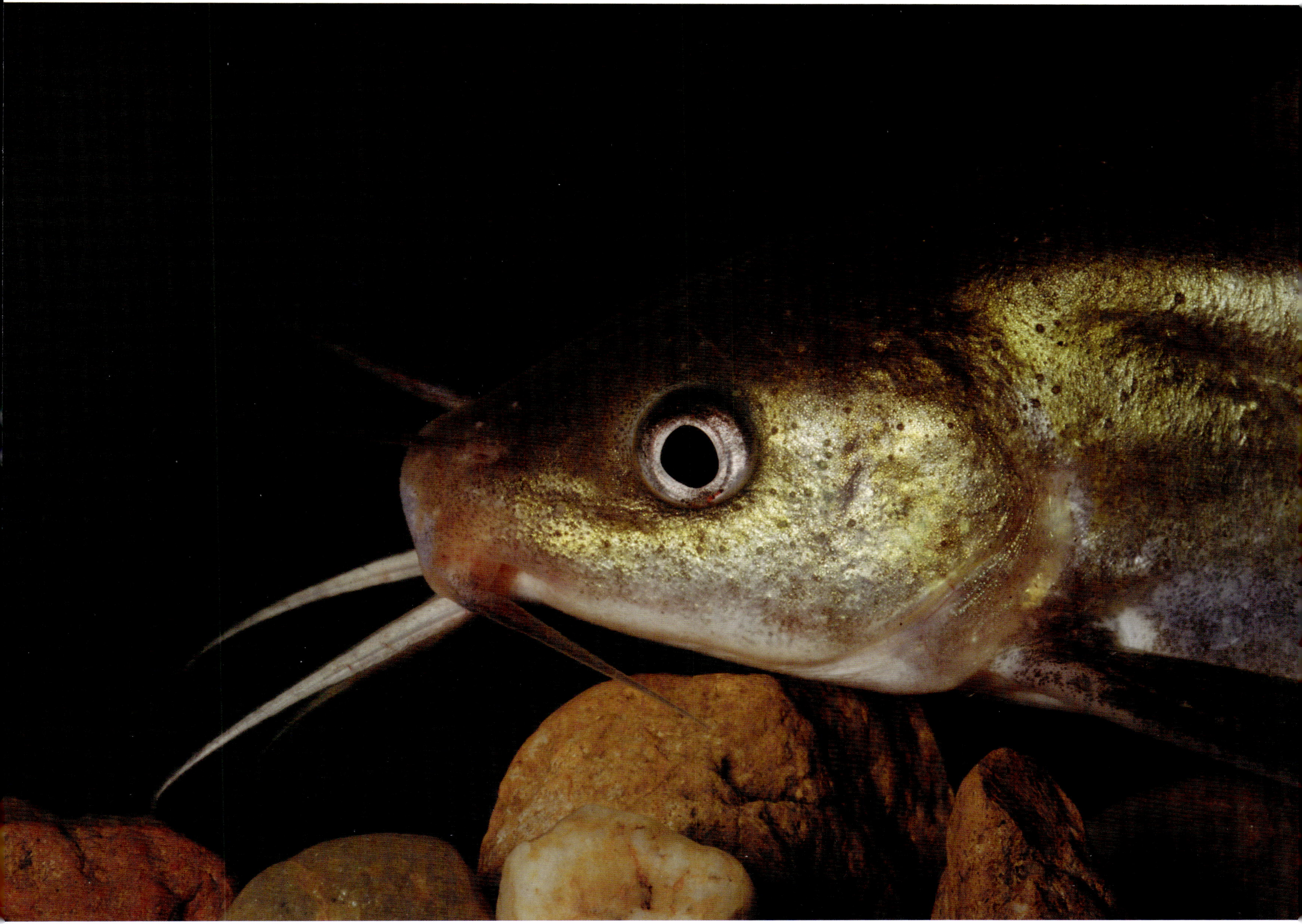

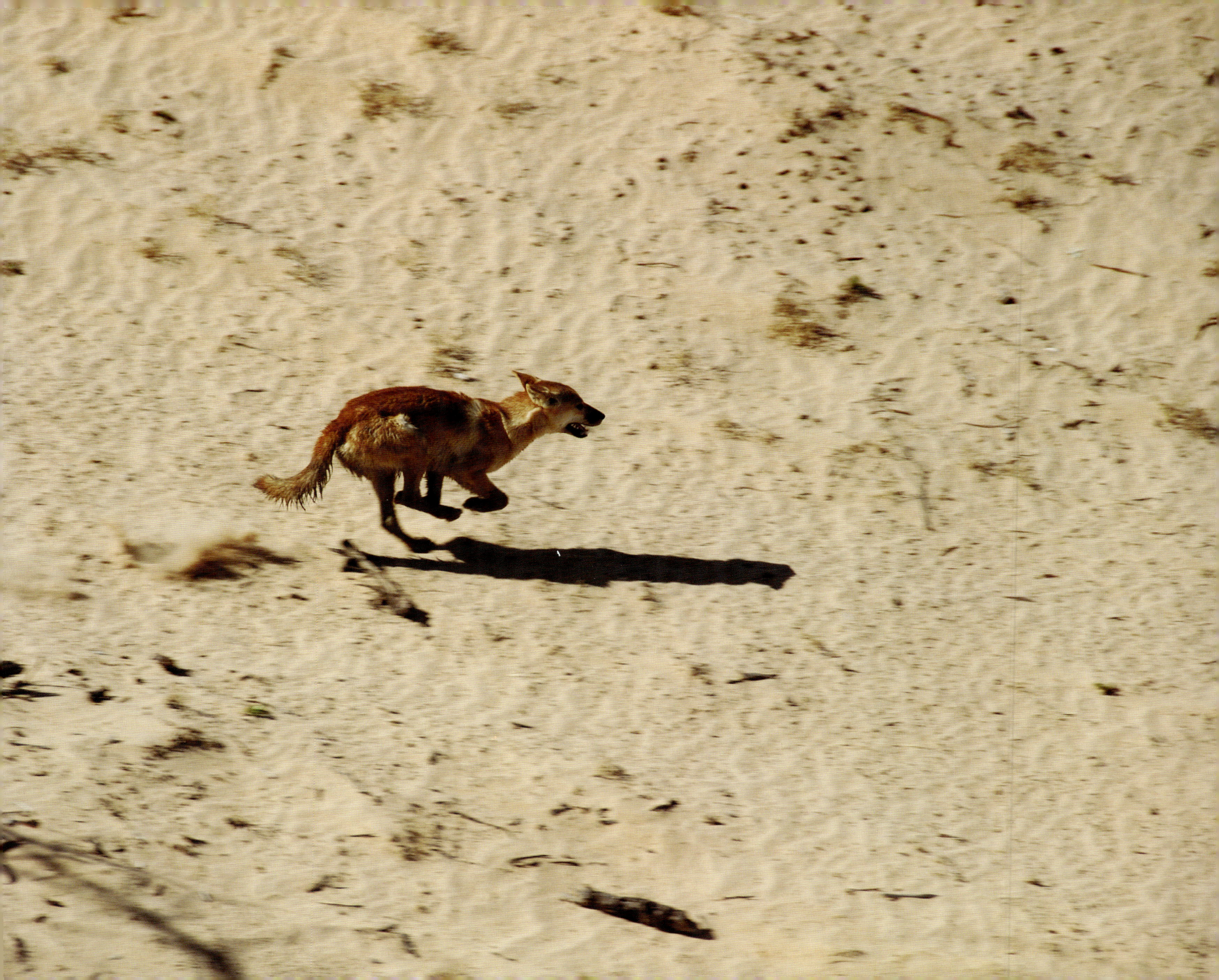

of river flows. Such disasters are a reminder of the critical importance of protecting the flows of the rivers of the Lake Eyre Basin.

In the mid 1990s, it was proposed to develop Cooper Creek for irrigation, widely thought to be for cotton, near the town of Windorah in the Channel Country of Queensland. The graziers of the Cooper fought the plan ferociously, knowing that to allow such a development would spell disaster for their grazing enterprises, which relied on the flows across the Cooper floodplain. Their understanding was also well attuned to the problems of the Murray–Darling Basin. They were joined by other strong voices: local councillors and MPs, environmentalists, scientists and many in the Australian community who warned of the dangers of interfering with this magnificent river system. It was the first time in Australia that a community had sucessfully protested about the development of an inland river for irrigation.

Governments soon responded, although at the time there had been considerable support for development from the Queensland Government. In 2000, the Lake Eyre Basin Agreement was signed and enacted by the South Australian and Queensland governments and the Australian Federal Government. The Northern Territory Government signed in 2004. The agreement promised to protect the flows of the mighty rivers of the Lake Eyre Basin for future generations. There was to be no large-scale diversion of water for irrigation. This agreement continues to guide policy and management by the signatory governments. Recently, the Queensland Government committed to declaring the rivers of the Lake Eyre Basin to be 'wild rivers', forever protected in Queensland. Australians have shown that we can lead the world in sustainable management by protecting the flows of the magnificent rivers that supply Lake Eyre.

Still, water remains the most important resource in this desert landscape. It will always promise wealth to individuals who can turn it into agricultural produce, a development path well trodden in the Murray–Darling Basin and many other rivers of the world. But it comes at great environmental cost. The temptation to develop the rivers of Lake Eyre will never go away, particularly as arguments about global food security increasingly gain currency.

Yet if we ever decide to dam or divert large quantities of water from the Cooper, Georgina and Diamantina rivers, future generations will not be privileged to see the great floods and the wildlife that make this region of Australia such a wonderful spectacle. Long may the rivers flow so that our children and grandchildren will still be able to enjoy the magnificent floods and everything they trigger as they course through the deserts of outback Australia.

A dingo on the run. Despite their capacity to scavenge, they too are reliant on sufficient food sources and can be significantly affected by the onset of the dry season and drought.

BREAKING THE DROUGHT

Flooding rains

Rex Ellis doubted he would ever see huge floods reach Lake Eyre again in his lifetime, especially as the new century heralded the worst drought in history. It took hold not just in Central Australia, but across the entire eastern half of the continent. Pastures withered and died, water ran short, and stock had to be moved or sold as the cattle stations tried to tough it out. Throughout the searing summers, and their fearsome dust storms, all eyes were cast towards the tropical north, hoping every year that the cyclone season would dump enough rain to get the rivers running towards the centre. At the beginning of 2009 it finally happened. Torrential rain blanketed the Gulf of Carpentaria leaving north Queensland awash. The flooding stretched all the way to Mount Isa and beyond. To the south, the bush telegraph crackled with news of the coming flows.

From his base in Birdsville, David Brook closely monitored the flood flow bearing down on Central Australia. He was constantly on the phone, calling landholders to the north of the town to check on flood heights, working out how much country would go under and whether there were any dangers posed to station homesteads, stock or small communities. There was much at stake for David Brook. His family runs five cattle

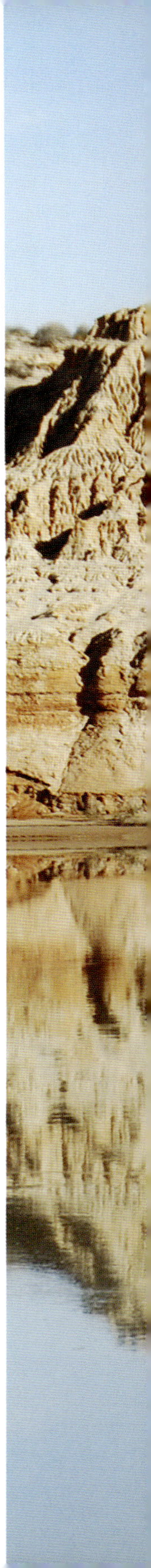

The rivers that enter Lake Eyre have carved paths through the desert so deep that in some places, such as the lower part of Cooper Creek, small cliffs have formed — reflected here with stunning clarity.

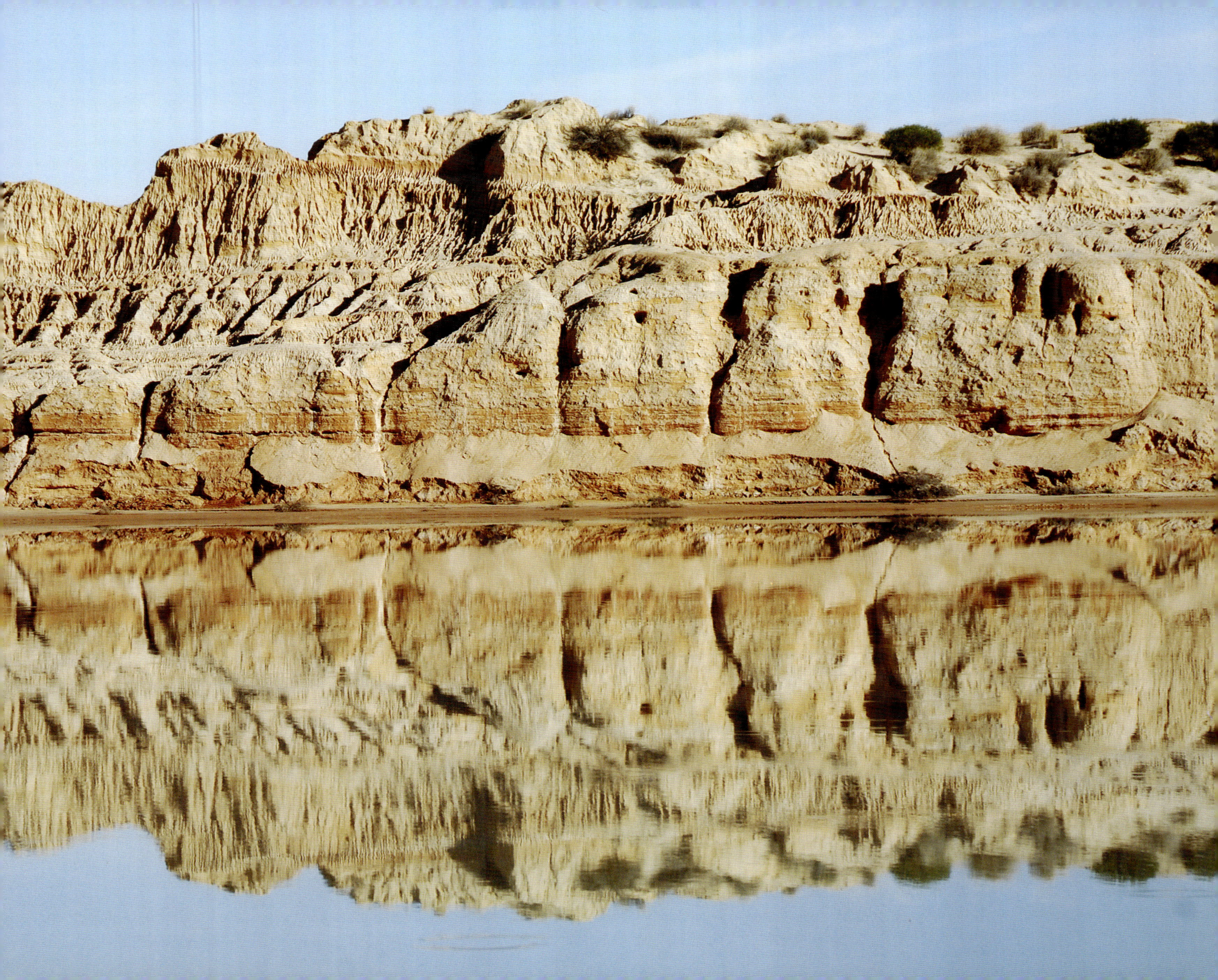

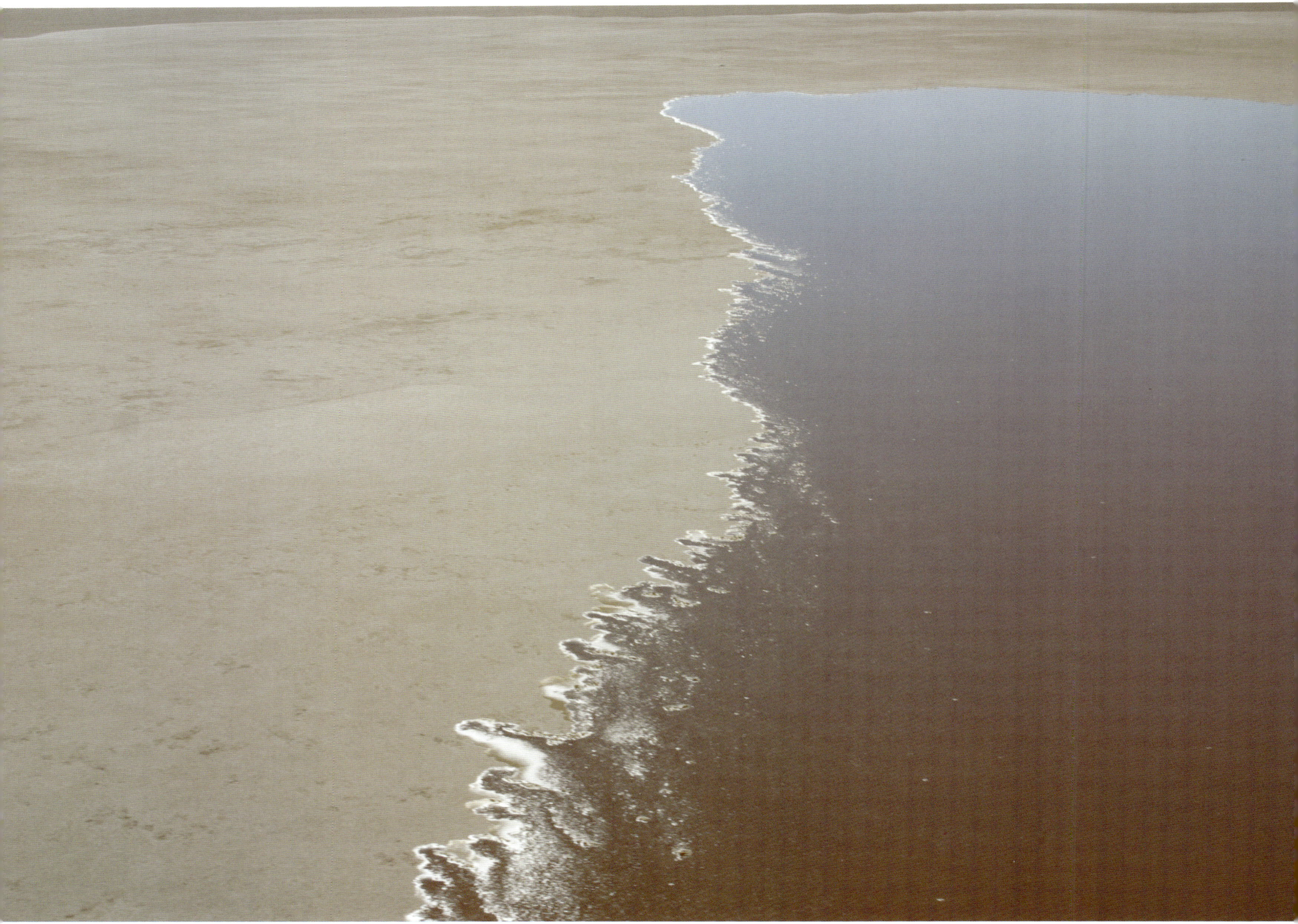

stations around Lake Eyre, covering more than 34,000 square kilometres altogether. But there was no panic. It can be a long wait between floods but the people of the outback are well accustomed to the massive inundation they face and the long wait for the water to pass. It's a very gradual drop from anywhere in the Lake Eyre Basin to the lake in the centre of the continent. The water drains very slowly. Upstream from Birdsville, the Georgina River had already spread so far beyond its banks that it was difficult to spot the course it usually followed. The tiny Queensland settlement of Bedourie was surrounded by floodwaters and emergency services workers were launching a flood boat to carry supplies to isolated stations. An enormous flow in the main channel of the Georgina River was not the biggest concern for the emergency personnel — rather it was the snakes that tried to swim to the safety of the boat. One worker armed himself with an oar to beat them away.

Ahead of the floodwaters, jackeroos took to four-wheel drives, motorbikes and horses to move cattle to high ground, with the help of mustering aircraft.

The water spread ever wider, soaking deep into the parched landscape. The Diamantina River to the east of Birdsville rose fast. All roads to the town would be cut for weeks to come. Out in the Simpson Desert, west of Birdsville, the Eyre Creek overflowed, sending fingers of water reaching out between the huge sand dunes. It was one of the most dramatic and incongruous sights of the outback flooding — streams literally finding their way through the desert.

At his home in Birdsville, David Brook explained his feelings as the flow stretched across the countryside:

> *Most people won't see this, they won't understand it. They'll look on a map and there will be a little blue line that says Eyre Creek or Diamantina River, and they will have heard of the desert and say you must be dreaming! The floods just bring life to everything. They excite us as they go past and rise. And when we see the water running freely we know that all the waterholes downstream will be filled, and the birdlife and fish and all that will get a real kick along.*

The slow-moving flood is a feature of the lake — rivers have to fill every lake and swamp and wetland before they can flow on, eventually creeping into Lake Eyre.

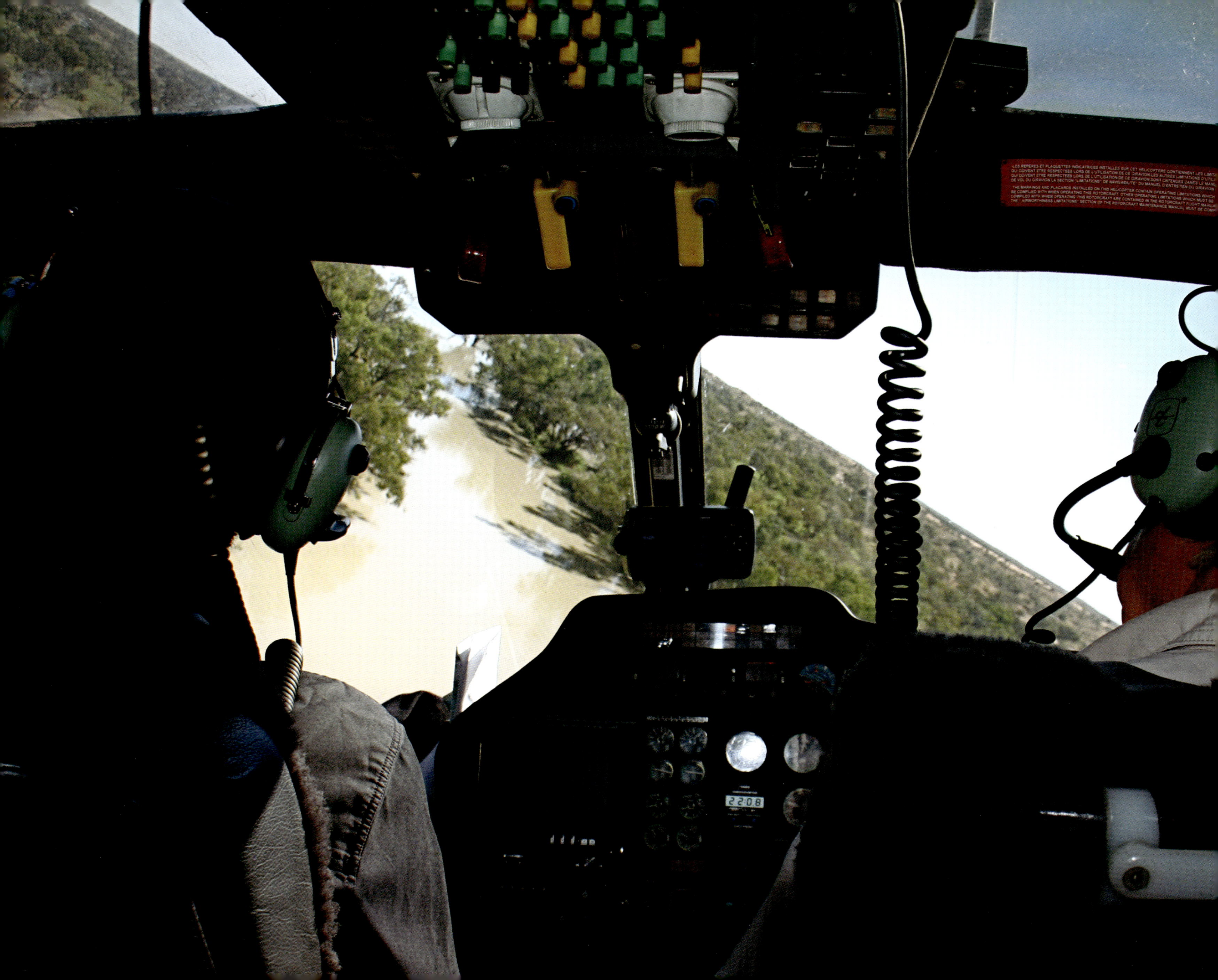

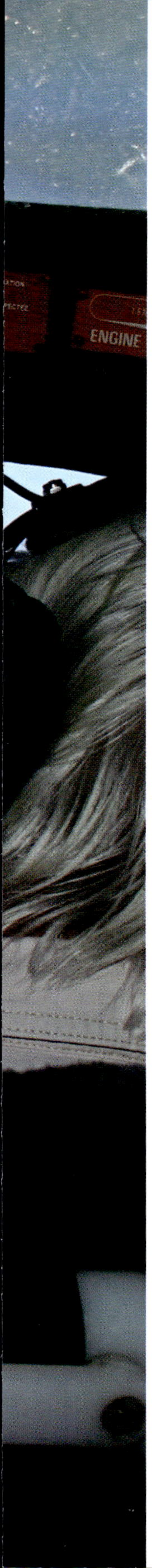

Travelling to Lake Eyre

In the ABC chopper as it flew out to Lake Eyre. Even today this remains one of the country's most remote areas; the trip in the chopper takes over seven hours with carefully thought out refuelling stops.

On a clear, crisp morning in May 2009, the ABC helicopter, with Gary Ticehurst at the controls, lifted off from its base in North Sydney. The chopper was packed with film equipment and supplies for a ten-day expedition to Central Australia. Camera operator Erik Havnen settled himself amongst the gear in the back of the chopper as it swung over the glistening harbour and its bobbing ferries delivering early-morning commuters to Circular Quay. Past the majestic sails of the Opera House and up over two excited groups of climbers as they made their way to the top of the Harbour Bridge.

The chopper followed a flight corridor west, past the Olympic Stadium at Homebush and then out over the Blue Mountains, with sandstone peaks bathed in the golden light of sunrise. There was a keen sense of anticipation about this ambitious filming mission.

We were headed to Innamincka, deep in the South Australian outback, but it would take about seven hours to get there.

Even with twenty-first century advances in communications, the coverage of news events in the most remote areas of Australia still presents huge challenges, especially for television. So when ABC News agreed that the Sydney-based helicopter should go to Central Australia to cover the floods there were high expectations. There was no doubt that the flooding represented the biggest break in the drought since the turn of the century; water was already streaming into Lake Eyre down Warburton Creek from the north for the first time in years. History was being made, but the filming opportunities were spread over a vast area. The logistics required careful planning. Fuel dumps for the chopper had to be organised well in advance at tiny communities and cattle stations dotted around Lake Eyre, and delivered by truck from Port Augusta, hundreds of kilometres away.

Our journey would take us over some of the great Australian place names — refuelling at Dubbo, Bourke and Tibooburra — crossing the Macquarie, Darling and Paroo rivers on the way. Neither flood nor rain had touched much of the country we flew over, and there was little sign that the coming winter would offer relief for landholders still locked deep in drought. The landscape deteriorated even further as we flew on from Tibooburra, in the far north-west of New South Wales, to Cameron's Corner, where the borders of New South Wales, Queensland and South Australia meet. Then it was on to Innamincka, a spot on the map next to a crossing on Cooper Creek, north-east of Lake Eyre.

In the early days, several stock routes joined up at Innamincka and a store was established in the late 1880s to trade with the drovers and the cattle stations in the area. In 1912, under the guidance of the Reverend John Flynn, the Australian Inland Mission opened a nursing station there, to co-ordinate outback medical care, eventually using the revolutionary communications of the pedal wireless and, by 1929, after tireless work by Flynn, what was to become the Royal Flying Doctor Service. But by the 1970s Innamincka was on its last legs. Like many other rural settlements, it suffered from the decline in numbers in the bush. The big labour force once prevalent on the outback cattle stations, so large that they had formed small communities, had long since dwindled. Higher wages and modern mustering methods, especially the use of helicopters and light aircraft, principally led to the labour cuts.

Innamincka was saved by new business generated by the oil and gas industry and tourism.

The place is still tiny, just a trading post and a hotel–motel, but during the winter there's a constant stream of four-wheel drives passing through the settlement as travellers make their way to and from the outback.

Innamincka is just downstream from the Burke and Wills Dig Tree, across the border in Queensland. The chopper provided a perfect view of what would have confronted the explorers when they stumbled around this area almost 150 years earlier. The sharp rocky plains and endless sand drifts of the Strzelecki Desert stretch off to the horizon and dip away to reveal the same dismal outlook. The scant vegetation was struggling to maintain

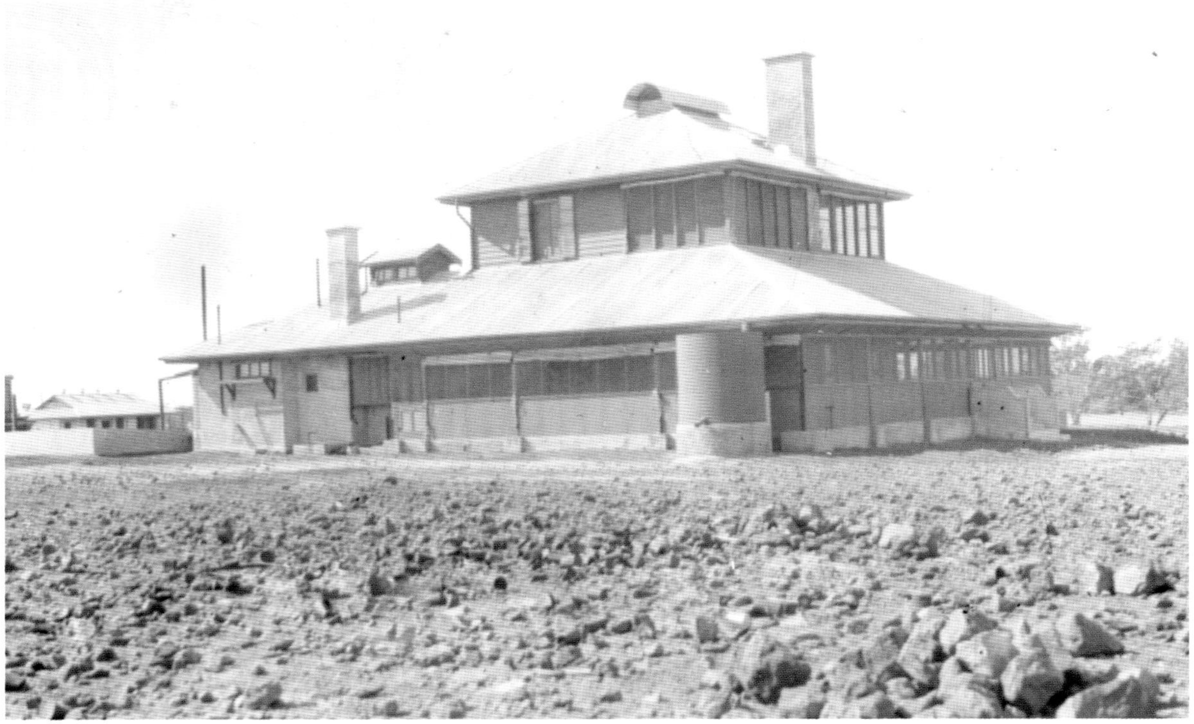

At the junction of several stock routes, a trading post was set up at Innamincka in the 1880s. In 1912, the Australian Inland Mission opened a nursing station (above) to coordinate outback medical care. Opposite: One of the essential means of communication in this remote region was the pedal wireless, seen here in use by the Reverend Fred McKay in the 1930s.

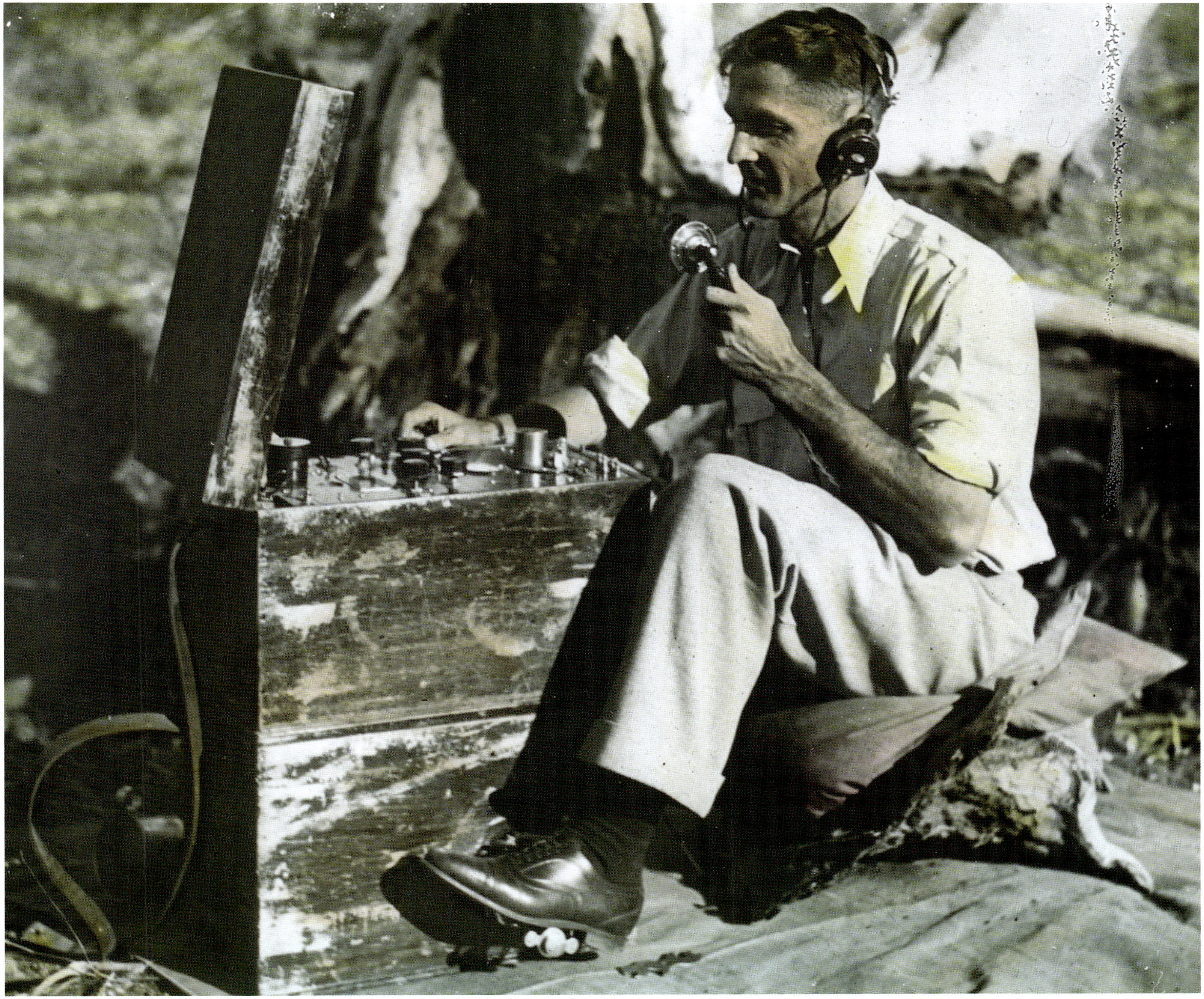

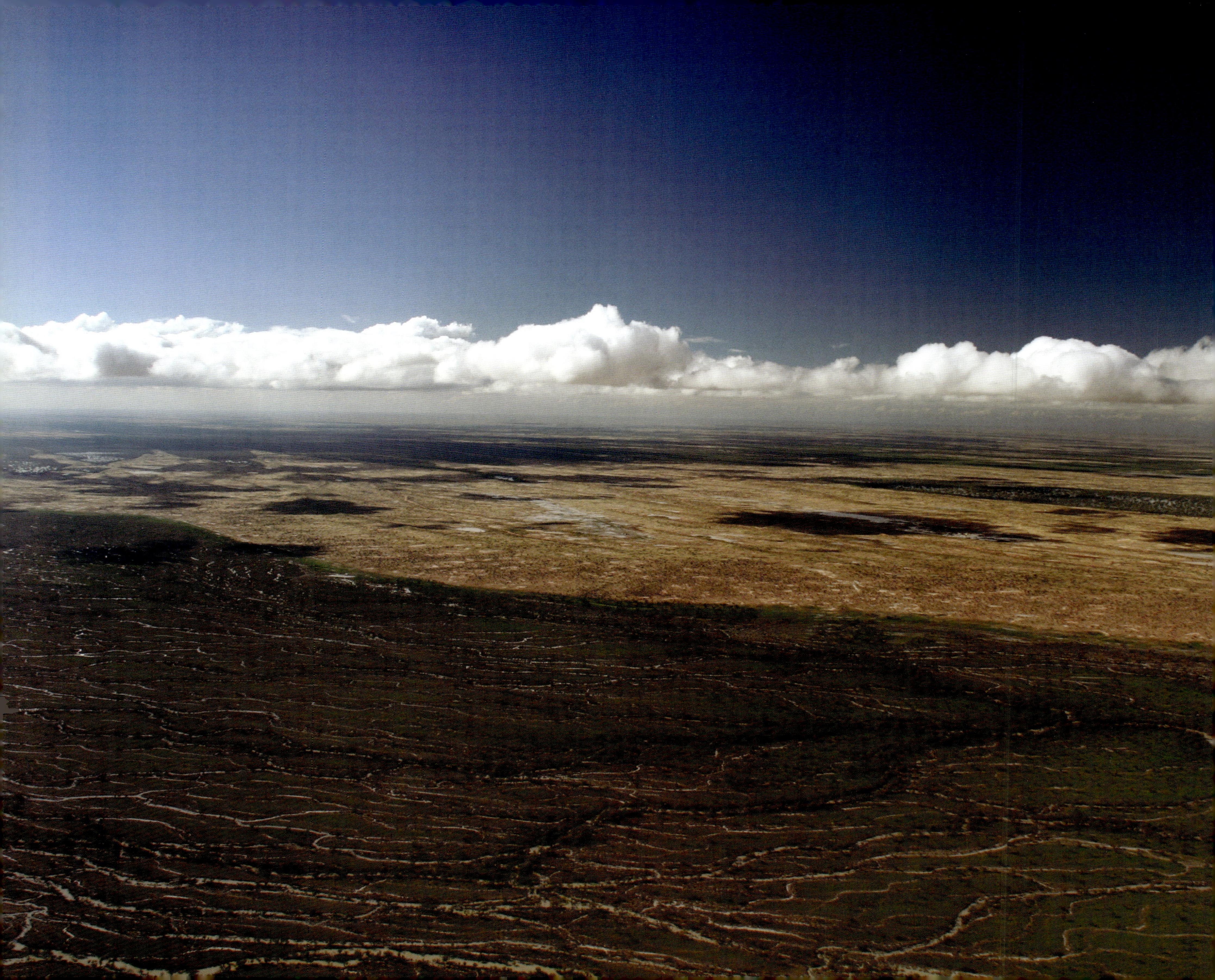

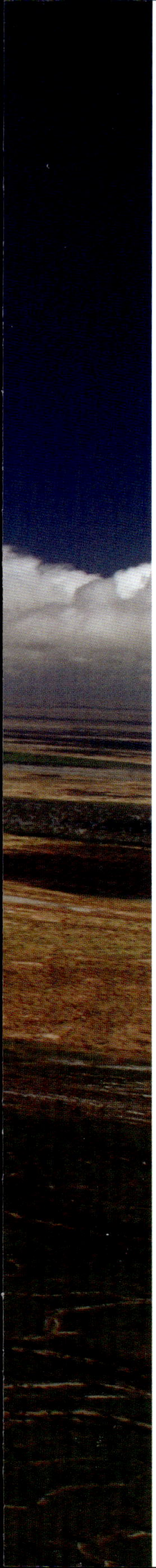

From the air there is a sharp divide between the arid desert landscape and the greener areas where creeks and rivers flow.

a grip in the arid landscape. But there was a distinct line of green curving away through the countryside, marking the course of the meandering Cooper Creek. Along the river it was very different. Even though there had been no rain in the region, the Cooper was flowing from big falls hundreds of kilometres to the north, in central Queensland, more than two months earlier. The waterhole next to the Burke and Wills Dig Tree was full, the place at the centre of their disastrous expedition eerily tranquil. Half a dozen pelicans were out on the water fishing, gliding along in tight formation. Everything happened in unison. They dipped their huge bills into the water at exactly the same time and seconds later they all popped up together, stretching their long necks high to gobble down the catch. On they drifted down the Cooper pursuing the fish in a remarkable display of synchronised feeding. Already the coolibahs, the river red gums and other vegetation hugging the banks of the Cooper were boasting shiny canopies. The flow had brought them back. But stroll 50 metres from the river and you were back in the drought.

From the Dig Tree the Cooper winds its way through the desert to Lake Eyre, but before it gets there it has to fill a huge series of lakes near Innamincka. Bearing north-west in the chopper from Innamincka we wondered where the flood had gone. All we could see was more of the same — the Strzelecki Desert disappearing into a big cloudless sky. Then, patches of green began to appear on the horizon and a huge flock of corellas wheeled away in front of us, the sun catching their wings as they turned. And a mob of about twenty wild horses — brumbies — which had been picking at the fresh pasture, galloped off into the dust of the desert. Floodwater had found its way there. A huge network of flowing channels soon opened up before us, the water trickling through a carpet of green, contrasting sharply with the reds and yellows of the surrounding dunes. It was all running towards a massive body of water — the Coongie Lakes wetlands — an environmental jewel in the outback spreading over almost two million hectares.

The bird migration mystery

Cooper Creek had topped up the wetlands and, for the first time in years, the birds were coming back. We descended to the biggest of the lakes in the system, flying across a big patch of bright yellow wildflowers blooming in the wake of the receding flow. Ducks had taken up early occupation, diving, honking and flapping as they feasted on the aquatic life that was now flourishing in the lake.

Twelve species of native fish are found in the Coongie Lakes and, when the water comes, hundreds of thousands of birds mysteriously find their way to this spot in the desert to feed and breed — including migratory birds all the way from the edge of the North Pole, in arctic Siberia. Among this massive array of birdlife are fourteen rare or endangered species. But after such a long drought there were deep concerns about how many birds would be left to take advantage of the flood. Professor Richard Kingsford, who has been conducting aerial surveys of bird populations across Australia for more than twenty years, has documented a worrying fall in numbers:

We've probably seen at least a 50 per cent decline in waterbird numbers over about a third of the continent over the last twenty to twenty-five years. A flood like this is just so important for actually building up numbers of things like pelicans and a whole range of different duck species — hard heads, grey teal, blue-billed ducks. And then we've got terns and ibis species, all going at a different phase out here — that's the incredible thing about these river systems.

The Coongie Lakes offered just a glimpse of what was to come. Professor Kingsford was conducting another bird survey in the region and had identified other spots where birds were now gathering in big numbers. Our course was set for a waterhole on the Diamantina River, north-east of Birdsville. We scanned the horizon for life as we tracked along the river waterholes, disturbing a big family of feral pigs revelling in the turn in the seasons. Off they charged, disappearing into an area of thick scrub before emerging to charge across

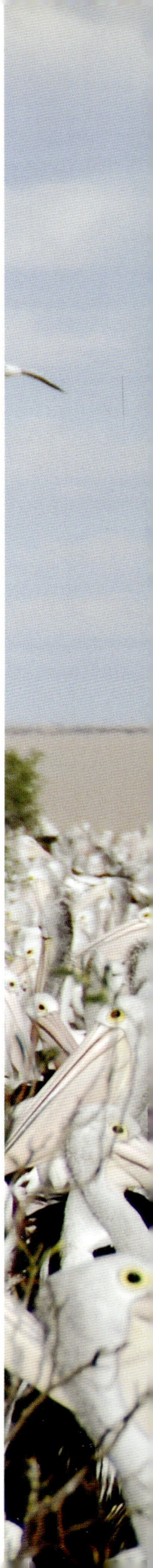

After the floods the lake area is like the Pitt Street of the bird world. Tens of thousands of pelicans gather to feed and breed on Lake Machattie, on the Georgina River.

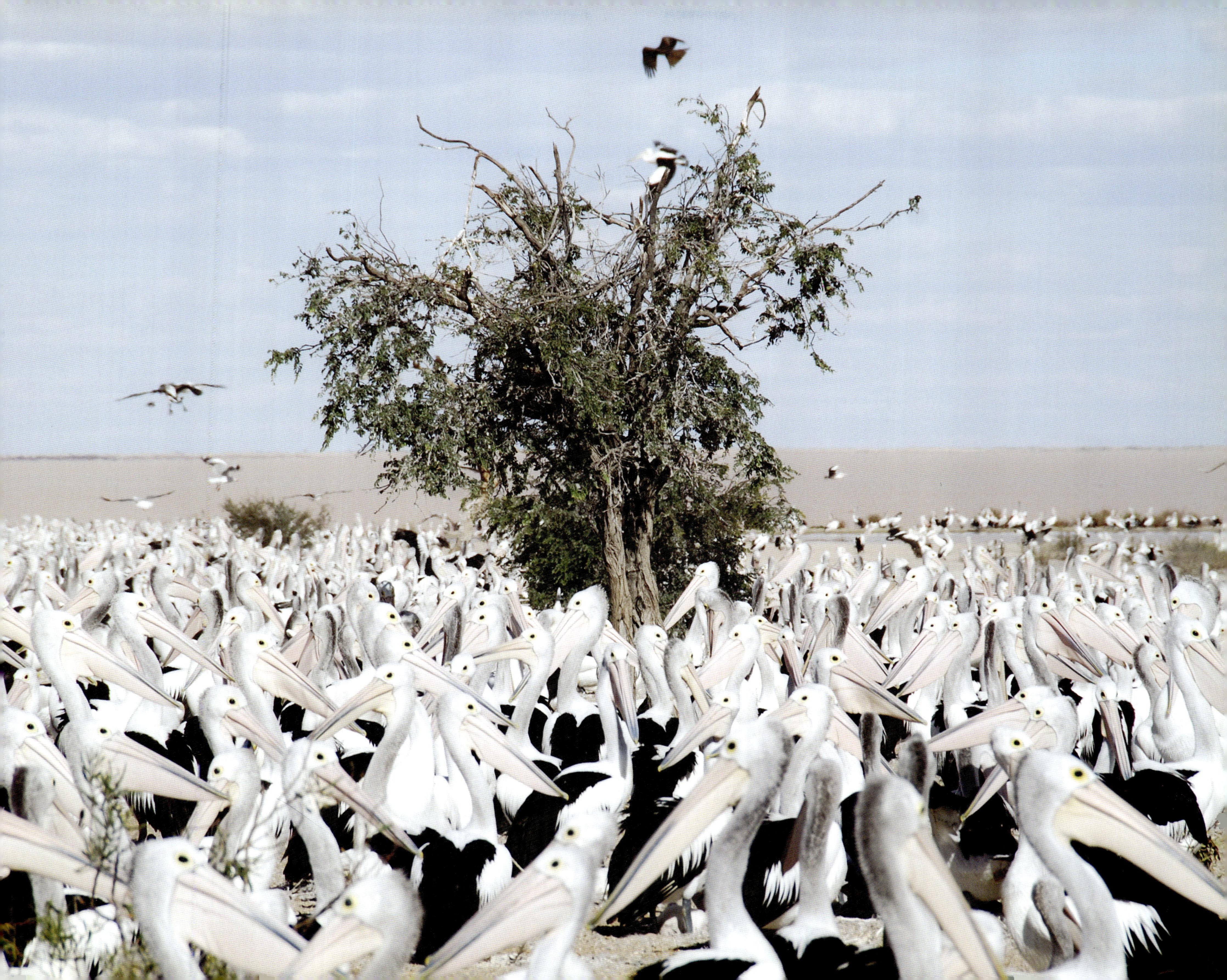

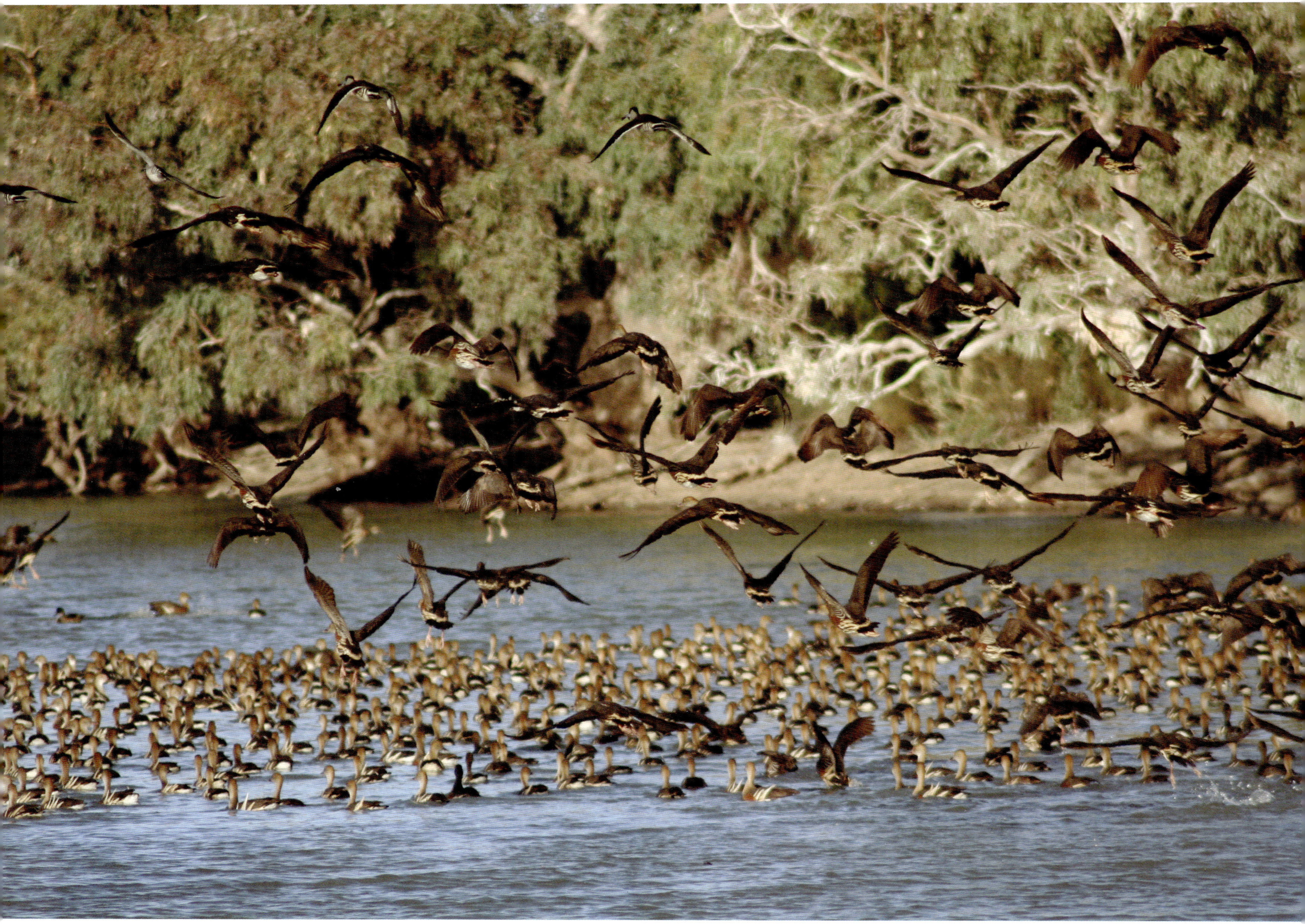

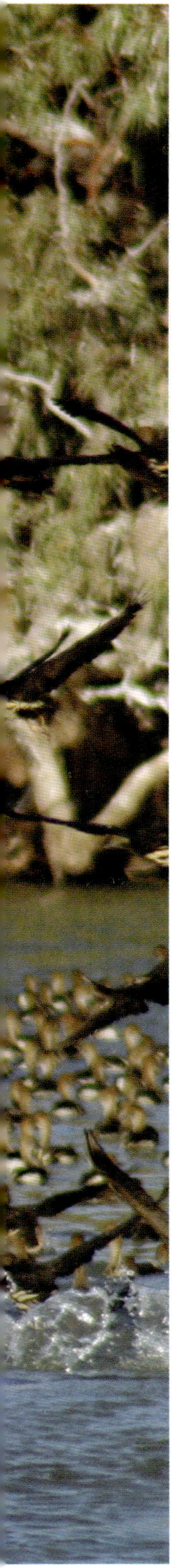

Vast flocks of plumed whistling ducks (Dendrocygna eytoni), *among other species, massed in the rivers and flooding waterholes as the Lake Eyre Basin came to life again in 2010.*
Overleaf (left): Plumed whistling ducks on a Diamantina River waterhole and (right) Australian pelicans and flying cormorants at dusk at a waterhole on the Burke River near Boulia, western Queensland.

a shallow channel, with the plump piglets bringing up the rear. Then the sky was suddenly alive with birds. Thousands of plumed whistling ducks lifted off the Diamantina, an enormous mass wheeling above the waterhole. We landed nearby and when they settled the birds presented an extraordinary sight — ducks from bank to bank, jostling for feeding space as they floated over the waterhole. Their high-pitched whistling calls filled the air.

Plumed whistling ducks are often found in the wetlands of the tropical north and, like other waterbird species, somehow know that the water has arrived in the arid heart of Australia — mystifying even to those who can trace their families back to the earliest inhabitants. Don Rowlands, an Aboriginal elder, says, 'I've yet to work it out for myself. I'm sure my ancestors would have had an answer in some of their mythical studies but I've never seen so many of these whistling ducks in one heap!' Rowlands has responsibilities to care for his ancestral homelands; he's a Queensland Government Park Ranger based at Birdsville, administering the Simpson Desert National Park, and a descendant of the Wangkangurru people whose homeland stretches through the Simpson Desert north-west of Lake Eyre. His ancestors established their communities around the artesian springs that have been bubbling up from deep below the surface of the earth for thousands of years. In flood times they would rest the country around the wells and spread further out — closer to Lake Eyre — to make the most of the bountiful hunting and foraging conditions.

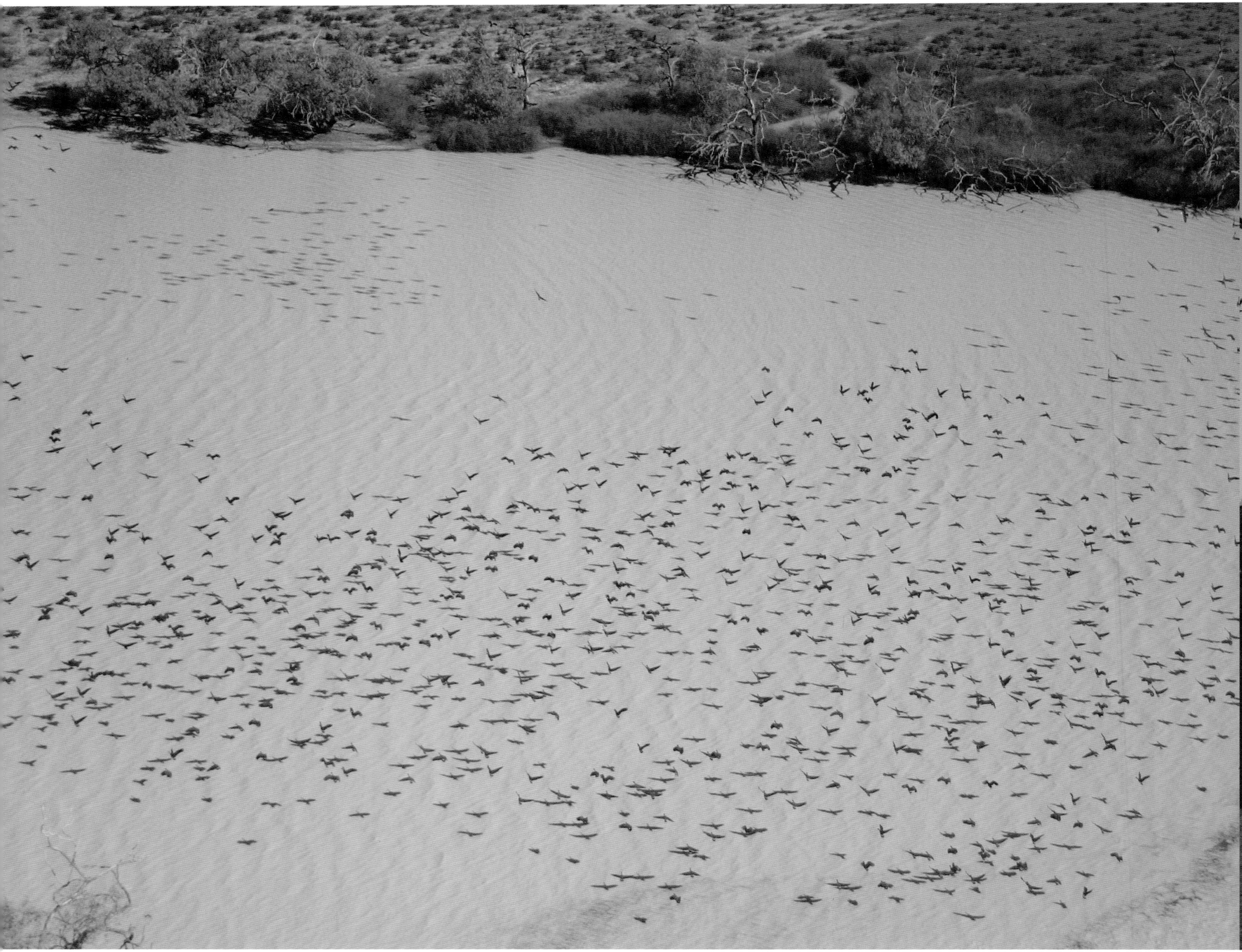
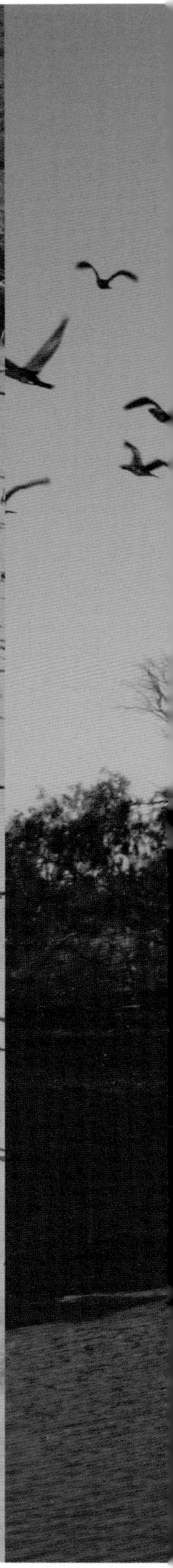

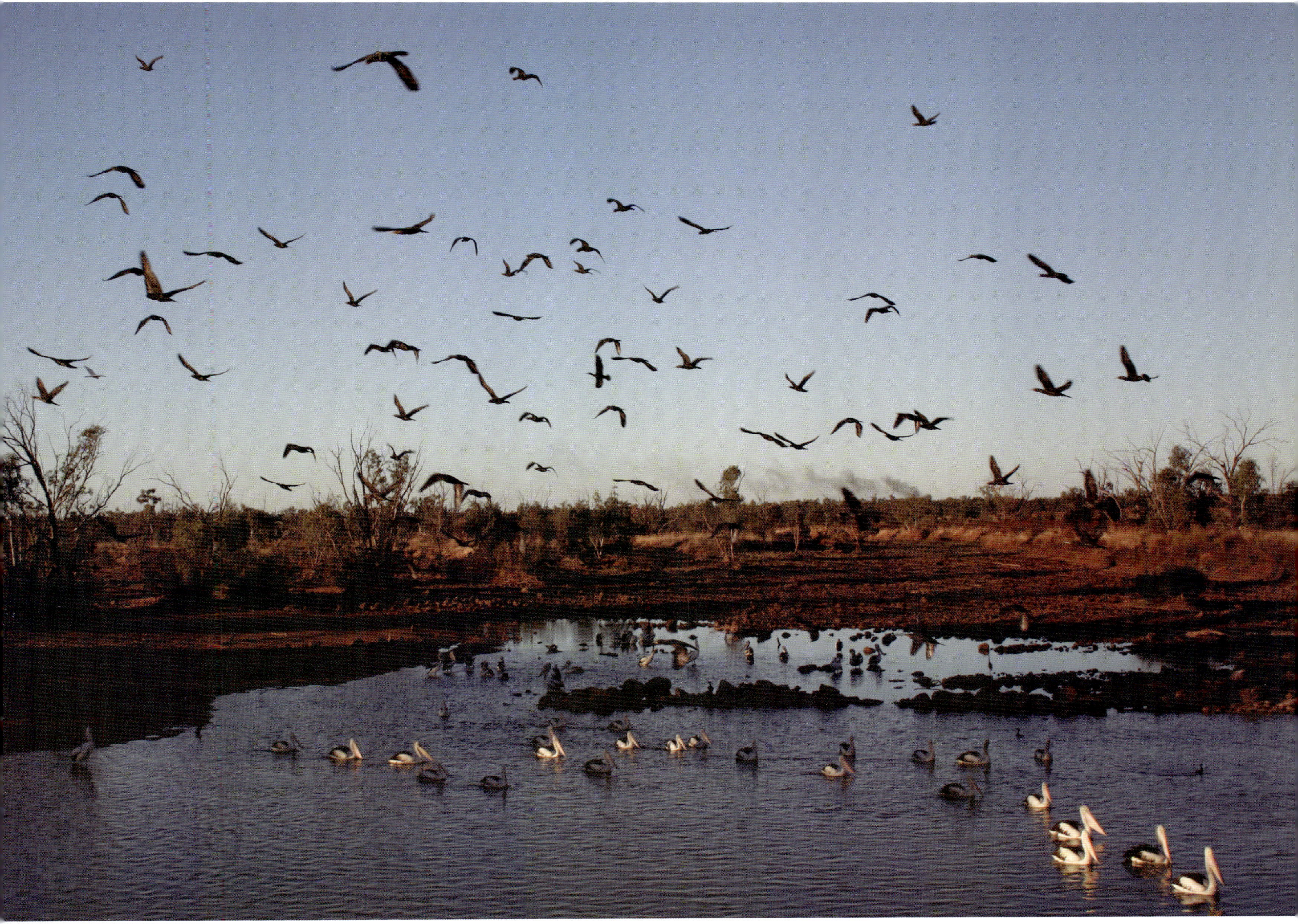

Proud parents sit guard over their ungainly chicks

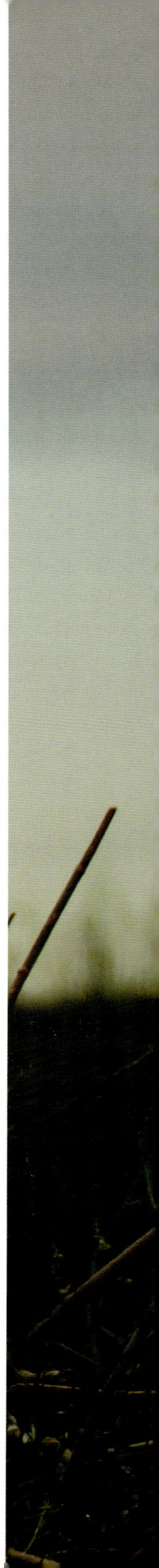

The floodwaters had topped up the waterhole, its banks were lined in green with an explosion of plant life, and out in the middle there was a feeding frenzy as birds swept in to pluck fish from the water or cruise with the flow, dining on the tiny forms of plant and animal life swept along in the river. Rowlands marvelled at the change in the seasons, imaging how the Birdsville waterhole would have sustained his ancestors for years after a flood:

> *We wait and wait and all of a sudden the water starts rising and it just seems to take on another look altogether. It's really exciting for me to see that the wildlife, the birdlife and everything, can survive out in this country that sometimes looks like it can never ever come back to what it can be. It reminds me of how my people used to live in this country. They depended so much on the good seasons to use this desert to its full potential.*

When the floods come to Central Australia it offers a narrow window for scientists to gather a deeper understanding of how the swift circle of life unfolds in the desert. The mass migration of birds to the outback is a case in point. Despite the usually long years between flood events, incoming birds not only know when the time is right to return, but they go back to the same breeding spots.

In May 2009, at the start of the big inland migration, Lake Machattie, north of Birdsville, running off the Georgina River, was targeted by pelicans — tens of thousands of them.

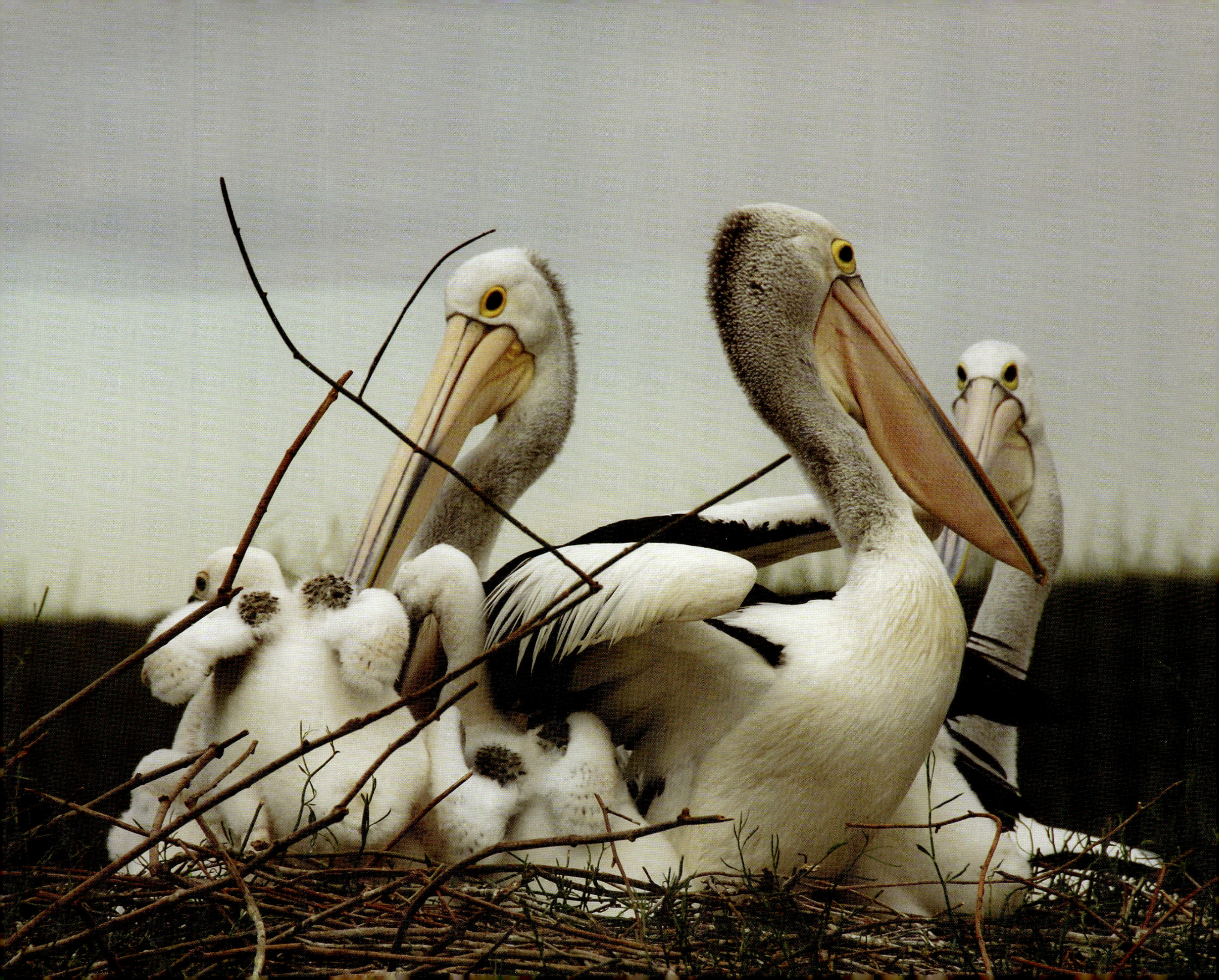

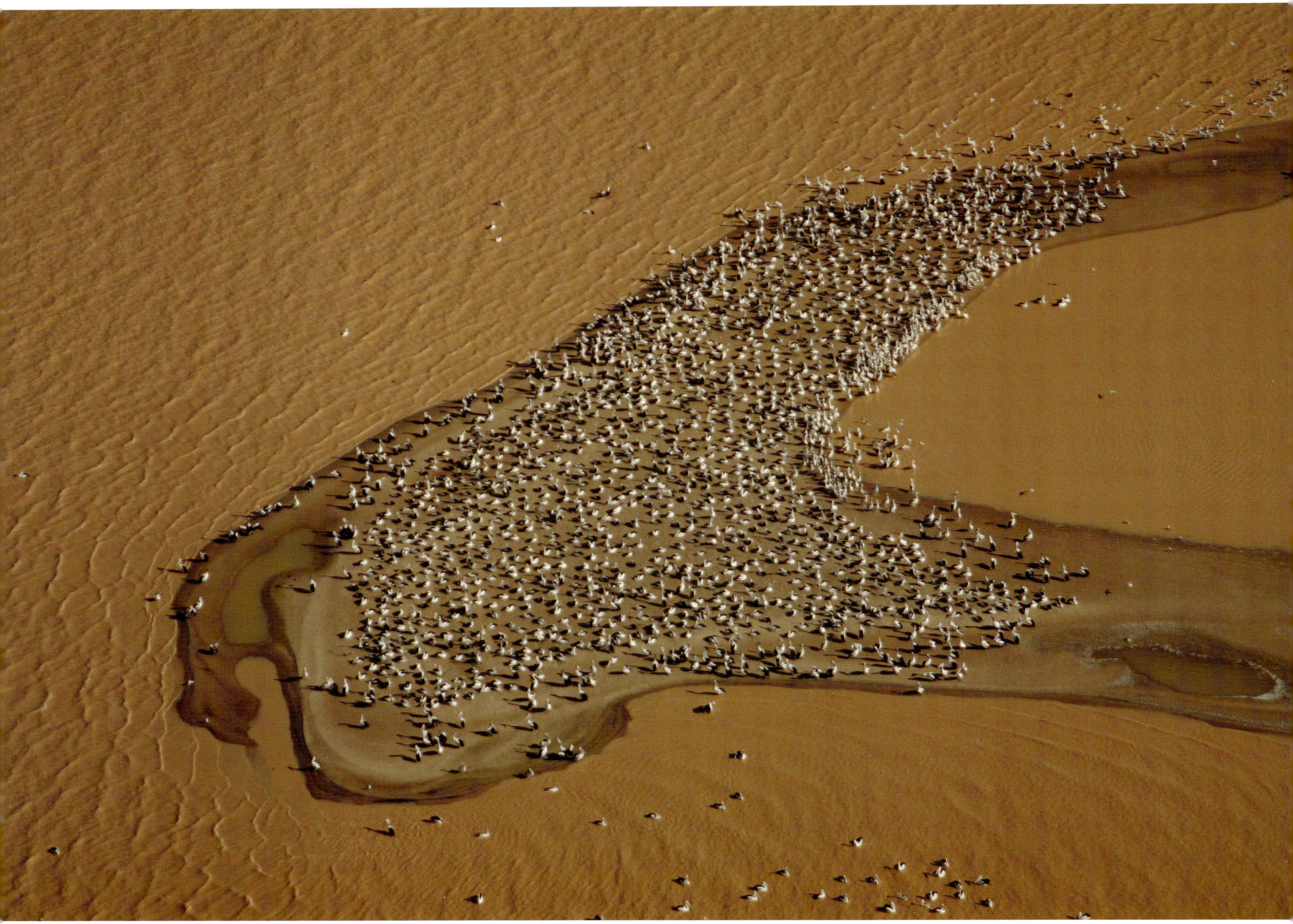

They crammed together on two sand dunes jutting out into the lake. There were fish supplies aplenty, providing perfect breeding conditions. Everywhere there were eggs and chicks, ungainly bald bundles hovering beneath their parents, trying to steady their stumbles by stretching out their tiny wings. There was a constant demand for food, the squawking from the young only silenced momentarily by the delivery of another meal from the lake.

But nature establishes a sense of order in the midst of all this mayhem, as Professor Kingsford explained. 'You've got all these little chicks that have just hatched out and basically each one has its own little territory which the parents defend and then they'll bring in the fish when they're feeding them.' Kingsford was greatly encouraged by what he was witnessing. It was one of the biggest pelican breeding colonies ever recorded in this part of the Lake Eyre Basin. 'There are probably 40,000 to 60,000 here. It's very difficult to know because they're so close together. It's great to see because there's so many places that these guys are feeling the pinch.'

Scientists can still only theorise about what triggers the influx of birds at flood times. Professor Kingsford explained:

> *We're just beginning to get some tantalising ideas. For example, we think these water birds are capable of travelling incredibly long distances in a very short time, so we think they could take reconnaissance trips to check out whether one of the rivers is actually running. And as you can imagine some of the chicks that hatched here are going to have imprinted on their minds that Lake Eyre Basin is a place to hang out when it's boom time, and they in some way can sense when there's a big rain depression coming across. That's what we think happens, but really we're just in the guessing game.*

For his part, Rex Ellis is happy for nature to retain one of the great mysteries of the outback: 'I reckon it's good that they don't know some of these things, and they probably never will!'

Just as astounding was the explosion in fish numbers. Native fish survive during the long drought years by finding refuge in the outback springs and in the drying waterholes along the rivers. When the flood comes, it sparks a frenetic breeding cycle. Fish in huge numbers are carried along by the floodwaters, taking their place in a food chain that suddenly erupts in the desert. As they feed on the micro aquatic life — plant and animal — the birds feast on them. Native fish are enormously resilient. Some are able to withstand huge temperature changes in order to cope with the cold winters and the searing summers. And they'll go to great lengths to follow the water wherever it goes.

In 2009, an enormous pelican breeding colony formed on a large lake on Eyre Creek. It numbered more than 100,000 nests.

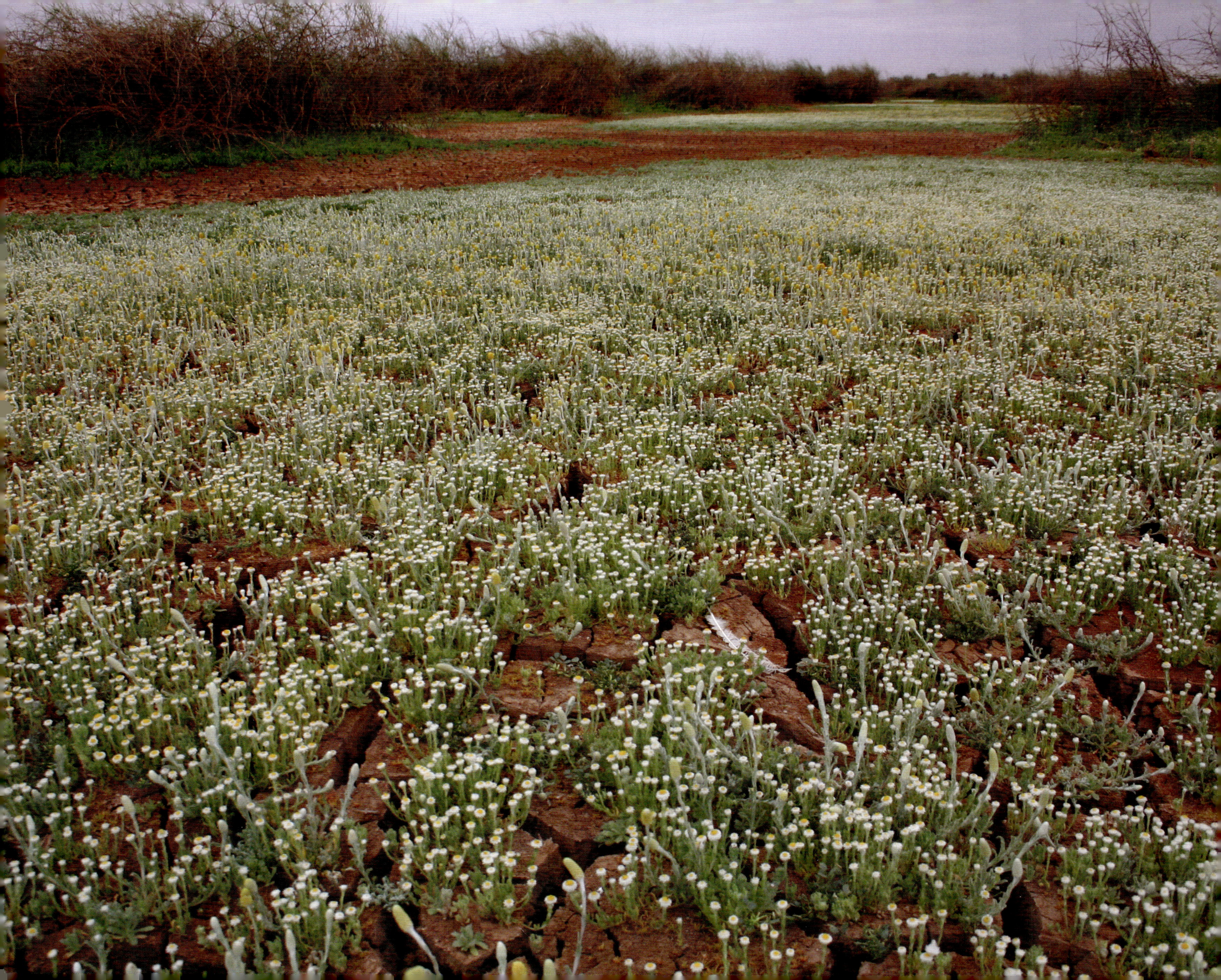

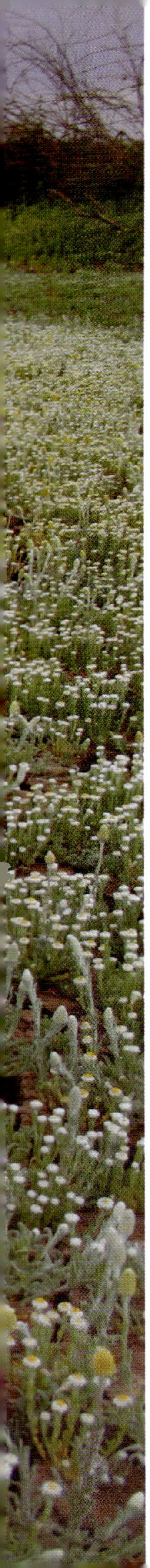

The desert wakes

After the floods, wildflowers emerge from the cracked earth of the Eyre Creek floodplain. Here, the common white sunray (Rhodanthe floribunda).

The desert had been jolted out of its long slumber. Life, on every level, had burst forth as the floodwaters coursed towards Lake Eyre. North of the lake, the Eyre Creek and the Diamantina River drained into an enormous system of channels known as Goyder's Lagoon. From the air there are few more spectacular sights than the braided channels forming intricate patterns, running through a vibrant green floodplain interspersed with splashes of purple, yellow and red from patches of wildflowers. From here the water funnelled into Warburton Creek and down to Lake Eyre. Parts of the desert had turned into rich grazing land. It was time to restock the country.

On Cowarie Station, stretching over 4000 square kilometres just south of Goyder's Lagoon, Sharon Oldfield welcomed home cattle she had trucked out in the depths of the drought to a property at Cunnamulla in Queensland. Warburton Creek, which runs through her property, offered new security of water and feed. There had been some very tough years on Cowarie. Before the long drought took hold, Sharon Oldfield lost her husband, Grant, in a plane crash and was left to bring up three young children and run the station. Challenge enough for anyone but her upbringing in Sydney had been far from the outback. After training to become a nurse she had decided to take an outback adventure and went to work in the Birdsville Hospital. Soon afterwards she met her husband and started a new life in the desert on the edge of Lake Eyre.

Much of Cowarie Station is desert. It was first settled in 1876 and became an outpost for the workforce that had moved into the area, including shearers, well sinkers, station hands and drovers. Cowarie

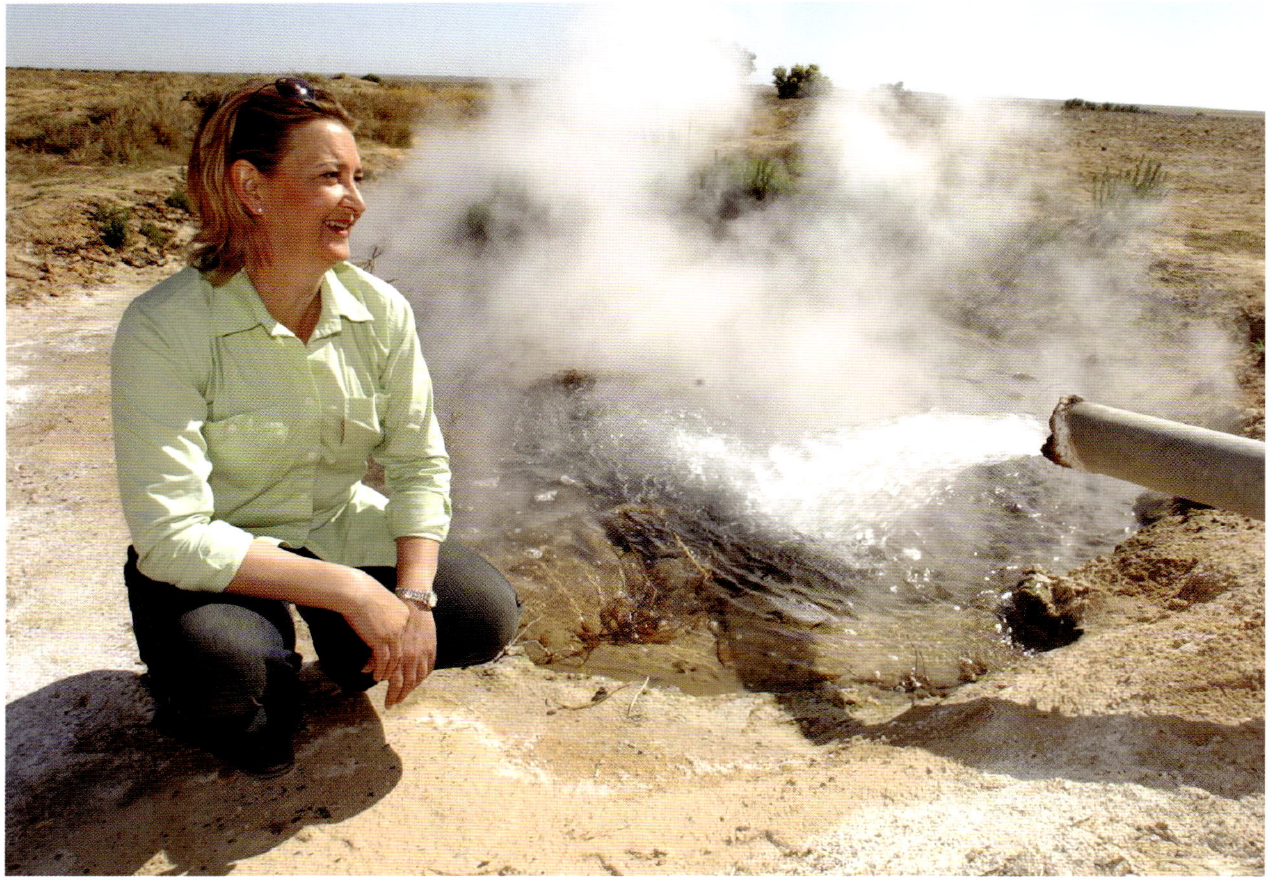

Pastoralist Sharon Oldfield (left), who has single-handedly managed the 4000 square kilometres of Cowarie Station through plenty of tough times. An inland sea of yellow wildflowers (Pycnosorus melleus) *(right) near Lake Eyre in 2010.*

even had its own post office — records show that 342 letters were received at the Cowarie Post Office in 1877. The property relies on the occasional floods to provide water and pasture growth along Warburton Creek. But so desperate did it become on Cowarie in 2008 that Sharon Oldfield was forced to send 2000 cattle away to save them. Just a patch of lawn, watered from an artesian well, prevented the drought from reaching right to the doorstep of the homestead, but nothing could stop the dust storms. Year after year it got worse. People in the outback who are accustomed to weathering the bad times began to wonder if they would survive this one.

Finally the flooding of 2009 put water back down the Warburton, reviving fortunes on Cowarie. It was an emotional day for Sharon Oldfield when her cattle were trucked back from Queensland. Looking out over the floodplains running down to Warburton Creek, with the cattle up to their knees in sweet new pasture, wildflowers bursting out in patches of yellow and purple, and the water running strongly, she declared, 'It's absolutely magnificent. The desert has its best dress on right now. It is a land of extreme variability and it's certainly a land of boom and bust cycles, unfortunately the bust had gone on for such a long time you just truly forgot what the boom looked like.'

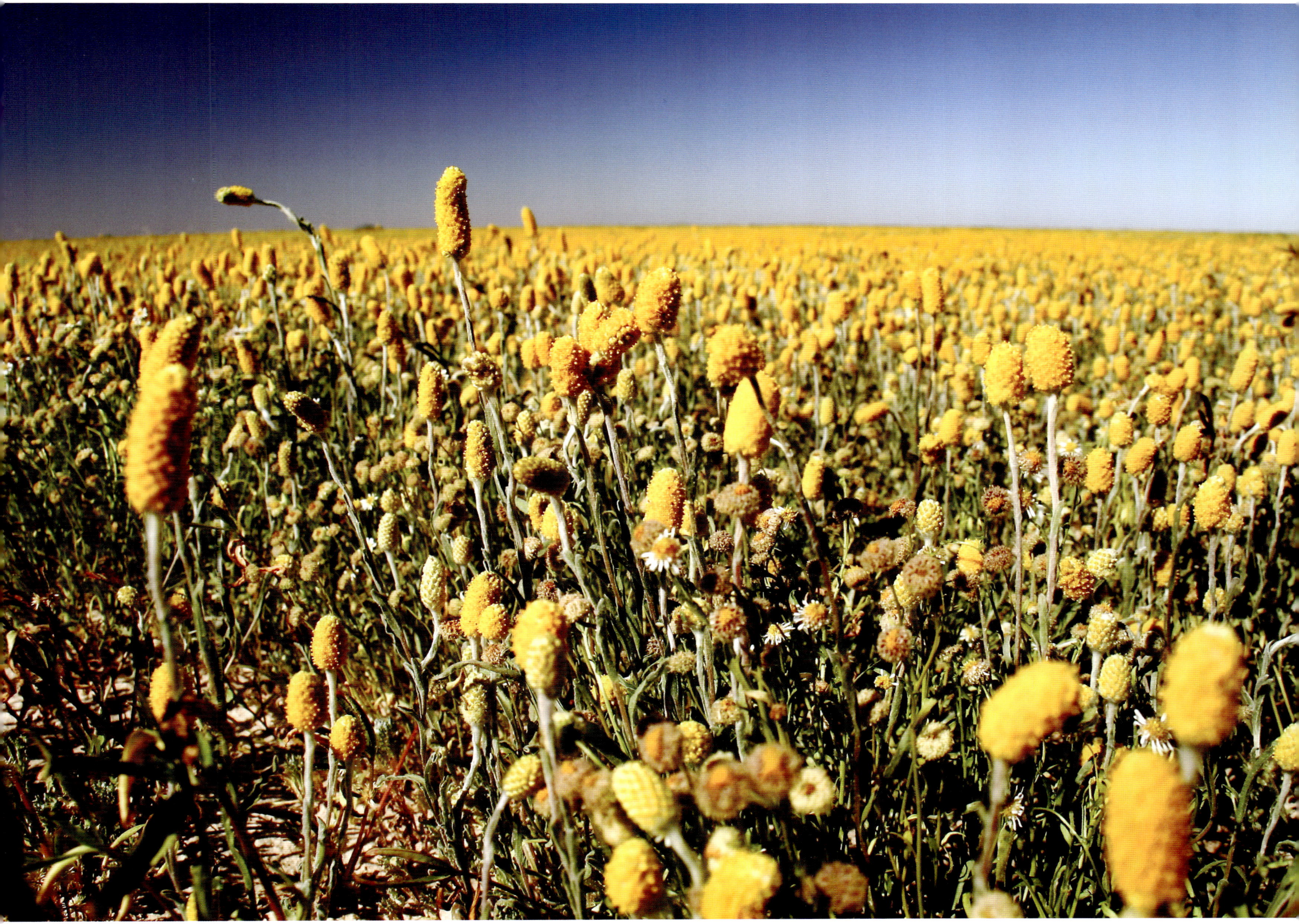

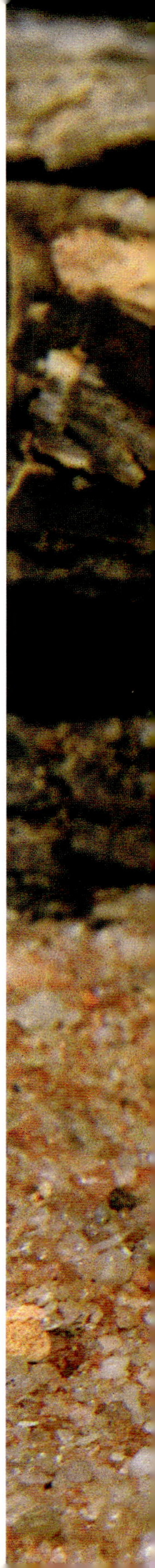

A fat-tailed dunnart (Sminthopsis crassicaudata).
Overleaf: In 2010, the floods once again spread over Lake Eyre, covering much of the lake.

Just below Cowarie, also on the Warburton, is Kalamurina Station. It's an even bigger property, covering more than 6500 square kilometres of desert country running all the way to Lake Eyre. Warburton Creek and a number of other waterways empty into Lake Eyre on Kalamurina's southern boundary, which is marked by the lake's shoreline.

Kalamurina was a struggling cattle station, purchased in the depths of the drought in December 2007 by the Australian Wildlife Conservancy, a nature group supported by donors anxious to see the protection of the environment. AWC has bought twenty-one properties across Australia to establish a network of wildlife sanctuaries. Much of Kalamurina is covered by the barren sand dunes of the Tirari Desert, but it also includes creeks, lakes and floodplains supporting a long list of threatened flora and fauna. The 2009 flood provided a perfect opportunity to show donors the big slice of Central Australia they had helped to preserve and groups were flown in to a campsite established in the sand hills beside the flowing Warburton Creek.

According to AWC's chief executive Atticus Fleming, Kalamurina is a hot spot for threatened wildlife: 'And Central Australia, and of course Australia, has the world's worst mammal extinction rate, so protecting a place like this is just so important.' Mammals considered to be at serious risk in the region include a native rodent, the dusky hopping mouse, which was once widespread through the interior but is now considered vulnerable, and two species of carnivorous marsupials, the ampurta and the kultarr. Surveys on Kalamurina have identified 160 bird species.

Scientists carrying out the survey work were excited about the boost the flow in Warburton Creek, and other waterways, would provide to the dwindling native animal numbers. And there are plans to reintroduce some species found to have already disappeared. Fleming explained: 'In five years time it would be nice to be back here and see this country as it was 100 or 150 years ago before a lot of the changes that came with European settlement. So it's about protecting what's here and restoring these ecosystems over time.'

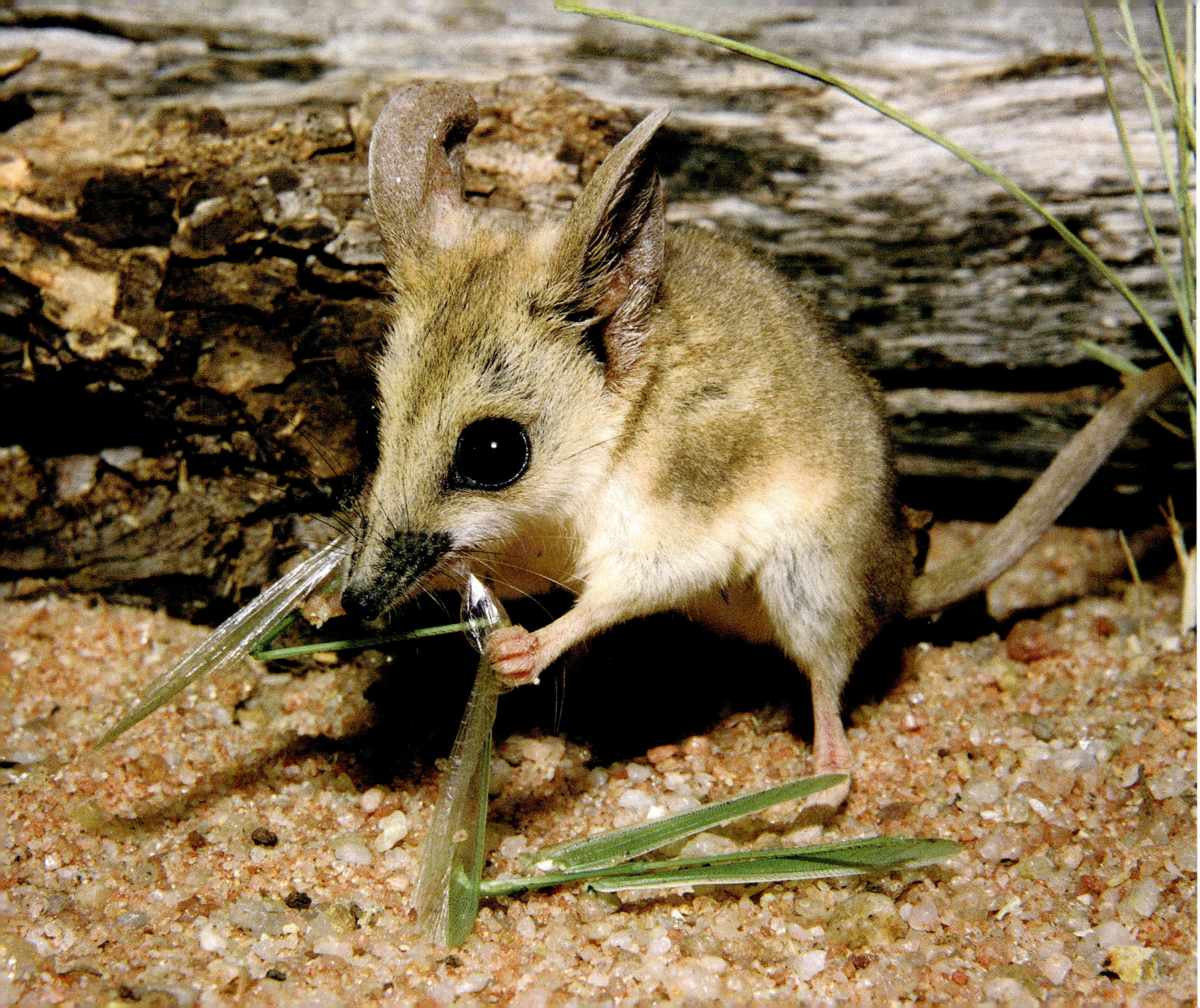

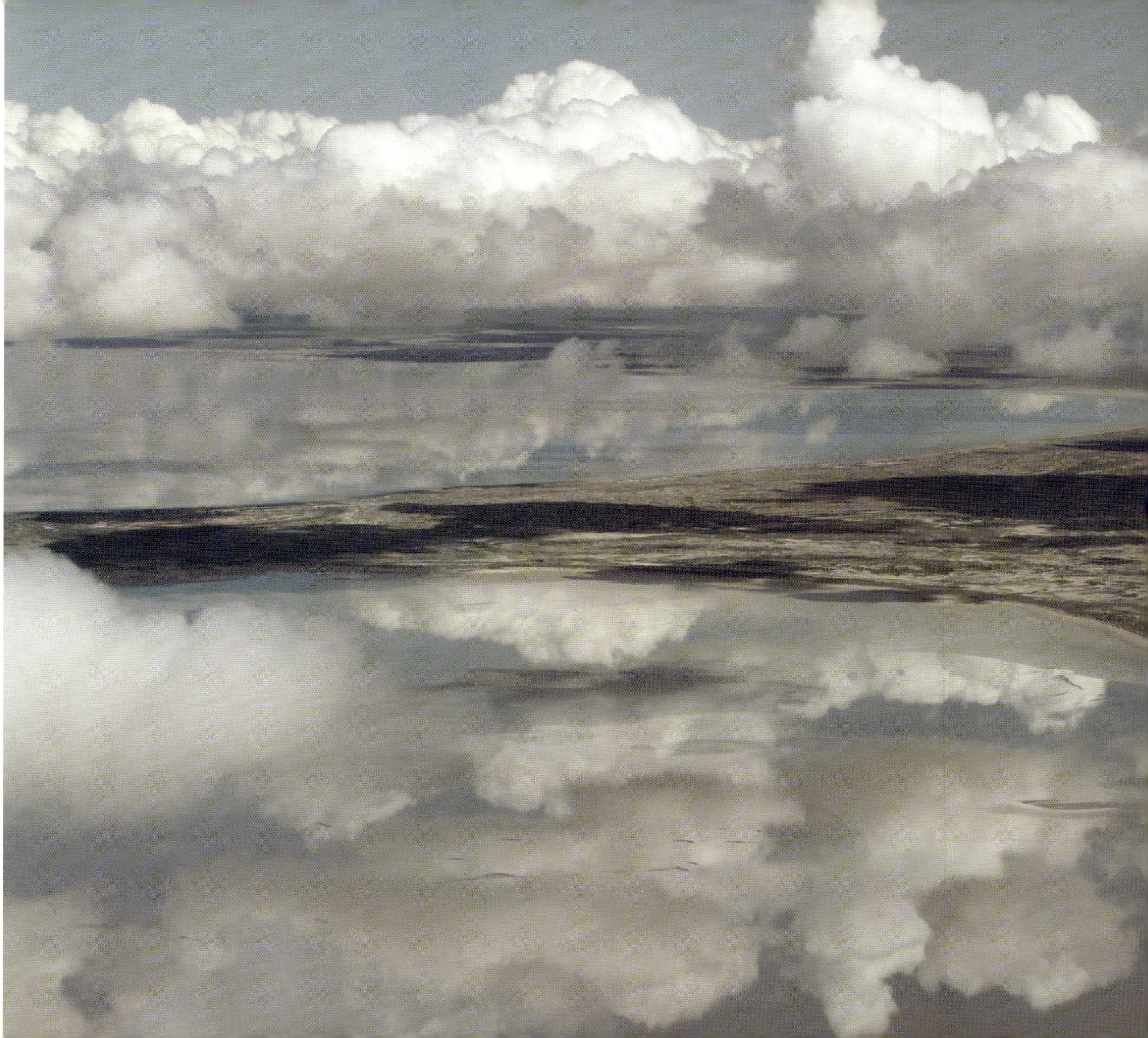

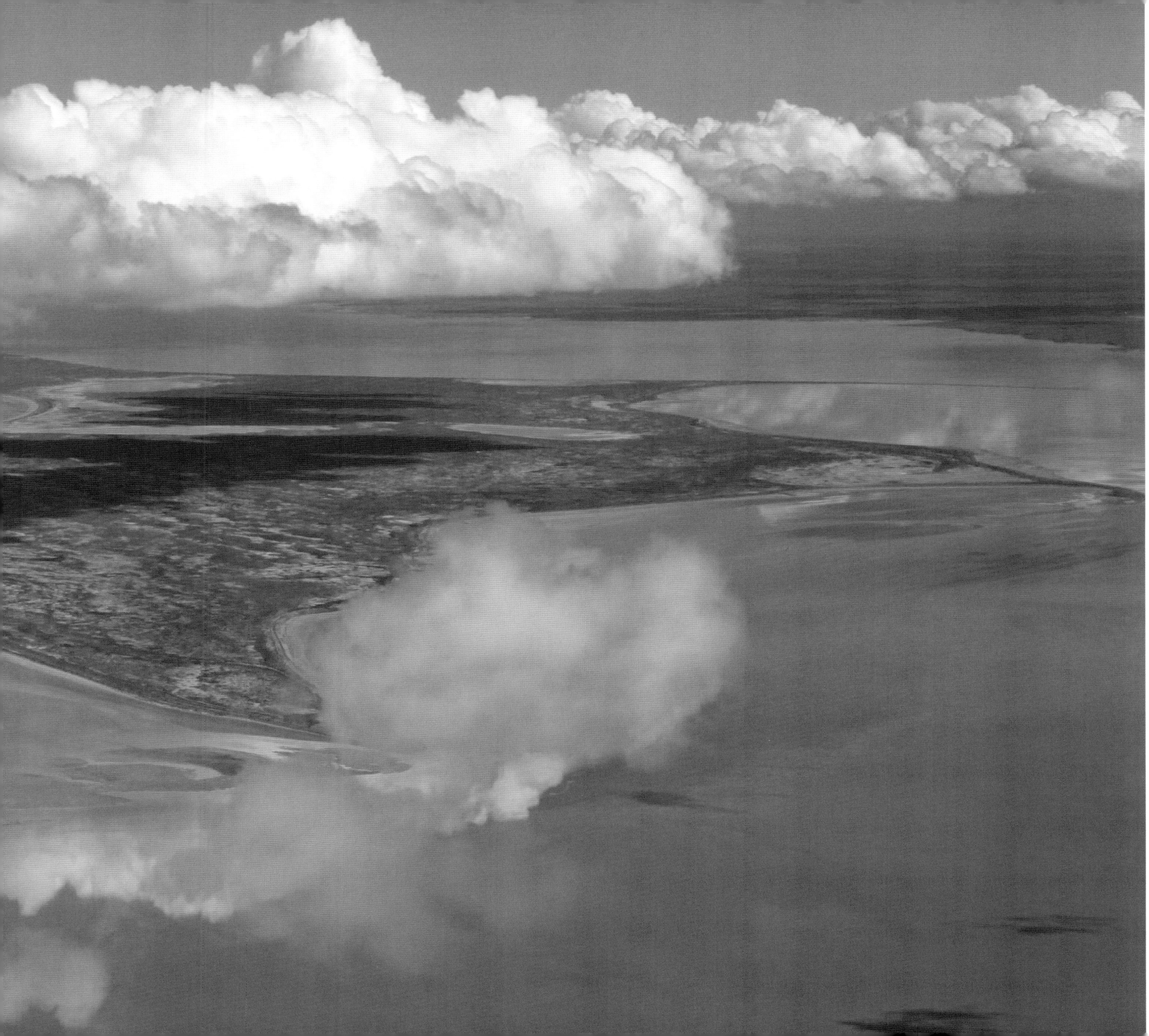

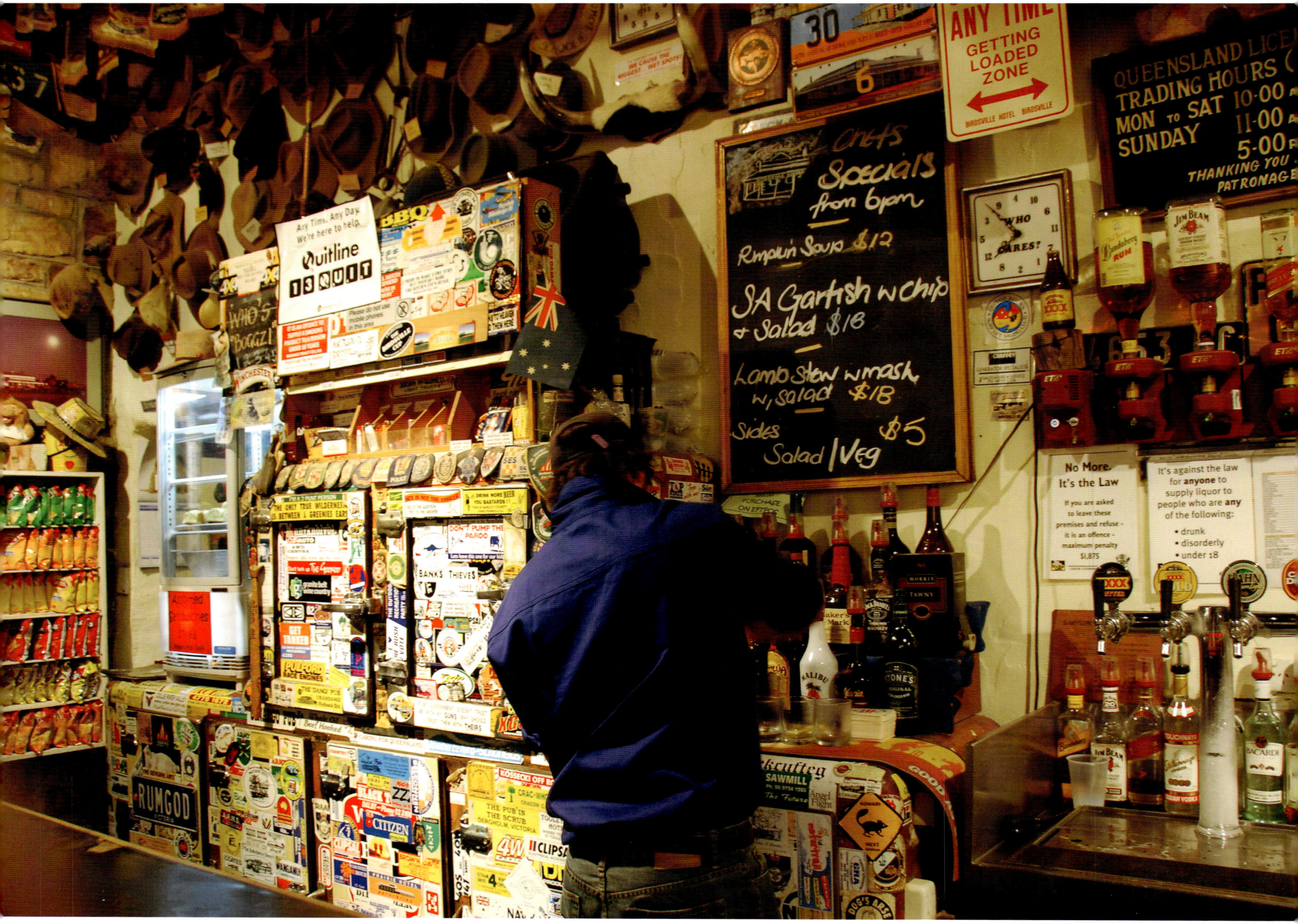
ANY TIME
GETTING LOADED ZONE
BIRDSVILLE HOTEL BIRDSVILLE
QUEENSLAND LICE
TRADING HOURS (
MON to SAT 10-00
11-00
SUNDAY 5-00
THANKING YOU
PATRONAGE
Chefs
Specials
from 6pm
Rmpkin Soup $12
SA Garfish w chip
+ Salad $18
Lamb Stew w mash
w, salad $18
Sides $5
Salad | Veg
Any Time, Any Day
We're here to help.
Quitline
13 QUIT
No More.
It's the Law
It's against the law
for anyone to
supply liquor to
people who are any
of the following:
• drunk
• disorderly
• under 18
RUMGOD
CITIZEN
BANKS THIEVES

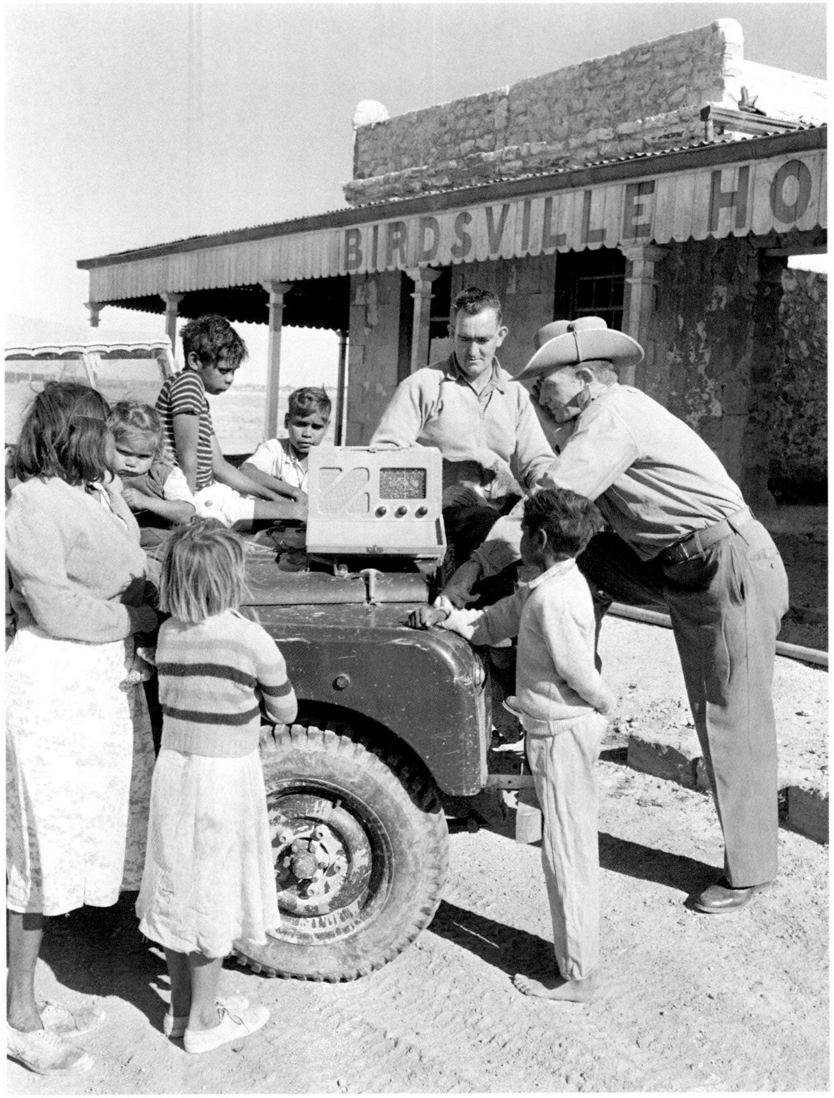

Opposite: Inside the Birdsville hotel — last drinks before far Western Queensland — the stockmen's hats and stickers decorating the wall tell of travellers past. Hub of the town (left) — Birdsville's policeman, the hotel's publican and other locals listen to the radio outside the pub in 1956.

The renewed optimism was carried through the outback by the floodwaters. 'From a pastoralist's point of view we get excited because we know that when all the water's gone we've got feed like this,' explained David Brook, as he pointed to the knee-high native grasses that now covered the river bank and stretched out across what had been a barren floodplain before the water arrived.

There was a buoyant mood among the stockmen and other drinkers in the famous Birdsville Hotel, the last stop for drinks in far western Queensland, just on the edge of the Simpson Desert. The Birdsville pub is part of bush legend, celebrated since the 1950s as the quintessential outback drinking spot, a cartoonist's dream. Here thirsty travellers could land their planes on the dirt strip and taxi right up to the front door.

In the bar, as is the tradition in pubs through the outback, the ceiling and walls are covered in the battered hats of stockmen who have graced the bar over the decades, a who's who of the station workforce of the area. This town of just 100 people once boasted three pubs. They were the days when the surrounding stations employed big numbers and droving teams walked the cattle to market through Birdsville. Then trucks replaced the drovers and modern management practices cut the workforce on the properties. But as the stockmen breasted the bar at the Birdsville pub in 2009, still in their wide-brimmed hats and swapping yarns, it seemed that little had really changed. The weather still dominated the discussion. All the talk was of the

A contented mob of Brahman cattle on the floodplain.

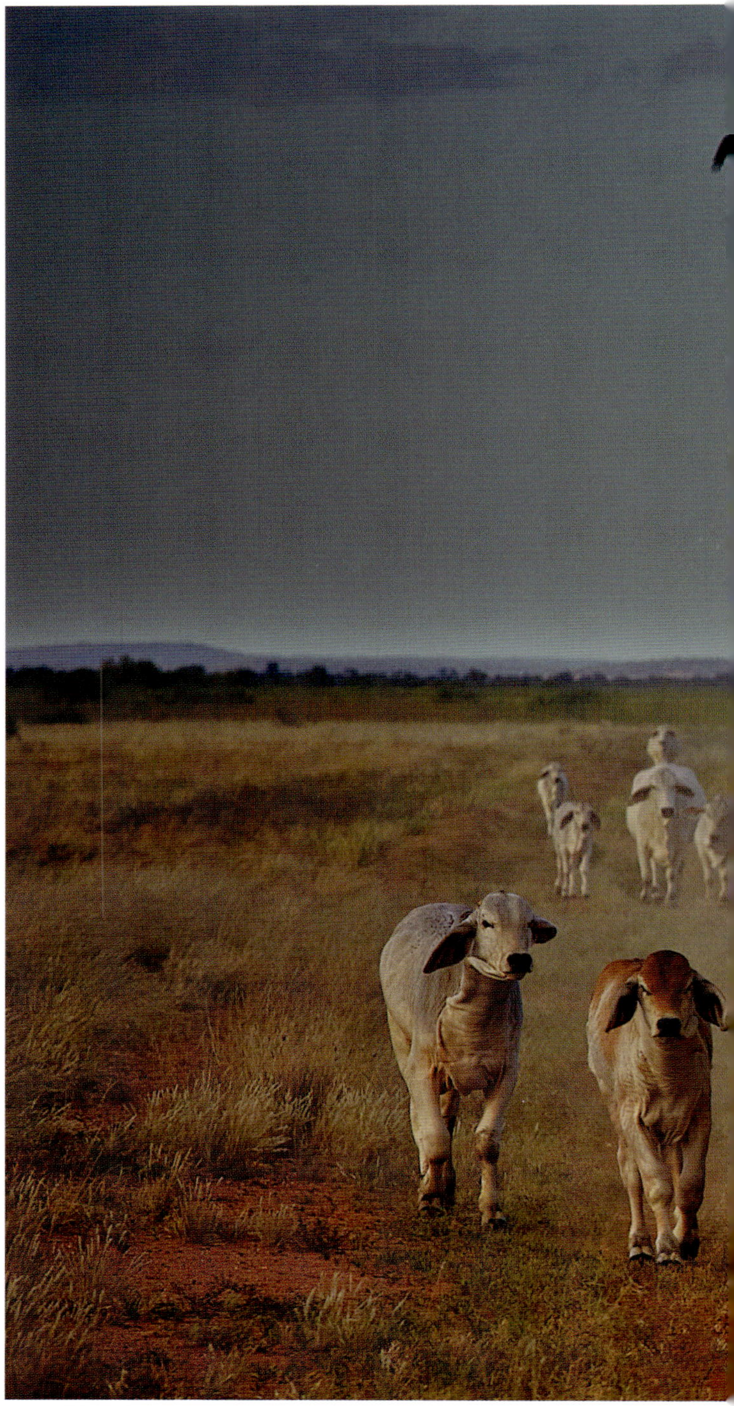

flood and the impact it would have. Everyone agreed it would be a shot in the arm for the cattle industry — which would give Birdsville a lift — and that it would probably provide a spark to the struggling tourist trade as well.

On a clear, still dawn, the sound of lowing cattle could be heard drifting across the sand dunes of the Simpson Desert, west of Birdsville. A mob of red and white Herefords, standing out against the yellow sand, were being coaxed along by stockmen on horseback and motorbikes. The cattle were coming off Adria Downs Station to play a support role in the annual Birdsville bronco-branding and rodeo event. The floods had injected considerable enthusiasm into the gathering. This would be a celebration of the changing seasons — and of the history of the cattle industry.

Bronco branding was developed by the early outback stockmen, who were forced to adapt to the vast size of the properties. They moved from camp to camp, mustering the cattle. Horsemen would keep the mob together while a stockman would go in and lasso a beast and pull it out to a team of jackeroos who would up-end it and brand it. The practice has faded out in the industry but the competition among the stockmen of today, to lasso and brand against the clock, remains fierce. And it's not just for the young. Even in his eighties, Charlie Rayment takes his place at the Birdsville event in a team that includes his grandson. Charlie Rayment grew up in the mustering camps when bronco branding was just part of the job. It's still second nature to him. He's lived on cattle stations in western Queensland all his life — apart from the time that he went away to fight for Australia in the Second World War. But even he was left to wonder when the rain would come again when the big drought enveloped the outback during the last decade: 'I think all of us that have worked in this country, I think we live on hope most of the time, hoping we'll live long enough to see another big flood.'

Beyond Birdsville and Goyder's Lagoon, the water that had coursed down Warburton Creek spread wide over the thick salt surface of Lake

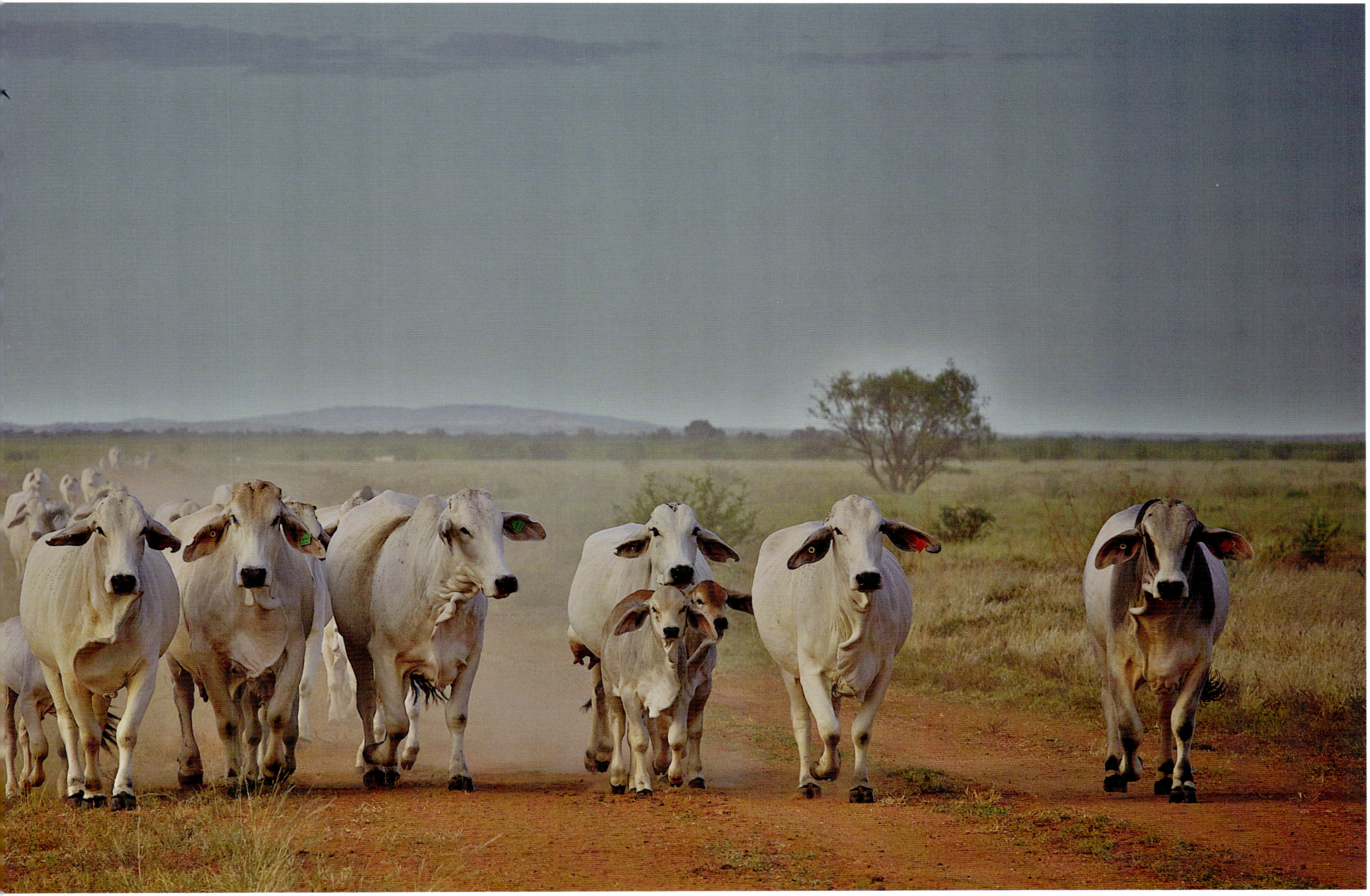

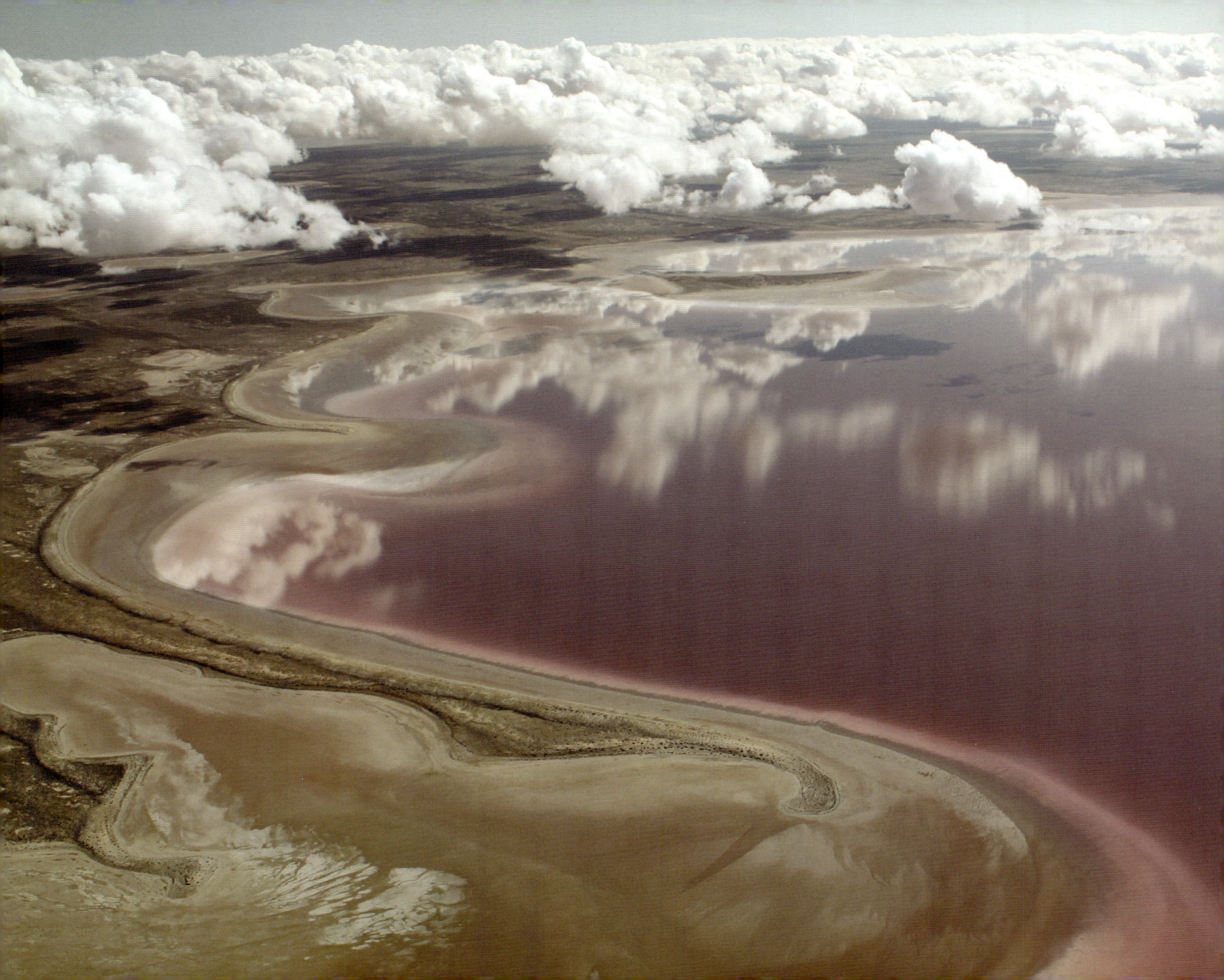

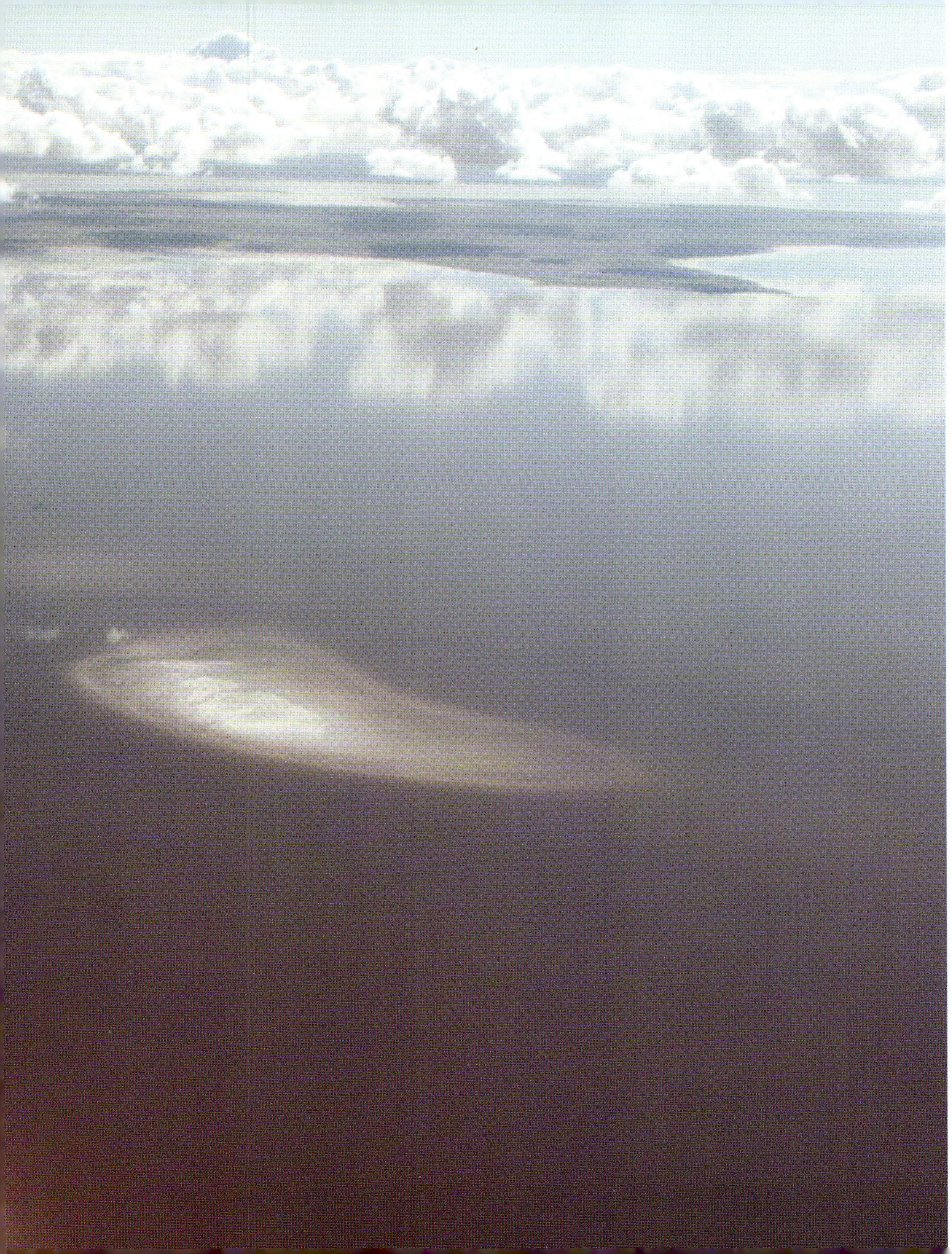

Pinks and browns and blues emerge when salt and fresh water interact in Lake Eyre. The algae (Dunaliella salina) *produces the pink hue when the lake is full, while islands of salt float like icebergs in the water.*

Eyre. The blinding white was now infused with other colours — shades of pink, blue and brown popped up as the salt dissolved in the fresh water. The stunning images changed with every shift of the sun.

Out in the middle of the lake, big chunks of salt, like icebergs, were caught in the brilliant blue of the waters. Where the water and the sky met a mirror image formed. On days when the lake and the sky merge into one it can become very tricky identifying the horizon — as some pilots have found to their cost, suddenly discovering they are in the water.

A colony of pelicans had established itself on a sandy ridge that was now an island in Lake Eyre. Other birds would follow — tracking the floodwaters, rich with fish and other food, down to the lake. The fresh supplies would support life until evaporation took hold as the summer heat arrived. The annual evaporation rate in the Lake Eyre region is a staggering 2.5 metres. As water in the lake drops, salt levels rise dramatically — becoming far too salty to sustain microscopic life, the fish or the birds.

Outback celebrations

The flooding of 2009 promised to deliver a spectacular spring in the outback. The transformation of Central Australia was almost complete. Replenished waterholes, lakes and rivers were pulsating with life and the rising heat had brought out a blaze of wildflowers on drying areas of the floodplain. The historic Lake Eyre flooding had become big news and the dust rose on the outback roads as travellers joined a convoy heading to the centre to take in the rare event. Many timed their adventures to coincide with Australia's most famous annual bush race meeting — the Birdsville Cup — which is held in early September. It had its beginnings in 1882, as a test of horsemanship between stockmen from rival stations in the area, but has grown over the years into a serious two-day race meeting to accommodate a long list of starters brought in by trainers from a wide area of regional Queensland. The bookies arrive in big numbers too.

Through the 1950s and 1960s, Birdsville became synonymous with the outback. The remote town, and its annual race meeting, captured the imagination of a generation of Australians and the Birdsville races are high on the 'bucket list' of many outback travellers. They arrive with every form of campervan, caravan and four-wheel drive. Space in the caravan park is booked out weeks ahead.

The races go by the appropriate slogan 'Where the dust never settles', and the meeting is still held on a track carved out of the dry floodplain just out of Birdsville. News of the flooding of Lake Eyre swelled the numbers in 2009. A record crowd of more than 7000 people — far above any previous attendance — descended on the tiny outback town. The airstrip was lined with aircraft, small and large, with people setting up camp under the wings. Outside the settlement people could be found camped all along the Diamantina River. In Birdsville, huge queues formed for food, fuel and showers. The Birdsville Hotel was under siege from thirsty visitors. Learning the lessons of earlier years, the stated pub policy is 'Drink and drop!' Only cans and plastic glasses are served. By nightfall drinkers are surrounded by a sea of

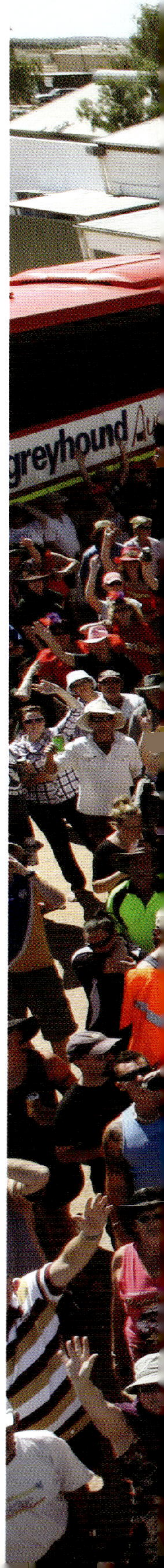

After the 2009 floods, the historic Birdsville races attracted a record crowd, which transformed the tiny outback town.

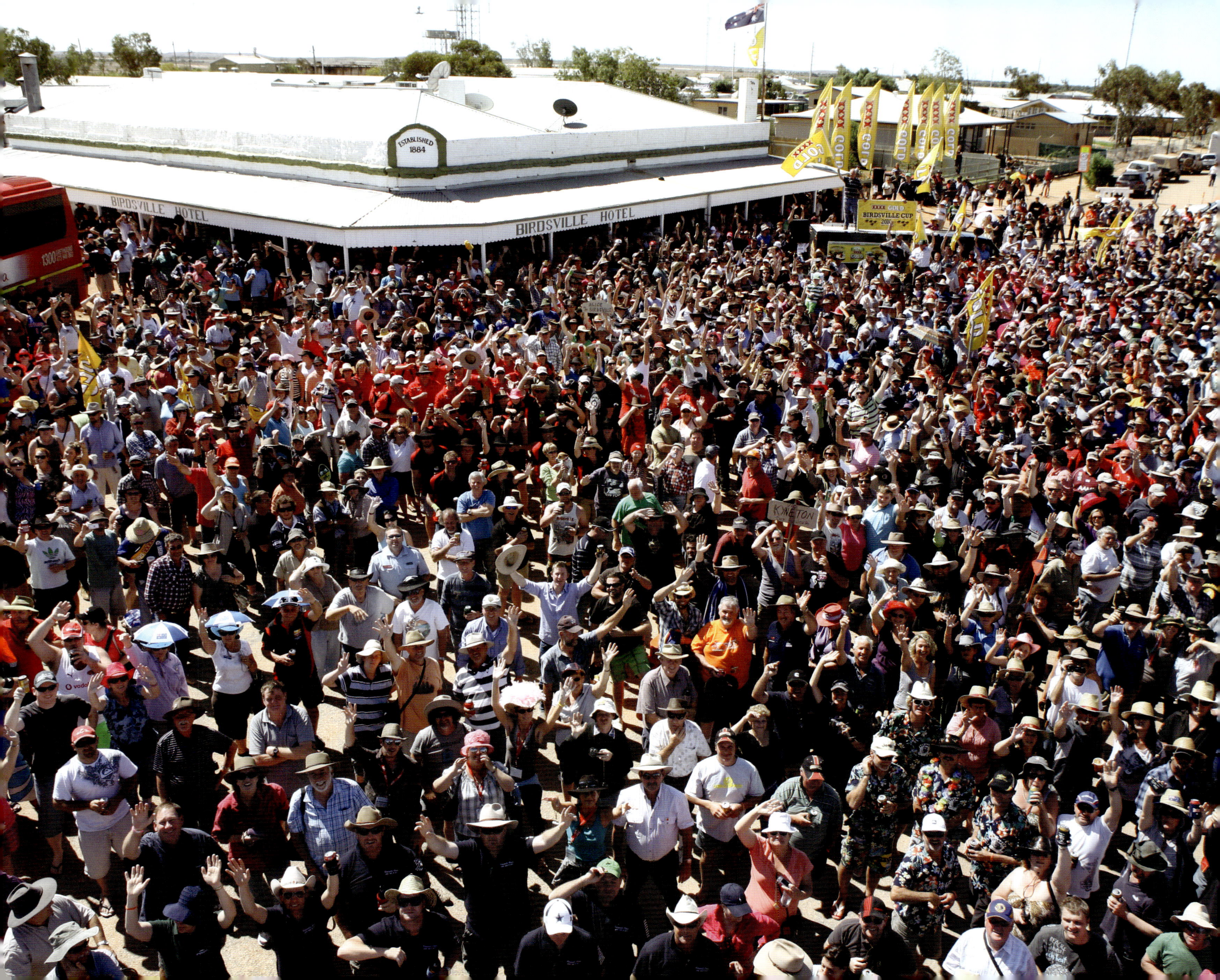

ESTABLISHED
1884
BIRDSVILLE HOTEL
BIRDSVILLE HOTEL
BIRDSVILLE CUP
KYNETON

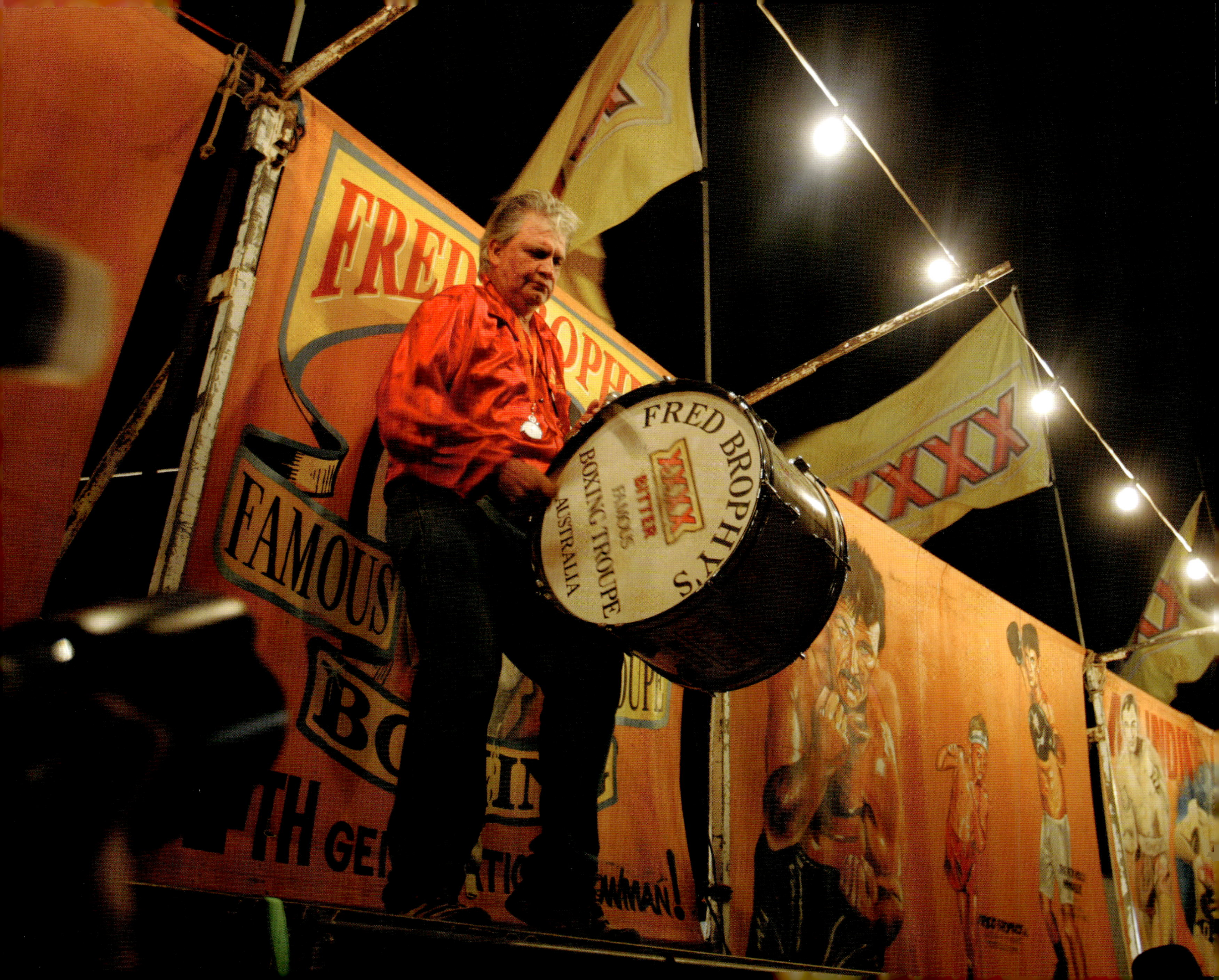

FRED
FAMOUS
FRED BROPHY'S
XXXX
BITTER
FAMOUS
BOXING TROUPE
AUSTRALIA
XXXX

Drumming up contestants to fight in his travelling boxing tent in Birdsville in 2010. Fred Brophy is an institution around outback Australia

crushed aluminium and plastic. It stays that way until 2am when the cleaning brigade moves in. By opening time the next day they've cleared the boards for the next onslaught. But there is seldom any trouble. The fighting is reserved for a big tent across the road from the pub.

'Ladies and gentlemen, my name's Fred Brophy and I'm the first referee in the outback. Give them a rally on the bells and drum.' The beating of a drum and the ringing of a bell signalled the night's entertainment in Birdsville. The last of the great outback boxing tents had opened for business. Out the front, high on a boardwalk, Fred Brophy, the old-time showman, was doing what he does best — pulling a crowd. 'This is where champions are discovered and we'll sort the men out from the women, and it don't make any difference if you win or you lose, this is where you earn yourself a reputation!' Brophy, flanked by his latest stable of boxers, has been travelling the outback for decades. He pointed to the images of former Australian boxing champions, including Tony Mundine, festooned on the colourful tent. 'All these fighters,' he proudly declared, 'All these old blokes before they fought for Australia had a fight in one of Brophy's boxing tents.' The boxing tents used to be a major sideshow attraction at the big city agricultural shows until questions started being raised about the long-term medical problems that might be associated with the sport — especially for the untrained pugilists plucked from a crowd.

Brophy's show has long been banned in New South Wales and Victoria on health grounds. But not in Birdsville, far western Queensland, and certainly not on the big race weekend.

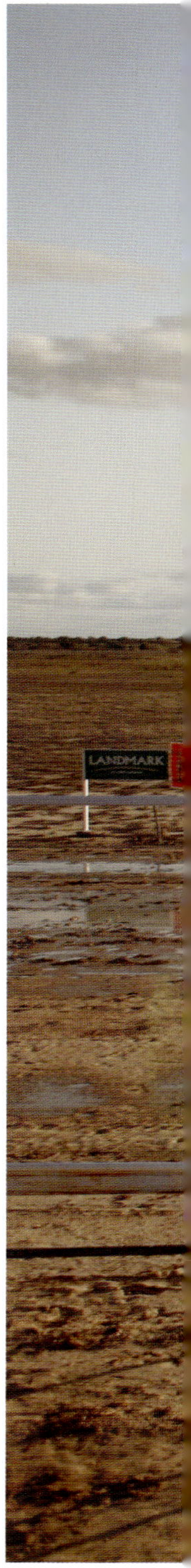

Washed out — the rains of 2010 put a dampener on the race meeting at Birdsville.

'I'm not going to change this boxing tent for anyone in Australia,' Brophy defiantly declared to the cheering crowd, 'No, that's the rule, because I'm just keeping it going — it belongs to everyone in Australia and there's no frills. What you see is what you get. Give them a rally on the bells and drums!' Two of his fighters, in their boxing silks, belted out the Brophy anthem with bell and drum as he cast an eye across the crowd for likely contenders.

Fred Brophy's boxers take on all comers but he insists that his fighters will only go as hard as they have to. It's the prospect of an upset that draws the people in, the chance that one of Brophy's boys will be collared by a stranger harbouring raw talent. And it does happen occasionally, much to the delight of the crowd. On Birdsville Cup weekend there was no shortage of contenders. The boardwalk quickly filled with young men keen to take a tilt at fame — or egged on by their mates to do so. Amongst them was Kenny Dowling, an Irishman working as a ringer on Cordillo Downs, a cattle station that takes up the north-east corner of South Australia. 'Tell me something,' asked Brophy as the Irishman clambered up beside him. 'Have you done any boxing?' Kenny shook his head. 'You haven't! Do you know where you are? Good luck to you … walk the plank … give him a rally on the bells and drums … welcome to Australia!'

The crowd pressed into the tent. The theatre continued inside with Fred Brophy playing ringmaster and referee. The bouts followed a familiar pattern. The challengers almost always come out flailing, hoping to land an early knockout punch. Brophy's boxers deftly evade, biding their time. Soon their opponents run out of puff, and by the final bell it's another points decision to Brophy's troupe. So it was for Kenny. He began like a threshing machine but ended up in an exhausted clinch. But he and the other contenders emerged with pride intact, knowing that their courage would be rewarded by their mates with a drink or two across the road.

The next day, Kenny Dowling made the long trip back to Cordillo Downs. It was still dry out there. The station lay between the flood flows that were working their way down

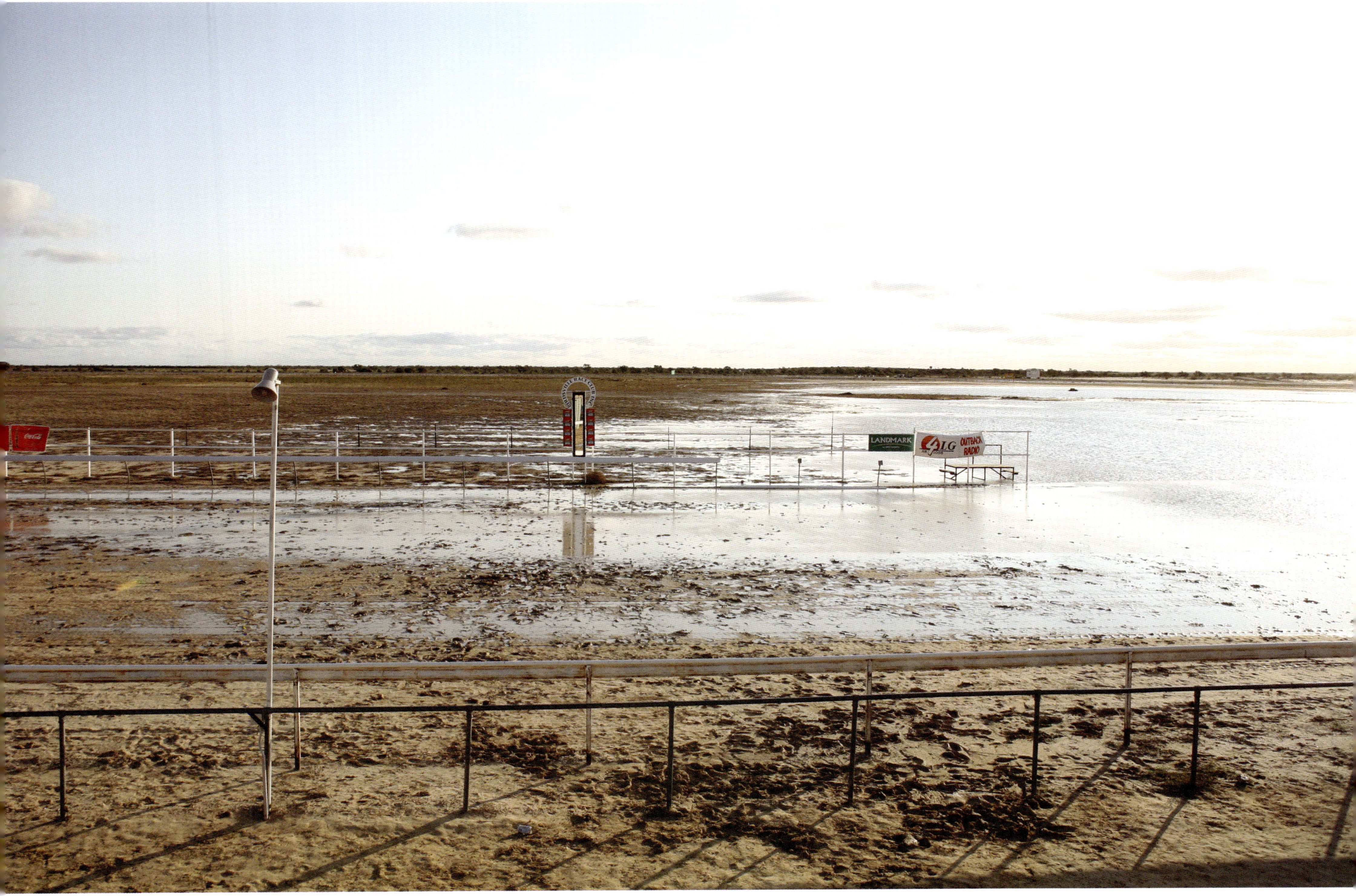
LANDMARK
OUTBACK RADIO

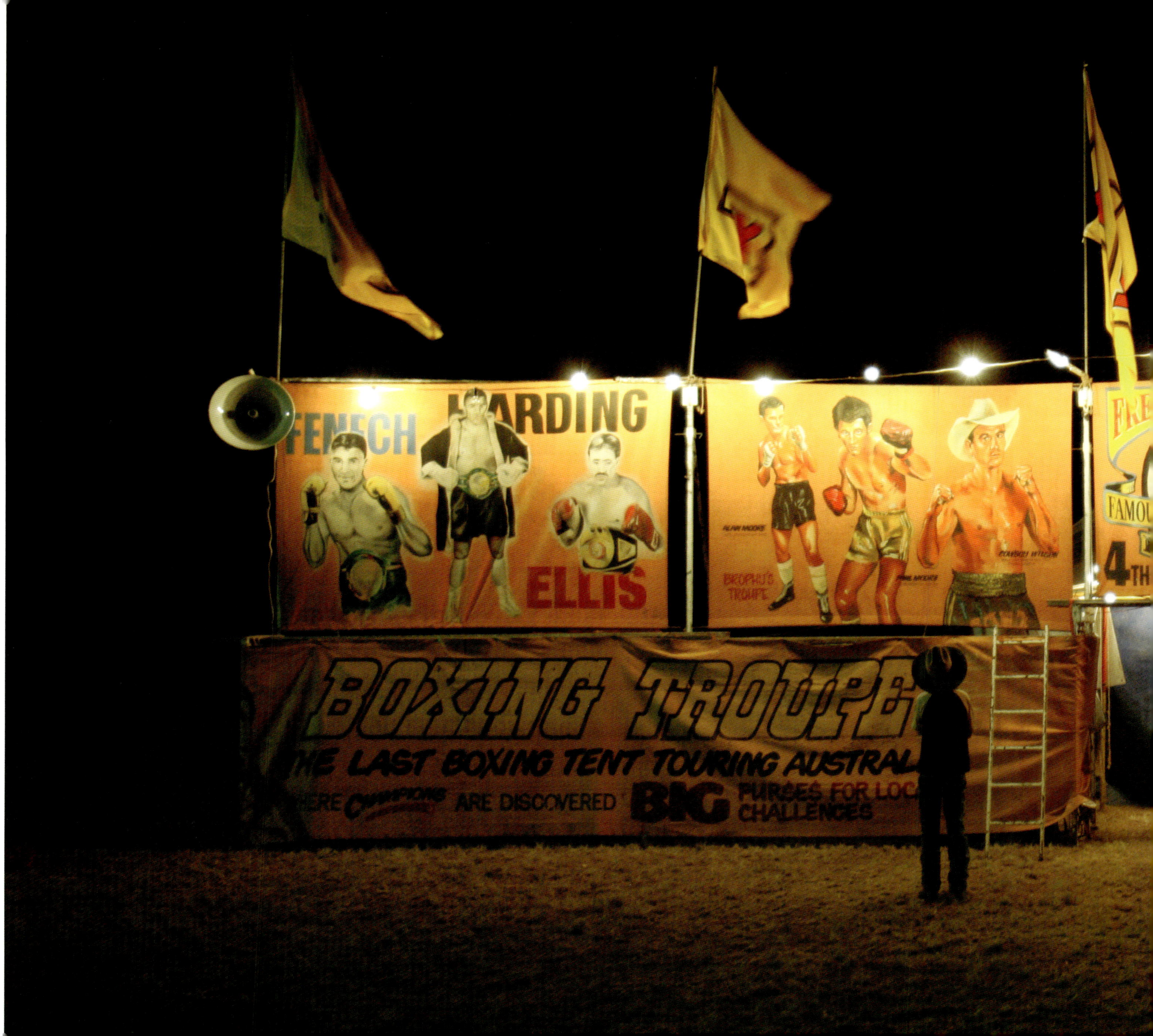
ELLIS
BOXING TROUPE
ARE DISCOVERED
BIG
CHALLENGES

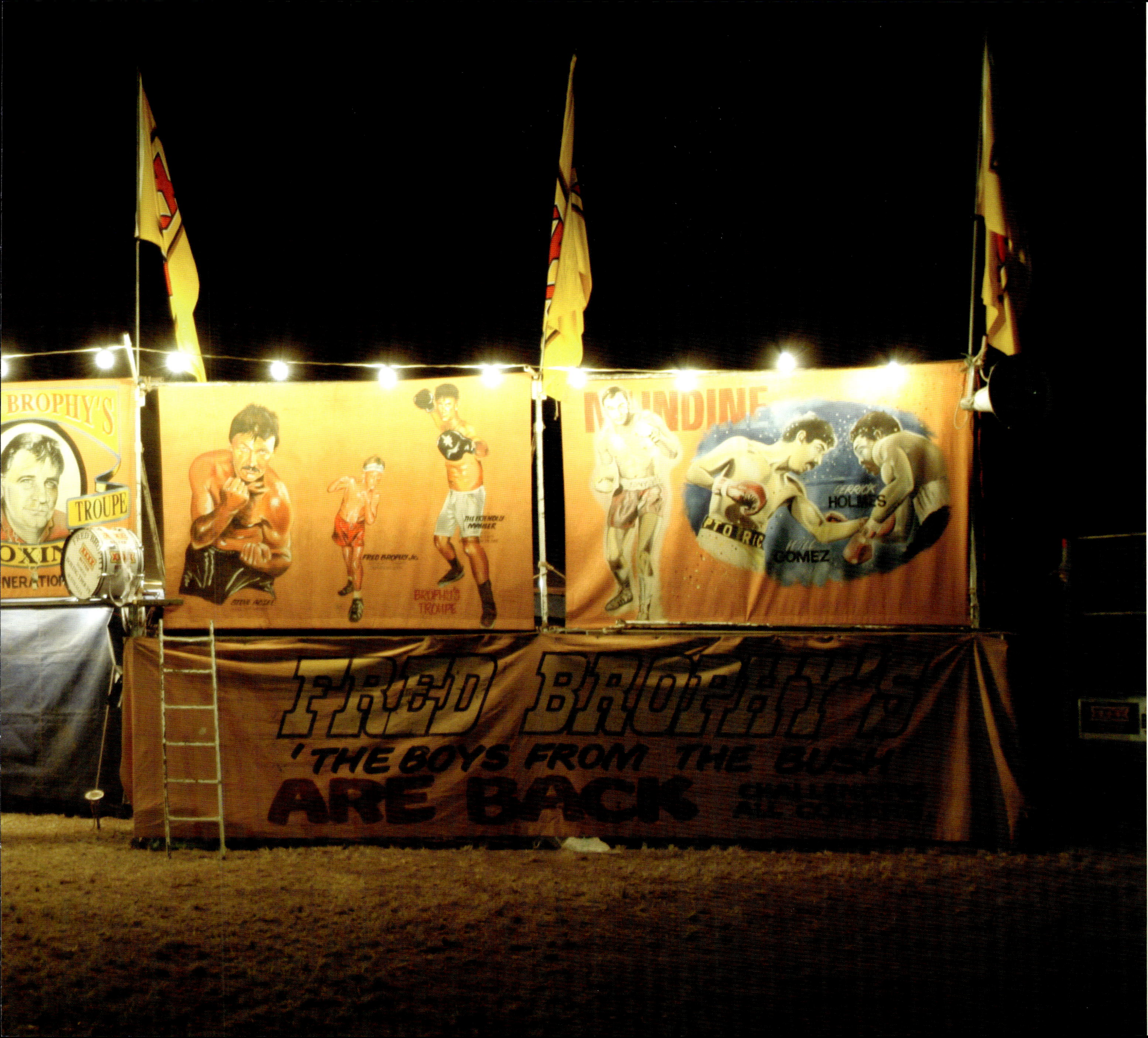
BROPHY'S
TROUPE
GOMEZ
FRED BROPHY'S
'THE BOYS FROM THE BUSH
ARE BACK

David and Nell Brook (right) and their son Anthony, his wife Janet and their family (far right).
Opposite: The old woolshed on Cordillo Downs.

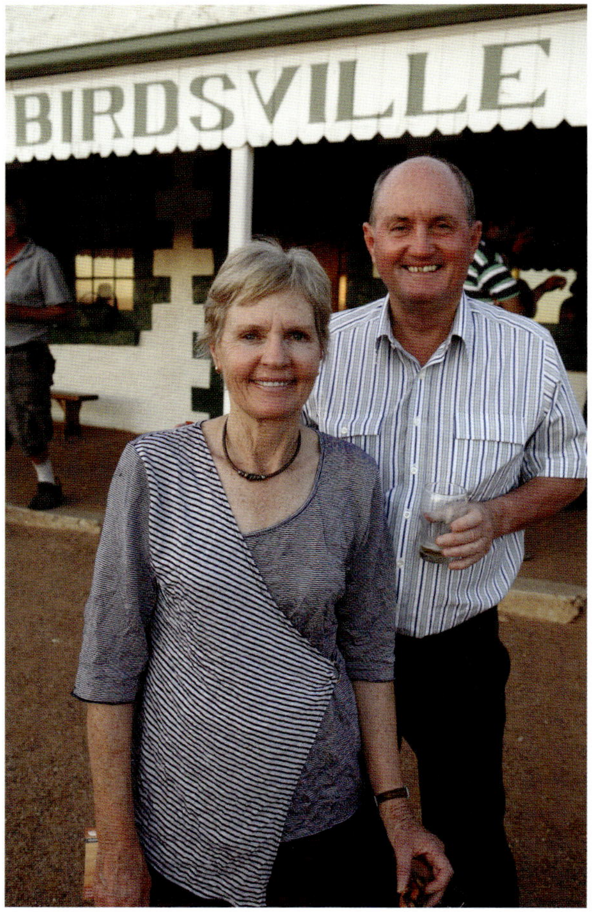

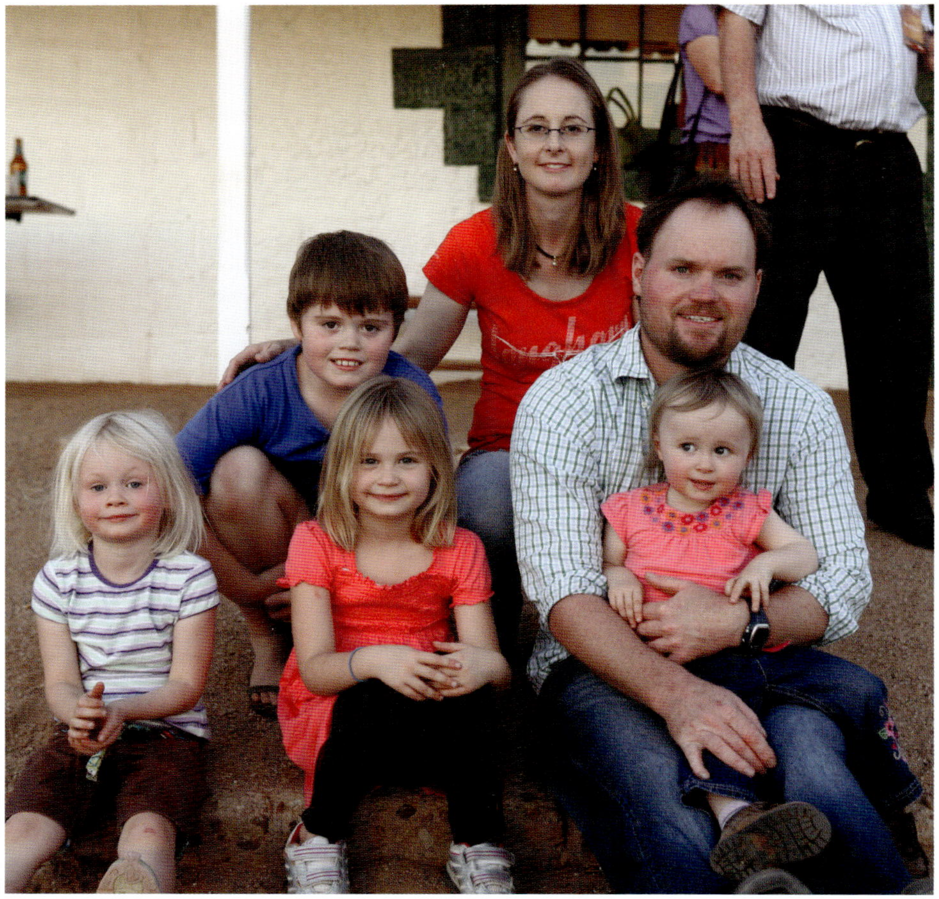

the Diamantina River and Cooper Creek, and there'd been no rain to bring relief to that corner of the outback. While other properties were restocking, cattle were still being moved off Cordillo Downs to greener pastures.

The homestead complex on Cordillo Downs is neatly laid out high on a gibber plain, on the edge of Sturt Stony Desert. The property covers close to 8000 square kilometres — one of the biggest of all the cattle stations in Central Australia. It was first settled in 1875, with cattle and sheep. The optimistic and resolute pioneers made good use of the rocky landscape, constructing impressive buildings in Dutch gable style, including a huge shearing shed with stands for 120 shearers. At one time the property was running 85,000 sheep. Building supplies and other stores were hauled in by the Afghan camel teams, which would then carry out the wool.

In 1885 the cameleers delivered an entire wool-scouring plant and steam engines to Cordillo Downs so the wool clip could be cleaned before it was shipped — removing the desert dust and other material, lightening the load enormously. The old steam engines and other pieces of machinery used in those early days can still be found dotted around the sturdy shell of the old shearing shed on Cordillo Downs. The property is now part of the Brook

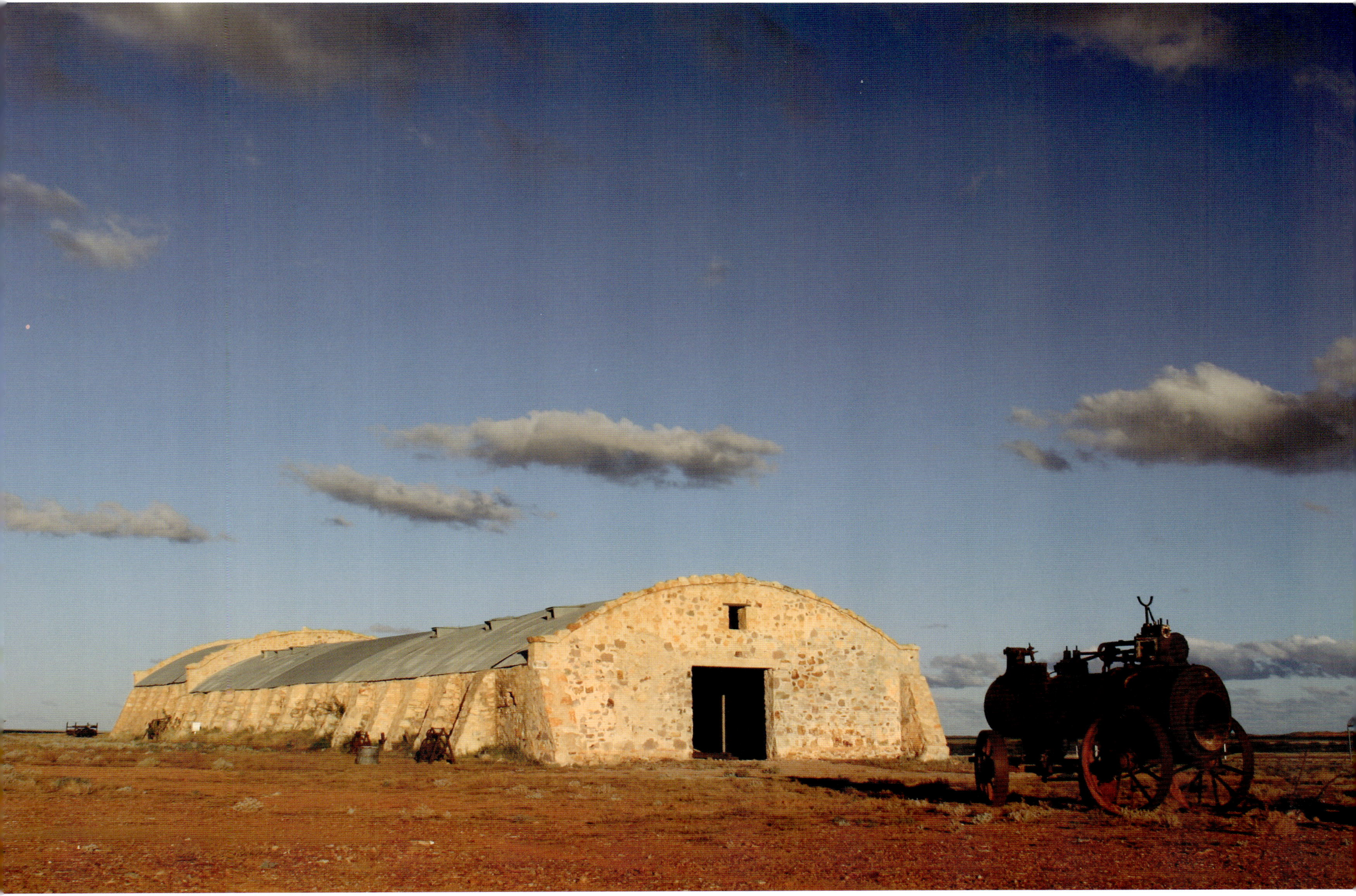

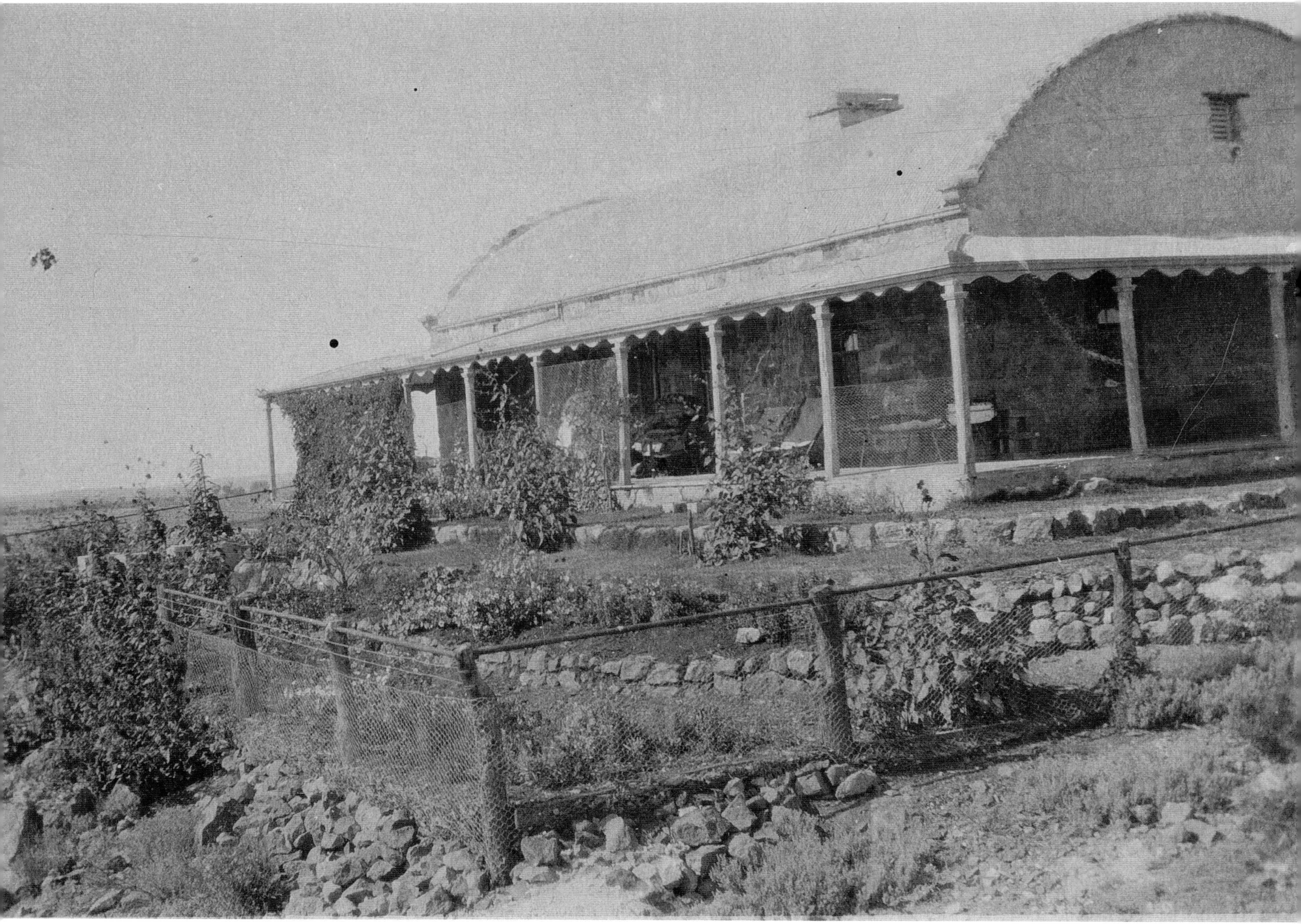

family portfolio and run by David Brook's son Anthony and his wife Janet. The station is still very isolated — almost 200 kilometres from the nearest town over challenging dirt roads.

It was a daunting enough journey from the other side of the world for Kenny Dowling and his Irish travel companion, Anne Marie Flattery, before they confronted the long dirt stretch to Cordillo Downs. 'Oh it's unbelievable compared to what we're used to,' says Kenny. 'Acres upon acres of sand and yellow grass compared to the small fields at home.' Kenny grew to love the freedom of mustering cattle on a motorbike over the sand dunes in the wide-open spaces. 'No matter how much you see on TV or how much you read about it, when you come and experience it you're struck by the beauty … isn't it lovely … it's relaxing compared to the hustle and bustle of the city.'

Irish backpackers have become an important source of labour in the outback, where it has become harder and harder to fill jobs. 'We've put ads in the papers and left them in for a month and got two people applying, so generally we'll take anyone,' quips Janet Brook. 'You've got to have people to run these places. You can't do it just as a couple, you need at least four or five people — for us that would be a minimum.' Janet and Anthony Brook built such strong links with the first Irish couple that came to work with them that they travelled to Ireland to go to their wedding. The couple later decided they liked the outback so much that they returned, basing themselves at Birdsville to work on stations in the area. But it has proved too much for others. Two Irishman who arrived at Cordillo Downs in the middle of a stifling summer barely unpacked their bags: 'Two brothers who came out, they only lasted a week. It was a bit warm for them. They probably weren't prepared for that, it's not everyone's cup of tea!'

Anthony and Janet Brook have four young children — Harry, Niamh, Megan and Emma. Given the isolation, there's no choice but to start their schooling at home.

What began as the School of the Air, using pedal radio, has developed into a classroom of the twenty-first century, with satellite links bringing children together for classes over the internet. On Cordillo Downs, and

The homestead on Cordillo Downs Station in the 1920s.

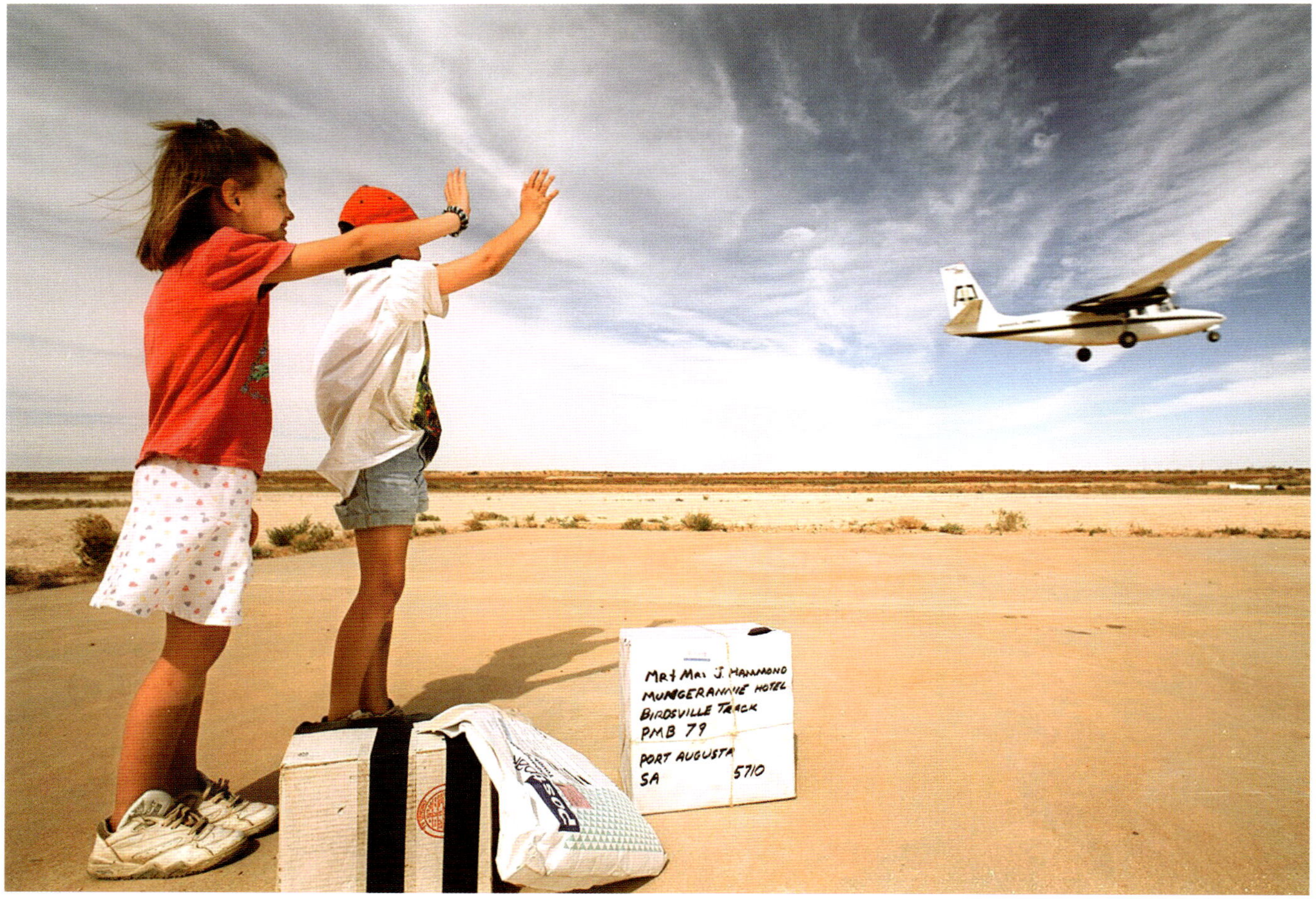

Waving goodbye to the mail plane (left) after it drops off Christmas mail at Mungeranie station on the Birdsville Track, the longest mail run in world. The isolation of outback life means that many children have been educated by the School of the Air. Where once pedal wireless was used (right, in 1951), these days internet and satellite links are the norm.

stations throughout the remote areas of Australia, separate classrooms are built to provide children with a sense of going off to school. Often a governess is employed to provide educational guidance. 'You've got to be really involved with your children's education,' says Janet Brook. 'It's not just a matter of sending them to school and things being fine, and having a look at their work at the end of each week, or having a look at their report card. You've got to be right on the ball with it.' Once outback children reach high-school age most are sent to boarding school.

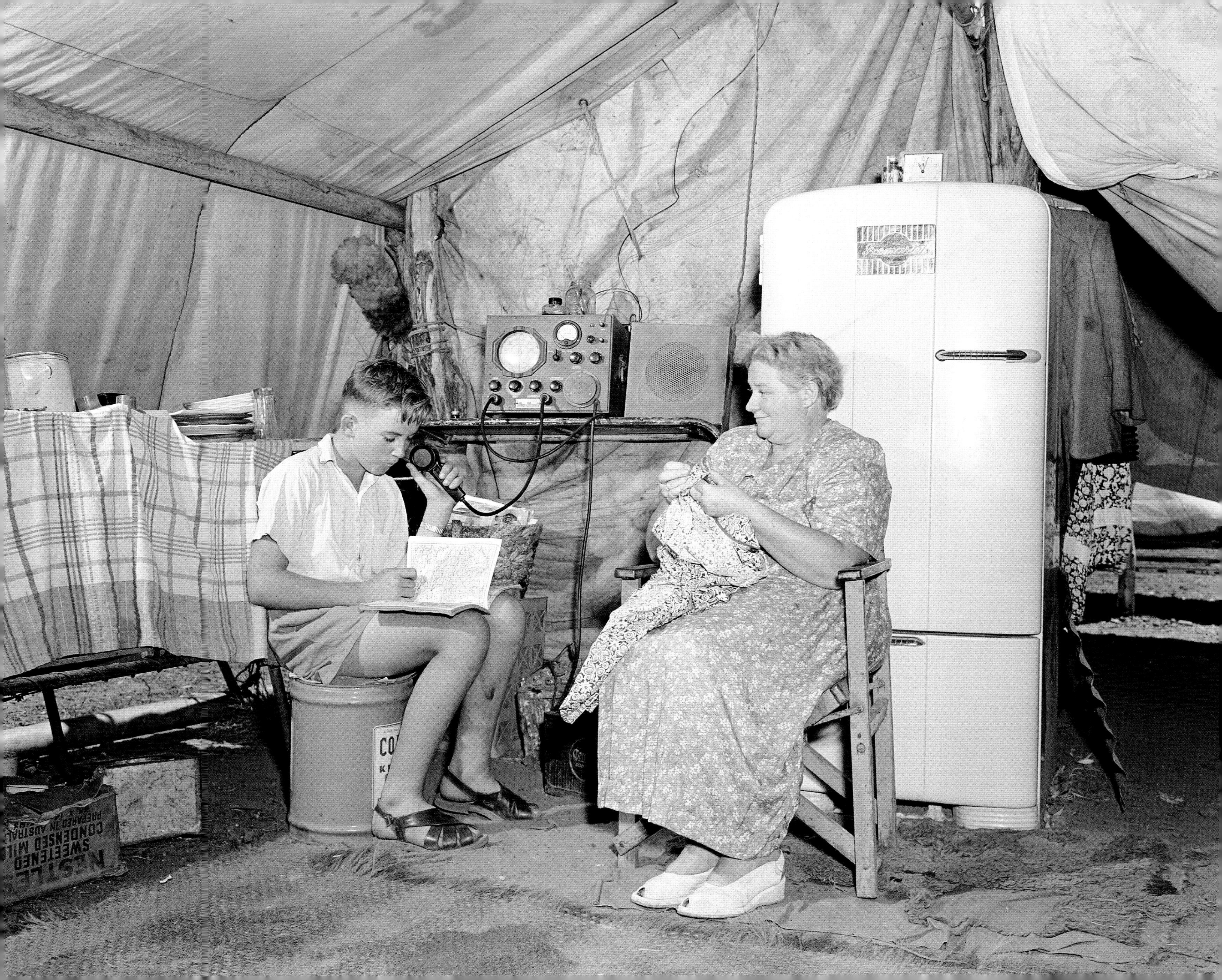

THE CYCLE TURNS

Summer returns

Away from the rocky plains of Cordillo Downs, the flow down the outback rivers had dropped. Life was beginning to be sucked out of the system. Fish numbers that had been supporting a huge pelican breeding colony in the lake north of Birdsville declined rapidly.

Disaster struck. Thousands of pelican chicks died of starvation, their bodies piled high under shrubs where they had jostled for shade. Others, weak and near death, struggled towards the water where hundreds could still be found, coasting across the lake, searching desperately for food. Just four months earlier a frantic breeding cycle had been in full swing here — now it had become a place of death.

Professor Kingsford joined us on our return journey to the lake. 'Unfortunately, they died because the parents abandoned them. Their parents probably had to go further and further to get their fish, and in the end they wouldn't have been able to get enough for the ones that died here.' It was the beginning of the bust that inevitably follows the boom in Central Australia.

Fish numbers continued to decline rapidly as water levels dropped in the lake with the rising heat of spring. Unable to find enough food for the new chicks, or themselves, the parents headed back to more reliable feeding spots away from the centre.

Nature can be brutal and uncompromising. But while thousands of pelican chicks perished at the end of the short breeding cycle, many more that had hatched earlier were able to follow their parents on the long journey to more secure food sources on other inland river

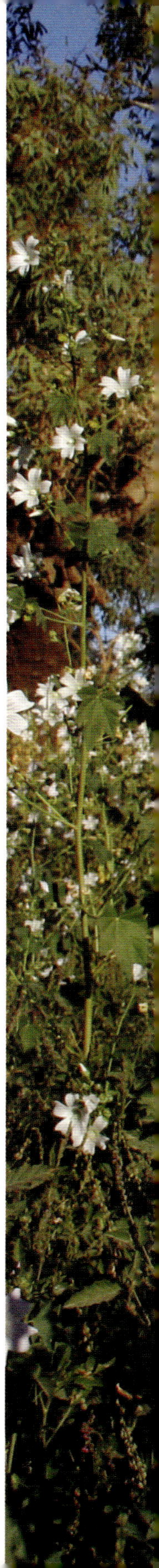

Once the floods pass, there is widespread germination, and soon a carpet of flowers on the riverbanks and floodplains of Lake Eyre's rivers, such as these native hollyhocks (Lavatera plebeia) *on the banks of the Diamantina River.*
Overleaf (left): Purple pussytails (Ptilotus sp.) *on the Cooper Creek floodplain and (right) yellow groundsel* (Senecio sp).

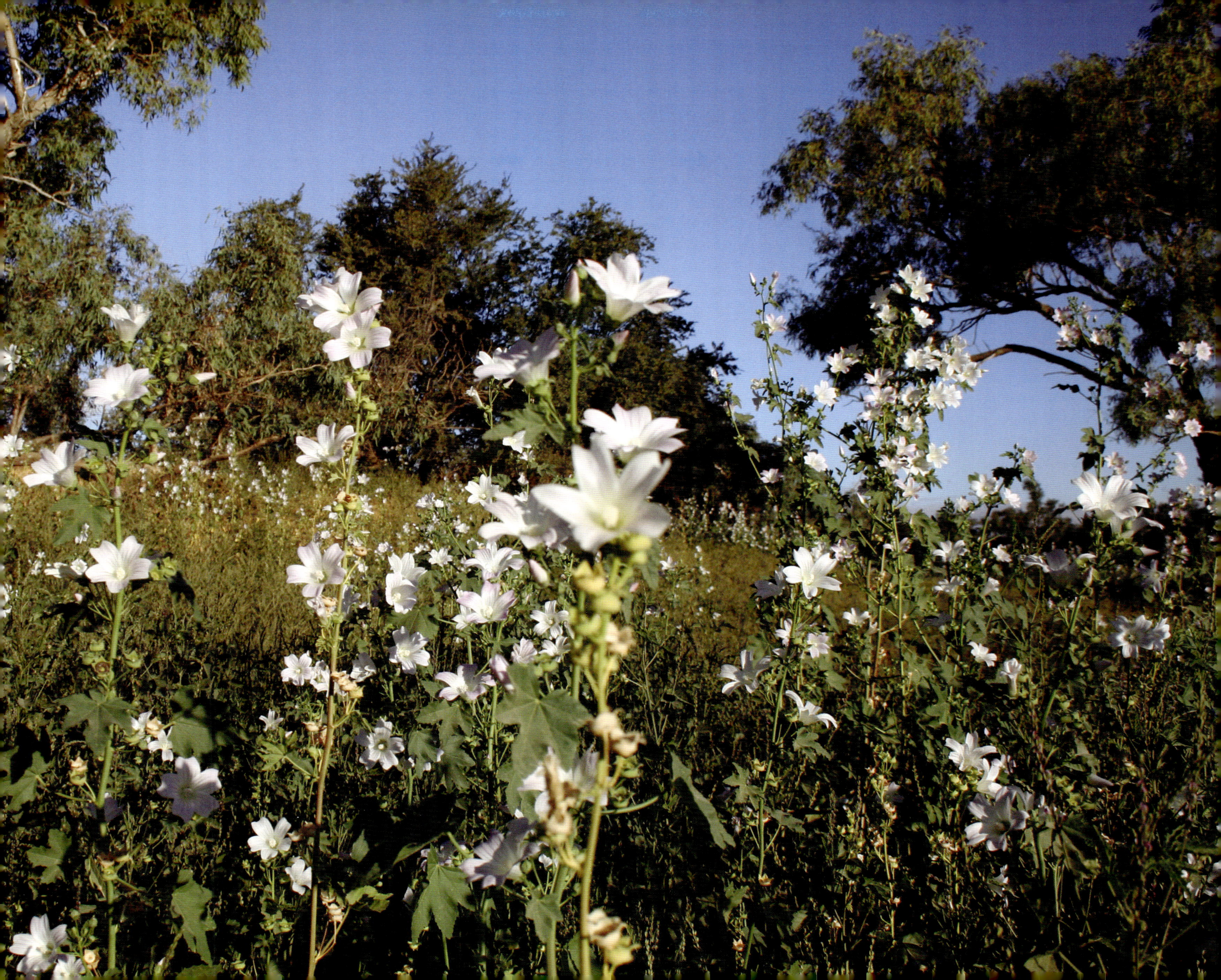

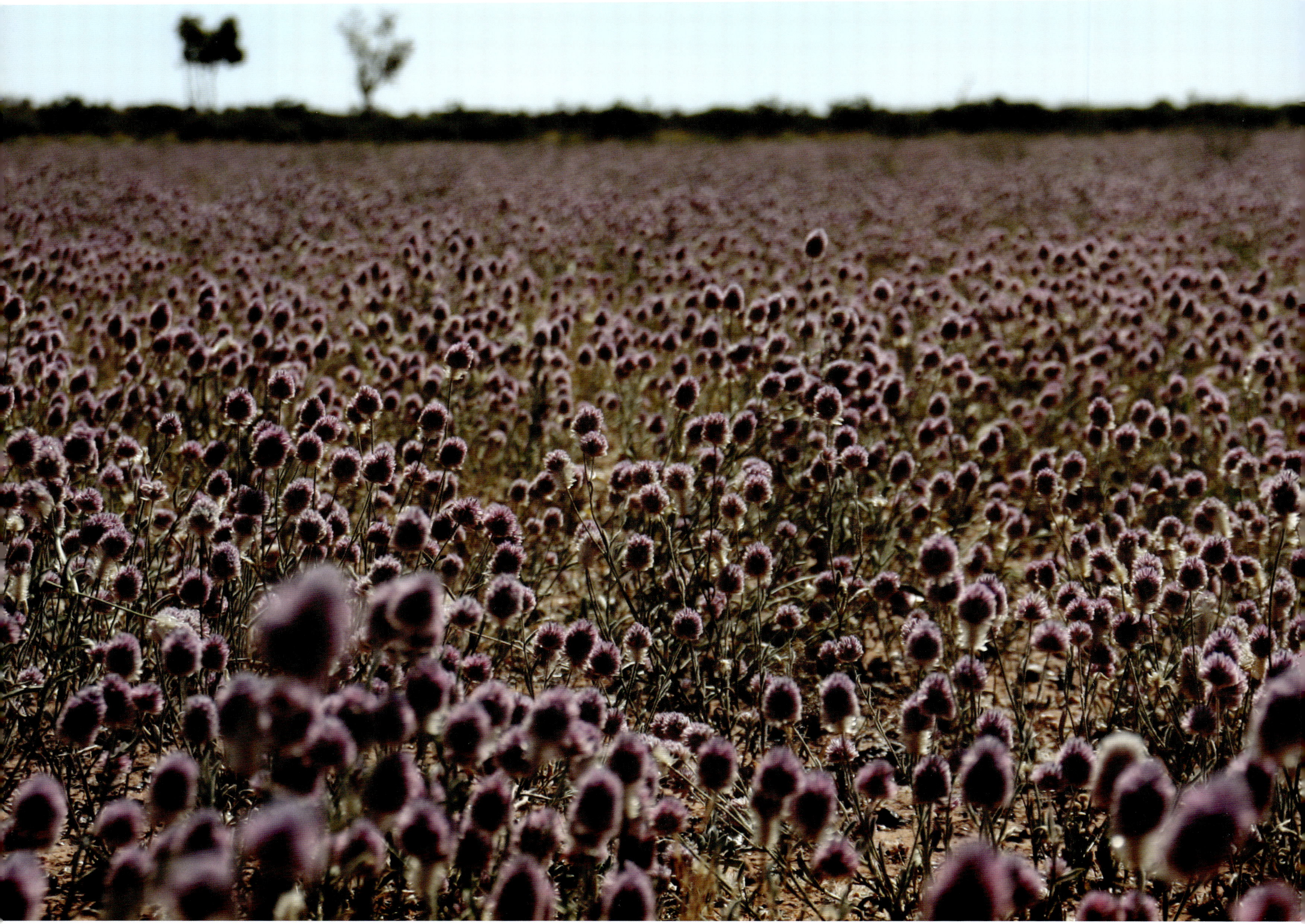

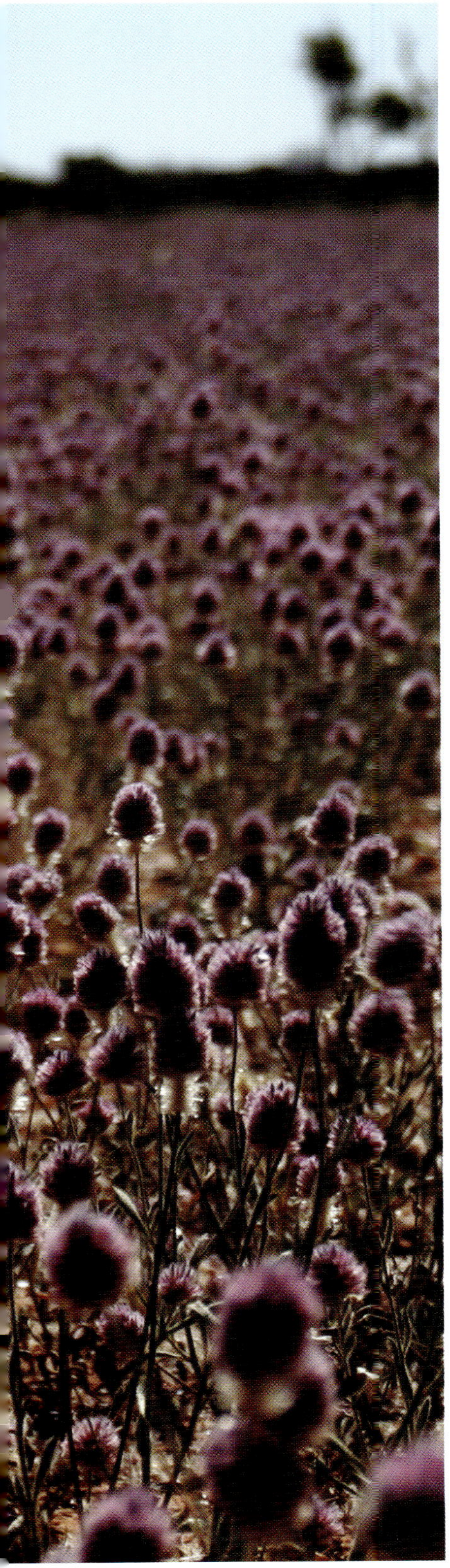

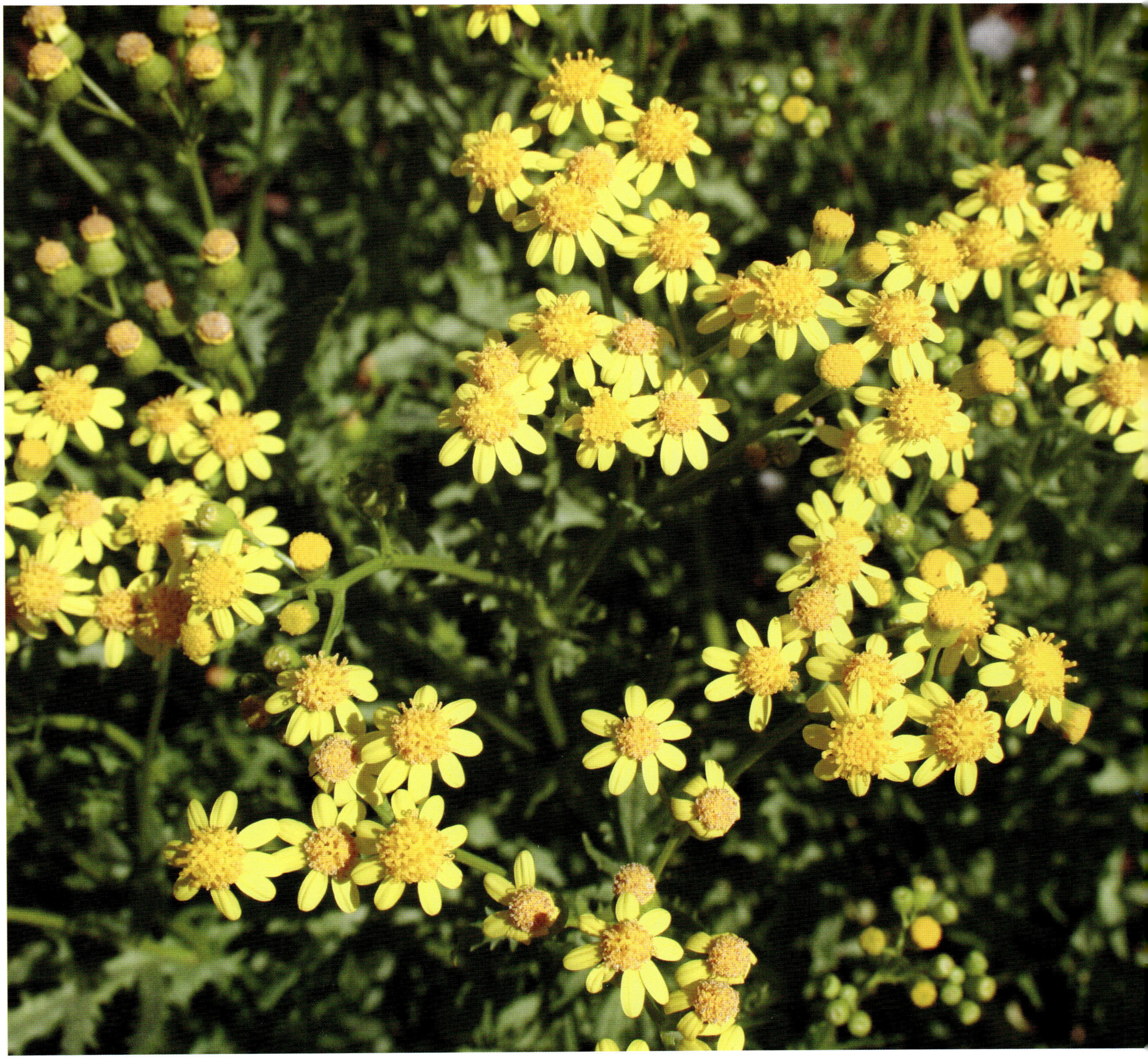

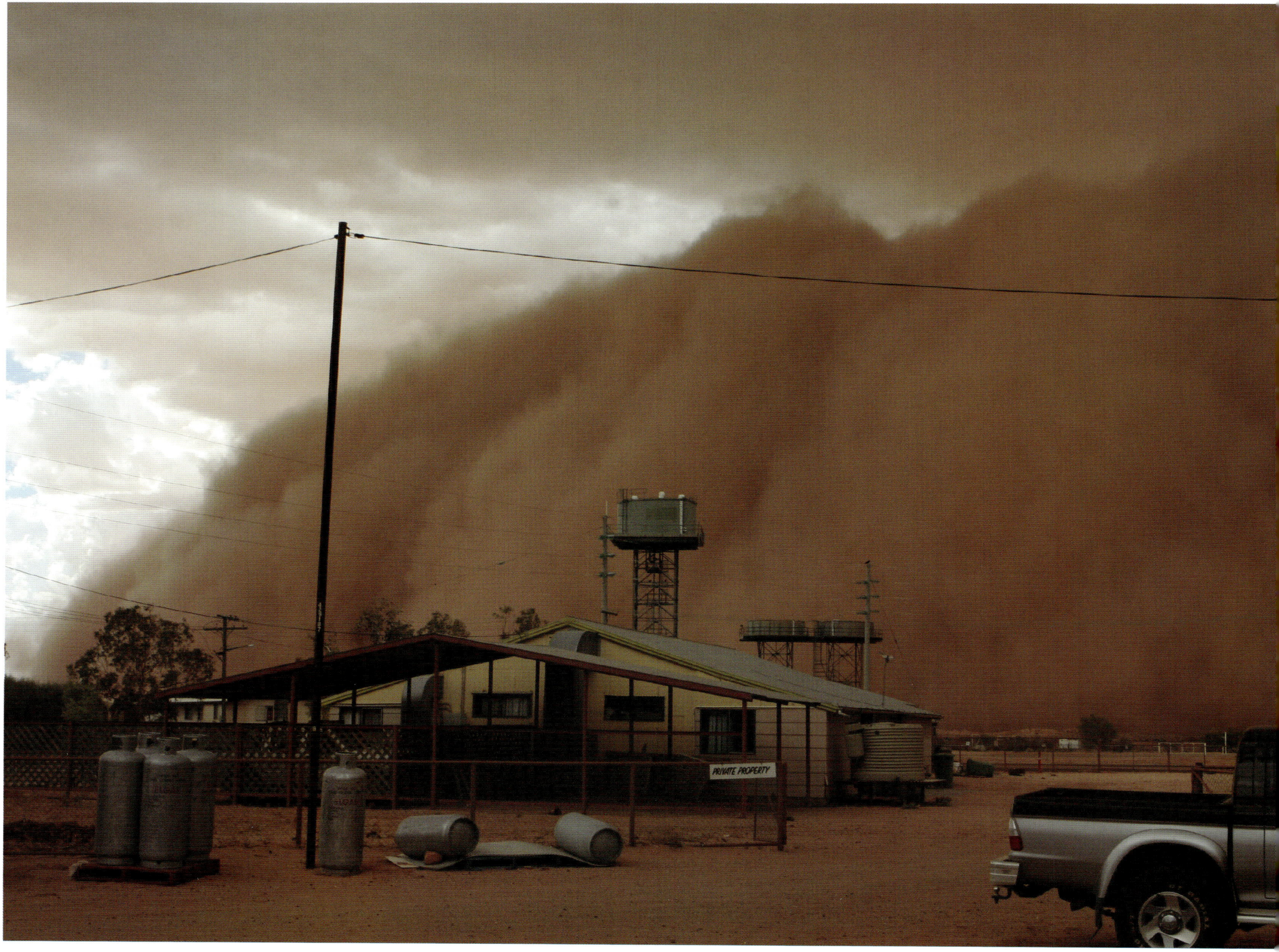
PRIVATE PROPERTY

A wall of dust rolls into Birdsville. The dust storms enshrouded the town and much of the outback.

systems and in coastal areas. Nature was operating on a number of different schedules on the floodplains. As the water drained away, another process started. The plant life began to germinate from the seedbeds laid down in the mud of previous floods. Right across the landscape there was a spectacular show of wildflowers, including big patches of pink daises, poached egg daises and billy buttons. Suddenly whole areas of the red outback were coloured in with pinks, purples, whites and yellows — all on a broad, green canvas. Wherever the water retreated, the plants took hold. This barren, windswept countryside, deeply locked in drought for so long, now took on the appearance of a lush garden.

But as temperatures rose in the spring, evaporation took a heavy toll. By October 2009, much of the water in Lake Eyre had dried out and dust storms were whipping across the surface. Much of eastern Australia experienced the drying of the centre firsthand. A weather front that swept across Central Australia picked up the desert sand in a huge cloud and carried it right across the continent. It was one of the biggest dust storms ever seen. As it swept east, the city of Broken Hill, in the New South Wales outback, was plunged into an eerie darkness in the late afternoon as the enormous wall of choking dust roared through the area, carried by gale-force winds. The dust storm spread over a front 1000 kilometres wide, eventually shrouding Sydney, Brisbane and much of the east coast. But it was only a tiny sample of what was being experienced on the cattle stations around Lake Eyre. There, the dust storms raged for days on end.

Swimmers take an early morning dip at North Sydney pool through the red haze that blanketed the city. The haze was caused by dust carried by overnight winds from the outback.

On Cordillo Downs, Janet Brook would no sooner clean up after one storm than be confronted by another. 'Well, if they reckon they had it bad in Sydney and Brisbane you should've been here that week,' she says. 'I think we had four dust storms that week, one after another. Back at the house I used a wheelbarrow and shovel to get rid of the sand on the verandah. It was not a fun time at all.' When the dust storms finally eased, landholders were confronted by a deeply scoured landscape — more barren and desolate than ever. They seriously questioned whether there would be any seeds left to germinate if and when the rain finally came to the drought-plagued area. As 2009 neared its end it seemed that another rare chapter in the flooding of Lake Eyre had already been written. In fact, it was just the beginning of the story.

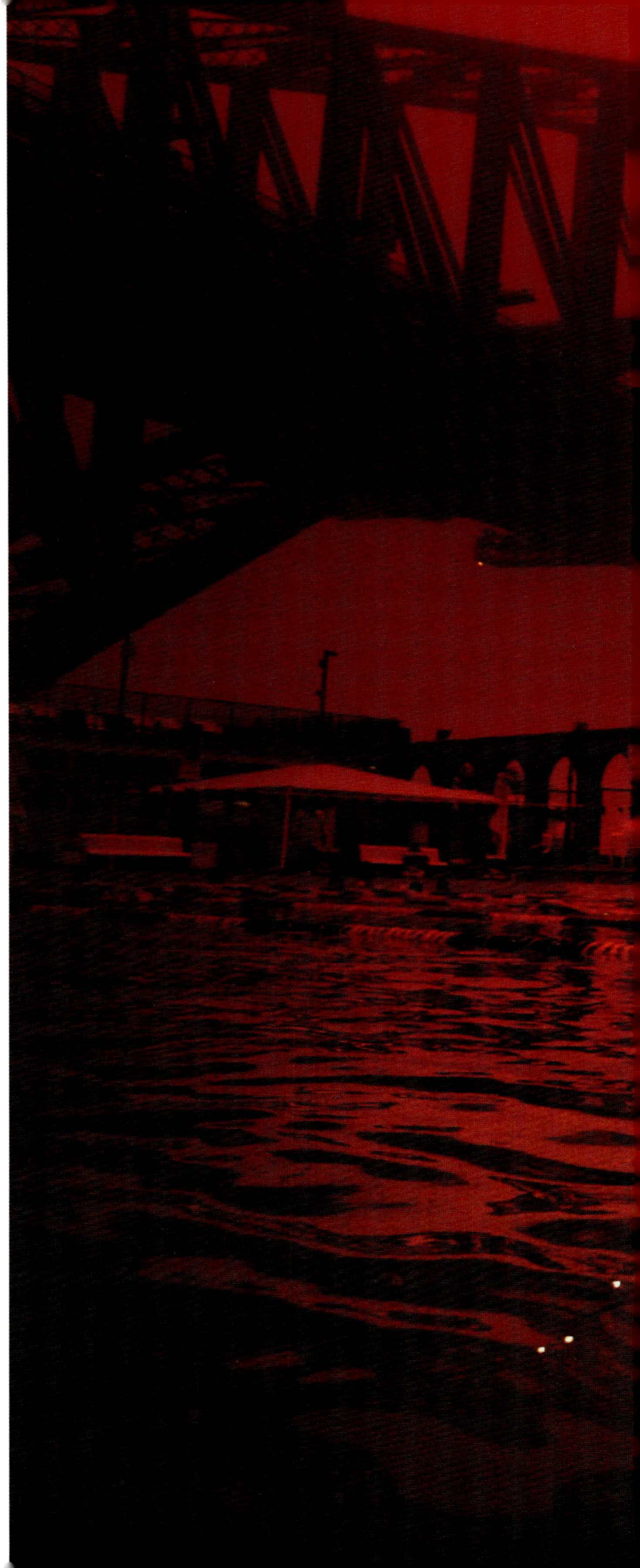

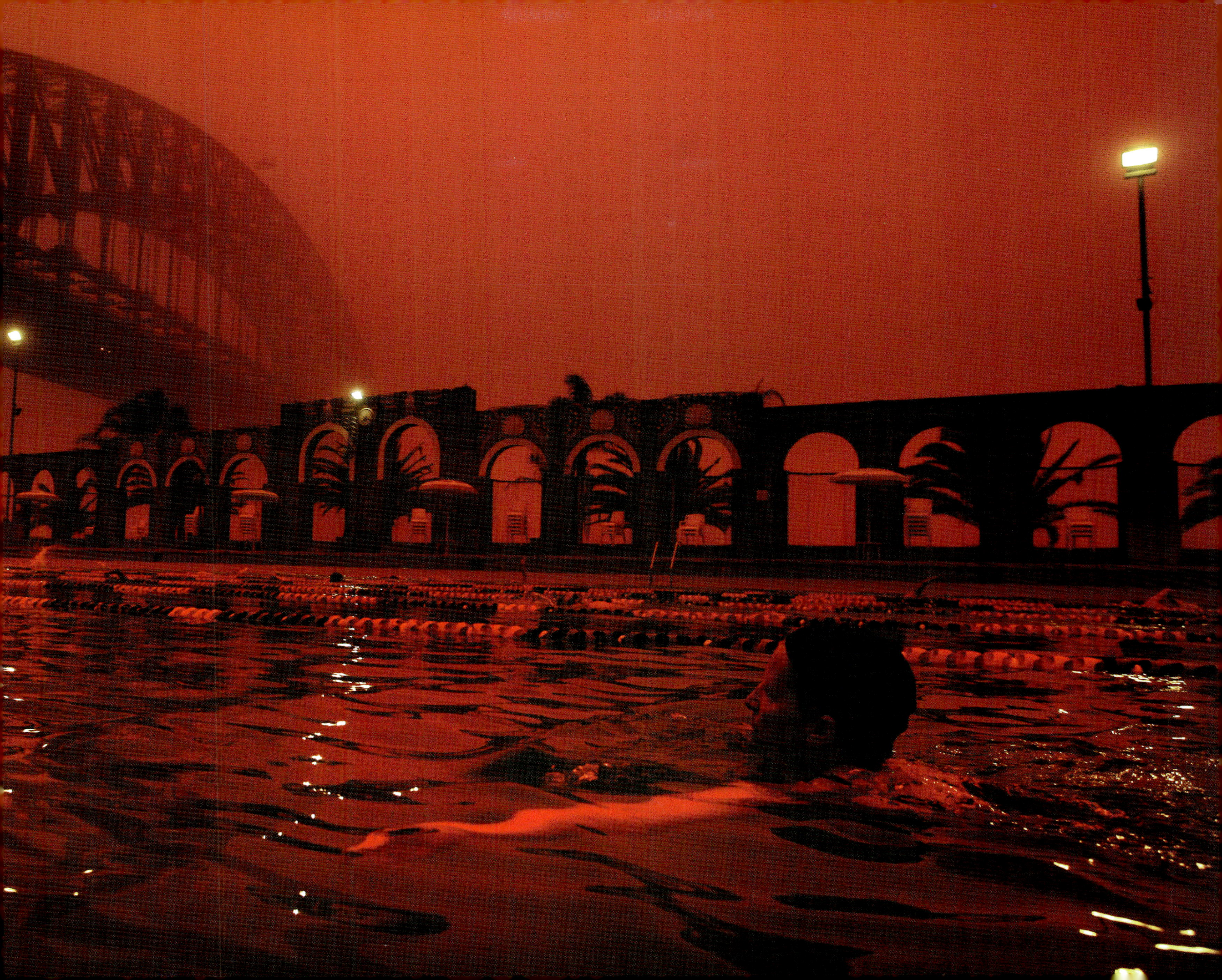

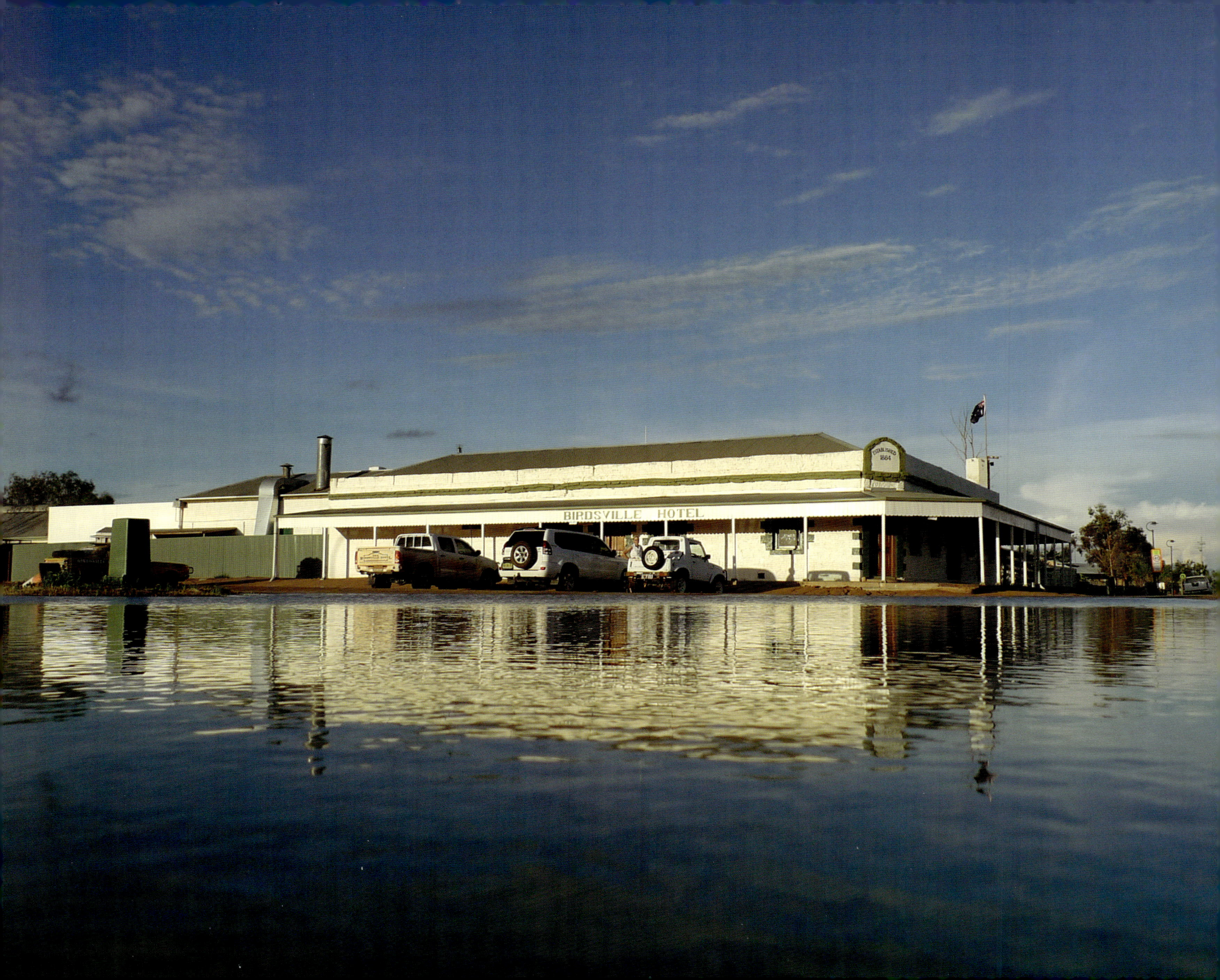
ESTABLISHED
BIRDSVILLE HOTEL

After the deluge

The pouring rains of 2009 delivered a year's worth of rainfall in just one day; outside the Birdsville hotel, it was wading season.

All around Lake Eyre it was expected that the summer of 2009–10 would return to its brutal worst. The indications were certainly there. Temperatures had been soaring since the spring and the massive dust storms had been relentless. But right across the outback, and big parts of eastern Australia, Christmas Day was to deliver a special gift — rain. It started at dawn in many areas and continued through the day. On Cordillo Downs and across the worst of the drought-affected areas of the Channel Country they tucked into Christmas lunch with extra relish, listening to the falling rain finally laying the dust. Enough rain fell to send water flowing down the dry creek next to the homestead on Cordillo Downs. The bush telegraph was crackling again as the far-flung stations compared rainfall figures and congratulated each other on a yuletide blessing. But there was much more to come.

'Everyone was just so amazed,' recalled Janet Brook at Cordillo Downs. 'They were really surprised, no one thought that they would see that much rain in their lifetimes again, it had been so long.' It had been the best part of a decade since there had been such heavy falls. The Brook children, ranging in age from one to eight, watched with wide-eyed astonishment — they had never seen rain like it on the property. And they were astonished to see a dry gully, running through the rocky landscape beside the homestead, suddenly carrying a torrent of water. The rain continued all over central and south-west Queensland, swamping the towns of Charleville, Roma, Saint George, Dirranbandi and Bollon. Further west, Birdsville recorded its highest rainfall in history.

One hundred and sixty-eight millimetres fell over a twenty-four-hour period — the town's average annual rainfall delivered in just one day! Streets in the town were flooded and running like creeks. Parts of the nearby Simpson Desert were inundated. All the waterways around Birdsville, including the Georgina and Diamantina rivers and Eyre Creek, flowed strongly again. And this time, Cooper Creek to the east was carrying a big flood too, streaming through Queensland and stretching out to every lake and waterhole across the Channel Country.

Caught in Cyclone Yasi's downpour in Cairns, Queensland, February 2011

In Windorah, beef producer Sandy Kidd revelled in it. He turned his battered hat into the driving rain, drinking in the view. The Christmas rain had already set the pasture shooting and he ran an approving eye over his sleek cattle chomping the wet, green grass. 'This just shows what this country can do. Eighth wonder of the world. It doesn't take much to turn it into the best grazing land in Australia — come back in a couple of months and it'll be even better!' Remarkably, waterways were coursing towards Lake Eyre for the second year in a row.

It promised to be the biggest flooding the centre had witnessed since 1974–75. The 2009 flood had brought relief to big areas but it had all come from river flows generated by rain in the far north. Now the rain fell right across the Lake Eyre region to benefit everyone. It sparked pasture growth everywhere and topped up all the desert waterholes. The last stubborn remnants of the long drought were being erased.

After the ABC's extensive coverage in 2009, this was not a story to be missed. So, in May 2010, for a third time the ABC chopper headed out from Sydney for an extended filming mission around Lake Eyre. All reports indicated that the birds were back, in even greater numbers than the year before. We were quickly able to judge that for ourselves.

After refuelling at Bourke on the first day of the trip, we headed north-west towards the New South Wales–Queensland border where the Bulloo River floods out to form huge wetlands. The flooding rains of the summer

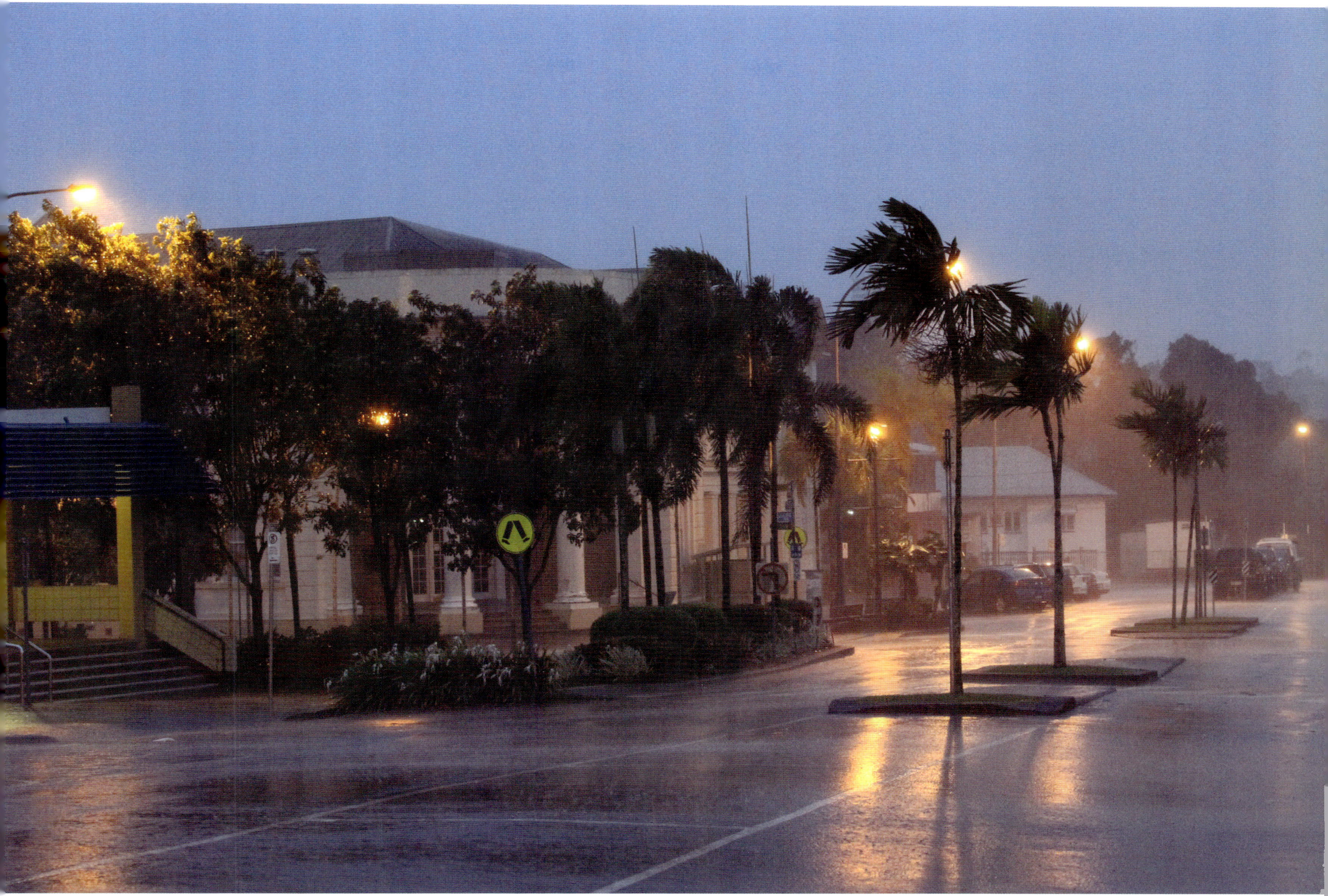

Through a break in the clouds, patches of transformed, waterlogged desert are visible

had set every river flowing across central and southern Queensland, all surging south towards New South Wales. The whole border area was under water. In the huge lakes that form the centre of the Bulloo wetlands there was an extraordinary sight. Thousands upon thousands of pelicans and straw-necked ibis were nesting together, crammed on lignum bushes running along the edge of the lake, next to a long sandy spit. The Bulloo wetlands are recognised as a major breeding area for waterbirds but there hadn't been an influx on such a major scale for ten years.

Pilot Gary Ticehurst tracked back with the chopper over the lignum as camera operator John Bean filmed. On and on we went, traversing the wetlands, dramatically revealing a teaming mass of birds, chicks and eggs in the nests below. On the open ground along the spit, hundreds more pelicans had laid their eggs and others were fussing around newly hatched chicks. We flew through more light rain as we headed for Epsilon Station, in the far south-west corner of Queensland. Country that had looked so forlorn a year before now carried a green tinge, with water shimmering in creeks that had been cracked and dry.

At Epsilon Station, Graham and Sharon Betts proudly took us to a big waterhole near the homestead. Weeks of consistent rain had filled it up and it was now supporting new bird life, including a gang of loudly squawking white cockatoos — the larrikins of the outback — dipping and turning in a series of seemingly impossible manoeuvres, as if they were trying to outdo each other, before jostling for perching space in a gumtree near the waterhole. Half a dozen calves kicked up their heels as they led a small mob of cattle down to drink. Graham Betts was a very relieved man. He had been forced to send most of his cattle away as the drought dragged on, unable to feed or water them. But the core breeding stock was still together when the rain arrived. 'We had to think like a sand goanna to keep them alive,' he says. 'Christmas Day we had 130 points (33 millimetres), and from then on it just started raining and got better and better — by the end of March the country was fully covered with feed — from nothing to fully covered, it's really good.'

The dissolved salt creates mirror-like effects across flooded Lake Eyre, 2010

From Epsilon Station all the way north to Cordillo Downs in South Australia the country had been revived. Sturt Stony Desert had seldom looked so inviting. In the hollows between the dunes, and even across the gibber plains, native grasses had taken hold. It was a pleasure now for Anthony Brook to take to the skies in his light aircraft, flying over the red sand dunes of Cordillo Downs, locating cattle for a mustering team on the ground: 'The pasture and grass is knee high compared to last year when we were shifting cattle off to other properties to make use of the floods. We don't have to do that this year. It's a one in twenty-five-year rain event — the country really won't get much better than it is now.' The mob of Herefords being brought together were in superb condition, thanks to the highly nutritious desert grasses. Janet Brook used a four-wheel drive behind the wandering cattle, with four-year-old Megan by her side: 'The kids come along — it's good for them and saves on the babysitting at home, and gets me out of the house. It's an absolute joy coming out mustering when it's like this. You're not worried about the condition of the cattle while they're walking along — it lifts your spirits actually when you see so much cover on the ground.'

East of Cordillo Downs, the Cooper was filling the floodplain as it worked its way through south-western Queensland. Water now streamed from the Cooper into Lake Yamma Yamma. Like Lake Eyre, it's usually a big flat pan, dry for years on end. But now it more closely resembled a wetlands in the tropical north. At the top of the lake a network of channels filtered clear blue water through a huge bright green swamp area and as the water swirled across the pan it created complex patterns in shades of

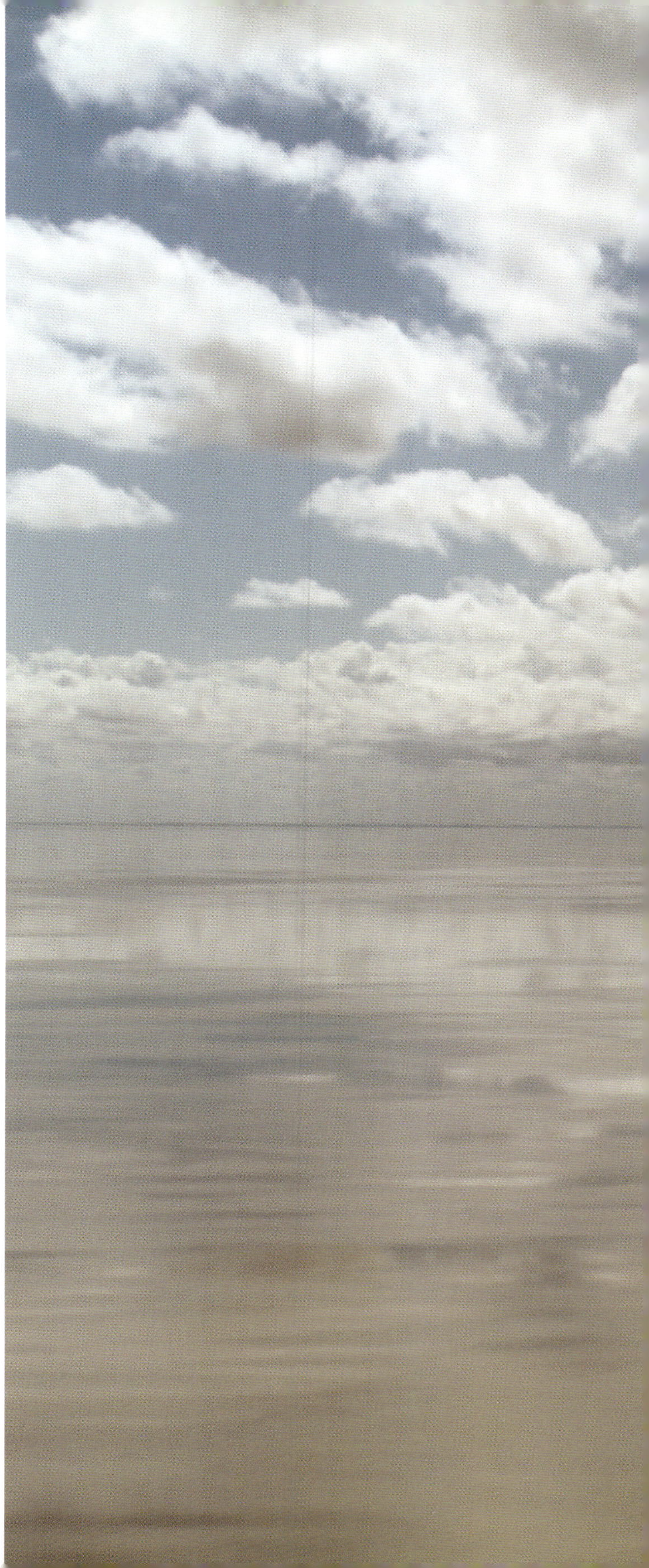

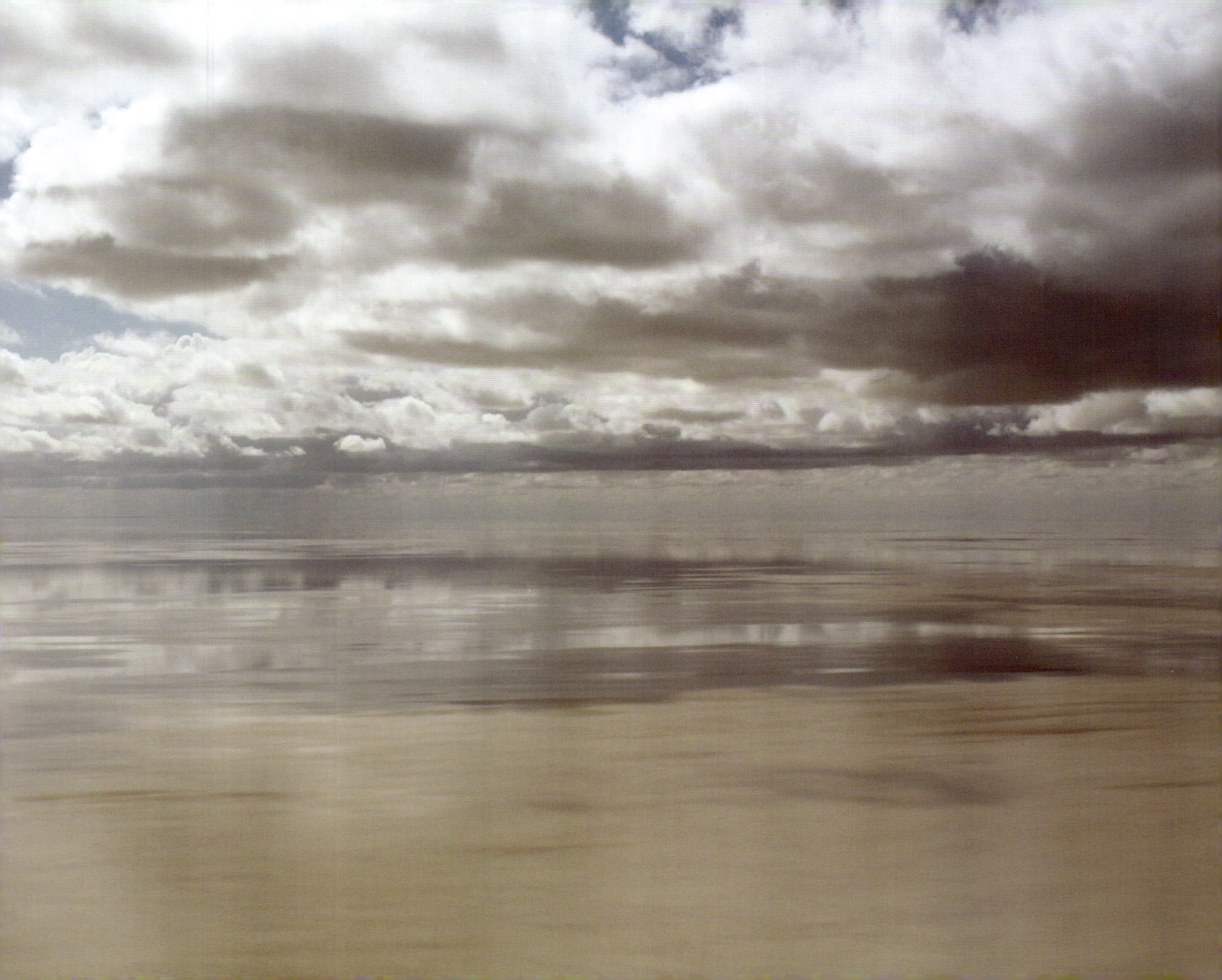

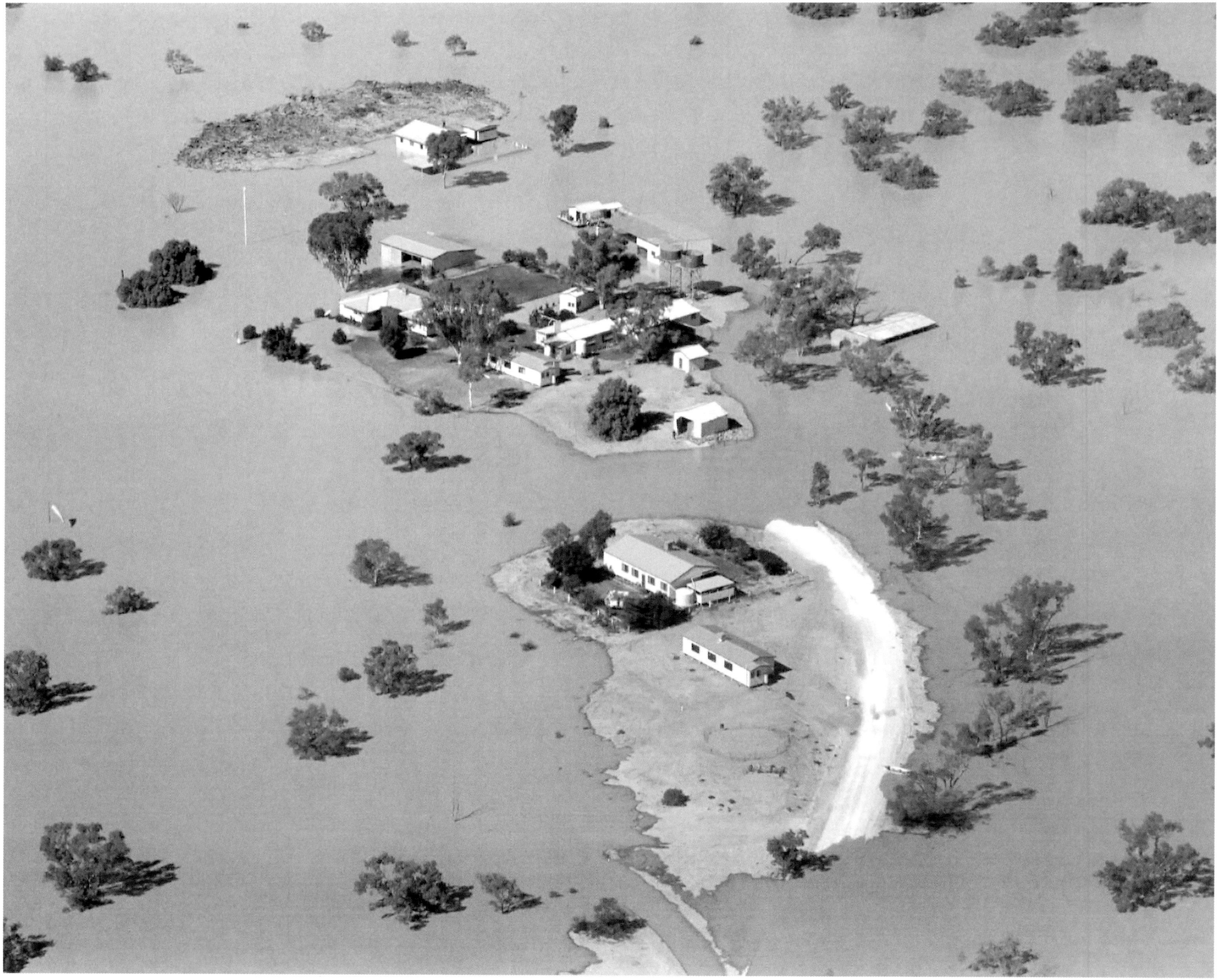

Innaminka homestead in South Australia, cut off by the rising Cooper Creek during the 1990 floods.

green, blue and grey. The colour contrasts were stunning. As the chopper descended over Lake Yamma Yamma it soon became clear that the birds had already discovered this patch of paradise. An armada of pelicans was out on the water, a squadron took to the air, and right through the lignum bushes and the tiny sandy islands of the lake there were eggs galore. This was another huge pelican breeding colony. If the pelicans had begun to build up their drought-depleted numbers in the flooding of the previous year this would surely make an even bigger difference.

Professor Richard Kingsford was excited about the prospects: 'These events are rare enough. But when you get a sequence of flooding, which is what we are seeing at the moment, it's just magnificent.' Central Australia wasn't shutting down in the usual expected bust phase; it was booming again. Lakes, waterholes and rivers were pulsating with life as nature went into overdrive. Waterbirds, in ever-greater numbers, descended on the outback to breed. The pelicans on Lake Yamma Yamma had food for months to come and took full advantage of the opportunity. It takes a month or more for pelican eggs to hatch and several more months for the chicks to grow big enough to make their exodus away from the outback. But with enough food left in Lake Yamma Yamma, the pelican colony could breed a second time — what's called double clutching. Pelicans had also returned to Lake Machattie, north of Birdsville, where the breeding event had come to such a disastrous end the year before. But curiously none of the birds had gone near the two sand dunes where so many chicks had died of starvation. There were only bones and feathers to be found there now. Instead, the pelicans were crammed onto a narrow, crescent-shaped

As the floodplain dries back, the waterholes of the rivers in the Lake Eyre Basin become refuges for fish, attracting flocks of cormorants and pelicans, such as these here at Annandale Waterhole on Eyre Creek.

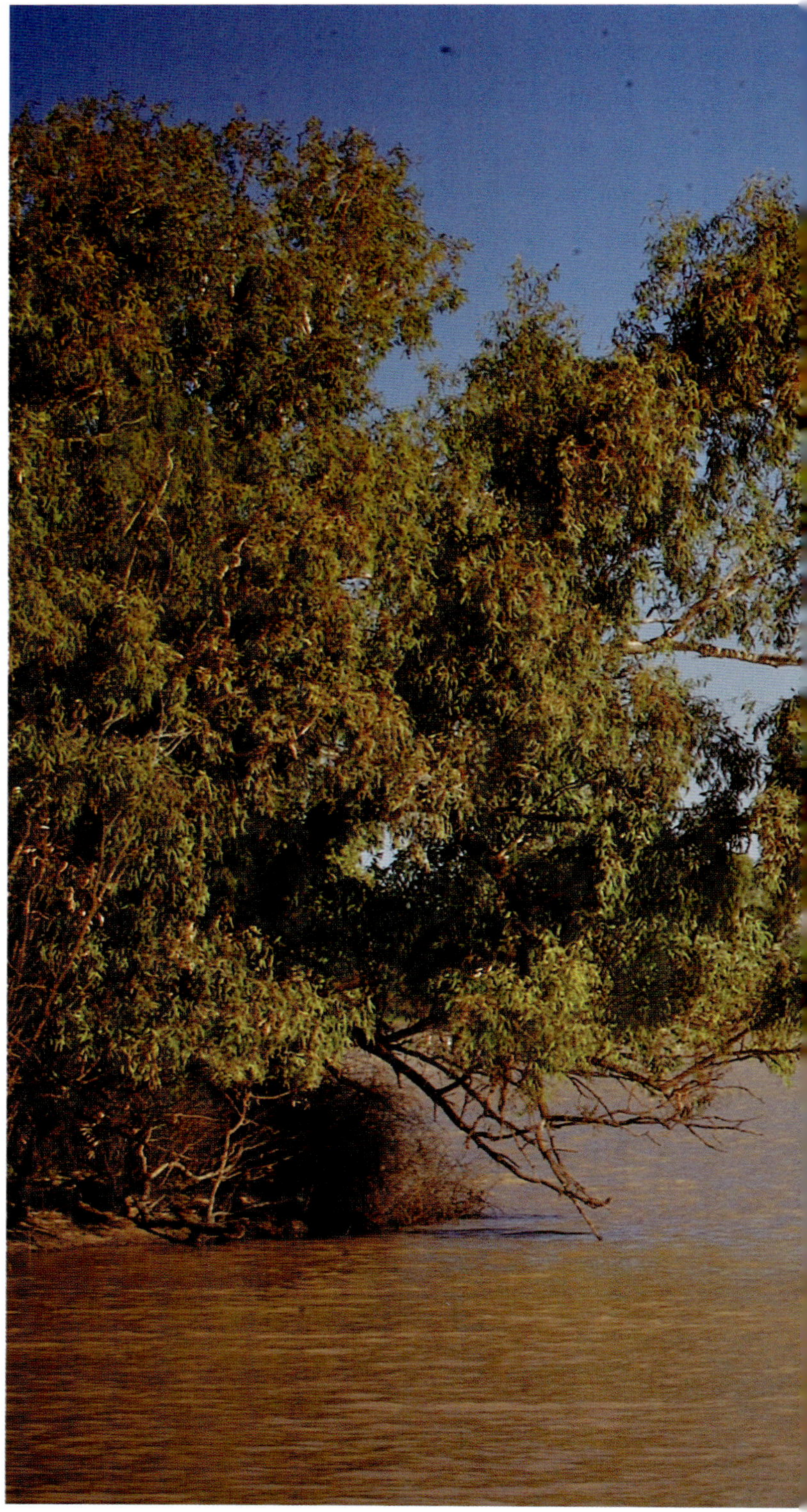

island, just beyond their old breeding spot. It begs the question, had they deliberately avoided a place of death? Professor Kingsford believes it is unlikely. The science suggests the birds simply choose the safest breeding spot in the lake where the danger from predators, particularly dingoes, is kept to a minimum.

The food supplies were more assured now. Fish had built up their numbers in the follow-up flood and it seemed the word was out. The trees dotted along the channels running through and around the edge of Lake Machattie were filled with nesting birds, cormorants and egrets, in their thousands. It was much the same at the Coongie Lakes wetlands, north-west of Innamincka in South Australia, but on an even bigger scale. Old nesting areas were re-occupied by birds that had travelled hundreds if not thousands of kilometres — a journey they had not made in years.

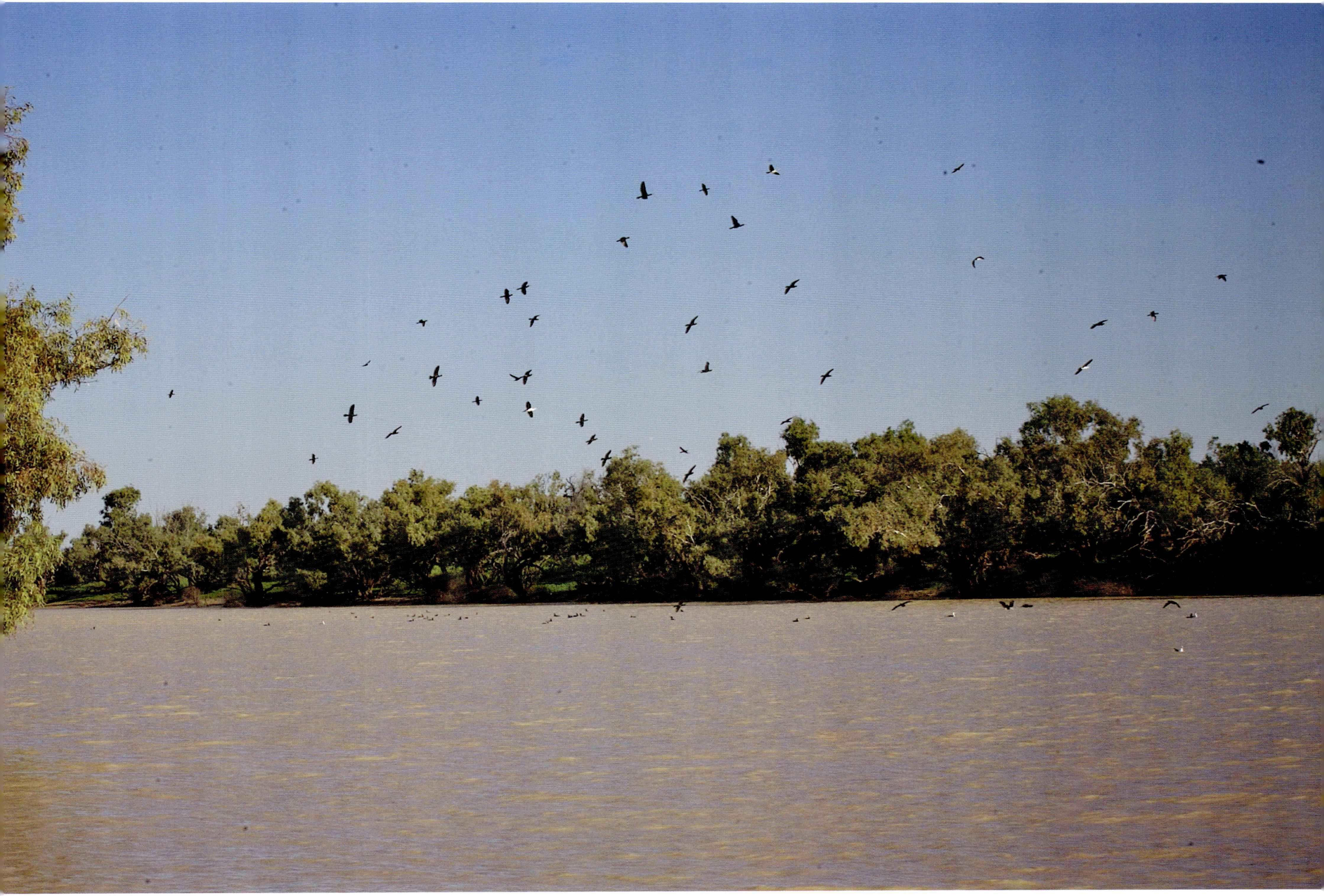

Slow flows the Cooper

On one level nature was working overtime, but on another it was following the unhurried pace dictated by the ancient, weathered landscape. Cooper Creek literally inched its way towards Lake Eyre. After it filled up the Coongie wetlands, and a string of other big waterholes near Innamincka, it still had an enormous journey to make. There were more big lakes to be topped up and a floodplain to be replenished. Finally, four months after the flood peak passed Innamincka, it snaked its way towards the Birdsville Track, just east of Lake Eyre.

The last time the Cooper had reached the Birdsville Track was in 1990. The track remains a crucial link for the communities and stations around Lake Eyre and everyone knows that once the Cooper gets to the track it will be cut for months. The solution is a desert ferry. A crossing point was identified long ago, back in the days when Tom Kruse had his mail run, upstream from the Birdsville Track. The South Australian Government eventually trucked a vehicular ferry to the crossing to ensure that the vital transport link could be maintained. The ferry was pressed into service in the floods of 1974, and again in 1990.

In the many dry years in between it had been gathering dust in the desert, a curious tourist attraction. When it was decided to recommission the old ferry for the Cooper flood of 2010, landholders complained that it was now too small and too slow to cope with the extra traffic and bigger trucks using the Birdsville Track. Nevertheless the decision stood, and the ferry was dragged back into the water, cables were reconnected across the Cooper and the road approaches graded.

Once a curiosity in the desert, the old ferry came into its own during the floods of 2010. If the Birdsville Track is cut by Cooper Creek's floodwaters, it can take months to reopen.

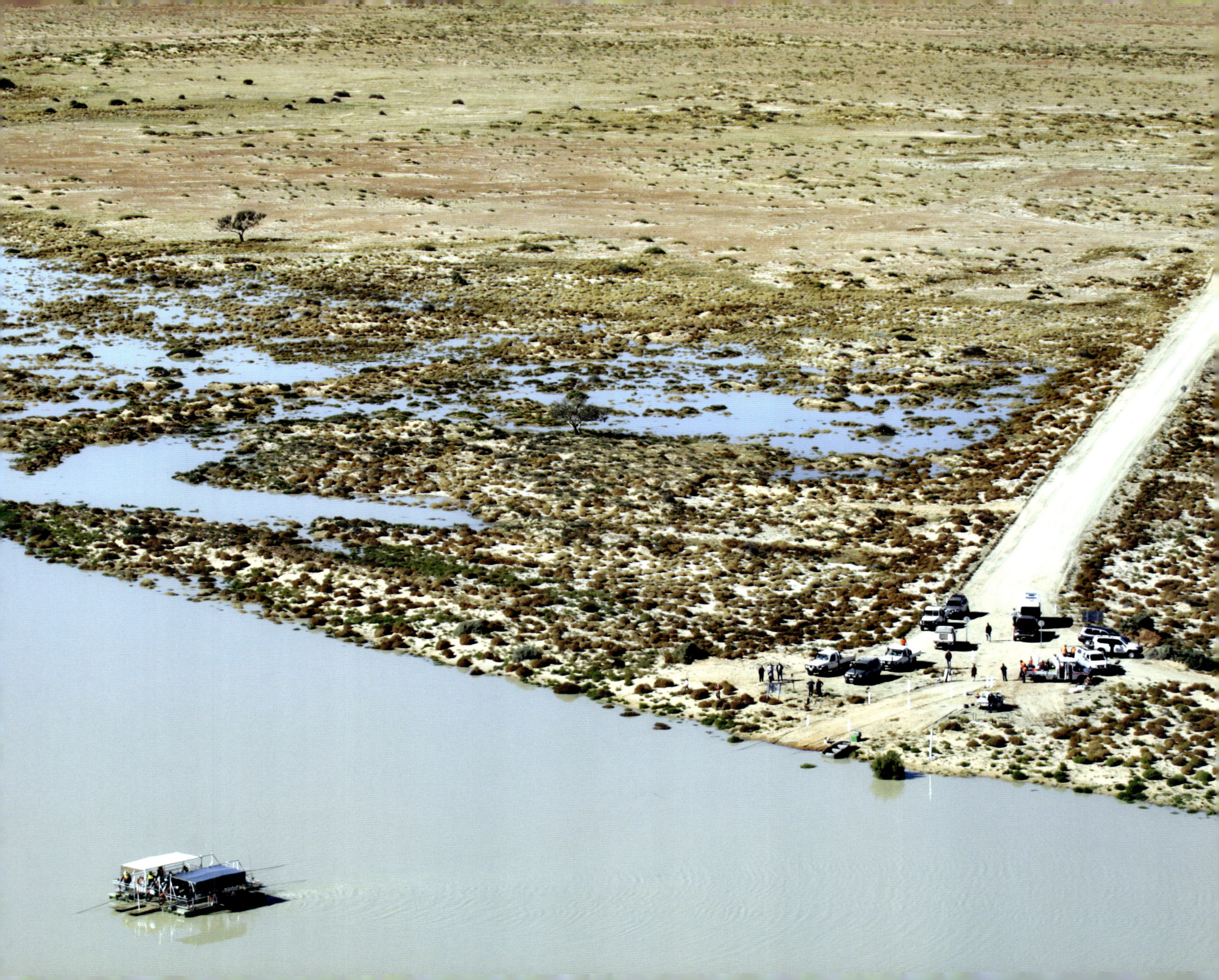

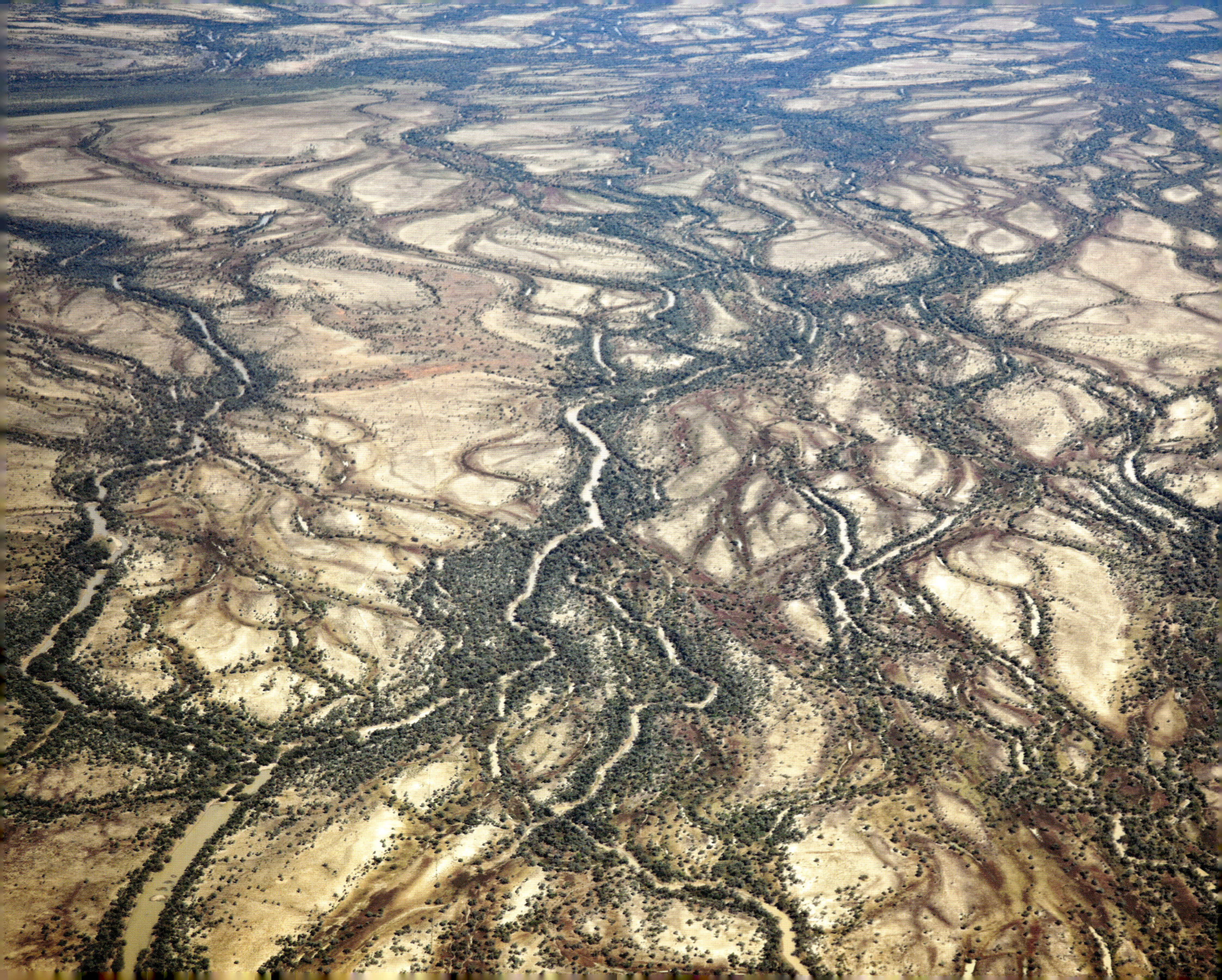

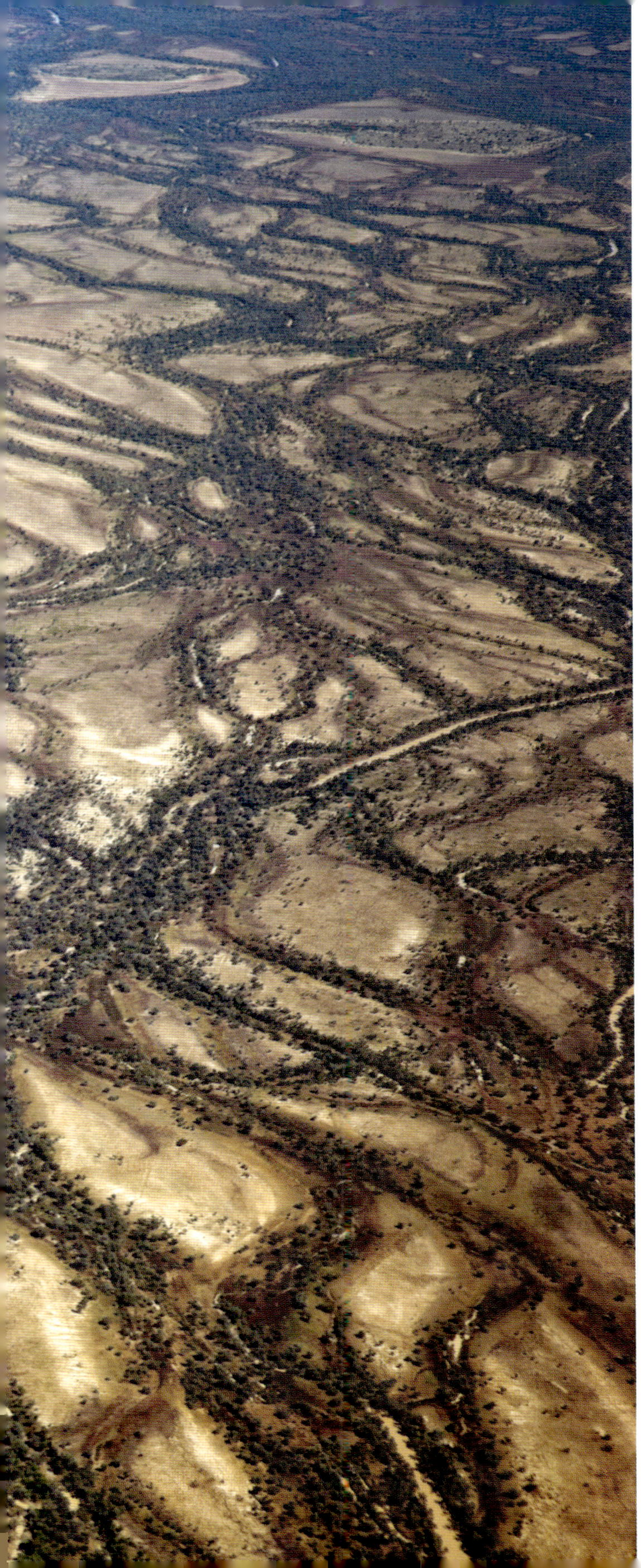

The channels of Cooper Creek north-east of Lake Eyre filled with water. Overleaf: As Coopers Creek dries out the colours in the landscape change to pastel hues.

As the work continued at the ferry crossing, so did one of the great guessing games of the outback — when would the Cooper reach the Birdsville Track? Every flood produces different water flows in the outback but because the Cooper flows to Lake Eyre so rarely it's even more unpredictable than the other rivers. Finally, on 1 June 2010, it started edging across the Birdsville Track. For weeks before, the progress of the Cooper had dominated discussion around Lake Eyre. Now that it had arrived the news quickly spread. People on both sides of the Cooper rushed to get across the gravel road before the water rose too high. Tourist buses ploughed through, along with camper vans, four-wheel drives with trailers in tow, and battered station vehicles. The Cooper Creek may move slowly but it carries an enormous volume. Within hours the water had risen to car bonnet height, swamping half a kilometre of the Birdsville Track. The authorities declared the road closed — and it would stay that way for another seven months. There was no rest for the work crews running the old ferry.

We filmed the history-making moment when the Cooper began flowing across the Birdsville Track and landed the chopper downstream to capture the start of the last leg of the flood, as it flowed on towards Lake Eyre. We were at the front of a river that stretched 1500 kilometres back through outback South Australia and Queensland. But there was plenty of time to observe it all. The Cooper still had to reconnect with an age-old pathway through the Tirari Desert before it got to Lake Eyre and that would take many more days. It was mesmerising to be at the flood front of one of the great outback rivers.

It was a trickle rather than a flow, moving at no more than slow walking pace. Near the Birdsville Track the head waters of the Cooper spread about 70 metres wide, surging and gurgling across the pockmarked floodplain — in and out of every crevice and depression, soaking deep into the landscape before gathering the momentum to go on. As the water crept across the landscape, spiders, beetles and a vast array of other insects scurried out of the cracks and hollows. A mouse left its run too late and was

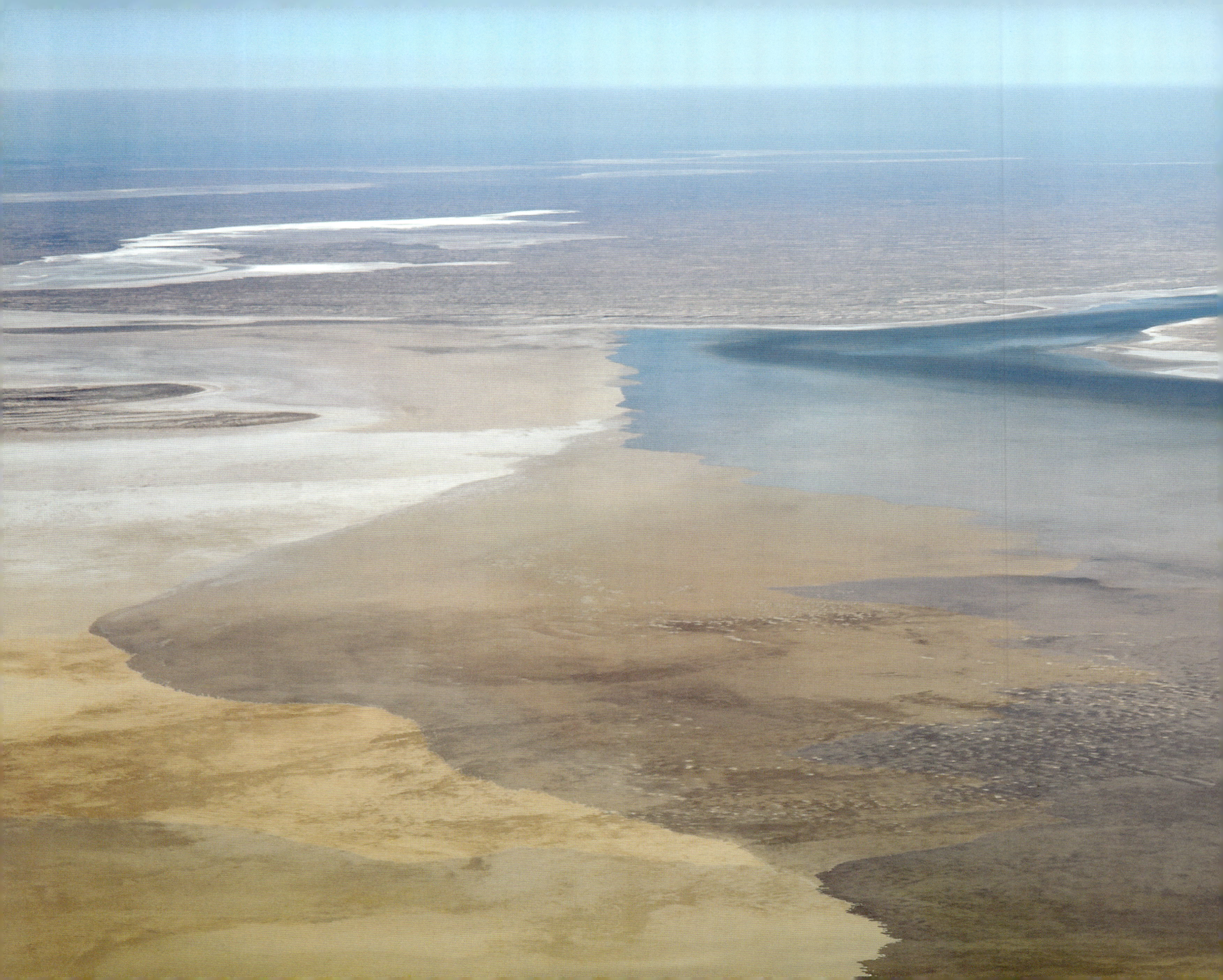

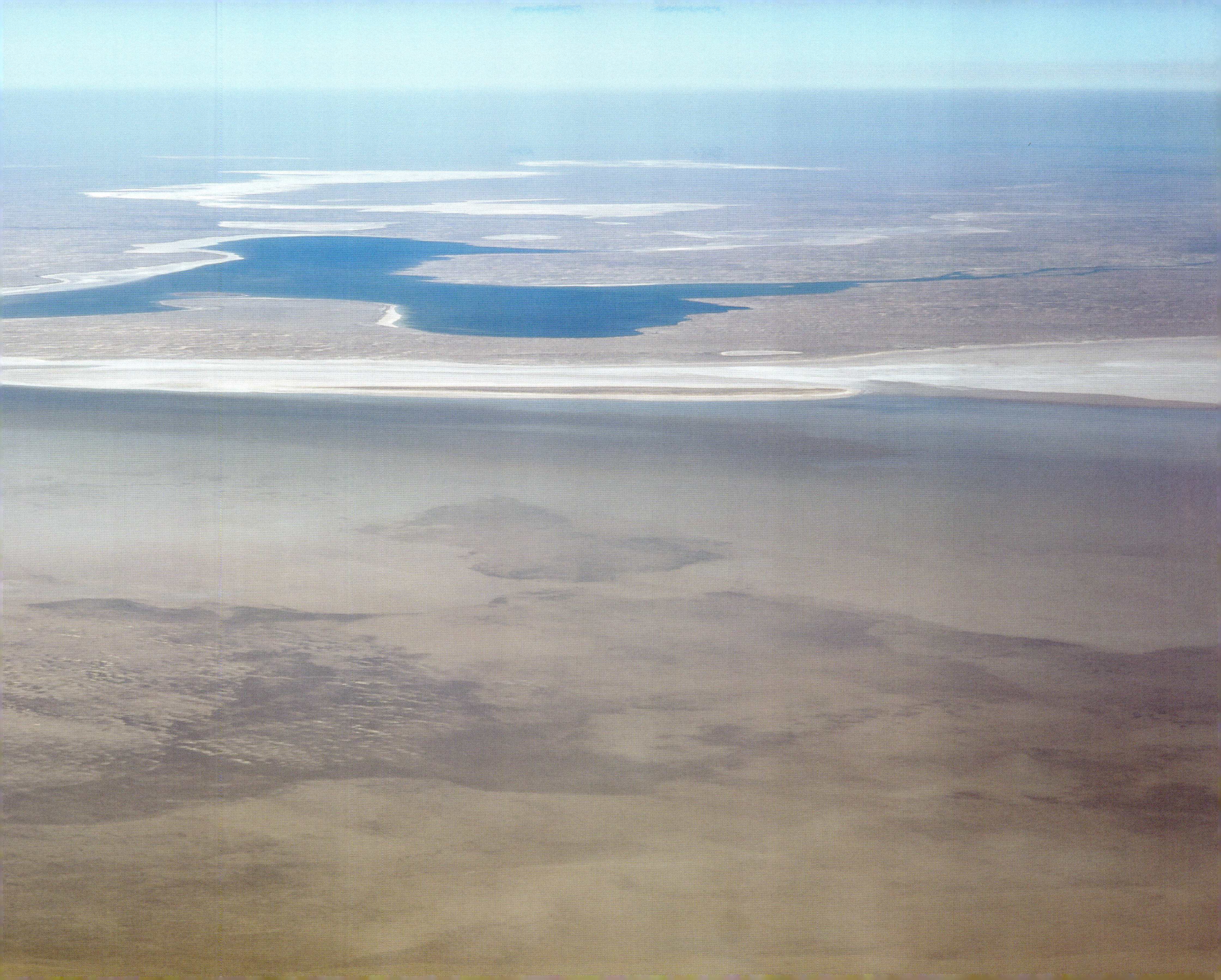

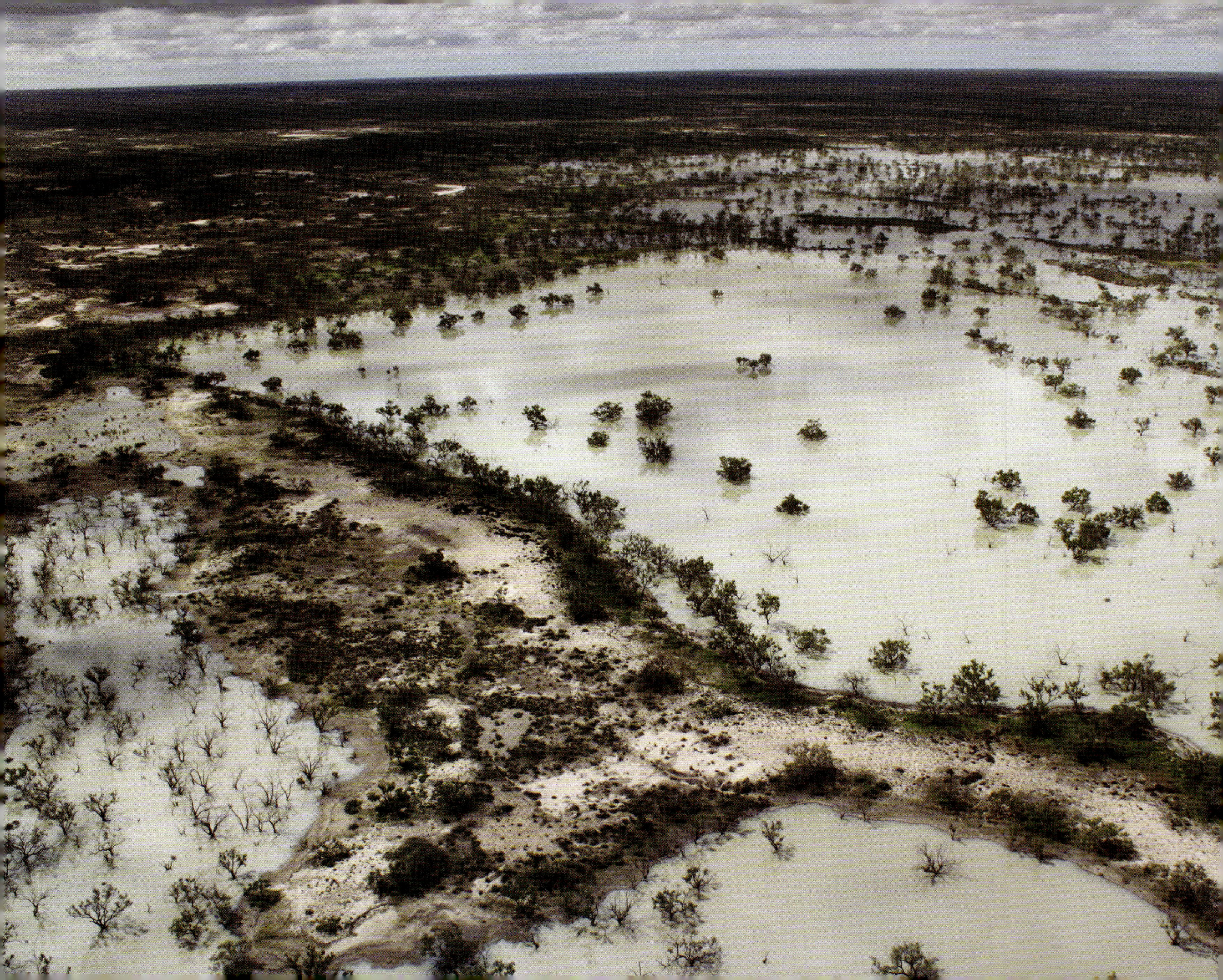

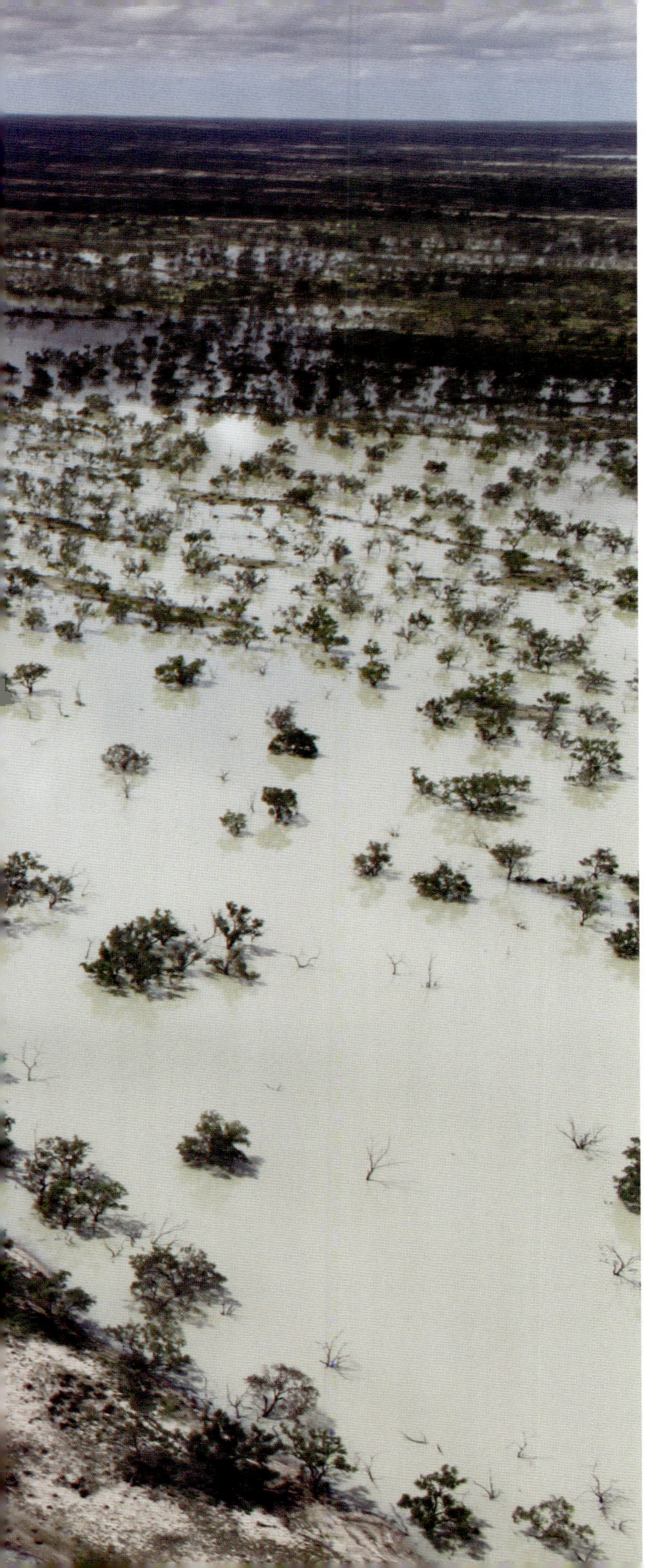

In 2010, the lower Cooper Creek flooded an expansive area of lakes and channels before emerging in a single channel to flow into Lake Eyre.

swept along by the water. The Cooper picked up speed momentarily as it funnelled down a narrow channel leading to the dune fields and then spread wide again, heading deep into the desert on the edge of Lake Eyre. Now there was a new guessing game in the outback — how long would it take for the Cooper to get to the lake?

Already the rivers from the north were delivering. Flows down Eyre Creek, and the Georgina and Diamantina rivers, had swamped Goyder's Lagoon and the water was streaming from there down Warburton Creek into Lake Eyre. The piggyback flood and the widespread summer falls had finally sent the drought into full retreat on Cowarie Station. Big areas of the desert now carried feed to add to the lush pastures that had taken hold in the station's flood country along the Warburton. The outlook from the homestead had changed dramatically for Sharon Oldfield: 'You're walking around and there's nothing on the ground, you can't see any seeds. And then it rains and there it is — it was just amazing and very exciting, and across the whole region you

Before it can run south through the sand dunes of the Simpson Desert towards Goyder's Lagoon, Eyre Creek must first saturate a large floodplain and lakes. Here the river flows through the floodplain eucalypts.

can hear the optimism in the voices of everyone you speak to. For the first time in years we're now able to genuinely plan for the future rather than just surviving.' Cattle were up to their knees in pasture and water in Goyder's Lagoon, contentedly grazing next to a huge, bright yellow patch of wildflowers. This country was usually indistinguishable from the surrounding desert, but now everything was covered in native grasses and wildflowers. Mini ecosystems were taking hold right across the landscape.

In swampy areas, purple swamphens darted about, picking away for herbs, seeds, insects and spiders. They, and a host of other wading birds, were offered the protection of a tangled mass of lignum shrubs, tall hardy perennials that grow through the wetland areas. Shadows constantly swept across the ground, created by a mass of whistling kites, birds of prey gliding on the thermals, filling the sky and waiting to swoop down on their victims. Small birds, mice, rats, frogs, lizards and even fish were in danger. Dingoes were on the hunt too. These were not the skinny, rangy native dogs normally found scavenging in the desert; rather they were sleek and well fed, bounding across the wetlands with pups in tow. They were making the most of the bountiful season to hunt and breed. It was a moving feast, as new life was triggered by the passing water, percolating through the maze of channels in Goyder's Lagoon on its way to Lake Eyre.

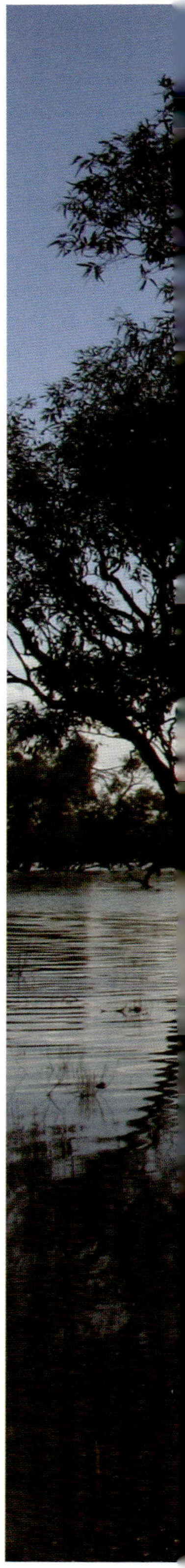

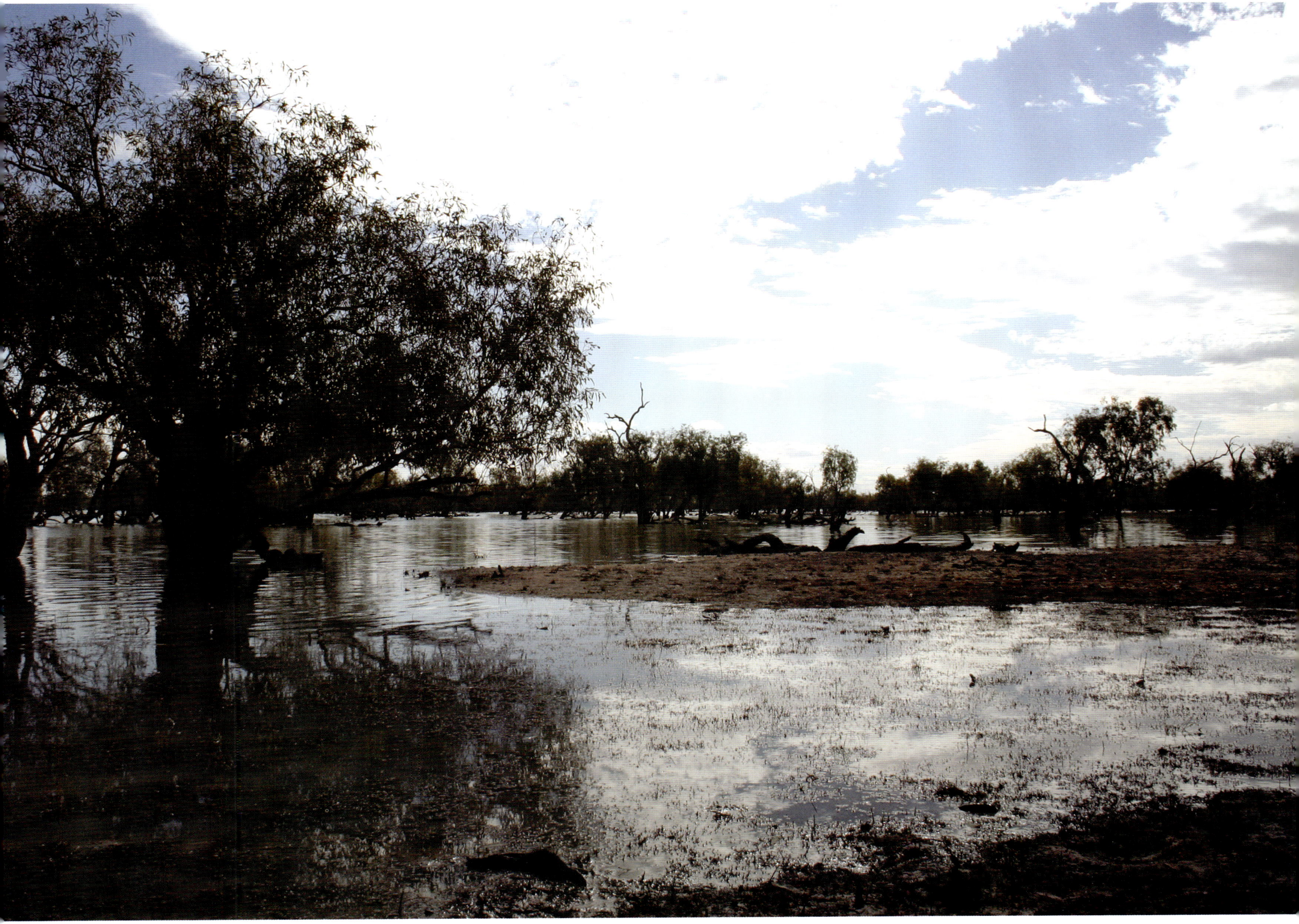

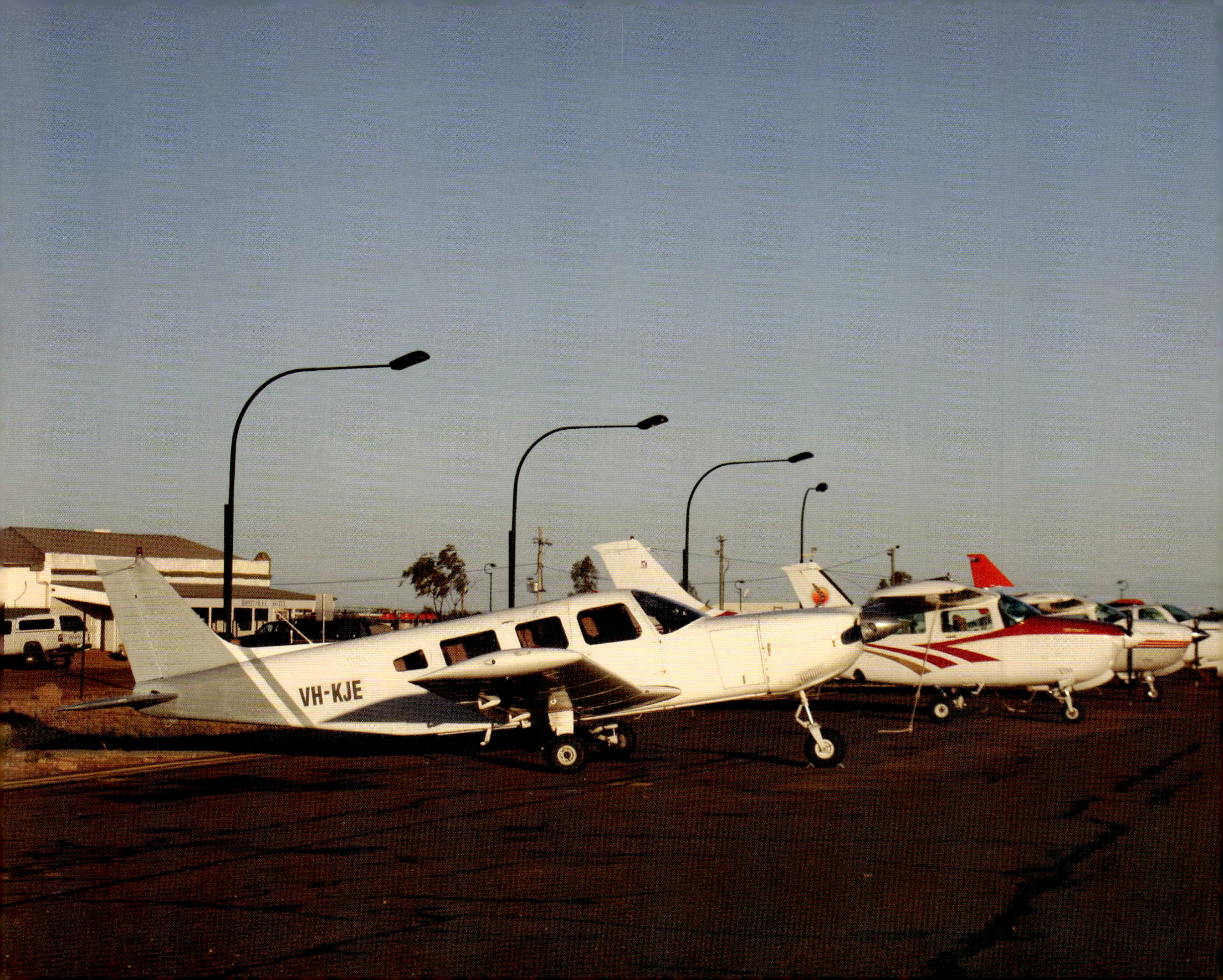
VH-KJE

In the carpark outside the Birdsville Hotel an everyday sight is aircraft carrying visitors keen to see the lake flood for a second year in a row.

The tourists flock

The flooding of Lake Eyre for the second year in a row created a tourist bonanza in the outback. There was a constant buzz of aircraft over Lake Eyre, as scenic flights took off from airstrips at Marree, to the south of the lake, and William Creek, to the west.

William Creek consists of little more than a pub, a caravan park and a few cottages. It started life as a cameleers' camp, when the overland telegraph was built along the Oodnadatta Track. The official population is three, including Trevor Wright. He's a pilot who took a gamble on establishing a business there during the floods of 1990. There were some very lean times during the drought years that followed, and Trevor struggled to find enough work from tourism and cattle mustering to keep two small aircraft in the air. He well recalls touting for business in the caravan park, trying to get enough passengers to fill a plane for a joy flight. At the height of the tourist boom in 2011 he could barely keep up with demand. He expanded his fleet to fifteen aircraft and recruited a team of sixteen pilots. Tiny William Creek was humming. Trevor Wright was not surprised by the tourist influx. He believes that Lake Eyre has become the most iconic destination for Australian travellers:

> *The Barrier Reef, Uluru and the Kimberley are big destinations but they rely on a flow of overseas tourists. The people who come to see Lake Eyre are Australians — campervans and four-wheel drives with mums, dads and kids, and many older travellers. They've seen and heard about the beauty of the lake in flood and the amazing kick it gives to the vegetation and the bird breeding and they don't want to miss out.*

North of Lake Eyre, Warburton Creek flowed strongly, cutting through the Simpson Desert to channel water into the lake from Goyder's Lagoon. It was an amazing contrast — a watercourse that had sat dry for years on end now streamed through the desert sand dunes. Out on the Warburton were three small boats, sitting low in the water and shielded from the

Rex Ellis takes his tinnie, a mate and his Jack Russell, Stubbie, out on Warburton Creek — or, as he prefers to call it, Warburton River — to witness the changed landscape.

sun and the weather by canvas covers. They were packed high with supplies and tourists. At the helm of one of the tinnies, tour guide Rex Ellis sat, occasionally offering directions by two-way radio to the skippers of the other boats. Beside him, eagerly observing progress was his constant companion, Stubbie the Jack Russell. Ellis was very much at home in this environment. Over more than forty years of adventures in the outback he's made close to thirty trips up and down the Warburton on the occasions it had flowed and he's more intrigued than ever by the desert watercourse: 'Cartographers call it a creek, which is demeaning. We call it a river — it's sometimes a river, so that's what it is!'

Cooper Creek finally joined the party. It rediscovered its old course through the last of the desert country and flowed into Lake Eyre for the first time in twenty years. The dead salt pan brimmed with life. Fish and other aquatic life swept down by the rivers spread across the lake as it continued to rise. The pelicans followed the rivers rich with food and established breeding colonies on islands in the middle of the lake. And the air filled with the screech of seagulls — deep in the outback! Only a sustained flood draws them away from the security of their coastal habitats, luring them to the centre of Australia to breed at Lake Eyre. Silver gulls claimed an island in the lake and gathered in their thousands. Nests set amongst the rocks covered much of the island. Everywhere there were eggs being guarded by squawking gulls.

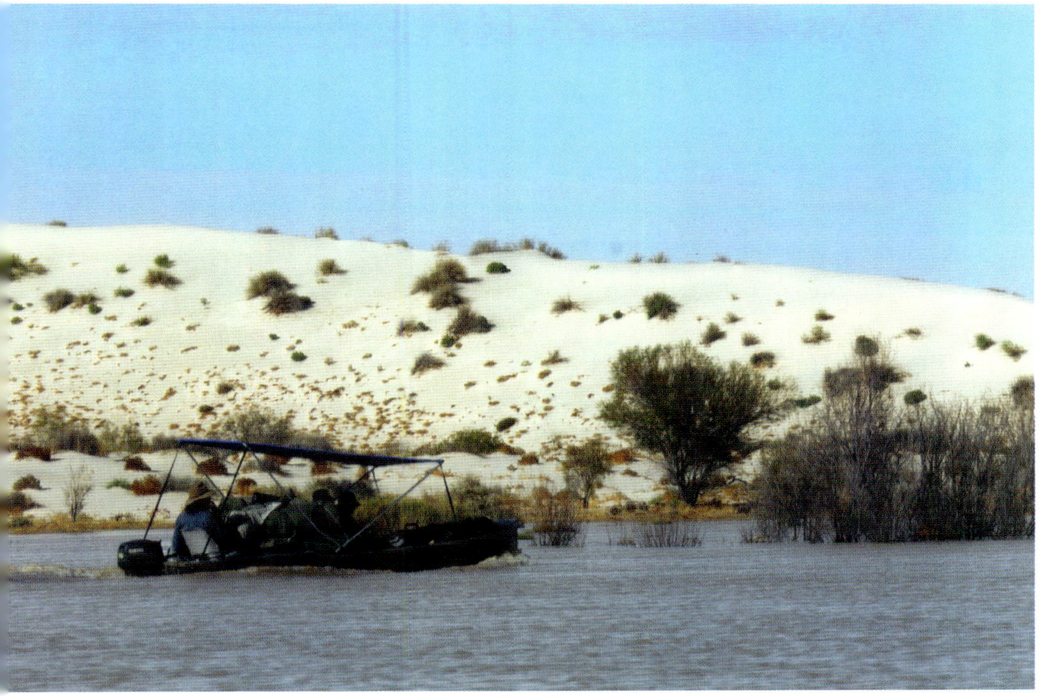

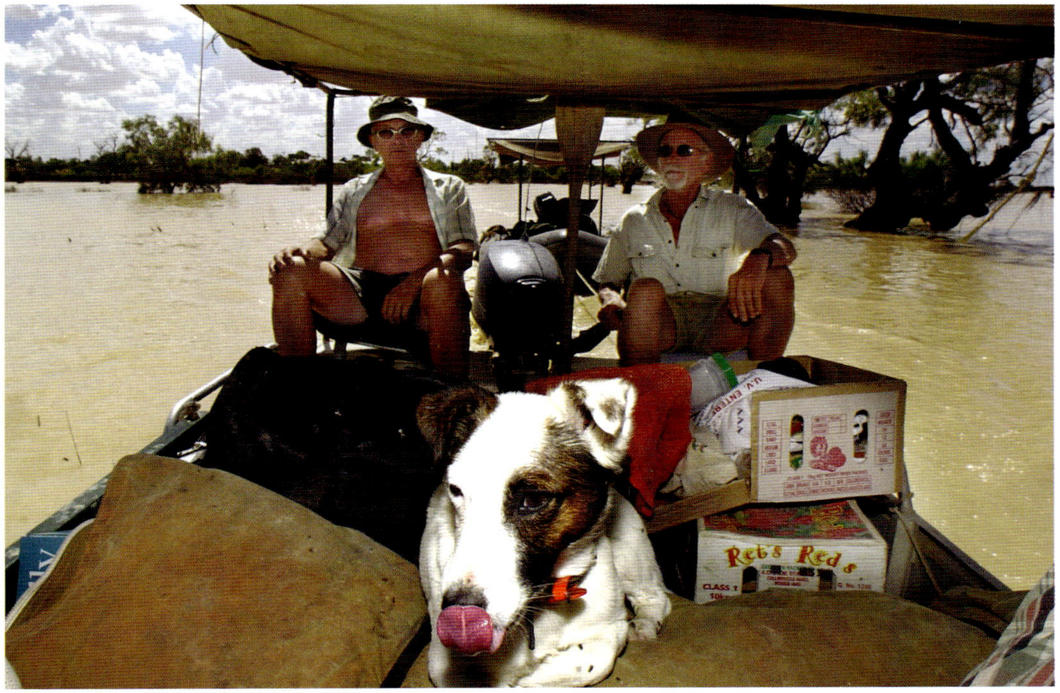
Reb's Reds

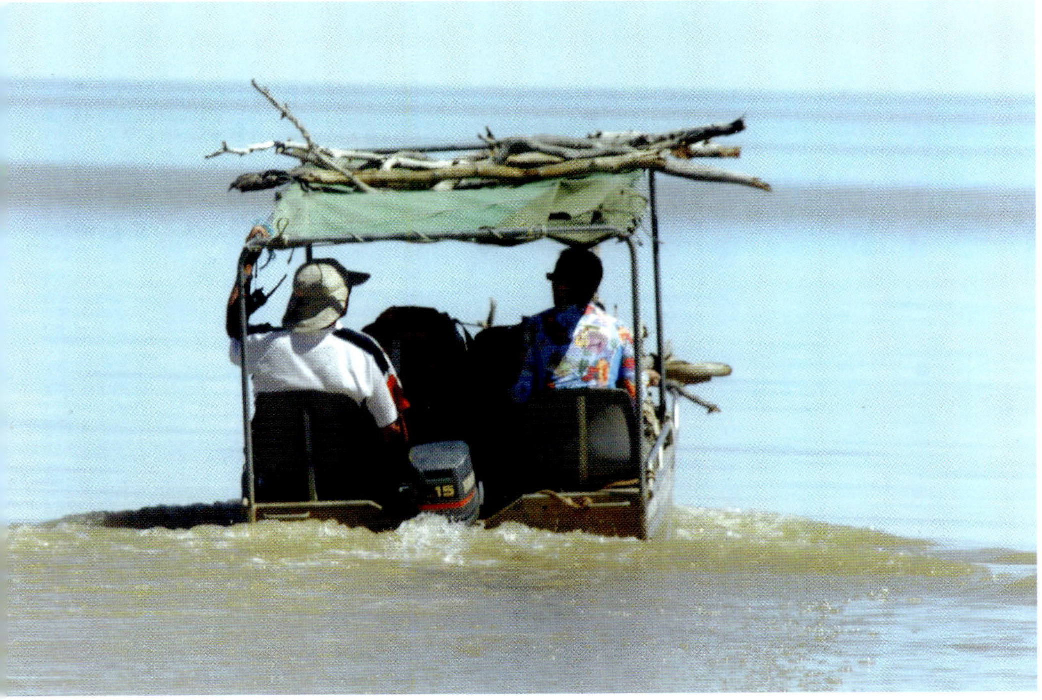
15

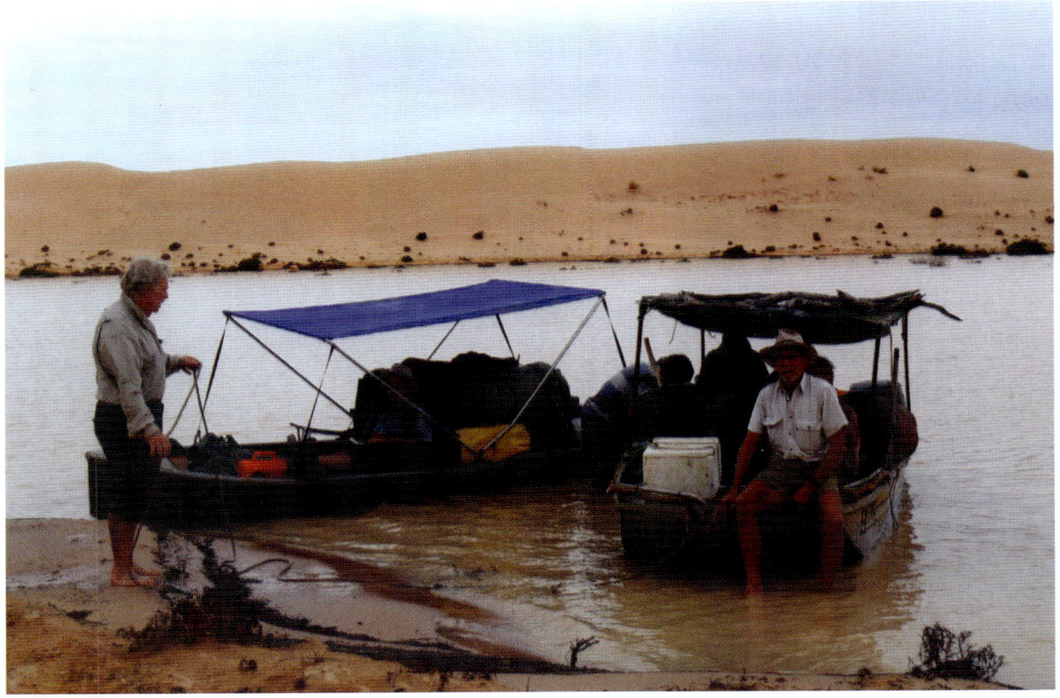

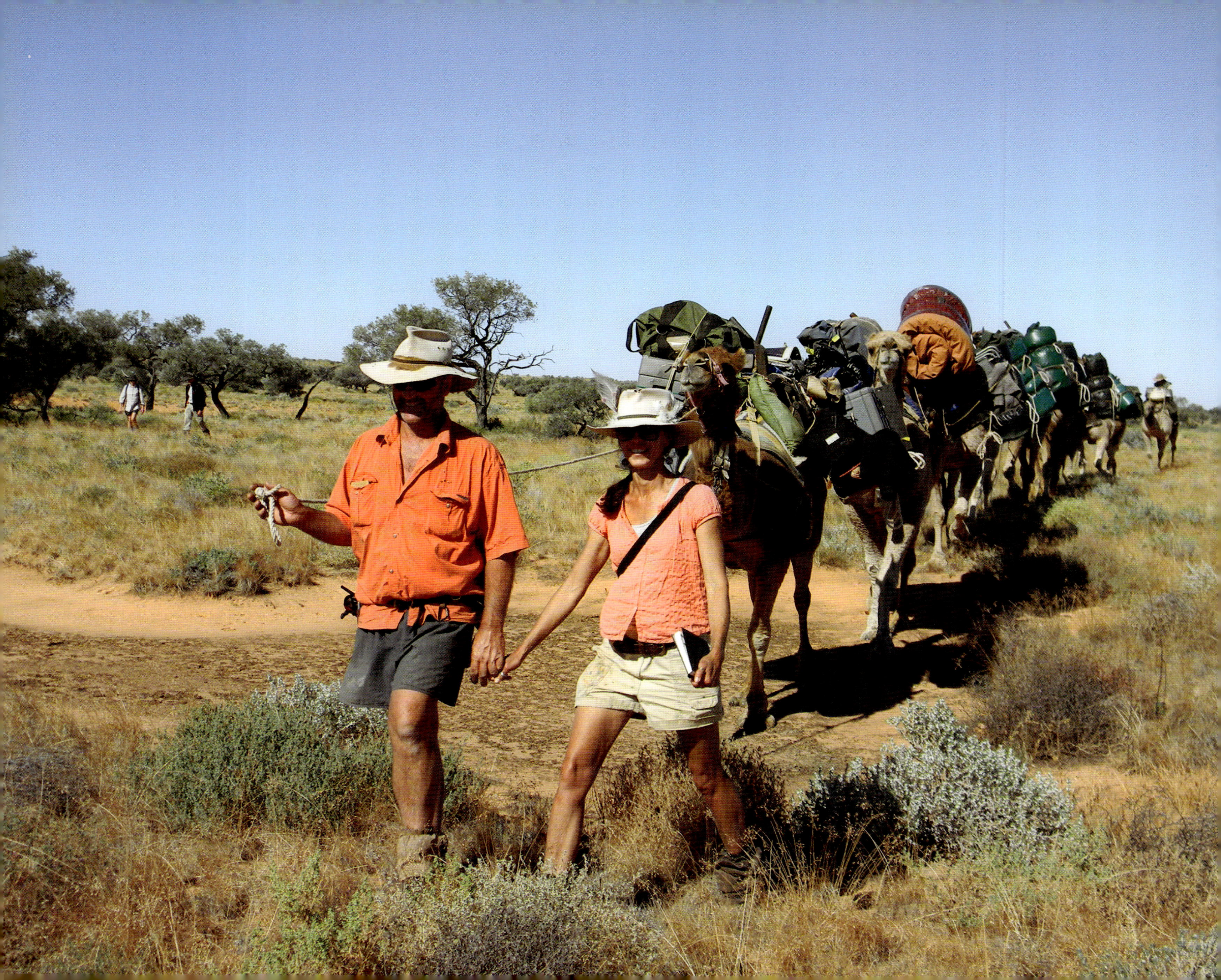

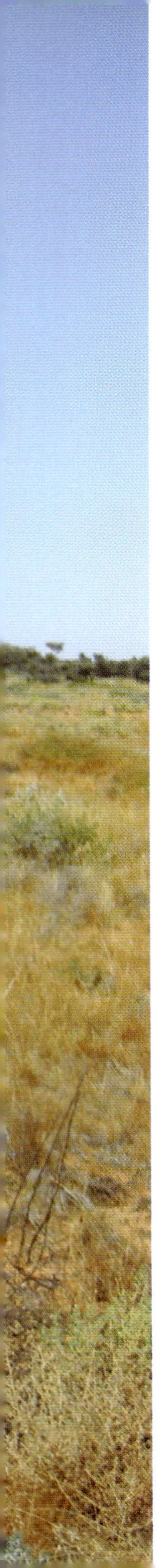

Cameleer Andrew Harper and artist Jo Bertini met and fell in love in the deserts around Lake Eyre. Bertini, who draws the landscape — and its animal inhabitants — obsessively, says the light is fantastic.

Chicks were breaking out of the shells, slowly pecking their way into the world. Others had already arrived — tiny feather balls herded together by protective parents.

Had the early explorers ventured out in a season like this, with water covering much of Lake Eyre, and seagulls overhead, they would have been forgiven for believing that they truly had discovered the inland sea.

They would have been pleasantly surprised by what they found in the deserts too. 'They could have been lulled into a false sense of security. They might have thought that this is the way it always is out here — look at this productive, fertile country — only to discover further down the track that it was going to turn dry again.' Latter-day cameleer Andrew Harper was referring to the Simpson Desert in the Northern Territory. This is normally some of the most desolate country in Australia but the big red sand dunes were now cloaked in native grasses and wildflowers. It was difficult to see the desert for the vegetation. 'It's a very rare event — we're so lucky to see it,' he said. 'Everything is rejuvenated: all the wildlife, particularly the birds, but also the insects, the bugs, the mosquitoes — the lot!'

Harper fell under the spell of the outback long ago and spends all his time organising new treks to areas where Europeans have seldom, if ever, set foot. 'Camels are the best way to do it, they can go where the vehicles can't … and there's nothing more relaxing I think than being able to string eighteen or twenty camels together and walk them through the desert — quietly, peacefully.' He hopes that his expeditions help to remind Australians of the big part that camels played in opening up the outback. And he believes they still have an important role to perform: 'Still the best way to explore the desert is on foot, using pack animals as your support, which is more environmentally friendly than driving around in a dozen four-wheel drives. It is very valid in this day and age in determining what's going on out there.'

Kindred spirits joined Andrew Harper on his expedition. Sydney artist Jo Bertini rode beside him at the head of the swaying camels, chatting and quickly sketching desert forms that caught her eye as she went: 'When you're with the camels you're connected to the landscape and you can stop and you can draw and stop and observe.'

The desert brought Andrew Harper and Jo Bertini together. She met him at a low point in her life, he invited her to join him on one of his camel expeditions and she discovered both love and inspiration. Now she attaches great importance to her annual treks into Central Australia:

> *For me, it's an analogy of offloading all my city baggage, problems and distractions. You load them onto the camel and you just become a solitary artist walking in the desert with no thoughts in your head other than being part of the landscape, connected to the landscape. It's the source where all my work comes from.*

After another day in the desert, Jo Bertini sat cross-legged on the edge of the campsite, dabbling in watercolours, her subjects the camels. They were free of their burdens and resting on their haunches. One rolled in the desert sand, lifting the dust into the soft glow of the late afternoon sun. 'Just looking now at the light on the camels, it's exquisite,' she said as she continued to paint. 'The light is fantastic and it gives you a different beast every time you see a camel like this in a different light.'

Beside the camp fire, under a brilliant full moon, Dr Mike Smith, the archaeologist, was in his own world, neatly documenting his findings from the day's trek in a small log book. In his many expeditions into the desert he had never seen it so lush. 'It's fantastic to see the pulse of life in the country, but as an archaeologist I like to see the bones of the country and they're all hidden now!' Camped next to a small range with a waterhole surrounded by Aboriginal rock art, he hoped that detailed research of the area might yield some more secrets about early human occupation of the Simpson Desert: 'It may be that we get a long record here of occupation, or it could be that this place has never been occupied in any sort of concerted form in the last 1500 years.' It's these intriguing unanswered questions about the deep past of the wild deserts that continue to drive Dr Smith. 'We're trying to document the great human story. It's the human story of Australia's deserts, 5 million square miles, 50,000 years of human history, one of the largest, autonomous hunter-gatherer traditions in the world.'

Next to Dr Smith, John Wilkinson nursed his nightly tipple. At eighty-nine he had shared a fair slice of human history himself, and had been taking camel treks through the Central Australian deserts for twenty years: 'I've always loved the bush and there's no better way of learning about the bush than walking through it.'

Wilkinson has lived in the bush all his life, starting out as a jackeroo on sheep stations, and later managing properties in the Riverina region of New South Wales. The camel treks have provided new motivation in his retirement years. 'It's something absolutely unique, being out with the camels and living in swags.

John Wilkinson has been enjoying camel treks through the desert for the last twenty years. He never gets tired of the way of life and is still discovering things he's never seen before.

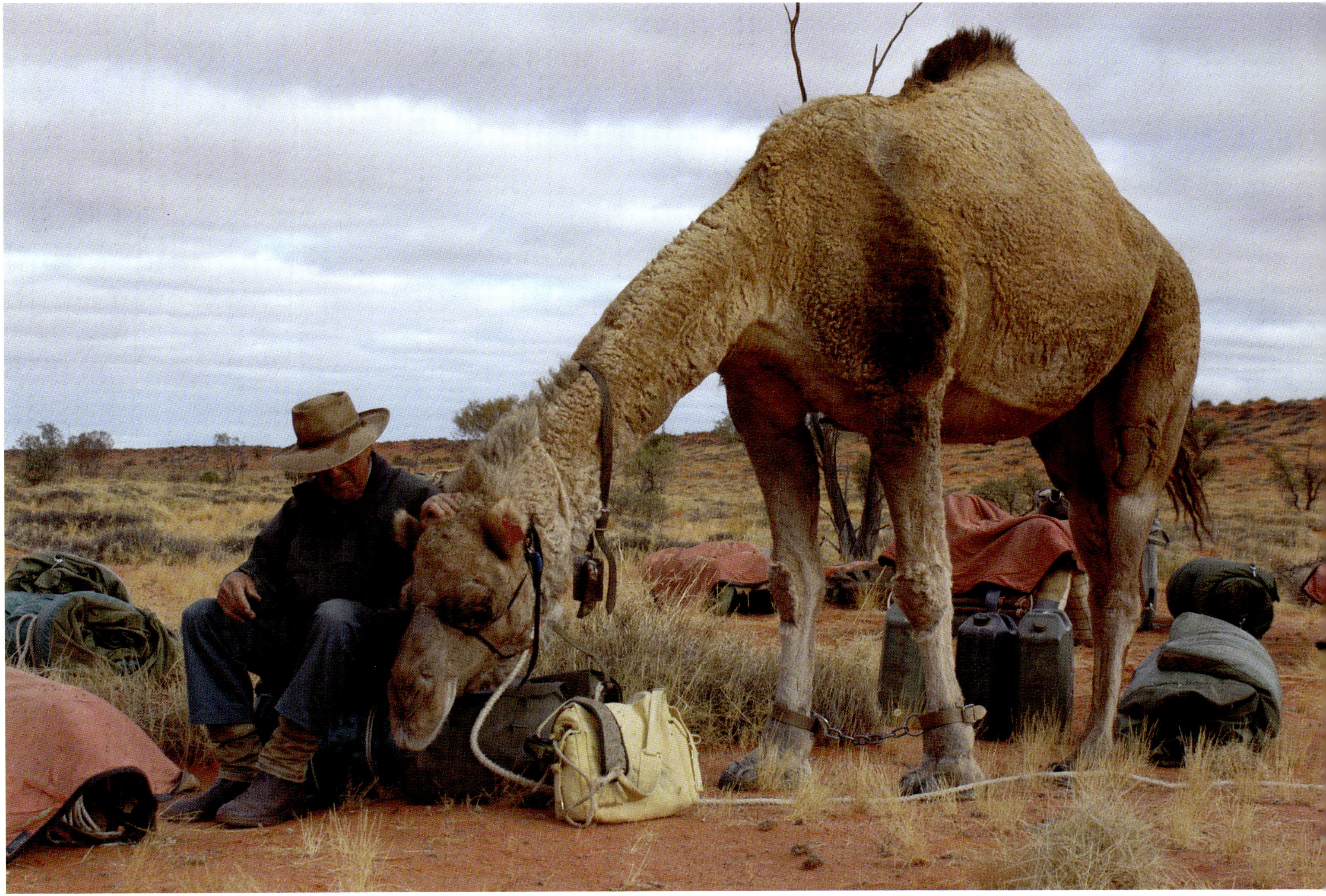

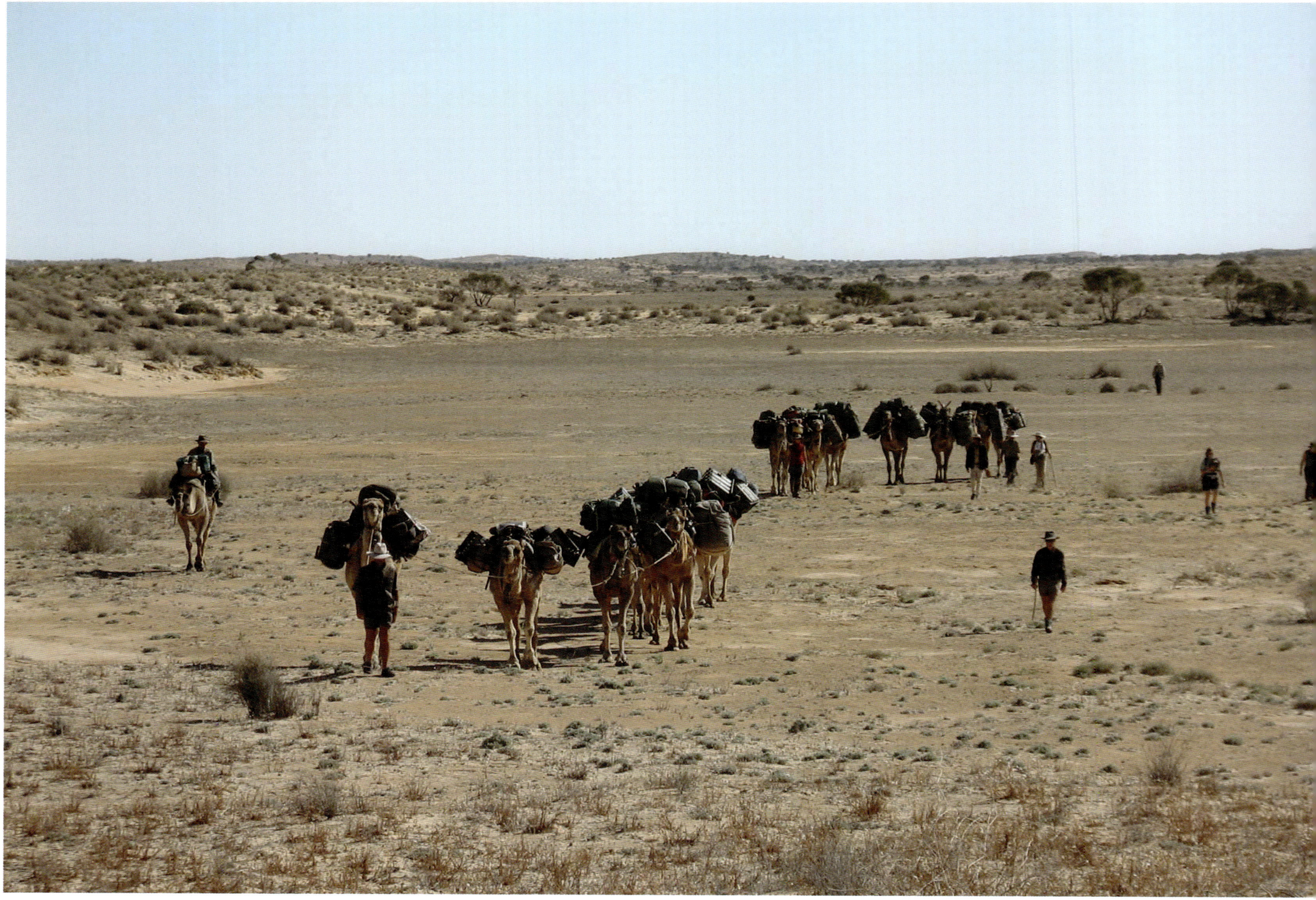

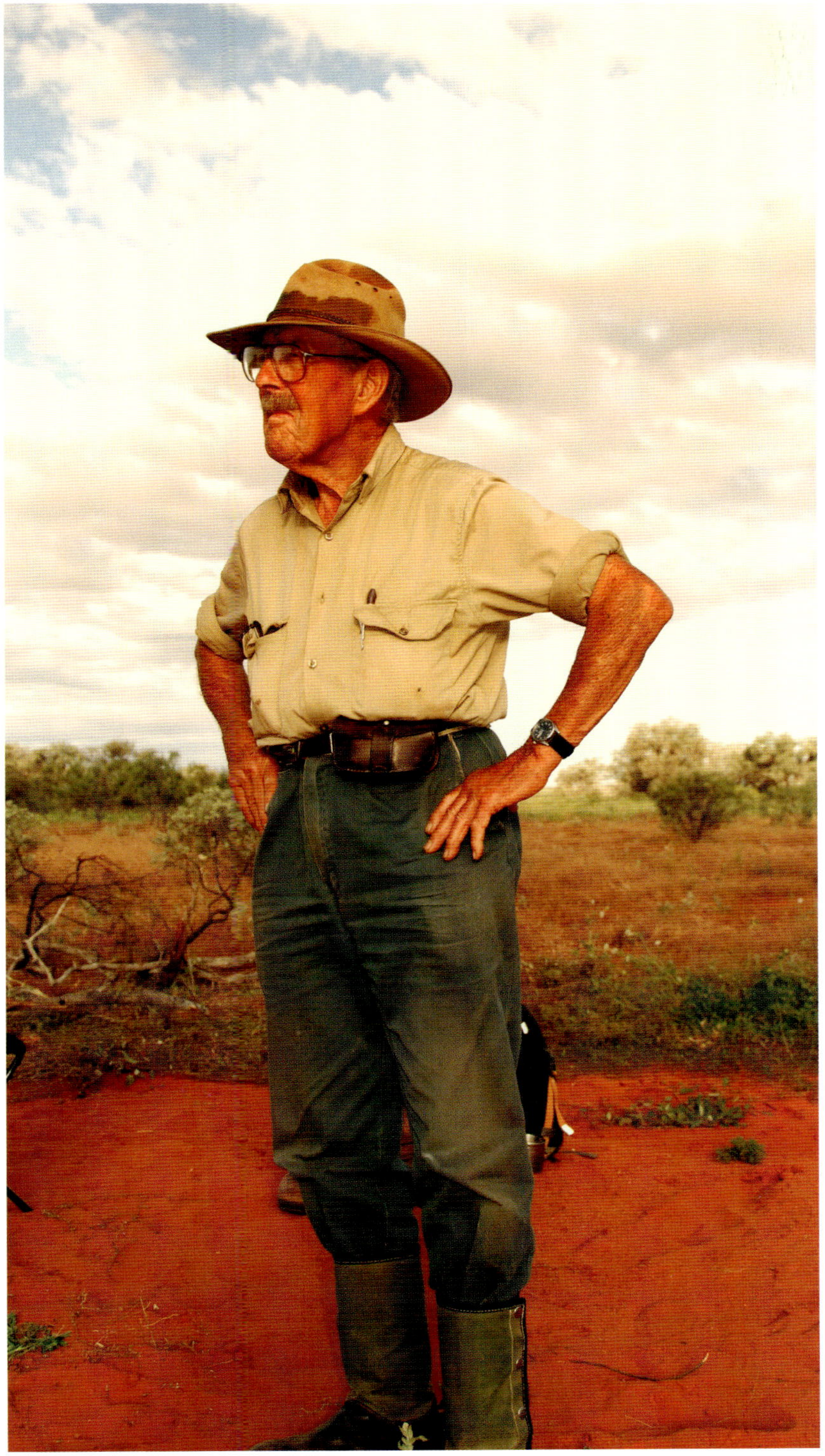

Opposite: Camels trek in the desert
Left: John Wilkinson

And the desert is absolutely amazing the way it recovers because a lot of these seeds would have been lying dormant here for years — I've never seen some of these plants.'

John Wilkinson cut a familiar figure in the desert, steadily pacing behind the camel train, using a sturdy staff fashioned from the bough of a tree for support. He did harbour one reservation about his desert adventures, however, and confessed with a laugh: 'The only time it's uncomfortable is getting out of the swag when it's raining on a cold morning — and that's a bugger!'

The rain kept falling in Central Australia. The widespread flooding in 2010 left many roads to the outback closed for weeks on end. In Birdsville it had been expected that another huge crowd would flock to the town's famous September race meeting, after the record attendance the year before, but the road closures caused major headaches. Only once since 1882 had the event been cancelled — when equine influenza stopped horseracing in 2007. The organisers optimistically went ahead with their planning for the 2010 meeting but only the hardiest travellers managed to get through the floods. Then, on the eve of the Cup, it bucketed down in Birdsville. The racetrack on the floodplain quickly turned to mud and then went under water. It was the first time in the proud history of the bush race meeting that the Cup had to be called off because of a wet track! But neither the visitors nor the bookies were deterred. The party continued at the drenched racecourse as the bookies offered punters wagers on races elsewhere around Australia. All roads out of Birdsville were cut. More than 3000 tourists were trapped in the town for another three days. There were no complaints from the publican of the Birdsville Hotel!

Beef producers around Birdsville couldn't remember a better time. Along Eyre Creek, west of Birdsville, on the edge of the Simpson Desert, a mob of Herefords was spoilt for choice. Every variety of native pasture was on offer. The grasses had taken hold on the sand dunes that run away from the creek, which was still flowing strongly from the outback flooding and rain. Jackeroos had to stand tall on their motorbikes to spot the cattle in the thick, high vegetation. The cattle seem to roll out of the lush surroundings to be mustered together and sent off to market. The road train drivers were astonished by the weight of the beasts. When one truckie finished a delivery, he rang Adria Downs Station to tell the manager, Don Rayment, that his 'hippos' had arrived safe and sound!

Lake Eyre was putting on its finest show. Visitors were able to get a tiny glimpse of what Central Australia might have looked like when all the rivers were running to a wetlands in the heart of the continent. Mesa-like ridges, which usually appear to be part of the endless desert, were revealed as imposing cliffs that form the age-old shoreline of Lake Eyre. And unremarkable sandy outcrops, dotted across the salt pan, were now impressive islands, playing host to a multitude of birds.

The water was almost 6 metres deep in parts of the lake, but it was so shallow in other areas that the water could be blown from one side to the other. One day the water would be up to the shoreline but if the wind turned it would quickly disappear out of sight. But it was the intricate patterns and ever-changing colours produced by the water swirling across the salt pan that fired the imagination. Tourists swarmed onto joy flights and, as the roads re-opened, they streamed to the centre, anxious to observe what may well be a once in a lifetime opportunity. Surely, after two years of flooding, Lake Eyre would soon revert to a dry, salty wasteland. But no one could have predicted what was to come in 2011.

The pink water of the lake reflects the high salt content; here a plane flies high overhead observing the astonishing transformation the floods have brought.

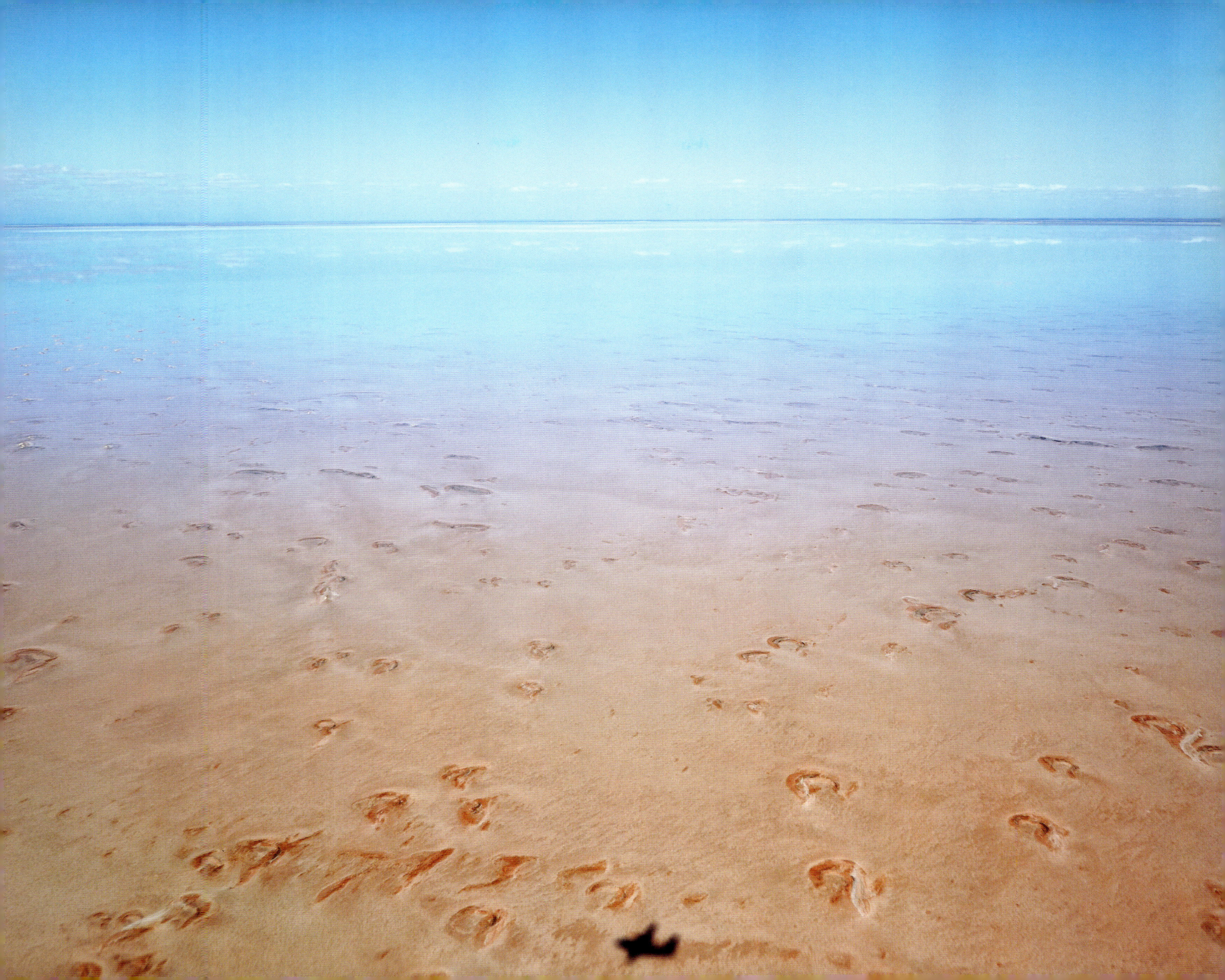

EPILOGUE

The grand finale

By the start of 2011, the El Niño weather event that had imprisoned eastern Australia in drought for so long was a distant memory. The cycle had shifted dramatically and now La Niña was in full command. Flooding rains had already wiped out much of the summer grain harvest in eastern Australia and rivers were again flowing from the northern tip of Queensland to Victoria. Water streaming down the Murray River was set to revive water supplies and struggling wetlands right down the system. Nowhere was the change in the seasons more welcome than at the mouth of the Murray River in South Australia. There, the estuary formed by a series of lakes and a long lagoon, the Coorong, was in desperate straits. As water levels had dropped the fish and marine life collapsed and the drying lake beds became acidic. A dredge worked around the clock to try to prevent the river mouth from closing over. But by January 2011, the relieving flows arrived in earnest and for the first time in more then six years, water flowed out of the Murray to the sea. But the relief came at a high price as communities in many areas of Victoria, New South Wales and Queensland battled to keep floodwaters at bay. Right through the summer, central and south-east Queensland confronted crisis after crisis, culminating with the tragedy produced by the torrent that swept through Toowoomba and the Lockyer Valley, and the flooding of Brisbane. Soon afterwards, Cyclone Yasi, the strongest storm ever recorded in Australia, bore down on the Queensland coast. It left a wide trail of destruction as it smashed coastal towns and tracked inland, eventually becoming a huge rain bearing depression sitting over Central Australia. For an incredible third year in a row, the rivers were again running to Lake Eyre.

Dramatic shifts in weather patterns have made the long drought a distant memory — the Warburton Creek channels form a trail of green through the desert, not too far as the crow flies from the Birdsville Track.

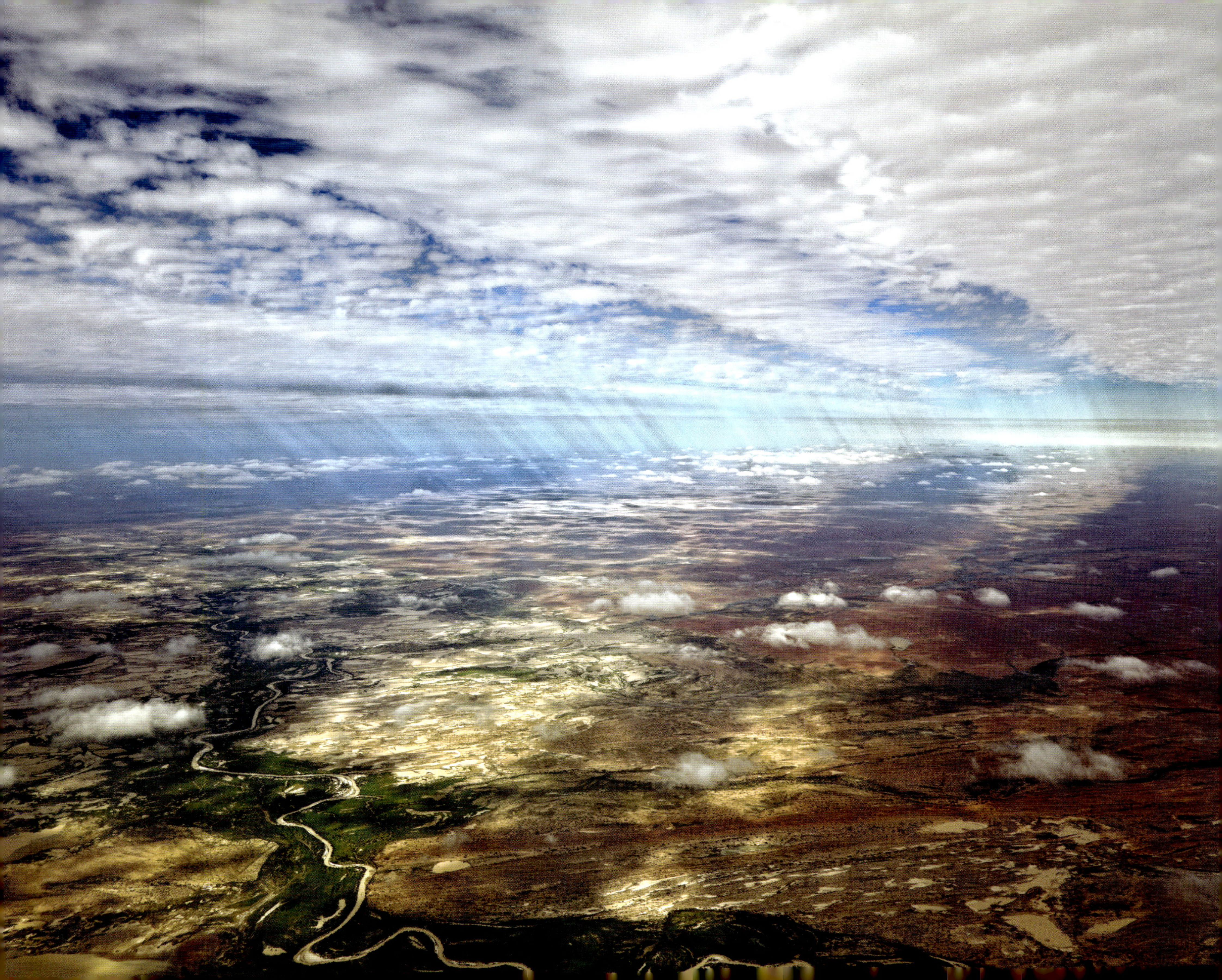

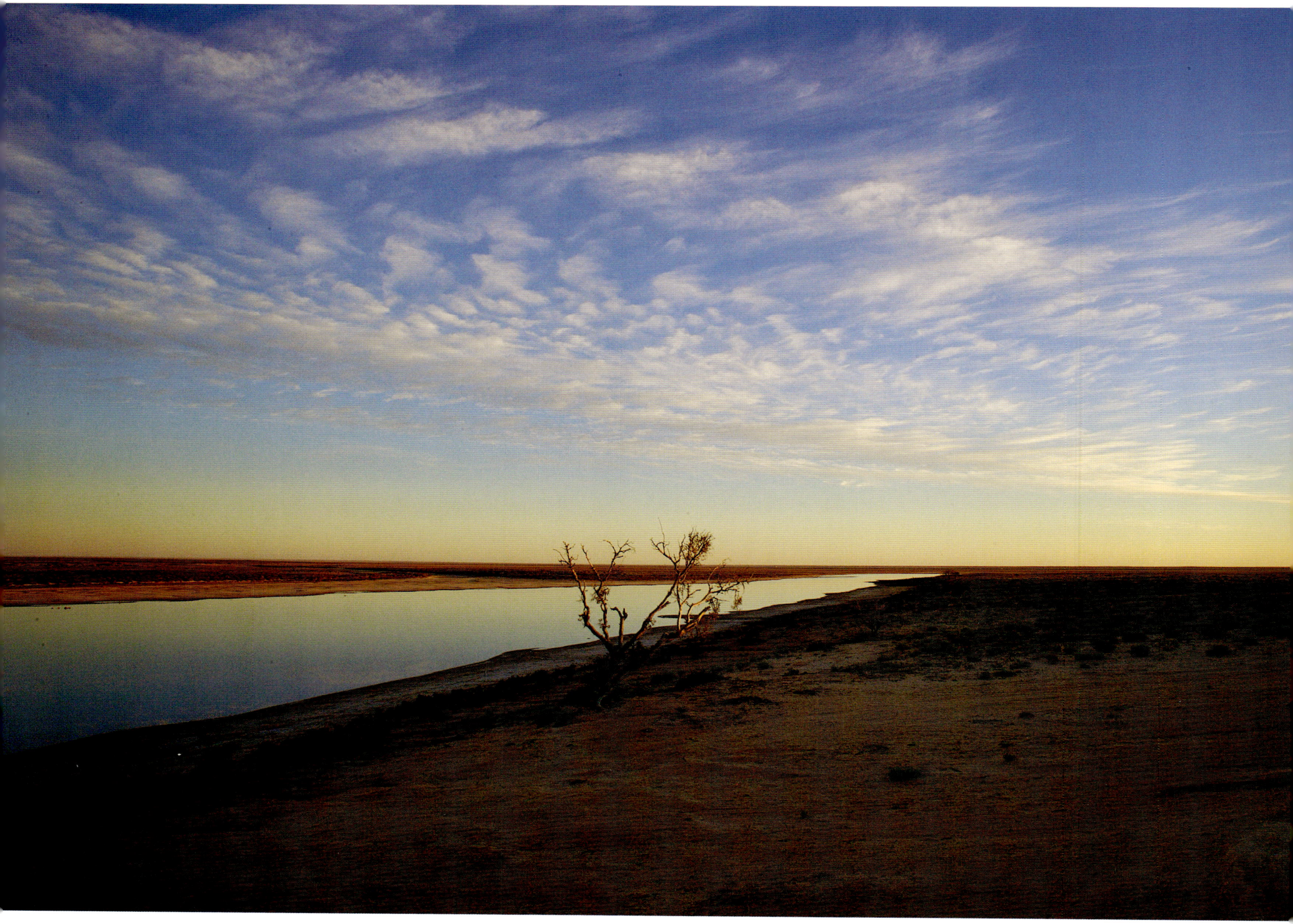

The flow of water through the intricate and often-hidden river and drainage systems in the dry red soils of Central Australia transform the dead heart during its boom and bust cycle. Lake Cadibarrawirracanna, to the west of Lake Eyre.

New rainfall records were set on some properties north of Birdsville. On Kamaran Downs, just northwest of Bedourie, 519 millimetres fell over just four days, more than two and half times above the average annual rainfall for the area. The long-time manager of Kamaran Downs, Trevor White, had never seen anything like it. His wife Cathy had to keep emptying the rain gauge into a bucket to measure out the torrential falls. Trevor White told ABC Regional Radio it was hard to believe the drought could end in such a dramatic way: 'Drought — what's a drought? We'll have to look it up and see what it is!'

On the edge of the Simpson Desert, the Eyre Creek again streamed through the sand dunes. Locals were astounded to see water reaching areas they had never seen touched by flood before. The monster sand dune west of Birdsville, Big Red, a famous landmark and tourist attraction on the track through the Simpson Desert, was suddenly an island in the desert. The flooding of 2009 had brought much-needed relief for the environment and cattle producers alike, the follow-up floods of 2010 were seen as an enormous bonus, but the events of 2011 had everyone reaching for the history books.

The whole of Central Australia was awash and scientists were left to marvel at nature as it went into overdrive.

Artist John Olsen travelled out to Lake Eyre again, this time accompanied by his son Tim, grandson James, and fellow artists Luke Sciberras and Guy Maestri. Olsen has made many painting expeditions to Lake Eyre since he was captured by the magic of the place in the flooding of 1974, and he remains entranced by the lake — the great void in the outback, as he calls it — intrigued by its many moods.

Luke Sciberras was struck by the place too. He is no stranger to the outback, having spent considerable time painting landscapes in far western New South Wales and the Flinders Range, which he said opened his eyes to the arid heart of Australia. But nothing prepared him for Lake Eyre: 'It completely surprised me how vast it is, how varied it is and how small my ideas were about it. The shift in tone and colour are so subtle that you just have to soak it up. It's one of the most beautiful things I've ever seen.'

On his return to Lake Eyre, John Olsen committed everything to memory as he studied the unfolding scene below — reacquainting himself with 'an old friend', as he put it. 'The heart of Australia is exposed to you. It's quite wonderful because you're projecting an empathy for how the landscape makes itself.' Olsen returned to his studio at Bowral in the New South Wales Southern Highlands to produce yet another series of works on Lake Eyre called 'Ruminations on an Empty Landscape'. Olsen describes it as a constant interplay of sky, land and water that he believes can only be captured from above: 'It's just as essential to observe the geological lay of the land from an aerial perspective as it is to peer into the crawling microscopic depths of a pond.'

Olsen insists that he can only provide part of the picture: 'I don't think anyone will ever capture it. You can just get parcels of it — the enormity of it and reasoning of it — it is so big that you only get little pieces of information.' To him, the lake is an eternal dilemma wrapped up in 'its complications and question marks'. But it still drives him on, even though he's now in his eighties.

Olsen is anxious to revisit the area to record when the inevitable bust that follows the boom — when the lake dries out and the desert reclaims the centre. It's a journey he believes everyone should make: 'Unless you see this you don't really know Australia. With all these beautiful colours, the scale of it, just majestic, it's a must see. In one's lifetime, to be a real Australian, you must see Lake Eyre.'

Even as Central Australia flourishes from the incredible sequence of these flooding years, the rising spring temperatures serve clear notice of what is to come. Soon water levels right across the Lake Eyre basin will begin to drop dramatically. Nature can turn swiftly and cruelly as summer takes hold. Chicks caught at the end of the breeding cycle will run out of food and perish. Fish will die too — unable to survive the rising salt levels in the receding waters of Lake Eyre.

Before too long all that will be left will be the glistening salt pan that so confounded and depressed the early explorers. But through the flooding years nature has gone a long way towards righting the environmental balance sheet left so deeply in the red by the long drought. Plant and animal life, on all levels, has bounced back. But more than that — nature has provided a down payment on the future. Flora and fauna in Central Australia now had a buffer to negotiate the next dry spell, as the cycle inevitably turns and the desert reasserts itself, in this, the heart of the most arid inhabited continent on earth.

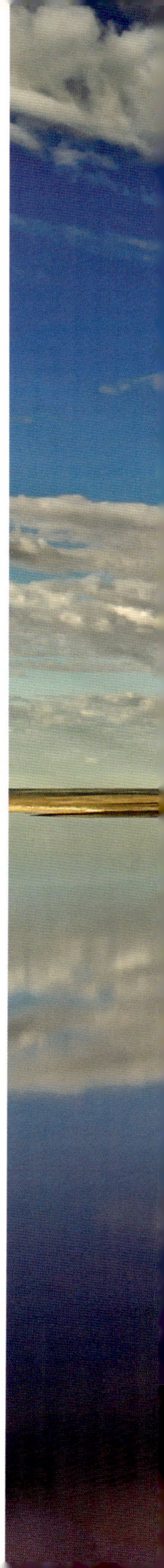

'You must see Lake Eyre — the beautiful colours, the scale of it, just majestic': John Olsen

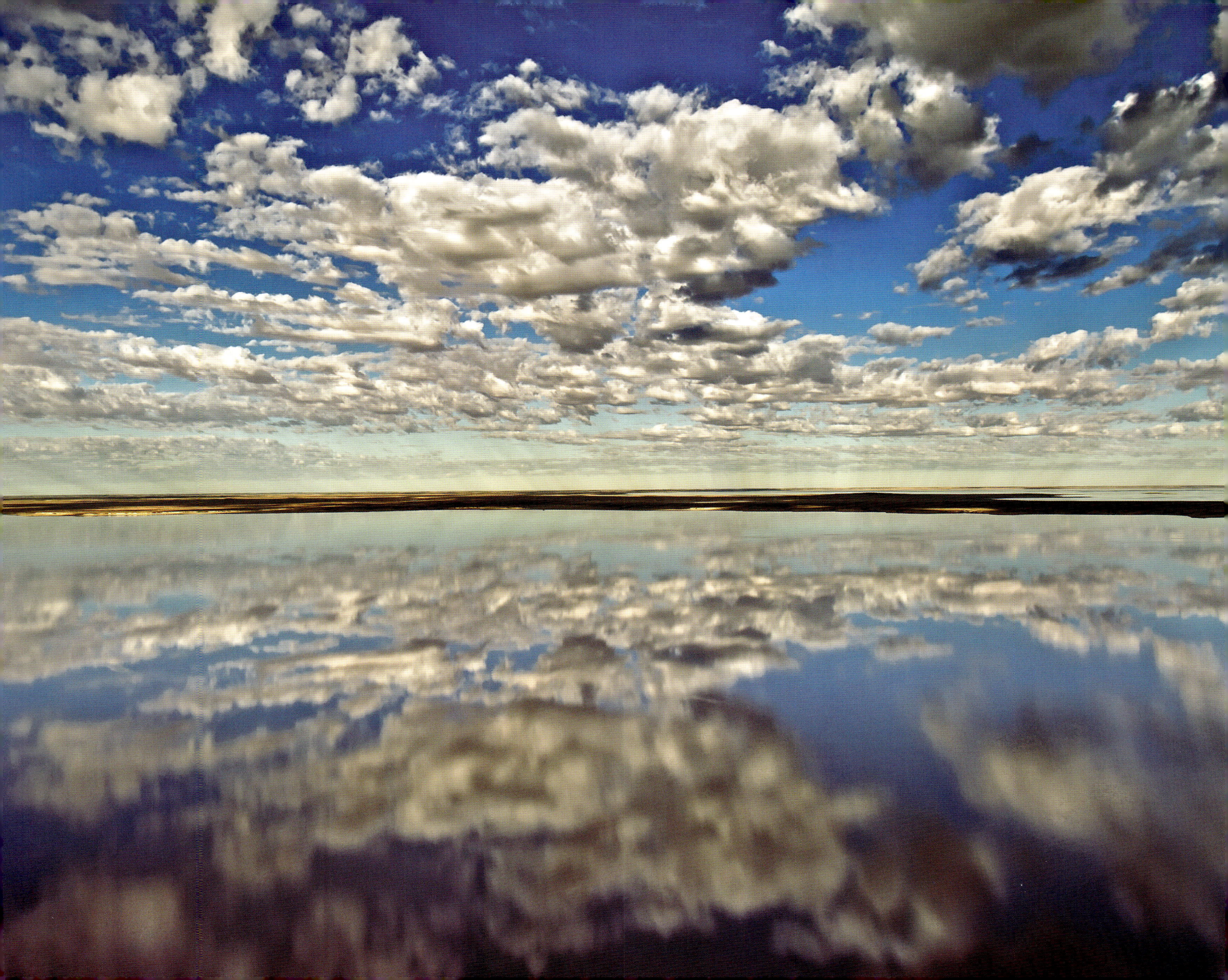

ACKNOWLEDGEMENTS

This book would not have been possible without the ABC. It blossomed out of extensive filming trips to Lake Eyre between 2009 and 2011 to cover the dramatic flooding in Central Australia for TV News and Current Affairs programs and produce two popular documentaries.

It is to the great credit of ABC News that crucial resources were made available to document one of nature's greatest displays in the remote heart of the continent. Special thanks go to the Director of News, Kate Torney and Don Lange, the Head of News Programming, for their continuing support for the Lake Eyre coverage as it stretched on from year to year. Much of the inspiration and drive for the filming missions was provided by producer Ben Hawke, who could see from early on that the drought breaking floods justified documentary length treatment. Peter Lewis, the Executive Producer of ABC TV's Landline, was a steadfast ally throughout. The ABC's Sydney based helicopter roamed far and wide on the long assignments deep into the outback, under the highly professional control of pilots Gary Ticehurst and Richard Howell.

Many gifted camera operators contributed to the coverage, including Erik Havnen and John Bean ACS, who captured the stunning television images around Lake Eyre – and many photographs. The creative finish to the documentaries, and many of the other Lake Eyre reports, was provided by the expert touch of tireless video editor Scott Monro.

ABC Books – HarperCollins – suggested that the historic flooding of Lake Eyre should also be documented in book form. I'm grateful to Amruta Slee, Susan Morris-Yates, Matt Stanton and Hugh Ford for their unwavering support and direction. A debt of gratitude is owed to Professor Richard Kingsford, who was involved in the ABC's Lake Eyre coverage from the beginning, and again contributed expert advice for the production of the book, as did Doctor Mike Smith, one of Australia's foremost archaeologists from the National Museum in Canberra.

The project was given a huge boost by the sheer enthusiasm of Australia's great landscape artist John Olsen, whose passion for Lake Eyre is deeply infectious. He generously embraced our efforts to tell the story of the flooding in film and book form, elevating our work to another dimension.

Many thanks must go to the people of Lake Eyre. Without their assistance and kind hospitality we could never have made our filming trips to the Centre. We are deeply grateful to David and Nell Brook in Birdsville, Anthony and Janet Brook on Cordillo Downs, Trevor and Cindy Mitchell on Muloorina Station, Sharon Oldfield at Cowarie Station, Graham and Sharon Betts at Epsilon Station, Bush Heritage's Ethabuka Reserve, Kalamurina Wildlife Sanctuary, Don Rowlands in Birdsville, Ross and Jane Fargher of Prairie Hotel in Parachilna and to the people of the tiny communities of William Creek, Mungerannie and Innamincka Many contributed photographs for the book including veteran outback adventurer, Rex Ellis, artist Jo Bertini, camel expedition leader, Andrew Harper and Karen Brook. It's from all these diverse sources that the rich story of Lake Eyre is told.

Finally, sincere thanks to my family, Maria, Jamie and Nick, for all their love and support as I immersed myself in an enthralling project.
Paul Lockyer 2011

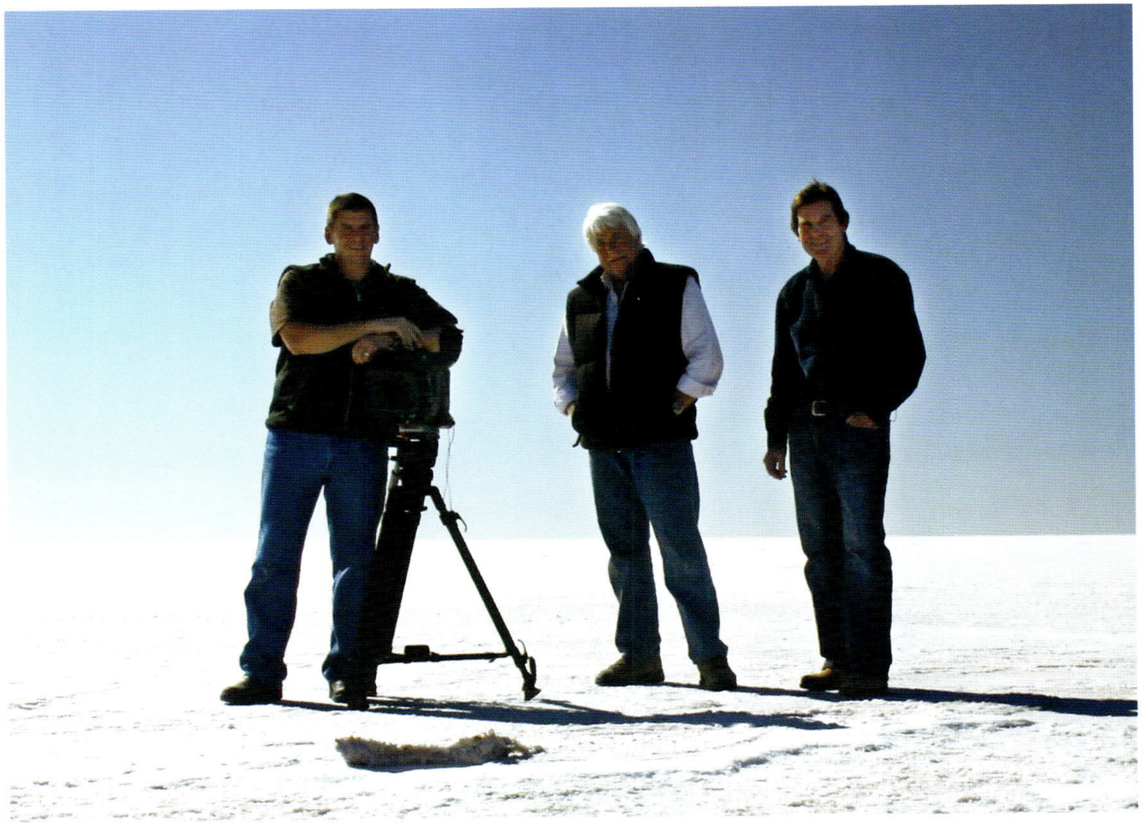

Bibliography

Bailey, J., *Mr Stuart's Track*, Pan Macmillan Australia, Sydney, 2006.
Bowen, J., *Kidman the Forgotten King*, Angus & Robertson, Sydney, 1995.
Dulhunty, R., *When the Dead Heart Beats Lake Eyre Lives*, Lowden Publishing Co., Kilmore, Victoria, 1975.
Dutton, G., "*The Hero as Murderer*", William Collins Limited, Sydney, 1967.
Ellis, R., *Boats in the Desert,* Central Queensland University Press, Rockhampton, 2006.
Hogg, G., *The Over-Landers,* Robert Hale Limited, London, 1961.
McGrath, S. and J. Olsen, *The Artist and the Desert*, Bay Books, Sydney, 1981.
Olsen, J., *Drawn from Life*, Duffy and Snellgrove, Sydney, 1997.
Pearson, J., *Bluebird and The Dead Lake*, Collins, Sydney, 1965.
Serventy, V., *The Desert Sea*, The Macmillan Company, Sydney, 1985.
Uren, M. and R. Stephens, *Waterless Horizons*, Roberts & Mullins, Melbourne, 1941.
Weidenbach, K., *Mailman of the Birdsville Track*, Hodder Headline Australia, Sydney, 2003.

Photographic credits

The publishers would like to thank the following individuals and institutions for their help and for their permission to reproduce the following images:

ABC Online 235
John Bean 34–35, 40, 49, 54, 146, 161, 181, 188, 216
Karen Brook 177, 179, 189 (both), 194, 197, 198
Ian Doyle Photography 78
Peter Elfes 4, 233
Rex Ellis 219 (top left, bottom left and right)
Angus Emmott 106, 109, 112, 113, 114, 117, 118, 121, 125, 135, 163, 169, 205, 230
Getty Images 18, 19, 89
Stuart Grant 22
The John Heyer Estate 79 (top right and left; bottom left)
Richard Kingsford 24, 29, 30, 103, 122, 126, 128–29, 132, 140, 150, 152, 153, 156, 158, 164–65, 170, 187, 189, 201, 212, 215
Kruse Family Archive 79 (bottom right)
Jane McRae 110 (all)
Motoring Picture Library, National Motor Museum (UK) 83, 86
Museum of Victoria 70–71
National Archives of Australia 39, 167, 185
National Library of Australia 33, 43, 55, 59, 60, 62, 64, 66, 75, 144, 145
Newspix 80, 85, 90, 93, 94, 160, 173, 174, 184, 190, 193, 197, 202, 206, 219 (top right)
State Library of New South Wales 68, 74
State Library of Queensland 178
State Library of South Australia 53 (left and right), 57, 72, 76, 81, 182
Gary Ticehurst 21, 98, 136
Laurie Whiddon 10
Kim Wirth 8–9, 13, 14–15, 26–27, 36, 46–47, 50, 100–101, 104, 208, 210–11, 227

Index

The ABC 'Wave' device is a trademark of the Australian Broadcasting Corporation and is used under licence by HarperCollins*Publishers* Australia.

First published in Australia in 2012
by HarperCollins*Publishers* Australia Pty Limited
ABN 36 009 913 517
harpercollins.com.au

HarperCollins*Publishers*
Level 13, 201 Elizabeth Street, Sydney NSW 2000, Australia
31 View Road, Glenfield, Auckland 0627, New Zealand
1–A Hamilton House, Connaught Place, New Delhi — 110 001, India
77–85 Fulham Palace Road, London W6 8JB, United Kingdom
2 Bloor Street East, 20th floor, Toronto, Ontario M4W 1A8, Canada
10 East 53rd Street, New York NY 10022, USA

ISBN: 978 0 7333 3064 3

Cover and internal design by Hugh Ford
Cover photograph courtesy of Peter Elfes Photography
Endpapers supplied by John Olsen
Typeset in 10/15pt ITC Caslon by Hugh Ford
Colour reproduction by Graphic Print Group, Adelaide
Printed and bound in China by RR Donnelley on 128gsm matt art

5 4 3 2 12 13 14

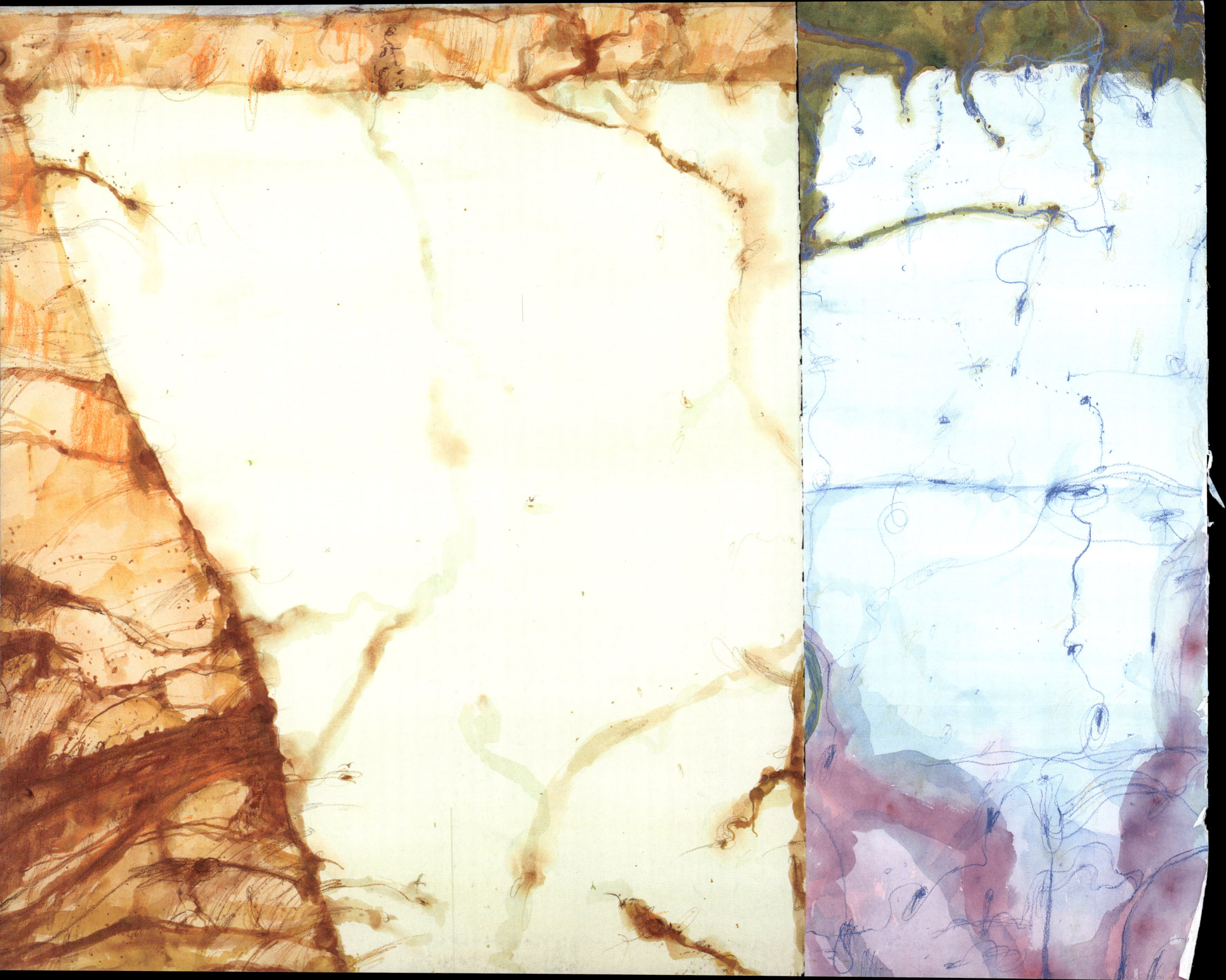